Little Queen

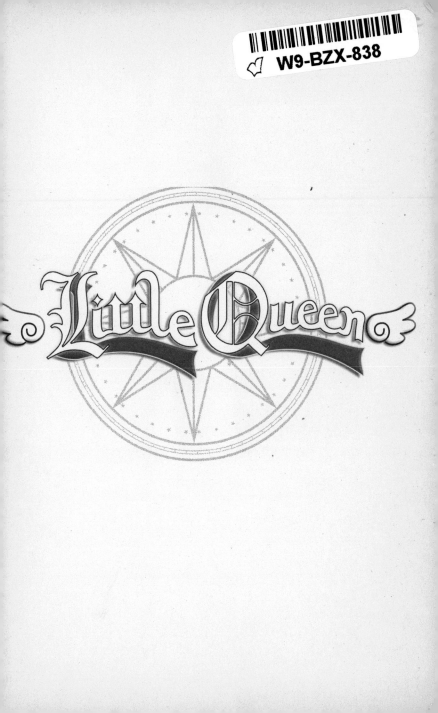

Little Queen Volume 4
Created by Yeon-Joo Kim

Translation - Jennifer Hahm
English Adaptation - Ethan Russell
Copy Editor - Stephanie Duchin
Retouch and Lettering - Star Print Brokers
Production Artist - Skooter
Graphic Designer - Louis Csontos

Editor - Bryce Coleman
Digital Imaging Manager - Chris Buford
Pre-Production Supervisor - Erika Terriquez
Production Manager - Elisabeth Brizzi
Managing Editor - Vy Nguyen
Creative Director - Anne Marie Horne
Editor-in-Chief - Rob Tokar
Publisher - Mike Kiley
President and C.O.O. - John Parker
C.E.O. and Chief Creative Officer - Stuart Levy

A **TOKYOPOP** Manga

TOKYOPOP Inc.
5900 Wilshire Blvd. Suite 2000
Los Angeles, CA 90036

E-mail: info@TOKYOPOP.com
Come visit us online at www.TOKYOPOP.com

ISBN: 978-1-4278-0205-7

First TOKYOPOP printing: November 2007
10 9 8 7 6 5 4 3 2 1
Printed in the USA

Volume 4
Yeon-Joo Kim

HAMBURG // LONDON // LOS ANGELES // TOKYO

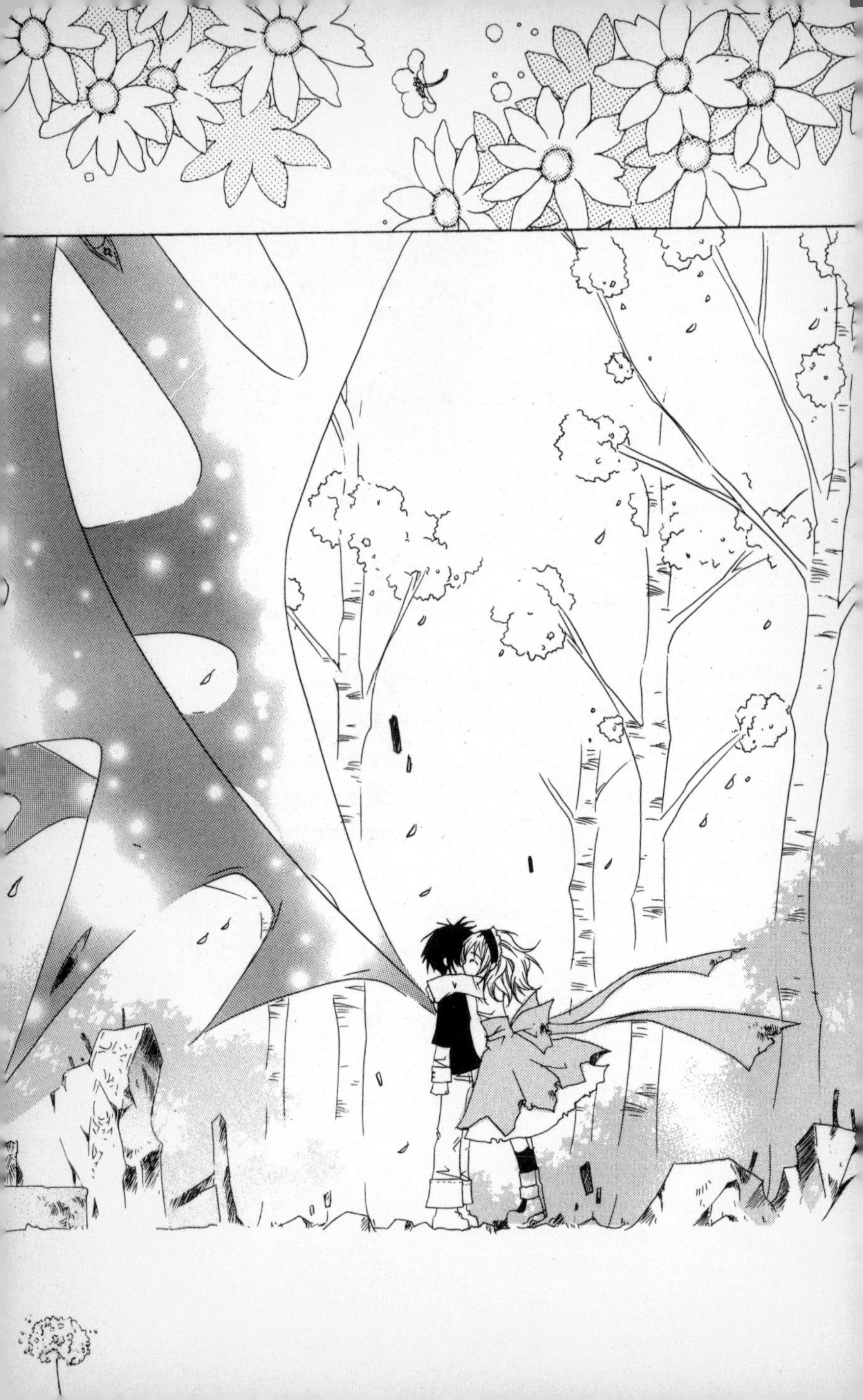

Previously in

As Rohini Academy's Queen of Light
competition moves into its final stages,
we learn more about the personalities
and pasts of our key players.
One of the more surprising stories is that
of Lucia. Considered aloof and somewhat
hard-hearted by her fellow classmates, Lucia
is, in fact, much more complicated than
her cool exterior would suggest. And as
Sejuru's dark past begins to close in around
him, there are hints that certain people at
the school may have ulterior motives for
keeping the supposed evil forces at bay...

CONTENTS

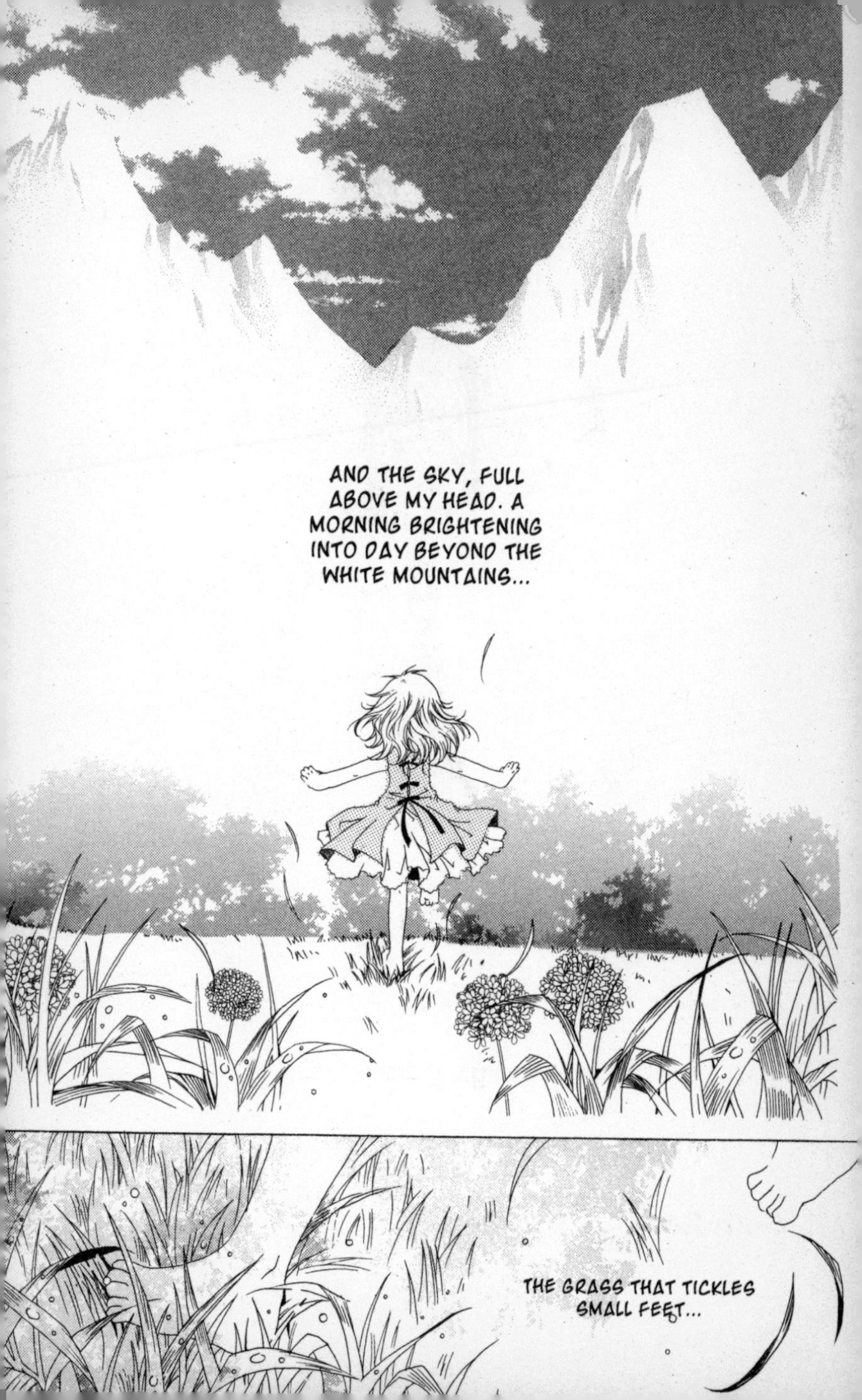
AND THE SKY, FULL ABOVE MY HEAD. A MORNING BRIGHTENING INTO DAY BEYOND THE WHITE MOUNTAINS...
THE GRASS THAT TICKLES SMALL FEET...

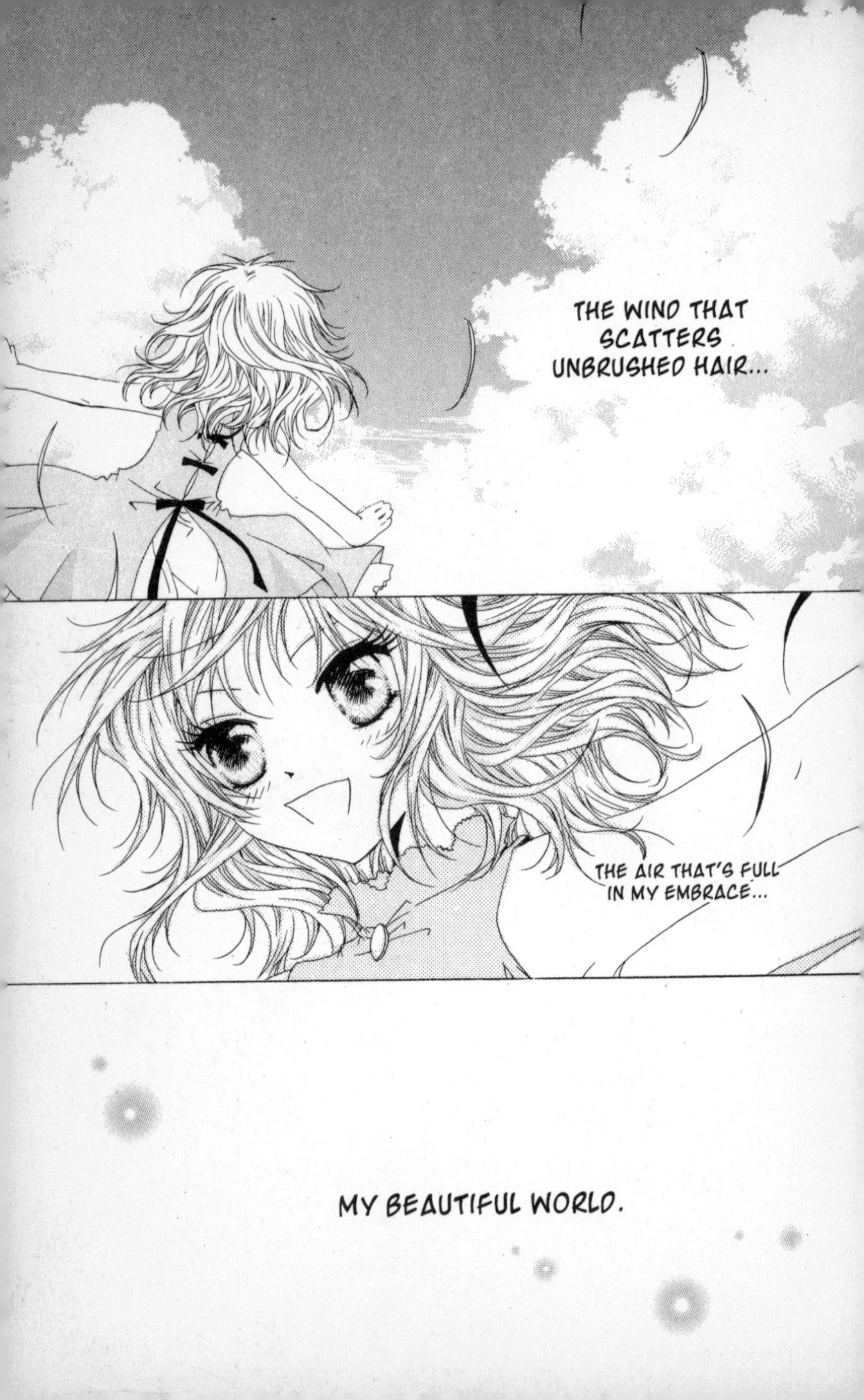
THE WIND THAT SCATTERS UNBRUSHED HAIR...
THE AIR THAT'S FULL IN MY EMBRACE...
MY BEAUTIFUL WORLD.

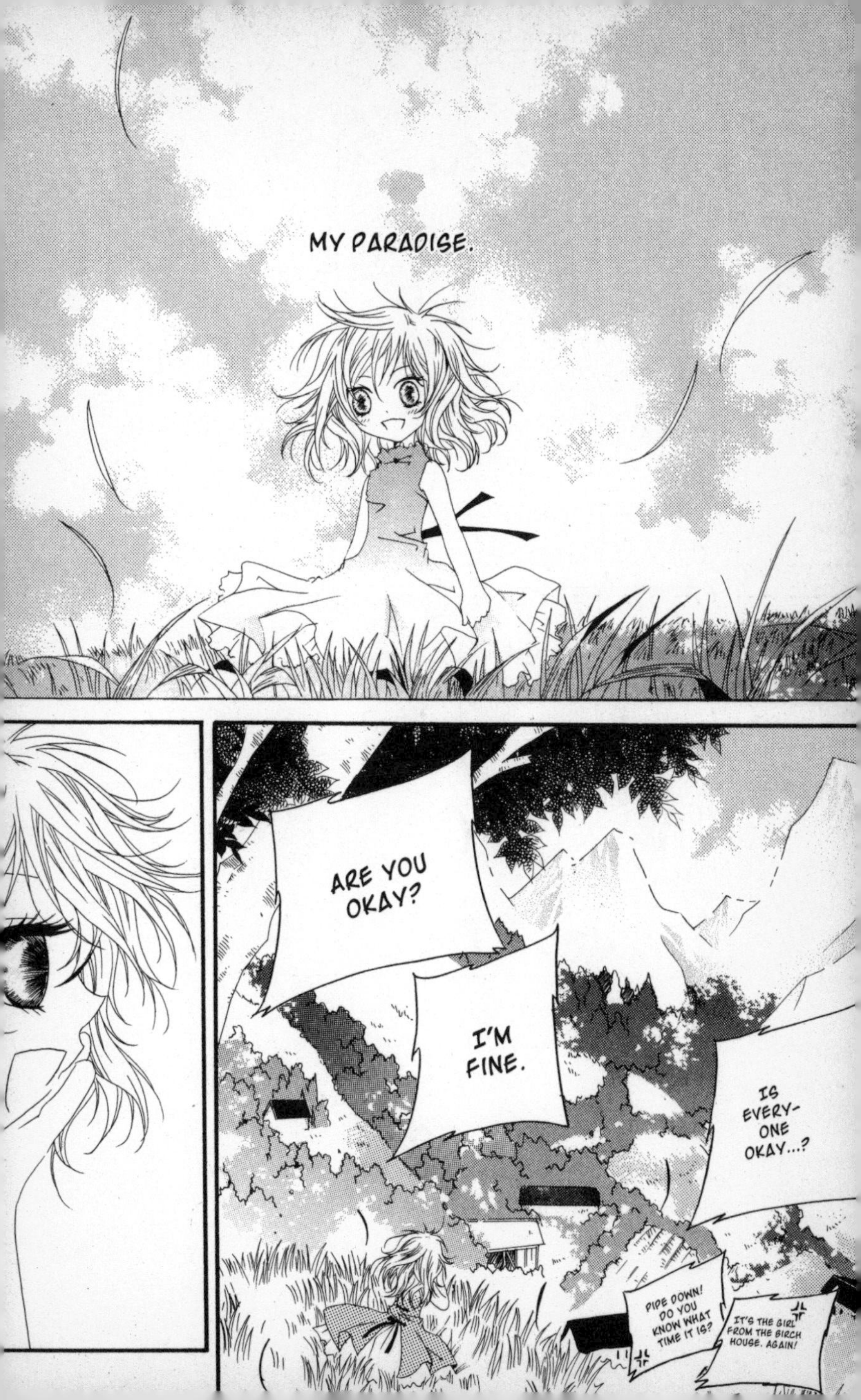
MY PARADISE.
ARE YOU OKAY?
I'M FINE.
IS EVERYONE OKAY...?
PIPE DOWN! DO YOU KNOW WHAT TIME IT IS?
IT'S THE GIRL FROM THE BIRCH HOUSE. AGAIN!

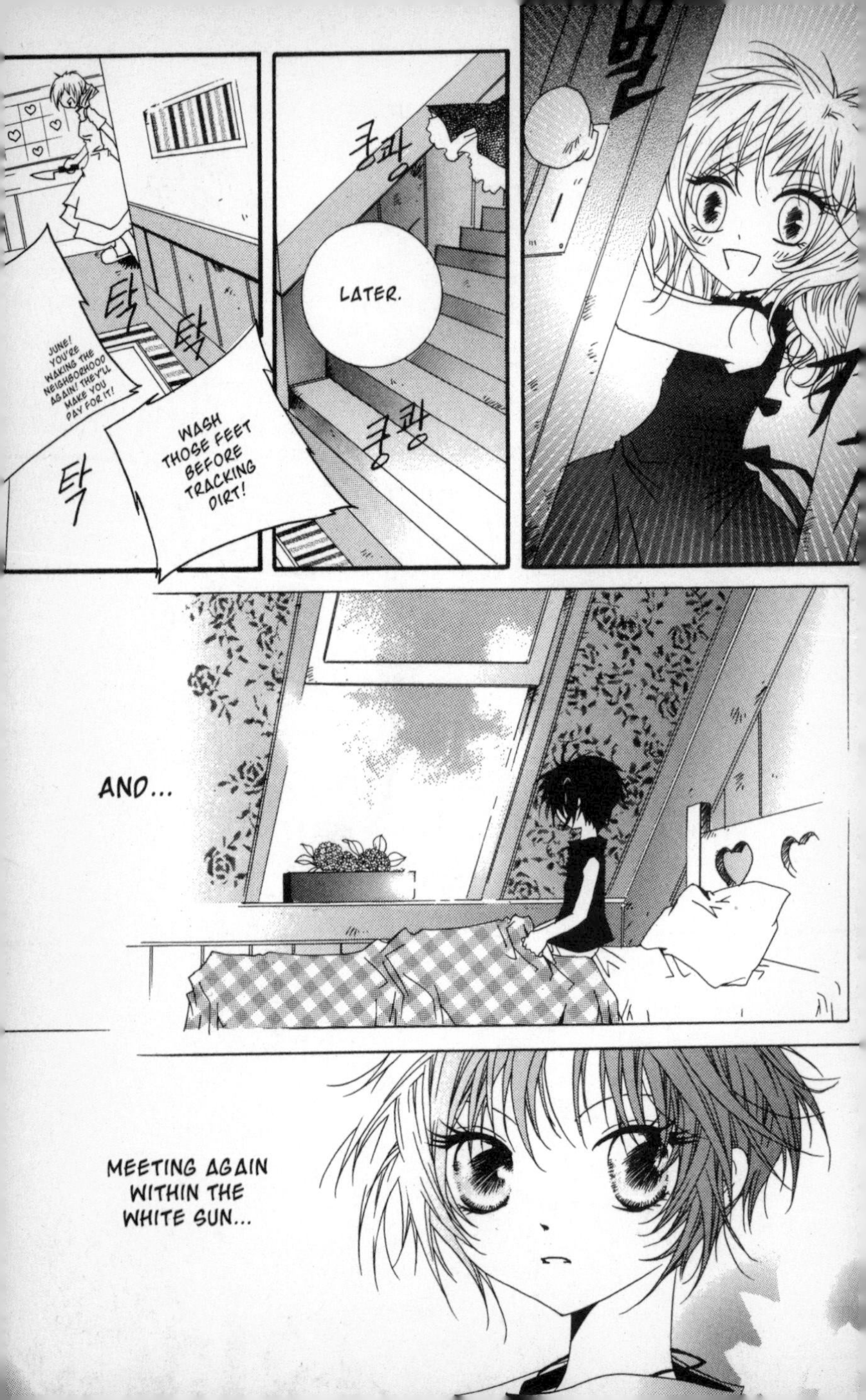
탁
June! You're waking the neighborhood again! They'll make you pay for it!
탁
탁
Wash those feet before tracking dirt!
쿵쾅
Later.
쿵쾅
벌
And...
Meeting again within the white sun...

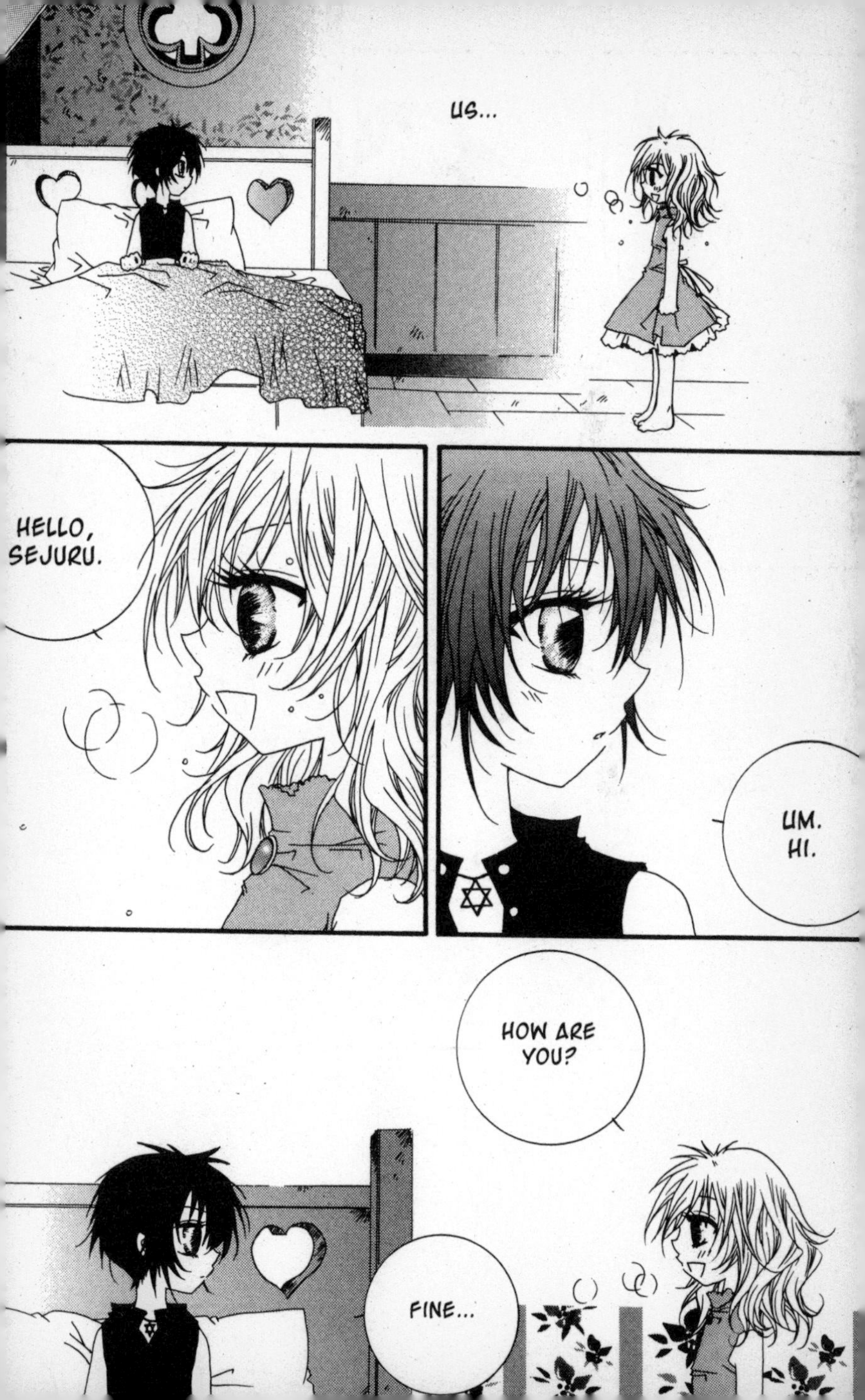
US...
HELLO, SEJURU.
UM. HI.
HOW ARE YOU?
FINE...

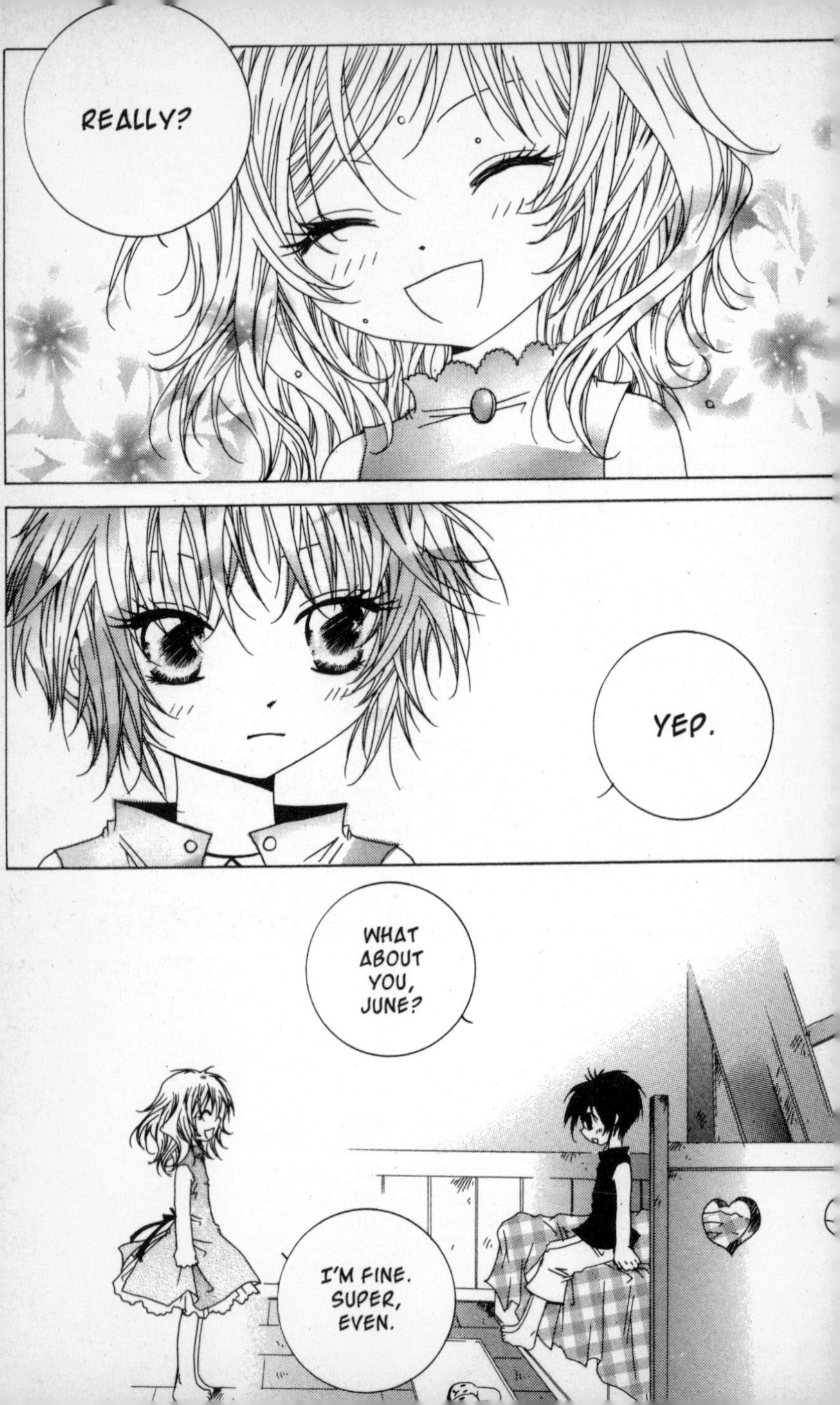
REALLY?
YEP.
WHAT ABOUT YOU, JUNE?
I'M FINE. SUPER, EVEN.

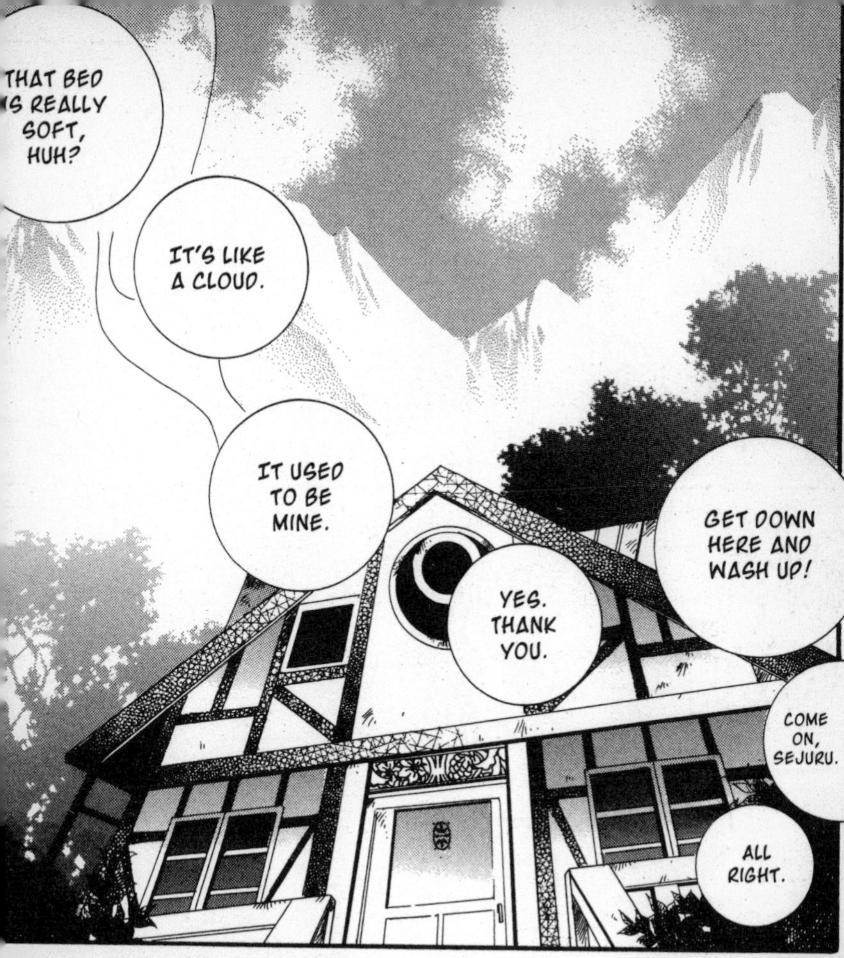
THAT BED IS REALLY SOFT, HUH?
IT'S LIKE A CLOUD.
IT USED TO BE MINE.
YES. THANK YOU.
GET DOWN HERE AND WASH UP!
COME ON, SEJURU.
ALL RIGHT.

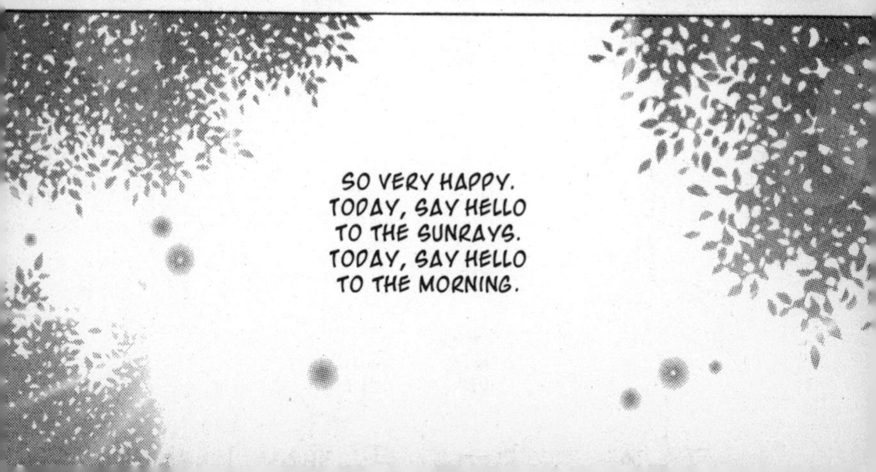
SO VERY HAPPY.
TODAY, SAY HELLO TO THE SUNRAYS.
TODAY, SAY HELLO TO THE MORNING.

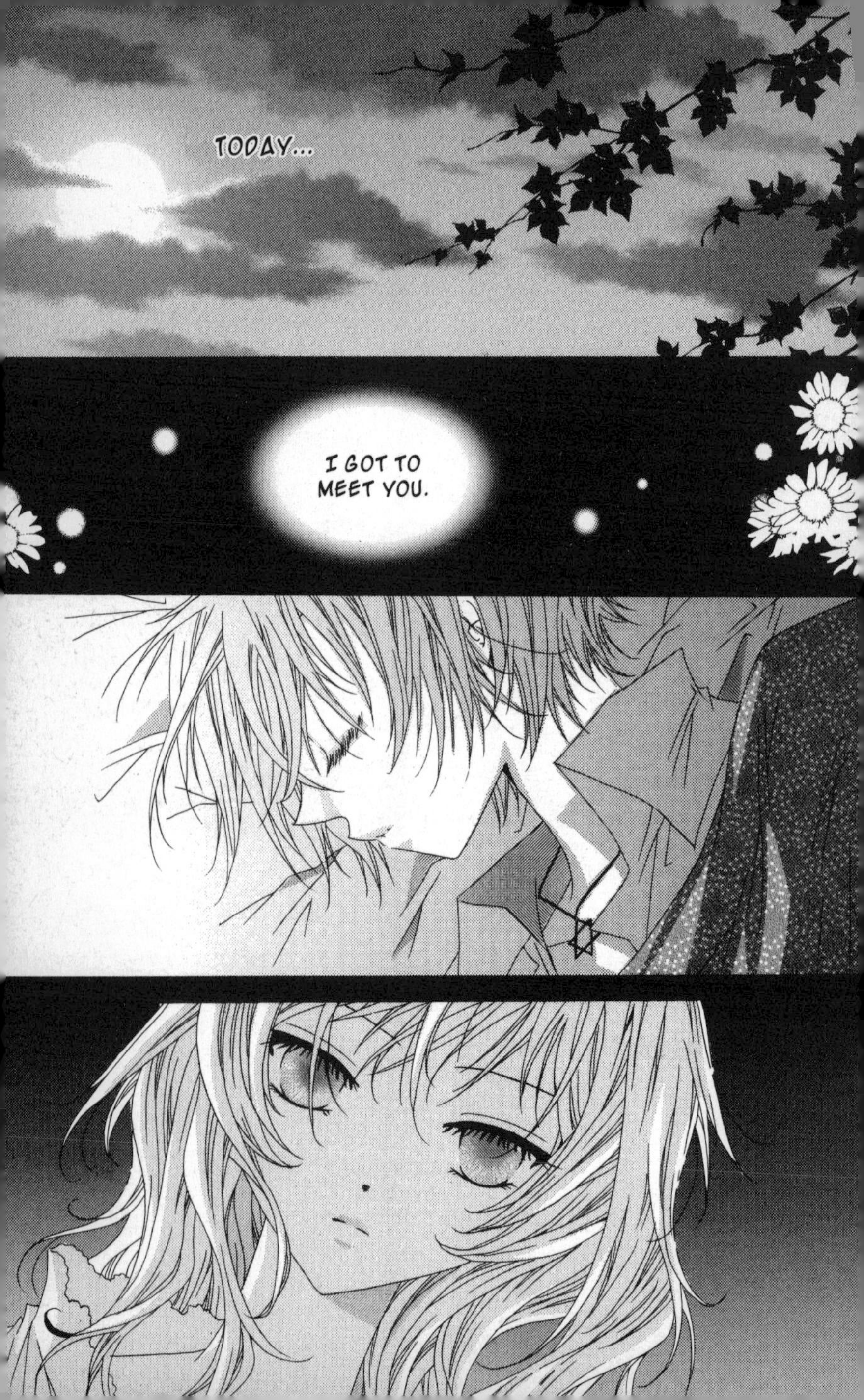
TODAY...
I GOT TO MEET YOU.

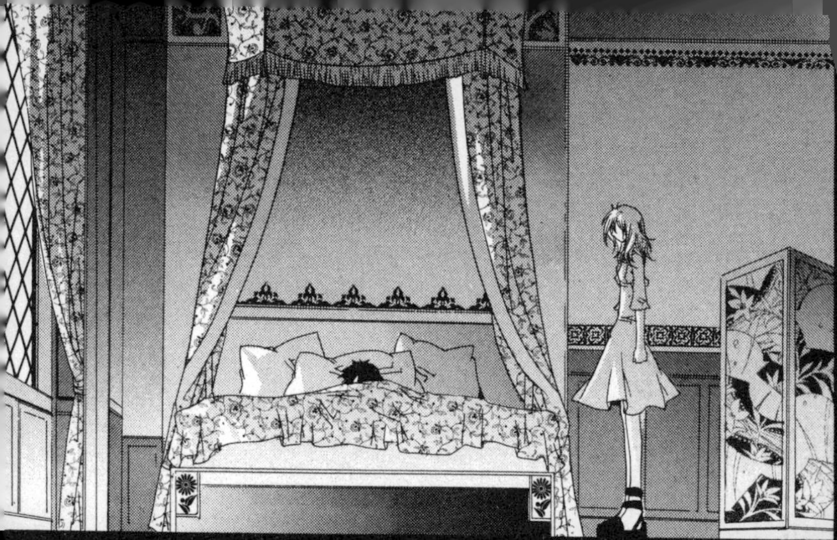

Say Hello to the Morning

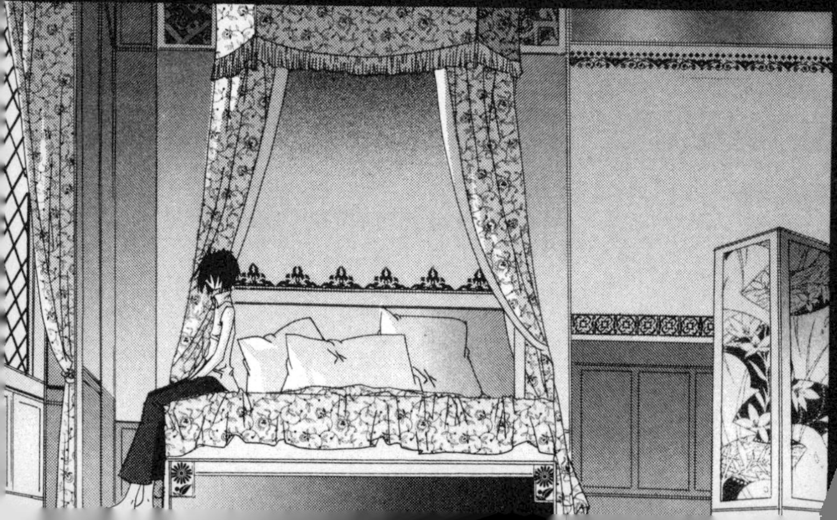

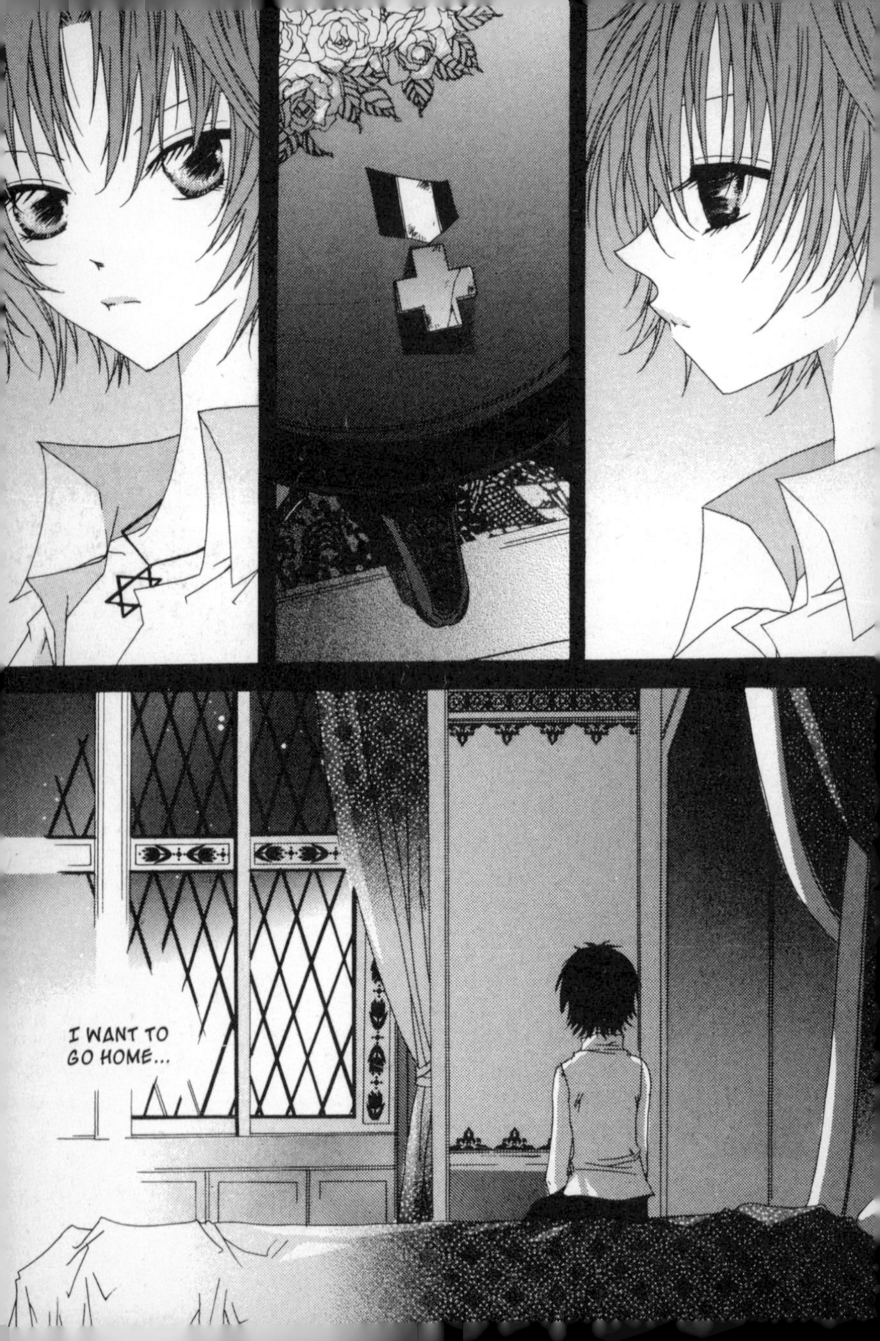
I WANT TO
GO HOME...

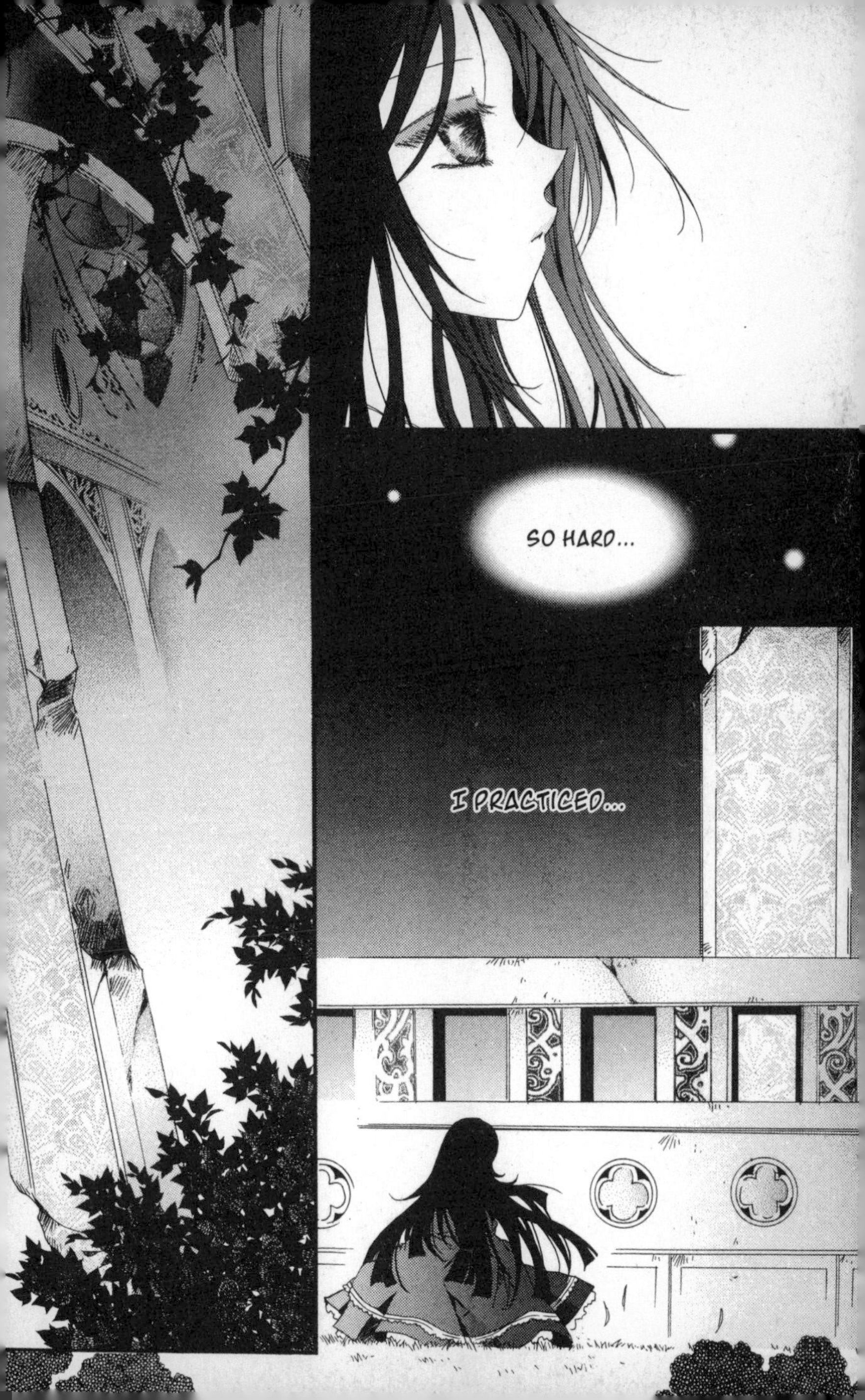
SO HARD...
I PRACTICED...

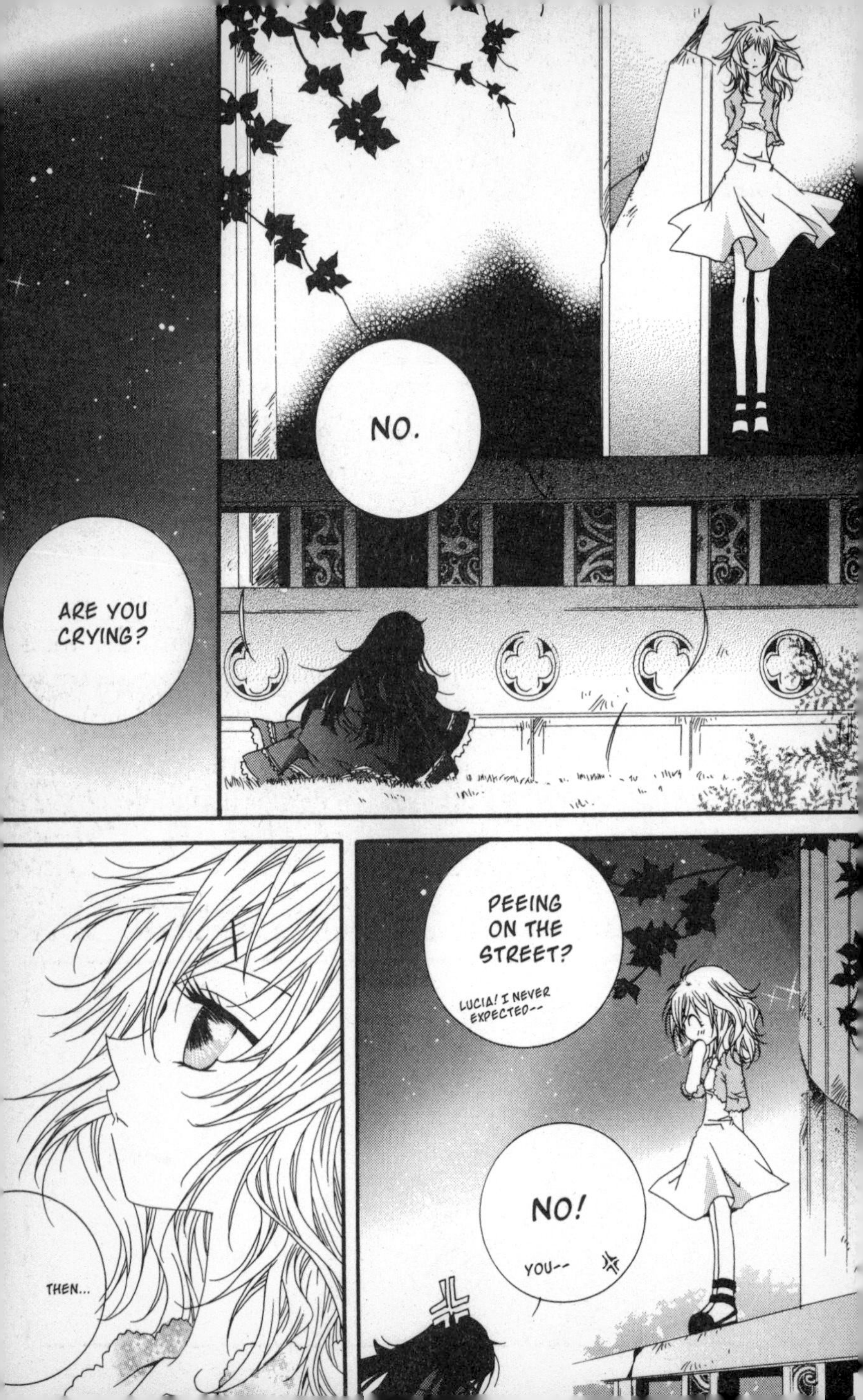
ARE YOU CRYING?
NO.
THEN...
PEEING ON THE STREET?
LUCIA! I NEVER EXPECTED--
NO!
YOU--

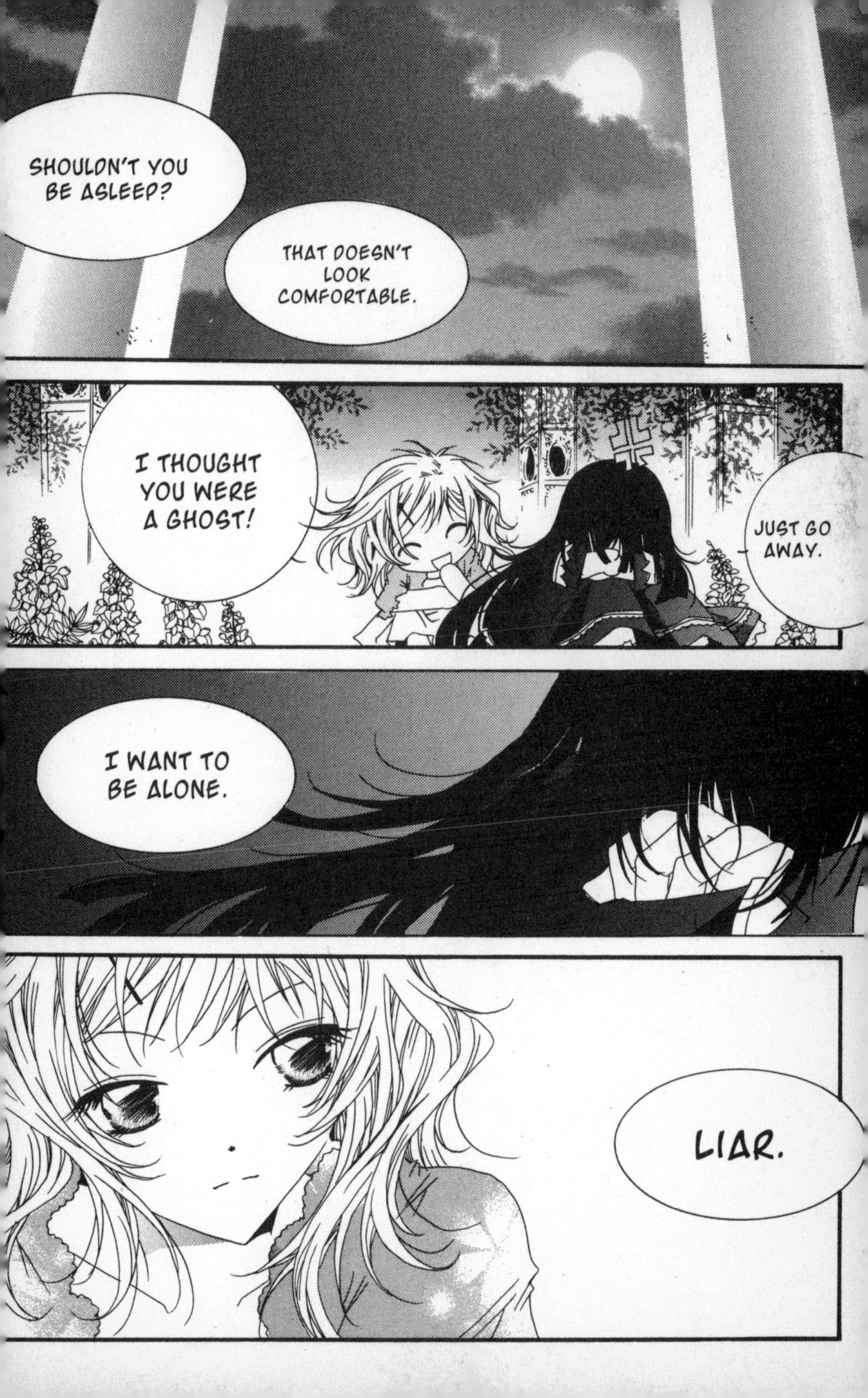
SHOULDN'T YOU BE ASLEEP?
THAT DOESN'T LOOK COMFORTABLE.
I THOUGHT YOU WERE A GHOST!
JUST GO AWAY.
I WANT TO BE ALONE.
LIAR.

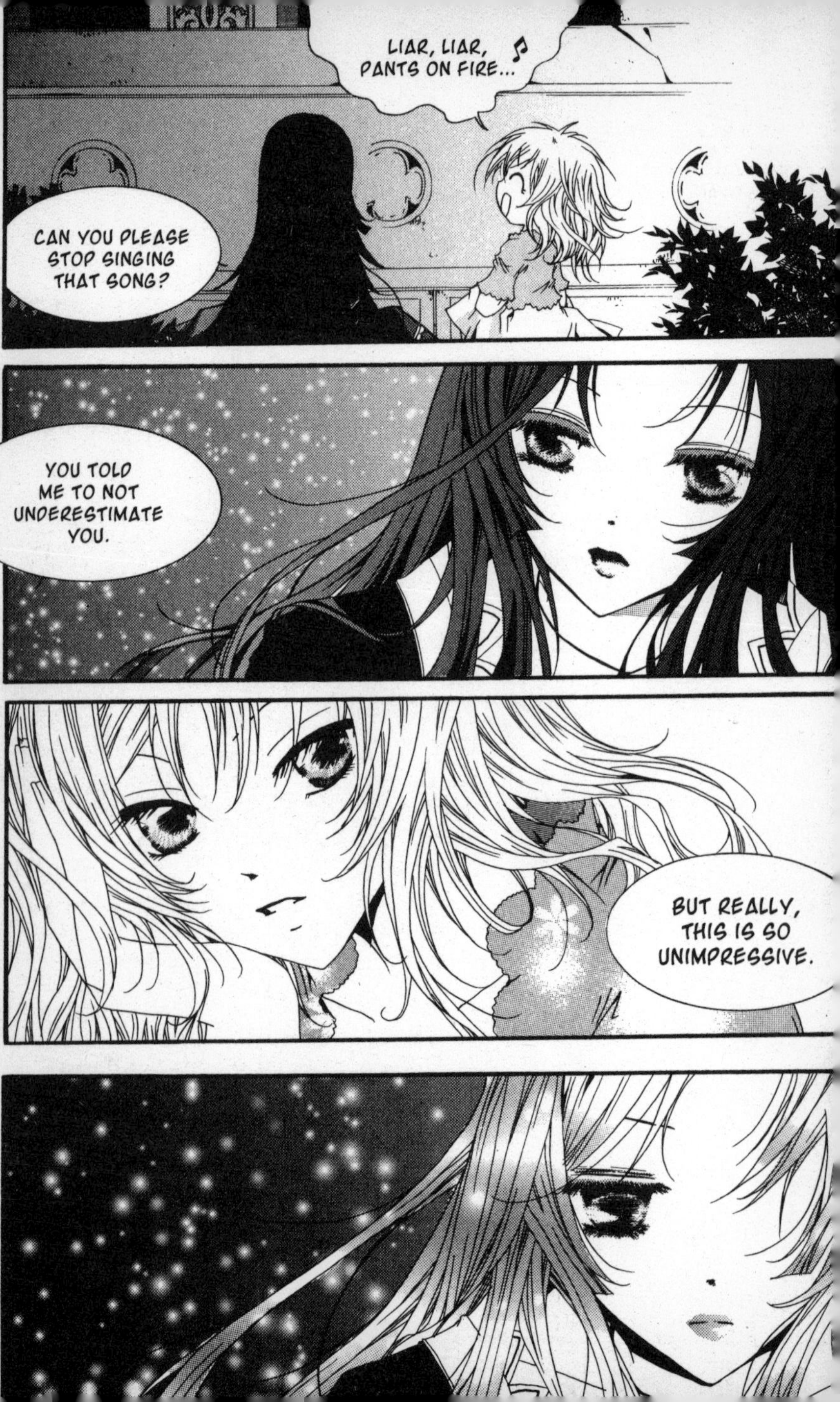
LIAR, LIAR, PANTS ON FIRE... ♪
CAN YOU PLEASE STOP SINGING THAT SONG?
YOU TOLD ME TO NOT UNDERESTIMATE YOU.
BUT REALLY, THIS IS SO UNIMPRESSIVE.

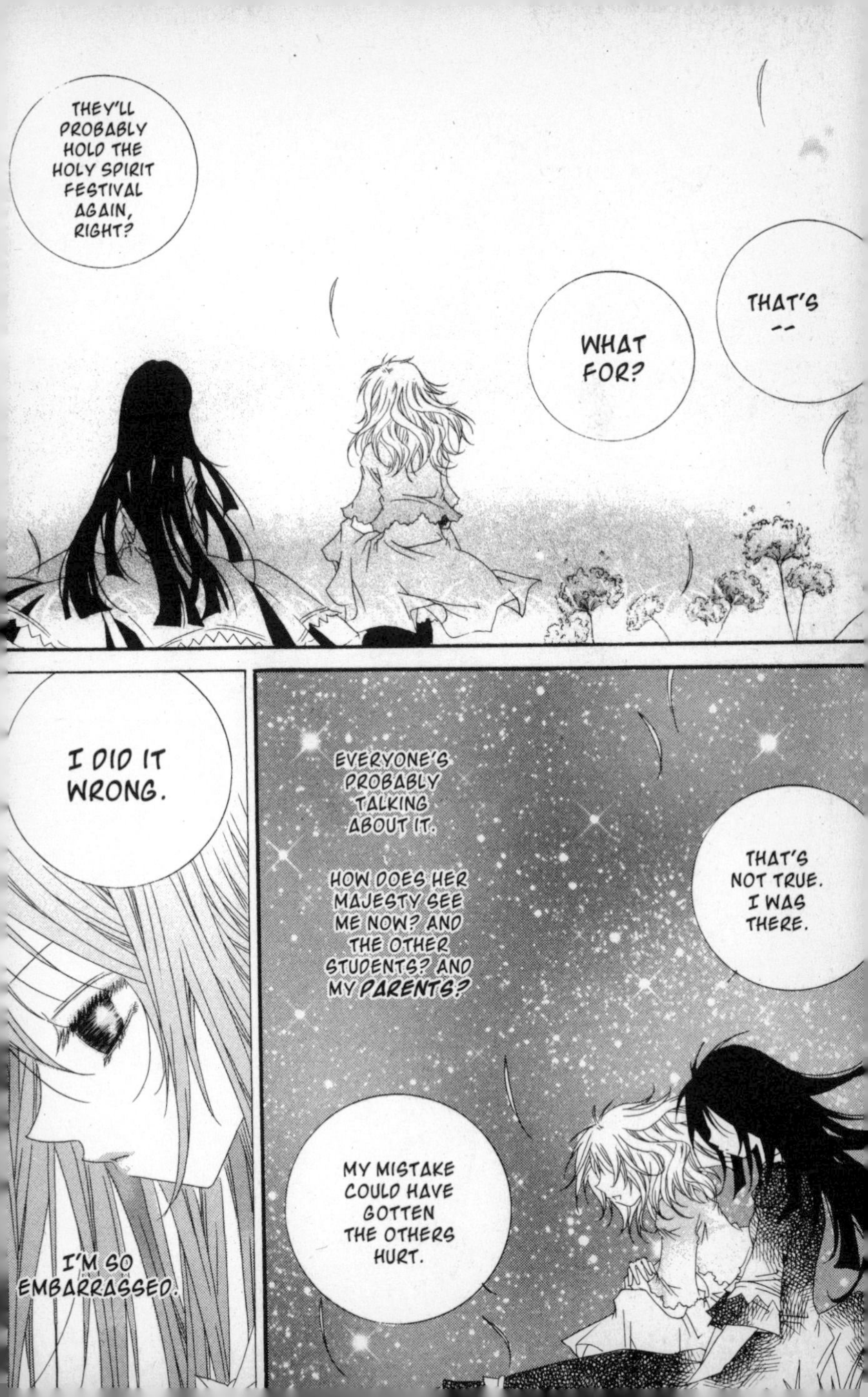
THEY'LL PROBABLY HOLD THE HOLY SPIRIT FESTIVAL AGAIN, RIGHT?
WHAT FOR?
THAT'S --
I DID IT WRONG.
I'M SO EMBARRASSED.
EVERYONE'S PROBABLY TALKING ABOUT IT.
HOW DOES HER MAJESTY SEE ME NOW? AND THE OTHER STUDENTS? AND MY PARENTS?
THAT'S NOT TRUE. I WAS THERE.
MY MISTAKE COULD HAVE GOTTEN THE OTHERS HURT.

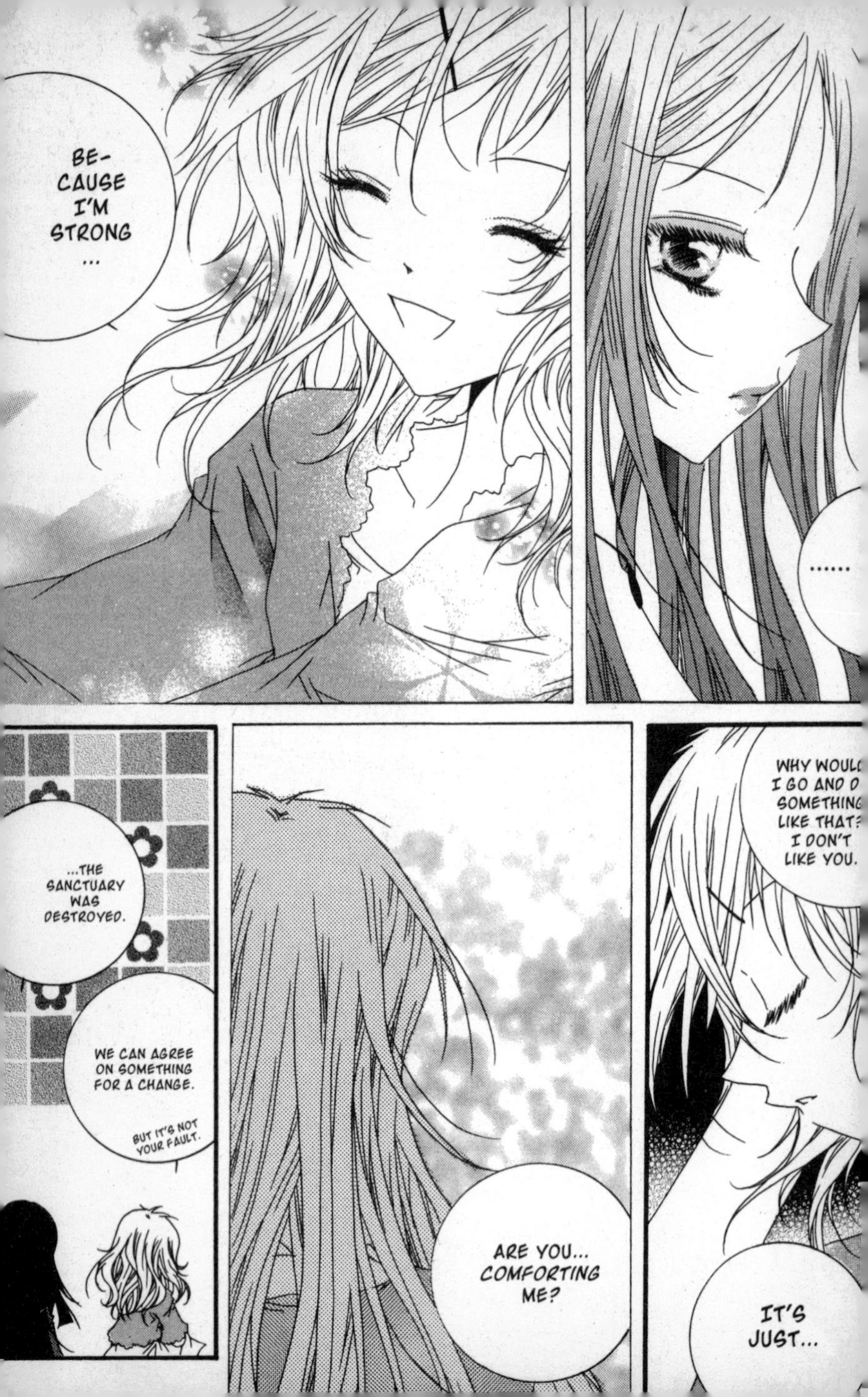
BE-CAUSE I'M STRONG ...
......
...THE SANCTUARY WAS DESTROYED.
WE CAN AGREE ON SOMETHING FOR A CHANGE.
BUT IT'S NOT YOUR FAULT.
ARE YOU... COMFORTING ME?
WHY WOUL I GO AND D SOMETHING LIKE THAT? I DON'T LIKE YOU.
IT'S JUST...

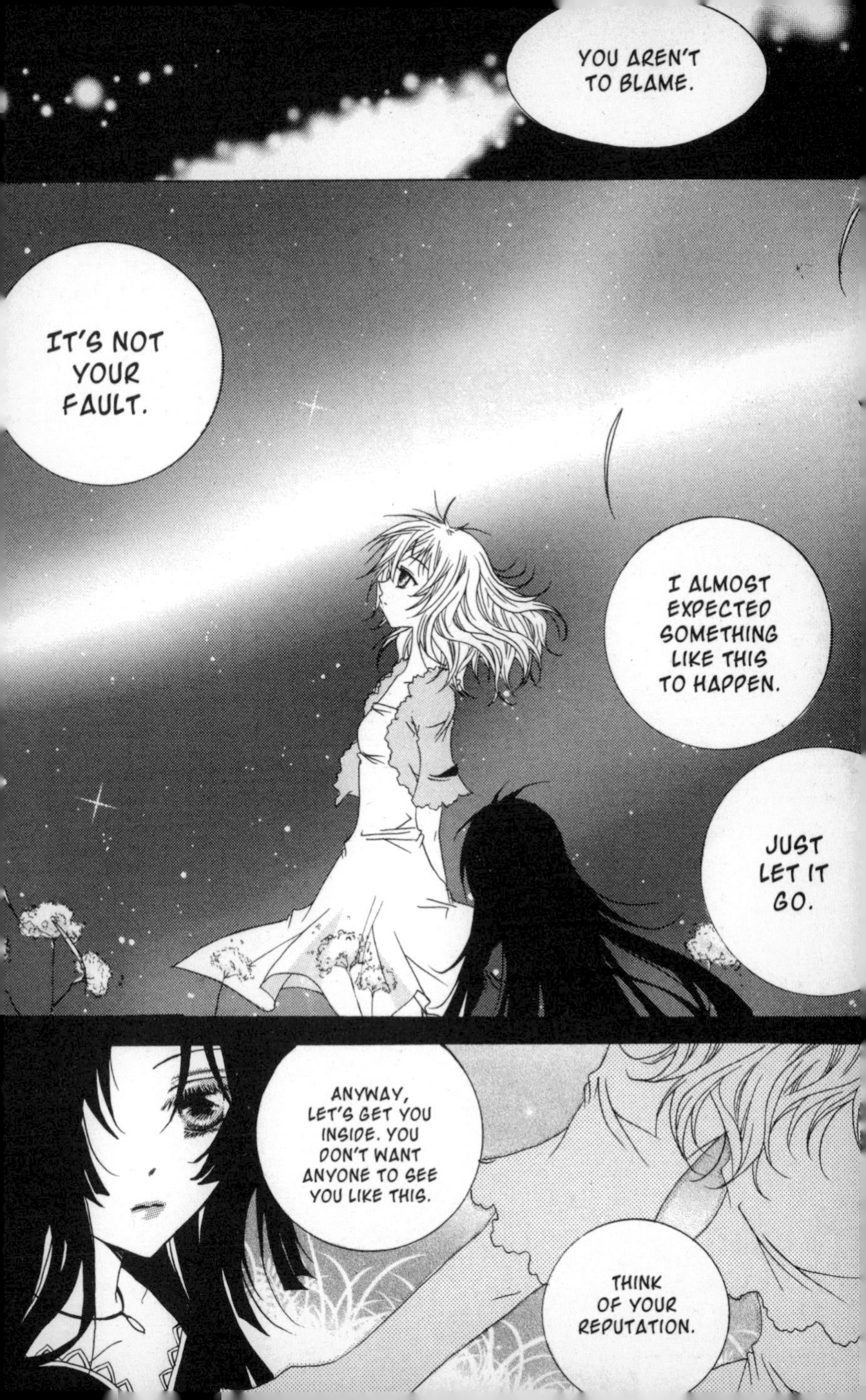
YOU AREN'T TO BLAME.
IT'S NOT YOUR FAULT.
I ALMOST EXPECTED SOMETHING LIKE THIS TO HAPPEN.
JUST LET IT GO.
ANYWAY, LET'S GET YOU INSIDE. YOU DON'T WANT ANYONE TO SEE YOU LIKE THIS.
THINK OF YOUR REPUTATION.

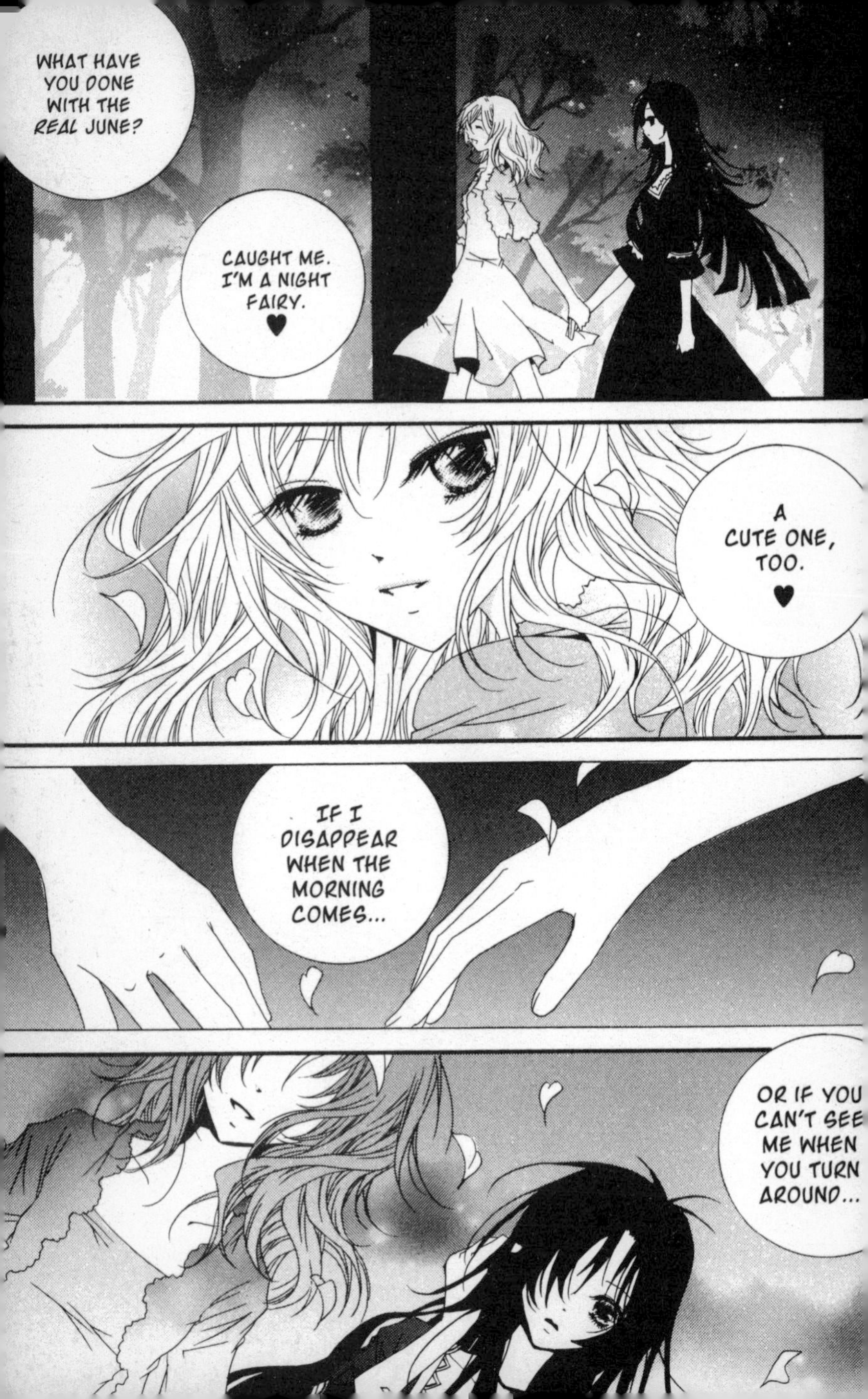
WHAT HAVE YOU DONE WITH THE REAL JUNE?
CAUGHT ME. I'M A NIGHT FAIRY. ♥
A CUTE ONE, TOO. ♥
IF I DISAPPEAR WHEN THE MORNING COMES...
OR IF YOU CAN'T SEE ME WHEN YOU TURN AROUND...

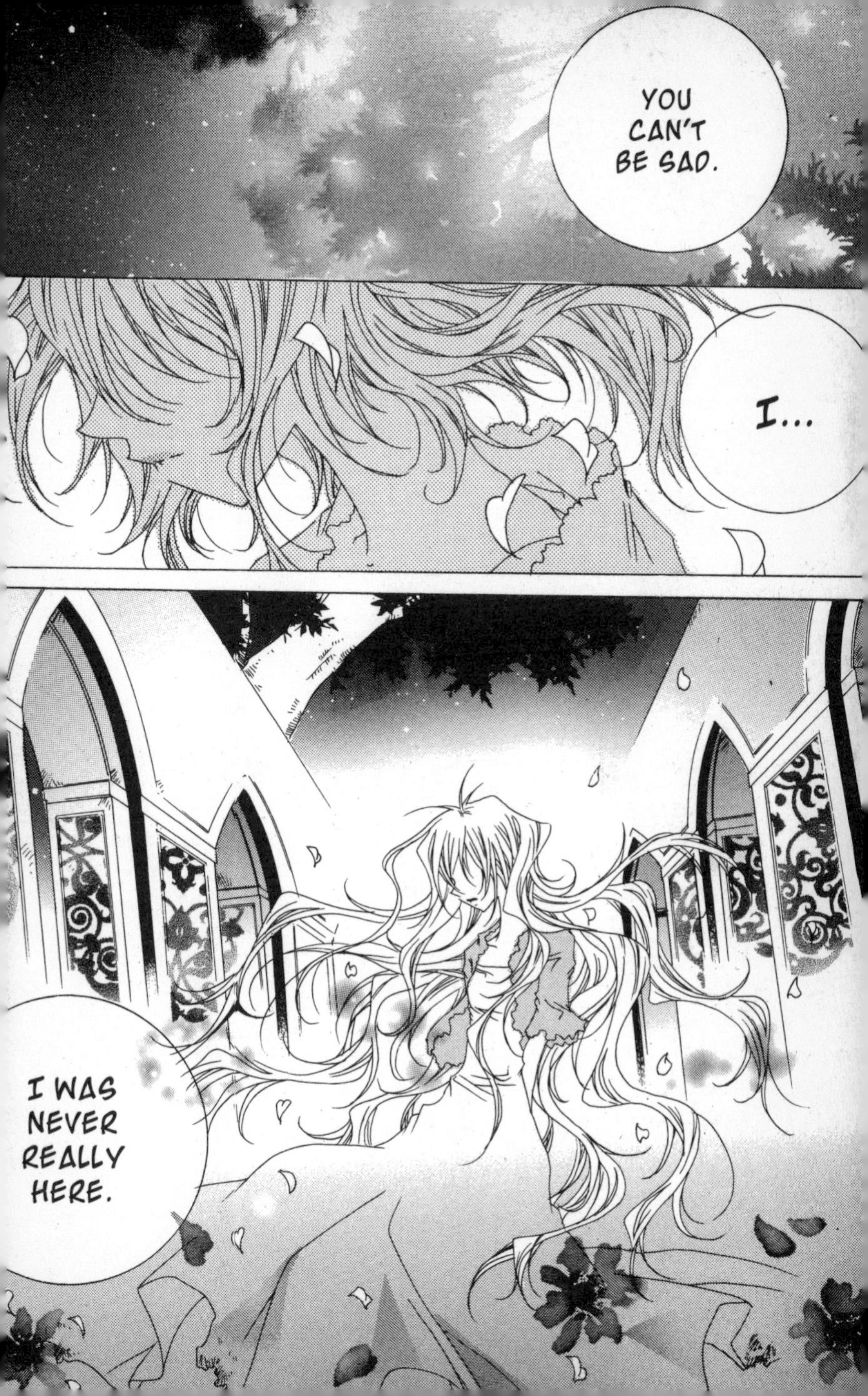
YOU CAN'T BE SAD.
I...
I WAS NEVER REALLY HERE.

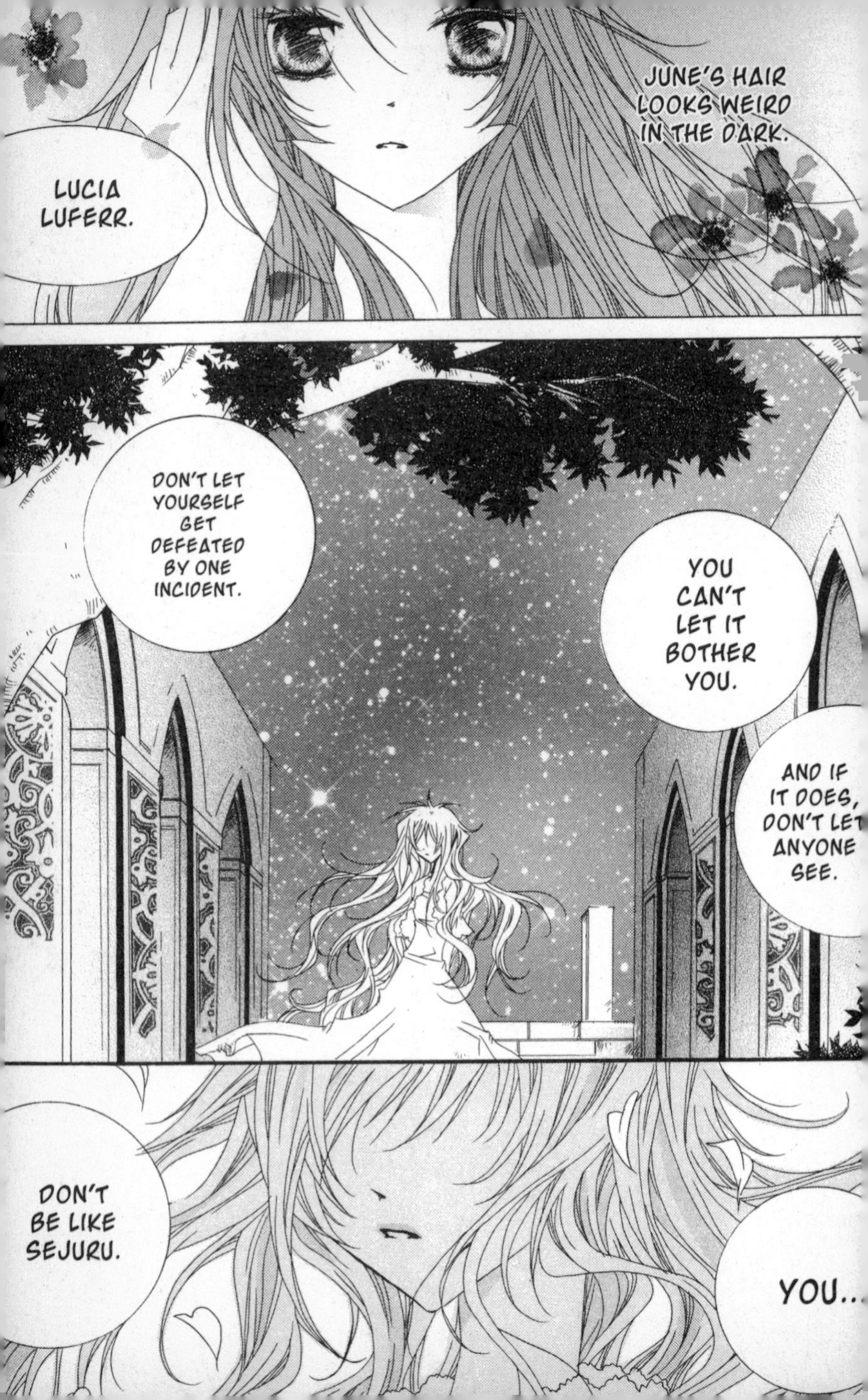
LUCIA LUFERR.
JUNE'S HAIR LOOKS WEIRD IN THE DARK.
DON'T LET YOURSELF GET DEFEATED BY ONE INCIDENT.
YOU CAN'T LET IT BOTHER YOU.
AND IF IT DOES, DON'T LET ANYONE SEE.
DON'T BE LIKE SEJURU.
YOU...

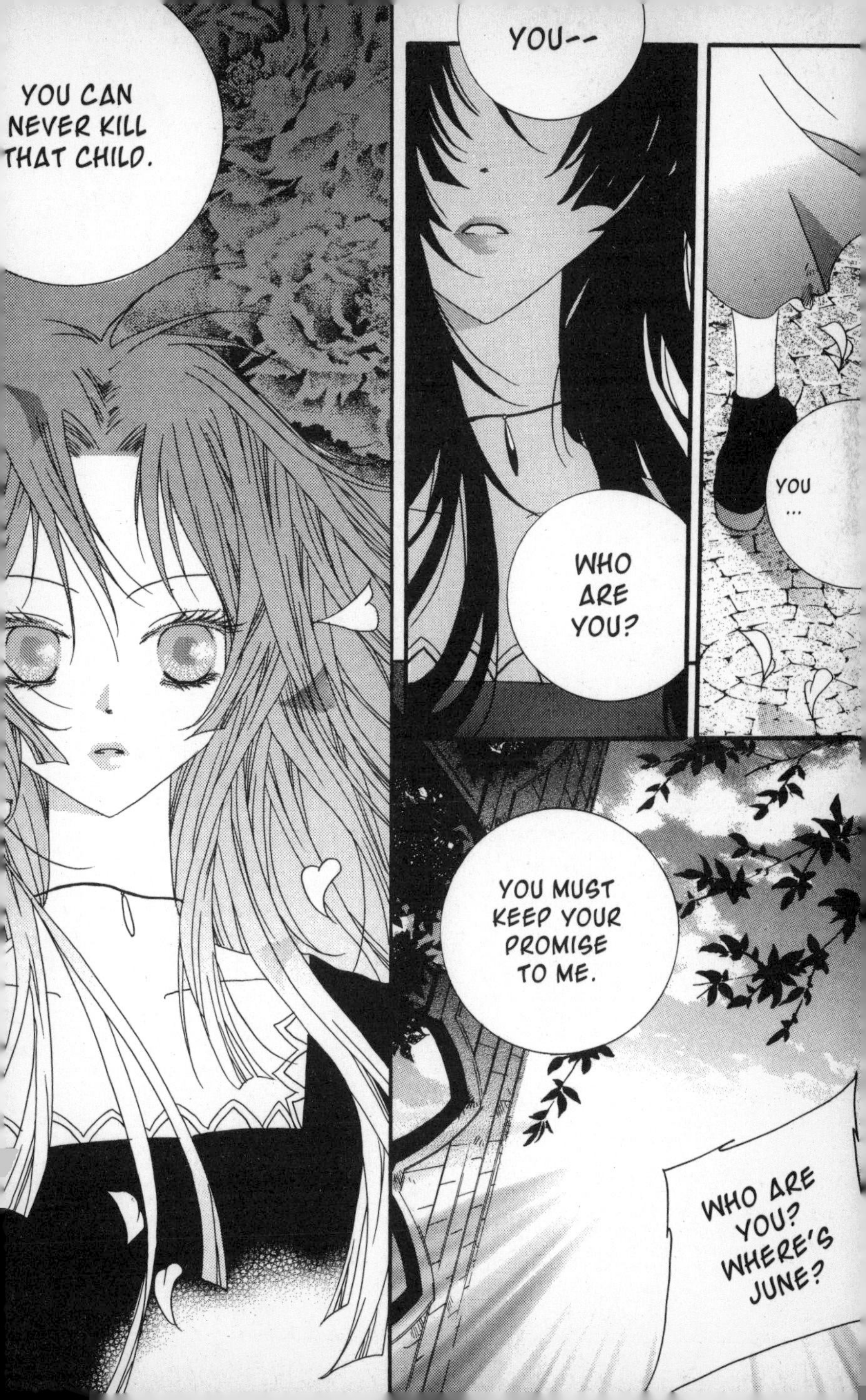
YOU CAN NEVER KILL THAT CHILD.
YOU--
WHO ARE YOU?
YOU ...
YOU MUST KEEP YOUR PROMISE TO ME.
WHO ARE YOU? WHERE'S JUNE?

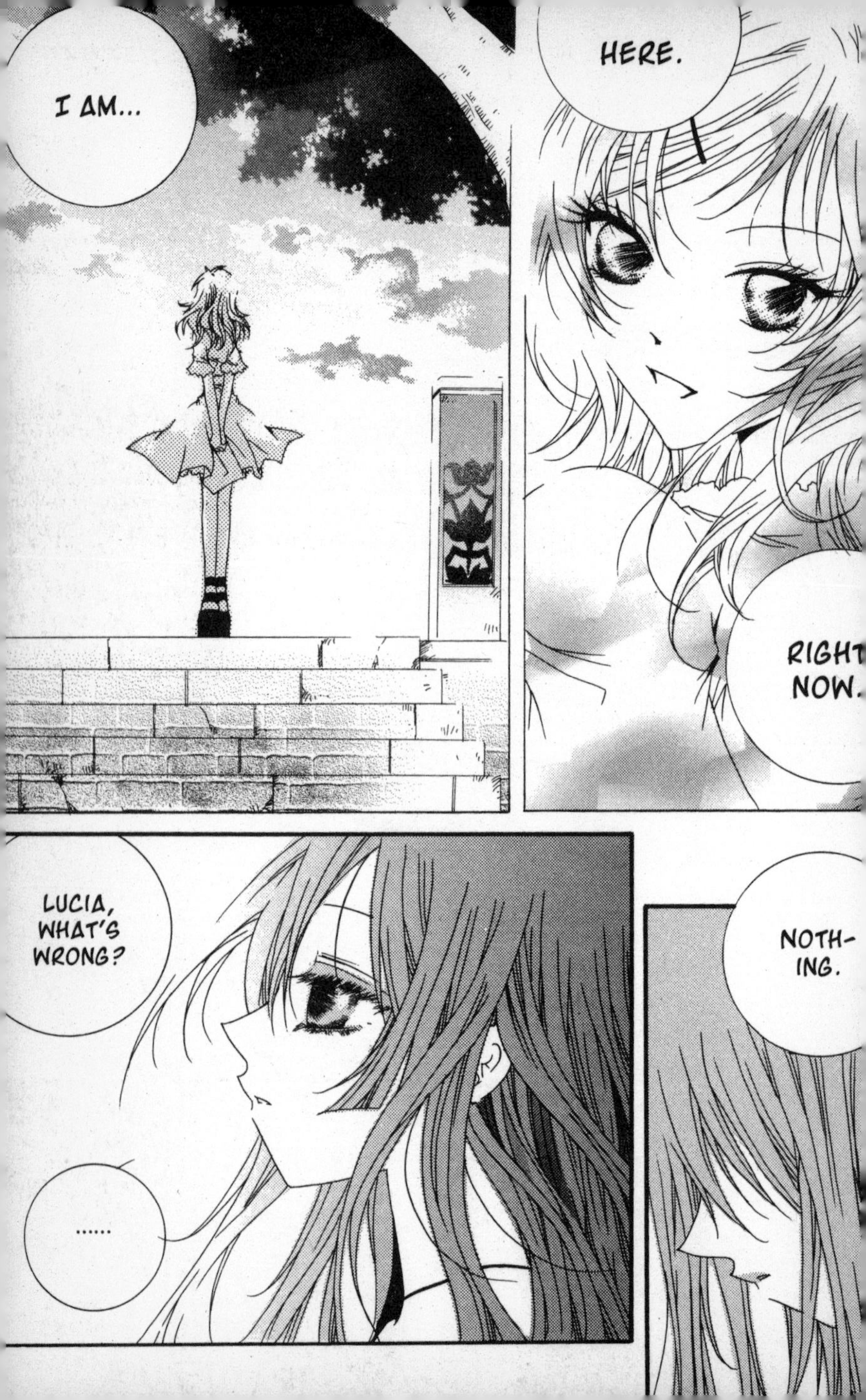
I AM...
HERE.
RIGHT NOW.
LUCIA, WHAT'S WRONG?
......
NOTH-ING.

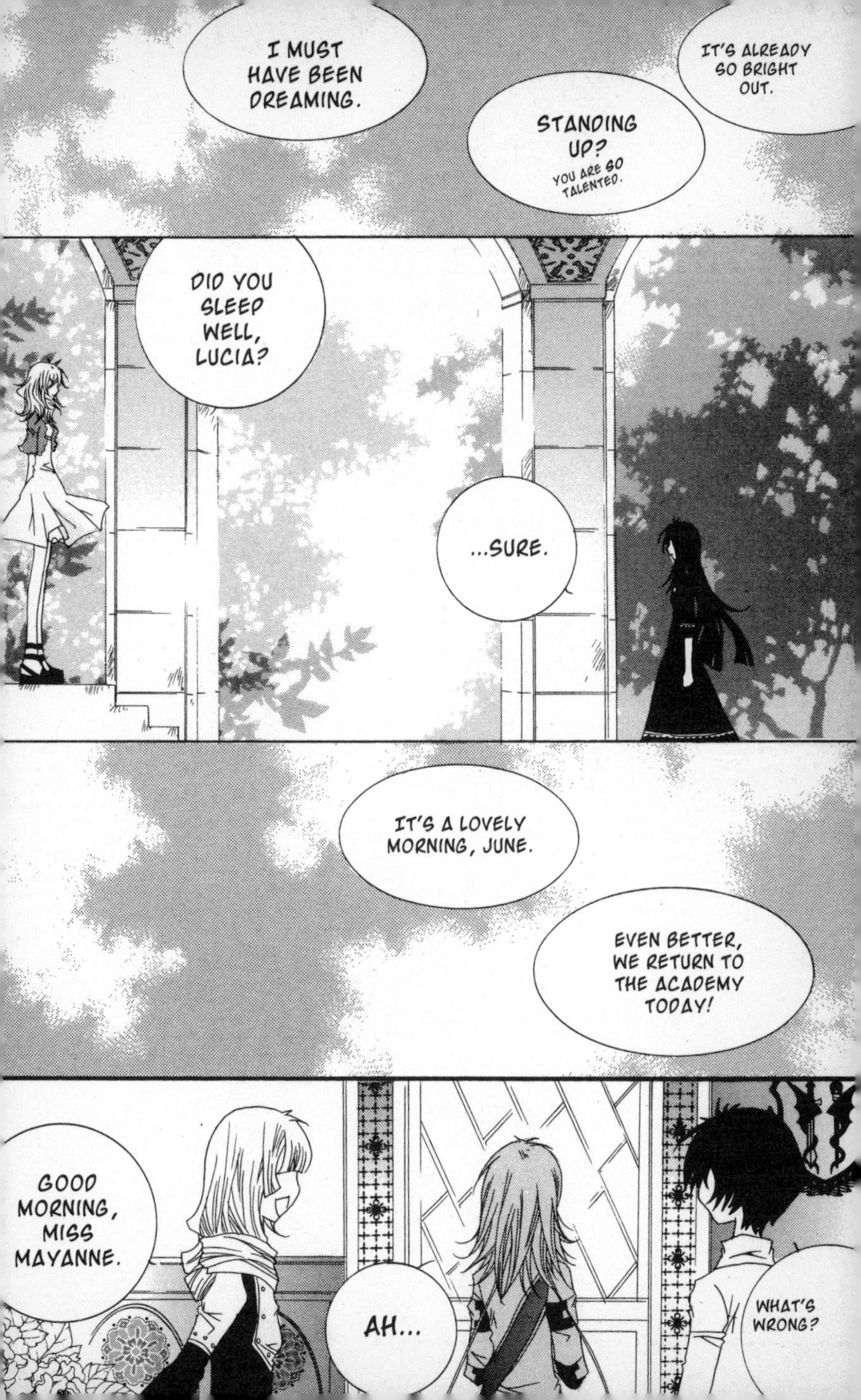
I MUST HAVE BEEN DREAMING.
STANDING UP?
YOU ARE SO TALENTED.
IT'S ALREADY SO BRIGHT OUT.
DID YOU SLEEP WELL, LUCIA?
...SURE.
IT'S A LOVELY MORNING, JUNE.
EVEN BETTER, WE RETURN TO THE ACADEMY TODAY!
GOOD MORNING, MISS MAYANNE.
AH...
WHAT'S WRONG?

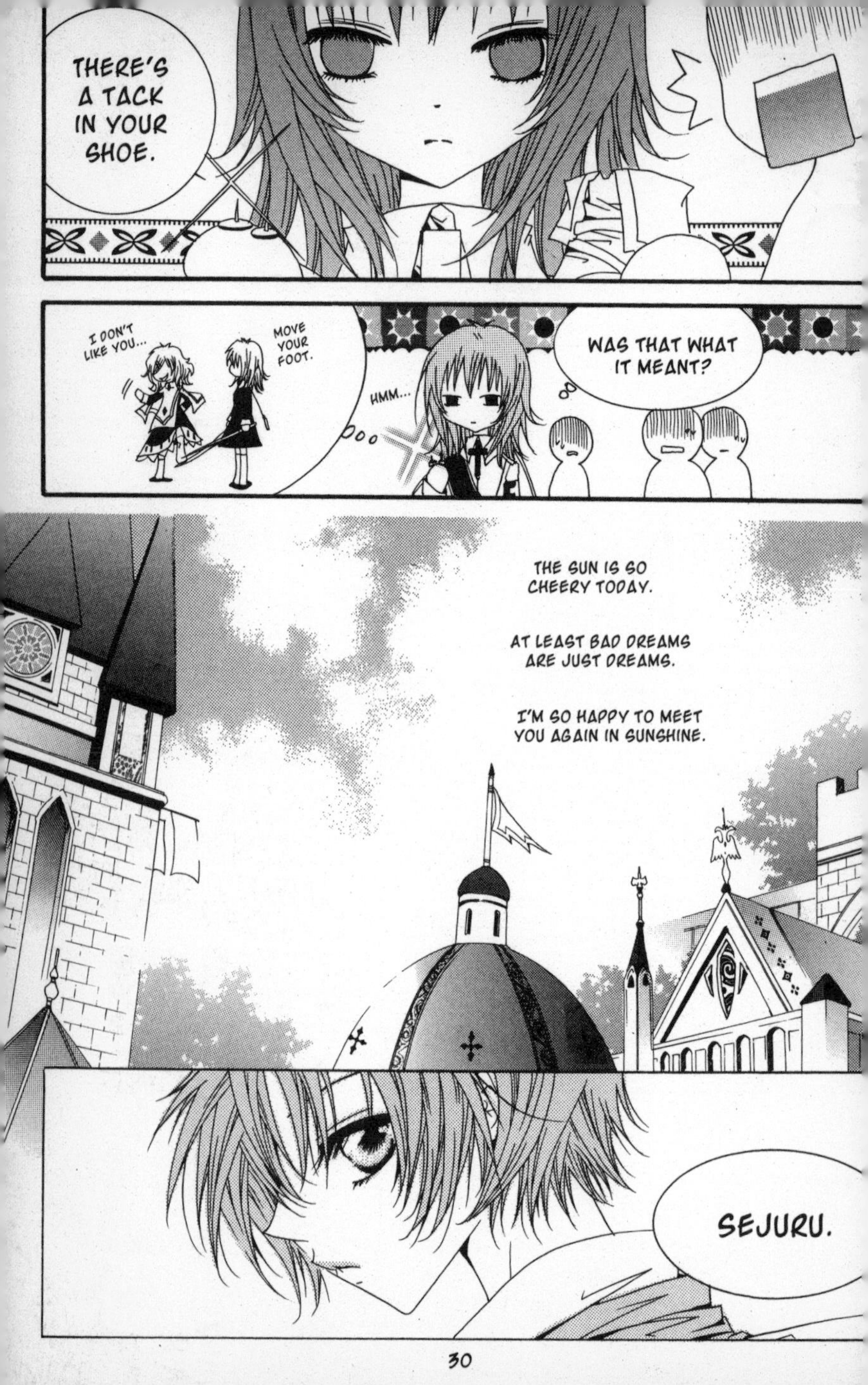
THERE'S A TACK IN YOUR SHOE.
I DON'T LIKE YOU...
MOVE YOUR FOOT.
HMM...
WAS THAT WHAT IT MEANT?
THE SUN IS SO CHEERY TODAY.
AT LEAST BAD DREAMS ARE JUST DREAMS.
I'M SO HAPPY TO MEET YOU AGAIN IN SUNSHINE.
SEJURU.

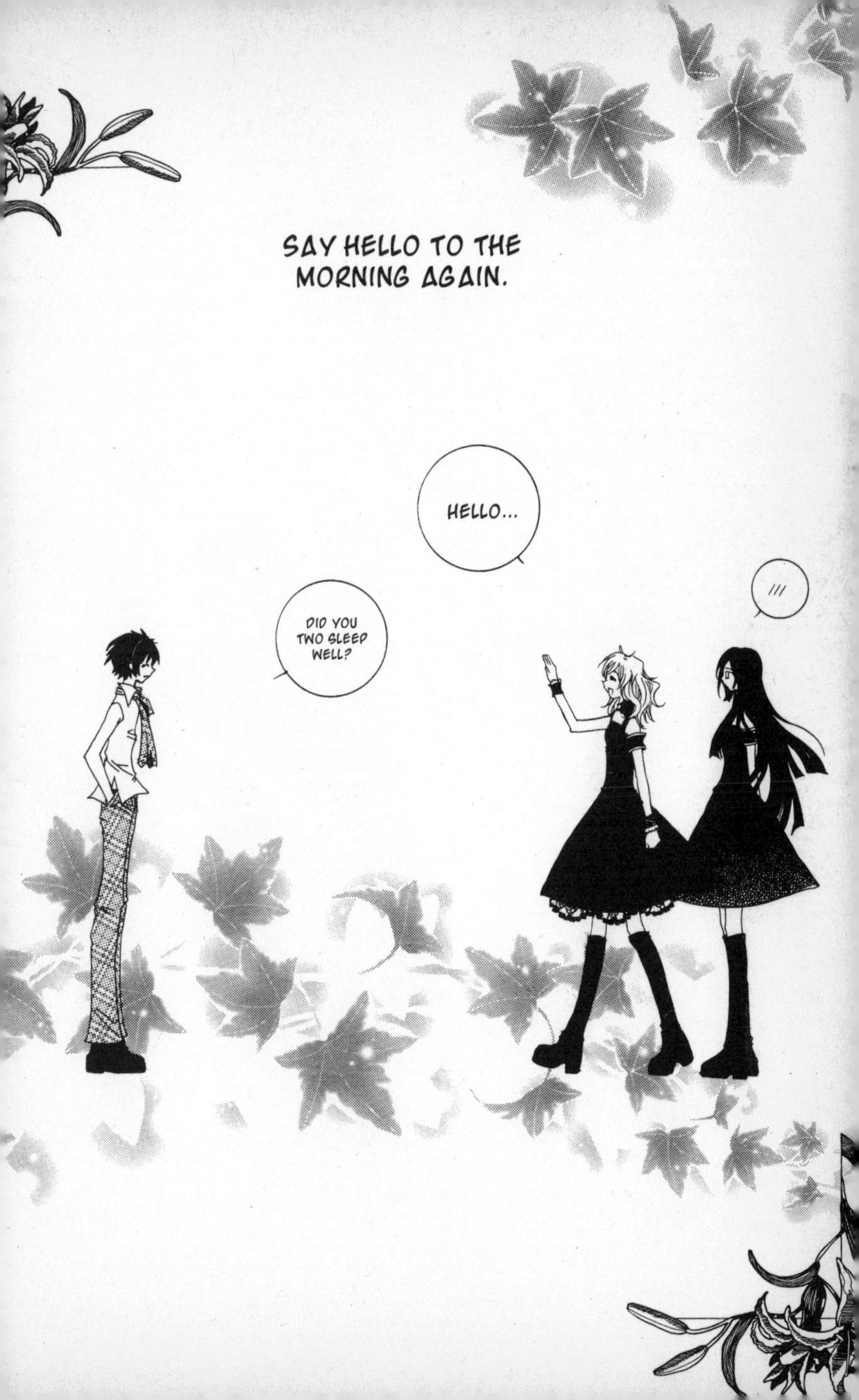
SAY HELLO TO THE MORNING AGAIN.
HELLO...
DID YOU TWO SLEEP WELL?

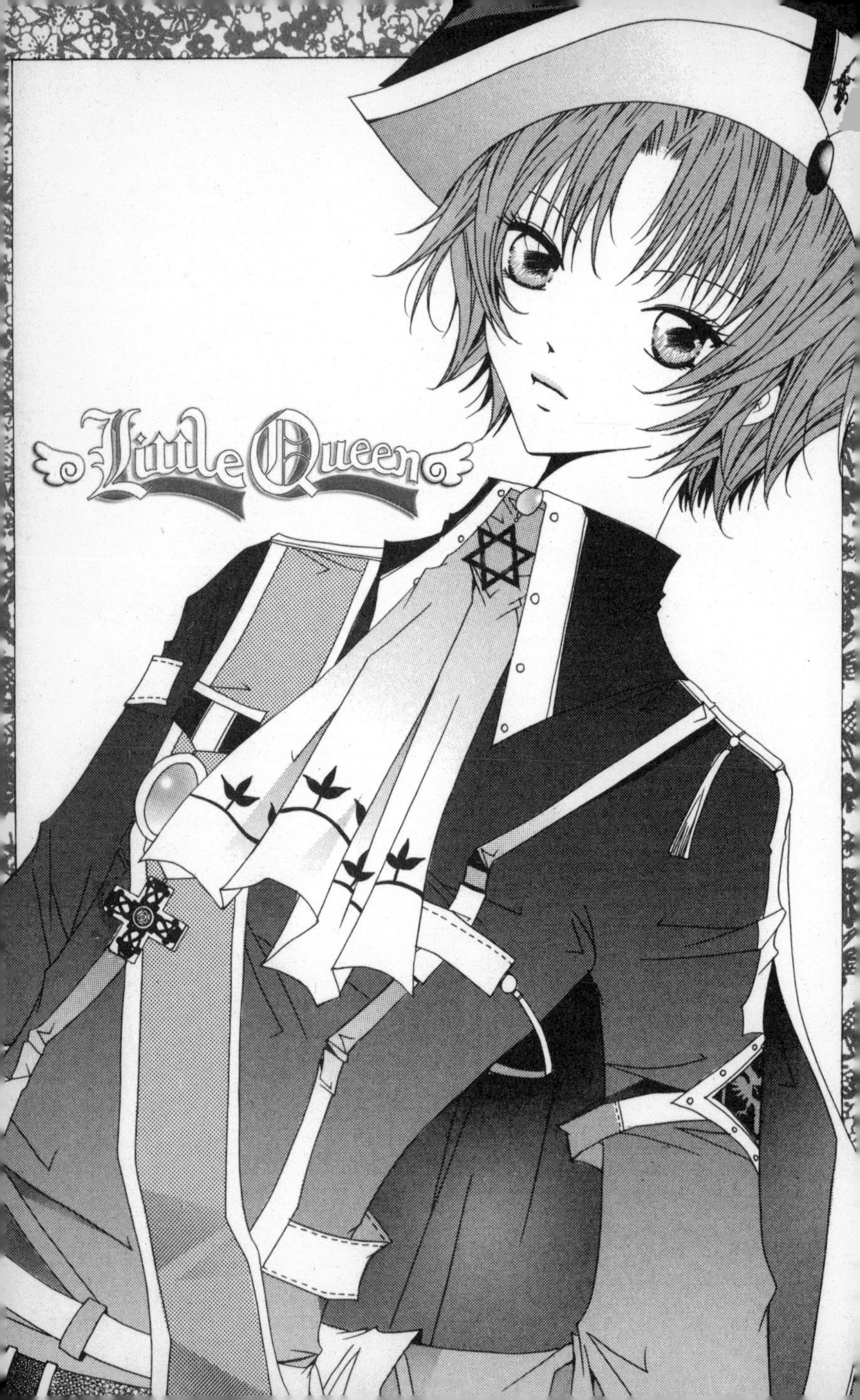
Little Queen

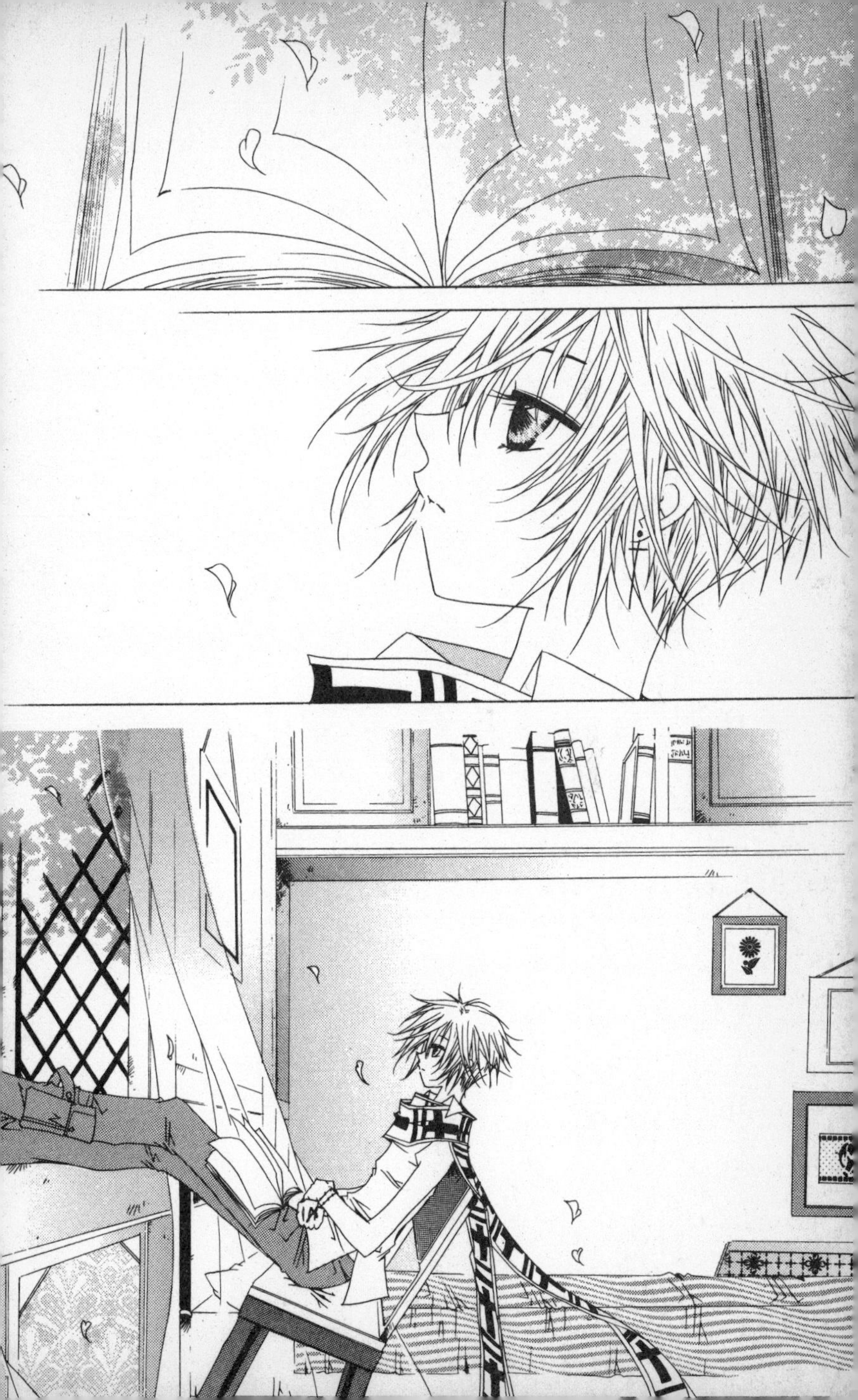

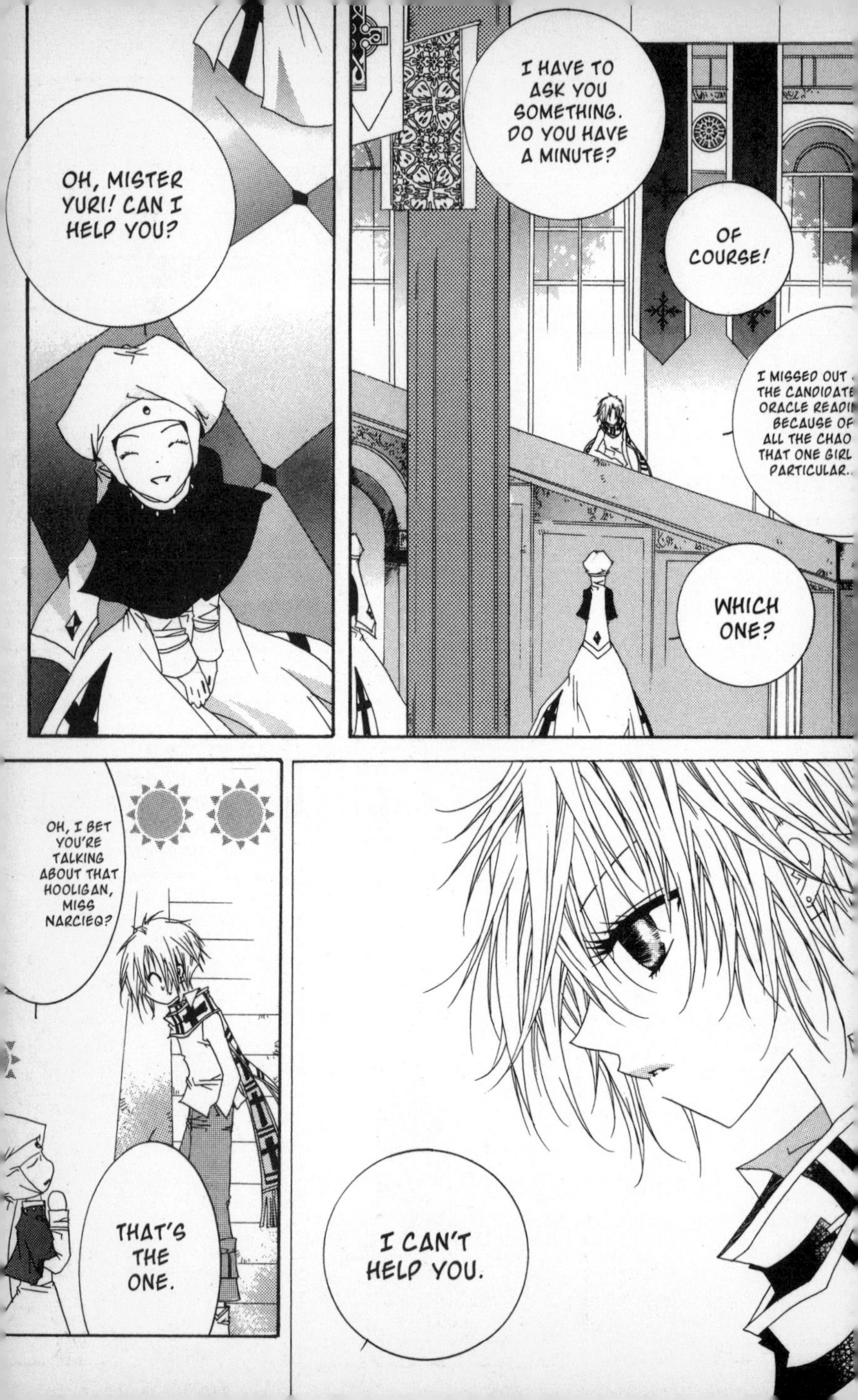
OH, MISTER YURI! CAN I HELP YOU?
I HAVE TO ASK YOU SOMETHING. DO YOU HAVE A MINUTE?
OF COURSE!
I MISSED OUT THE CANDIDATE ORACLE READI BECAUSE OF ALL THE CHAO THAT ONE GIRL PARTICULAR..
WHICH ONE?
OH, I BET YOU'RE TALKING ABOUT THAT HOOLIGAN, MISS NARCIEQ?
THAT'S THE ONE.
I CAN'T HELP YOU.

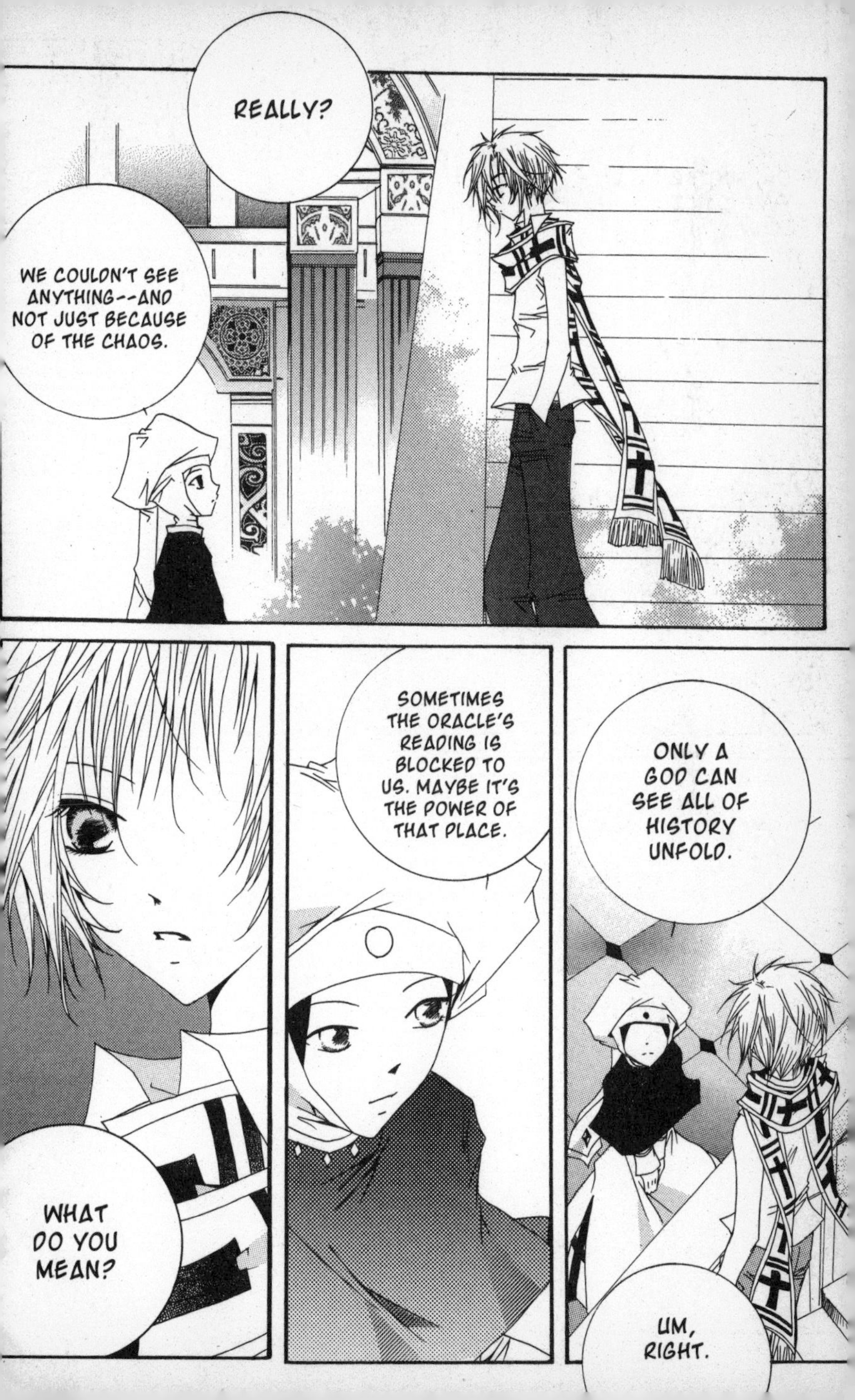
REALLY?
WE COULDN'T SEE ANYTHING--AND NOT JUST BECAUSE OF THE CHAOS.
WHAT DO YOU MEAN?
SOMETIMES THE ORACLE'S READING IS BLOCKED TO US. MAYBE IT'S THE POWER OF THAT PLACE.
ONLY A GOD CAN SEE ALL OF HISTORY UNFOLD.
UM, RIGHT.

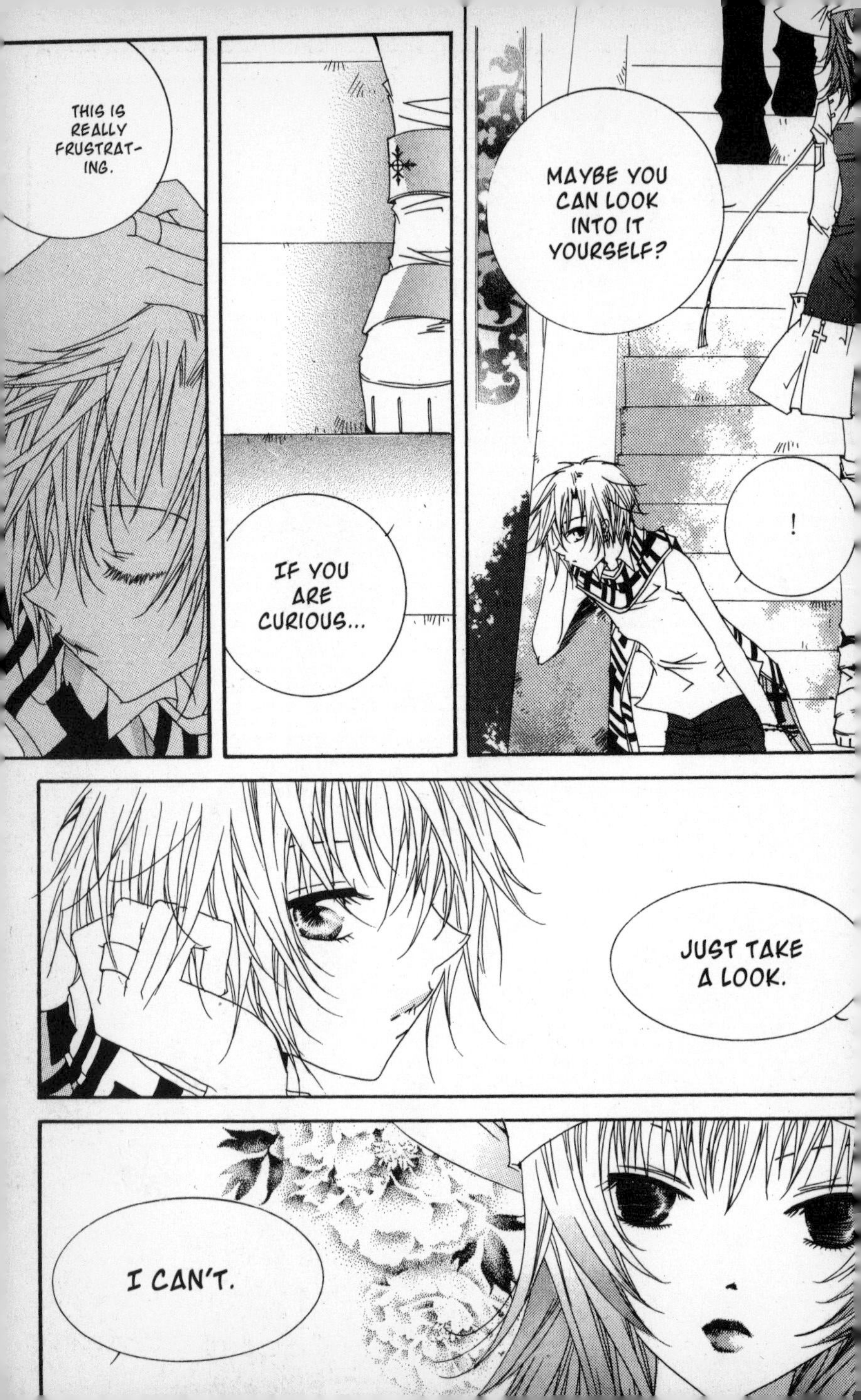
THIS IS REALLY FRUSTRAT-ING.
IF YOU ARE CURIOUS...
MAYBE YOU CAN LOOK INTO IT YOURSELF?
!
JUST TAKE A LOOK.
I CAN'T.

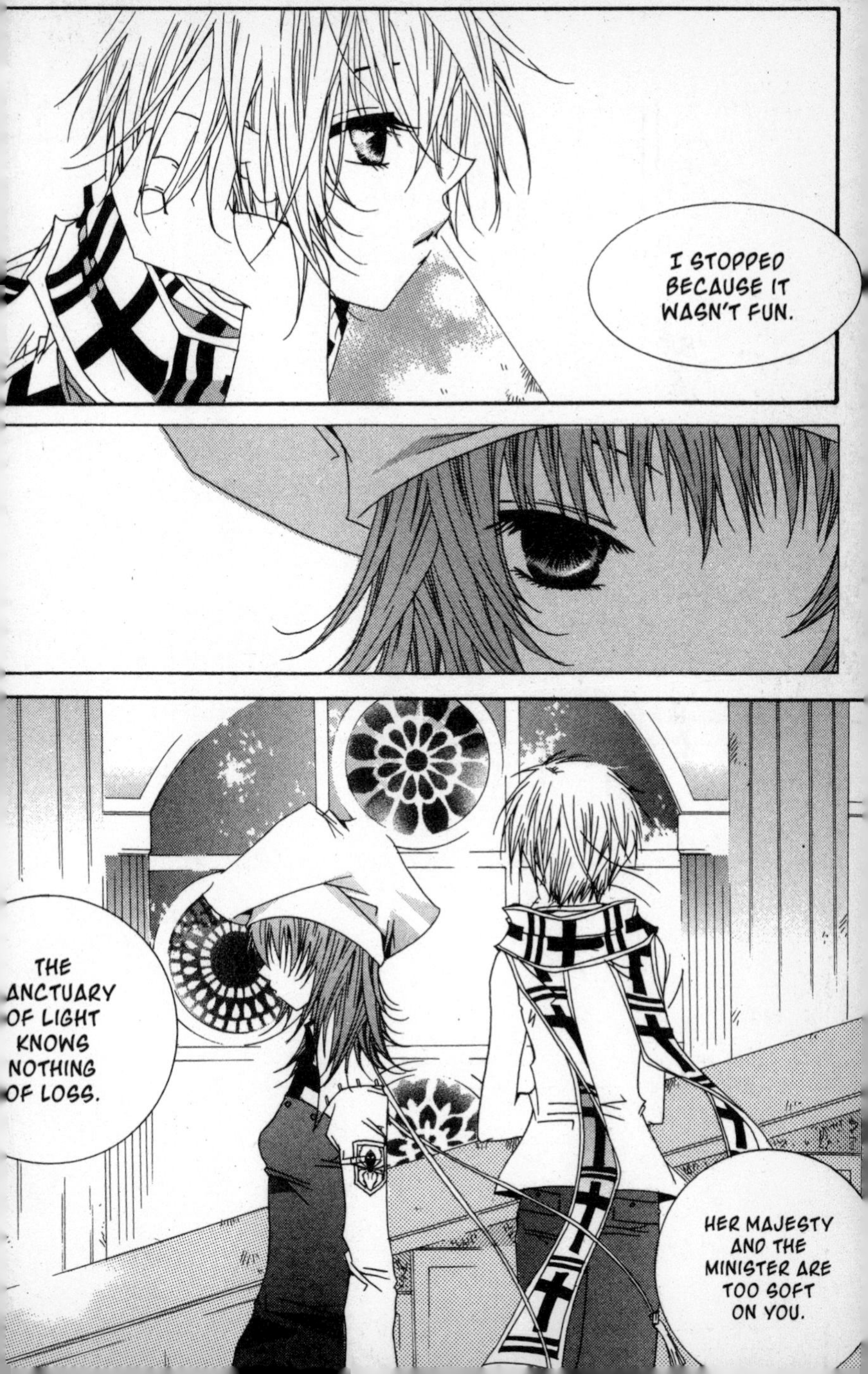
I STOPPED BECAUSE IT WASN'T FUN.
THE ANCTUARY OF LIGHT KNOWS NOTHING OF LOSS.
HER MAJESTY AND THE MINISTER ARE TOO SOFT ON YOU.

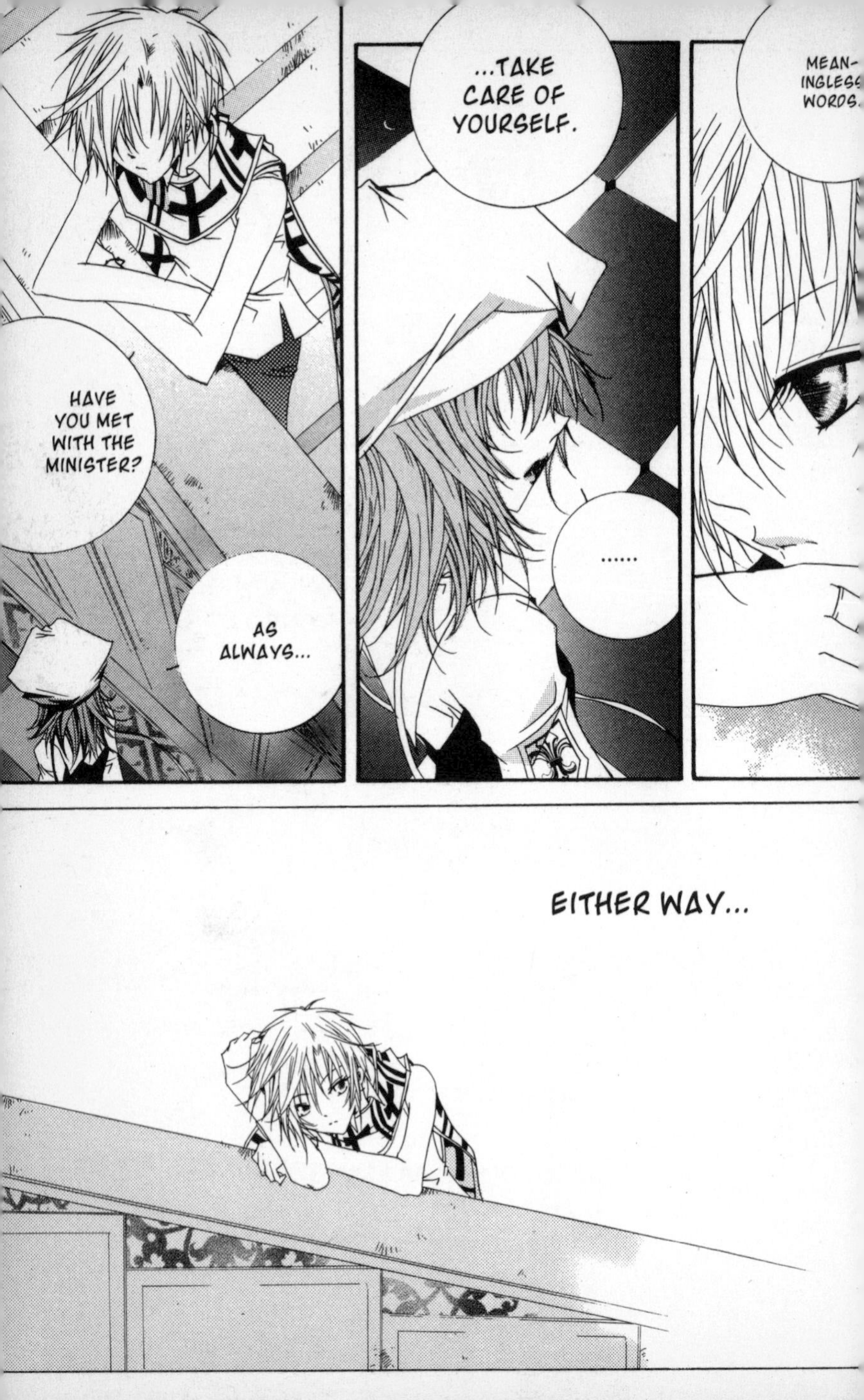
HAVE YOU MET WITH THE MINISTER?
AS ALWAYS...
...TAKE CARE OF YOURSELF.
......
MEAN-INGLESS WORDS.
EITHER WAY...

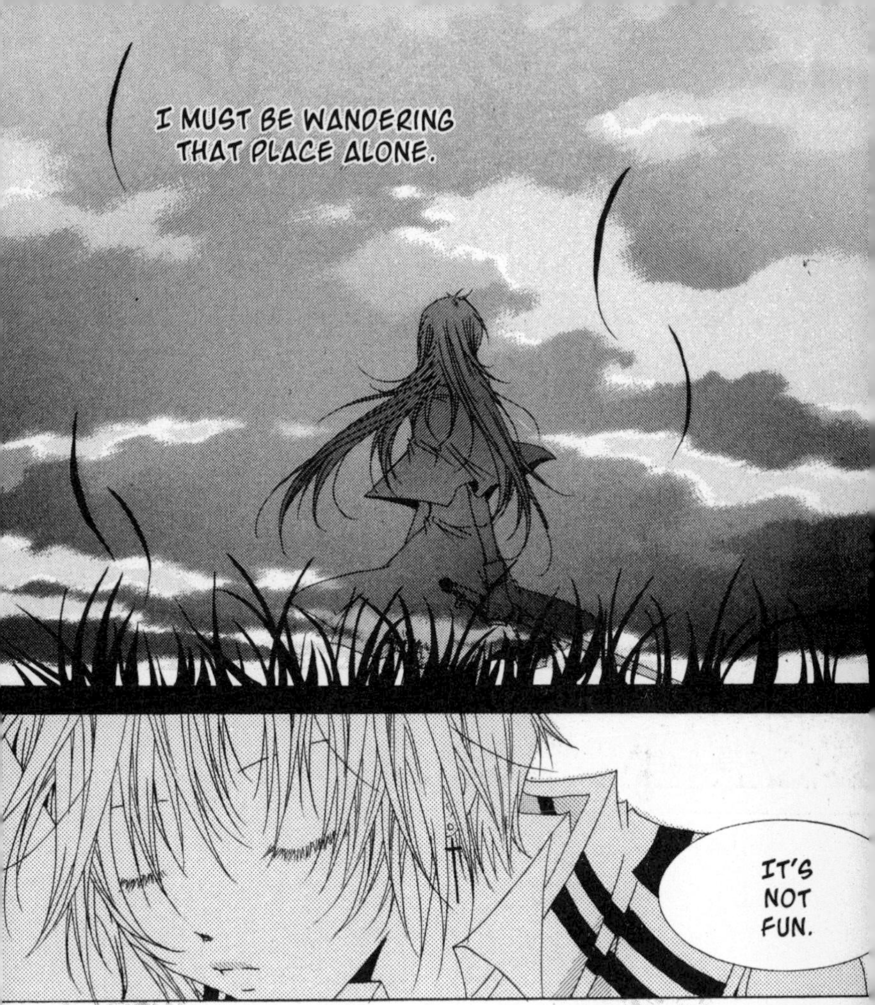
I MUST BE WANDERING THAT PLACE ALONE.
IT'S NOT FUN.

Your Eyelashes Hanging Low

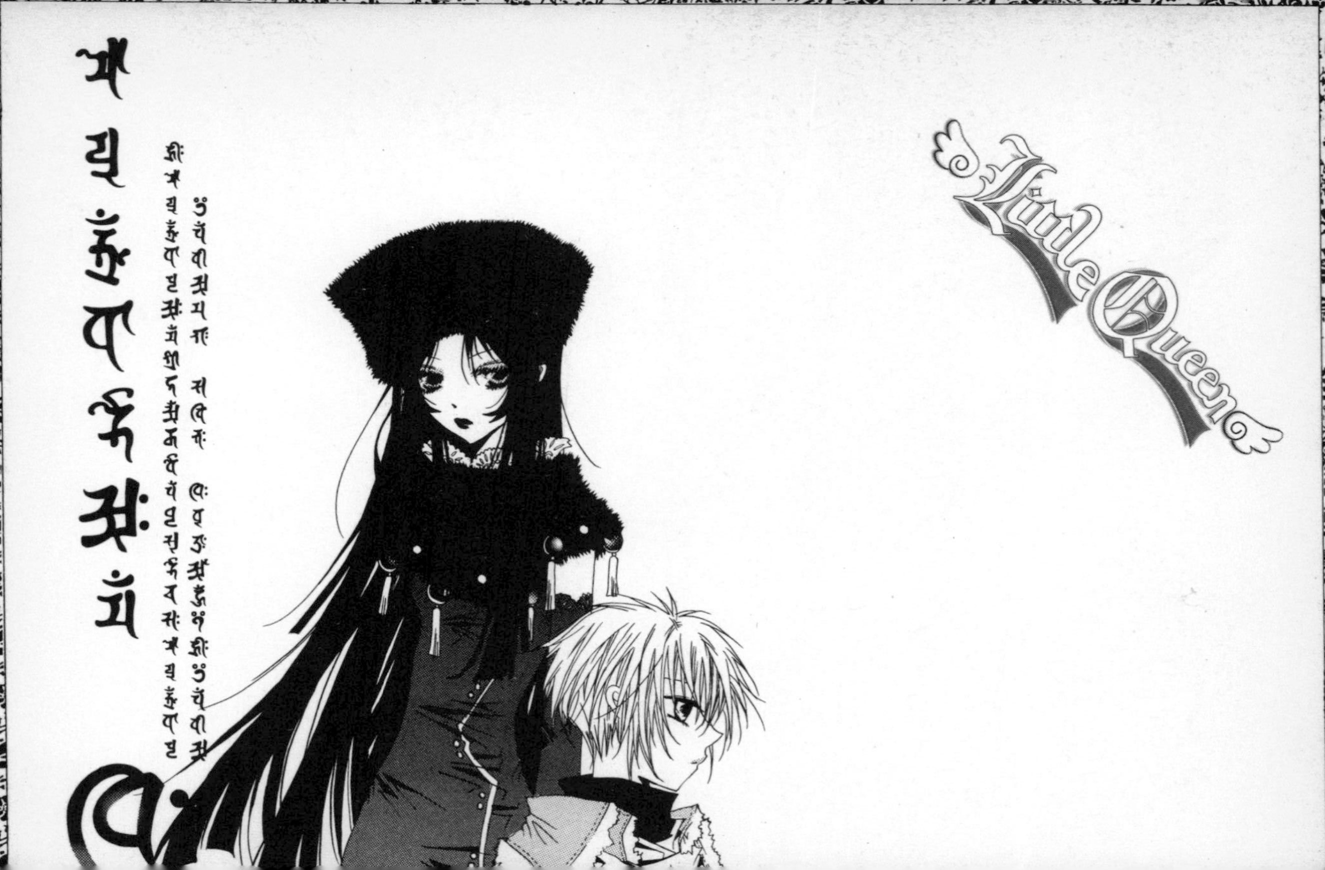
Little Queen

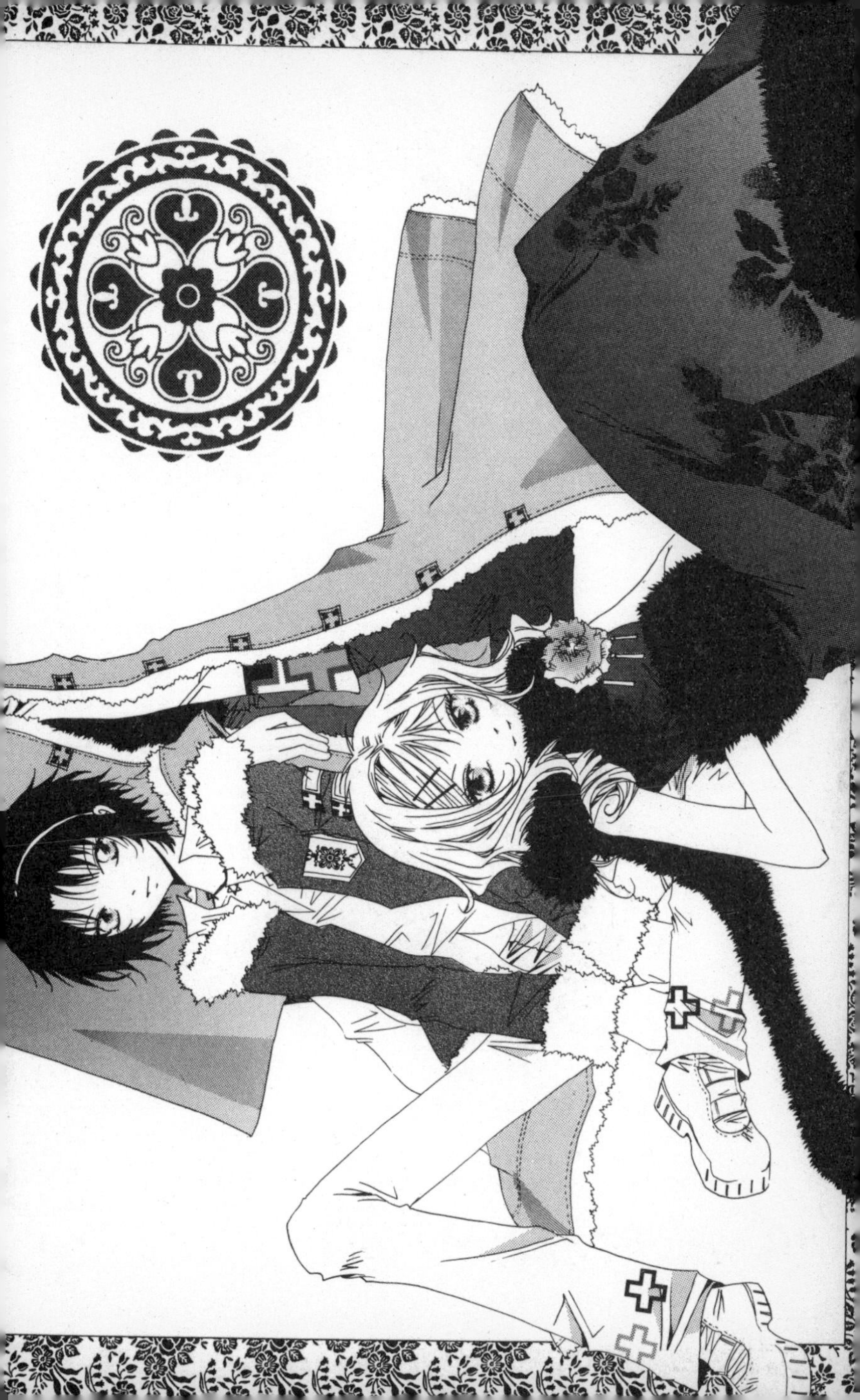

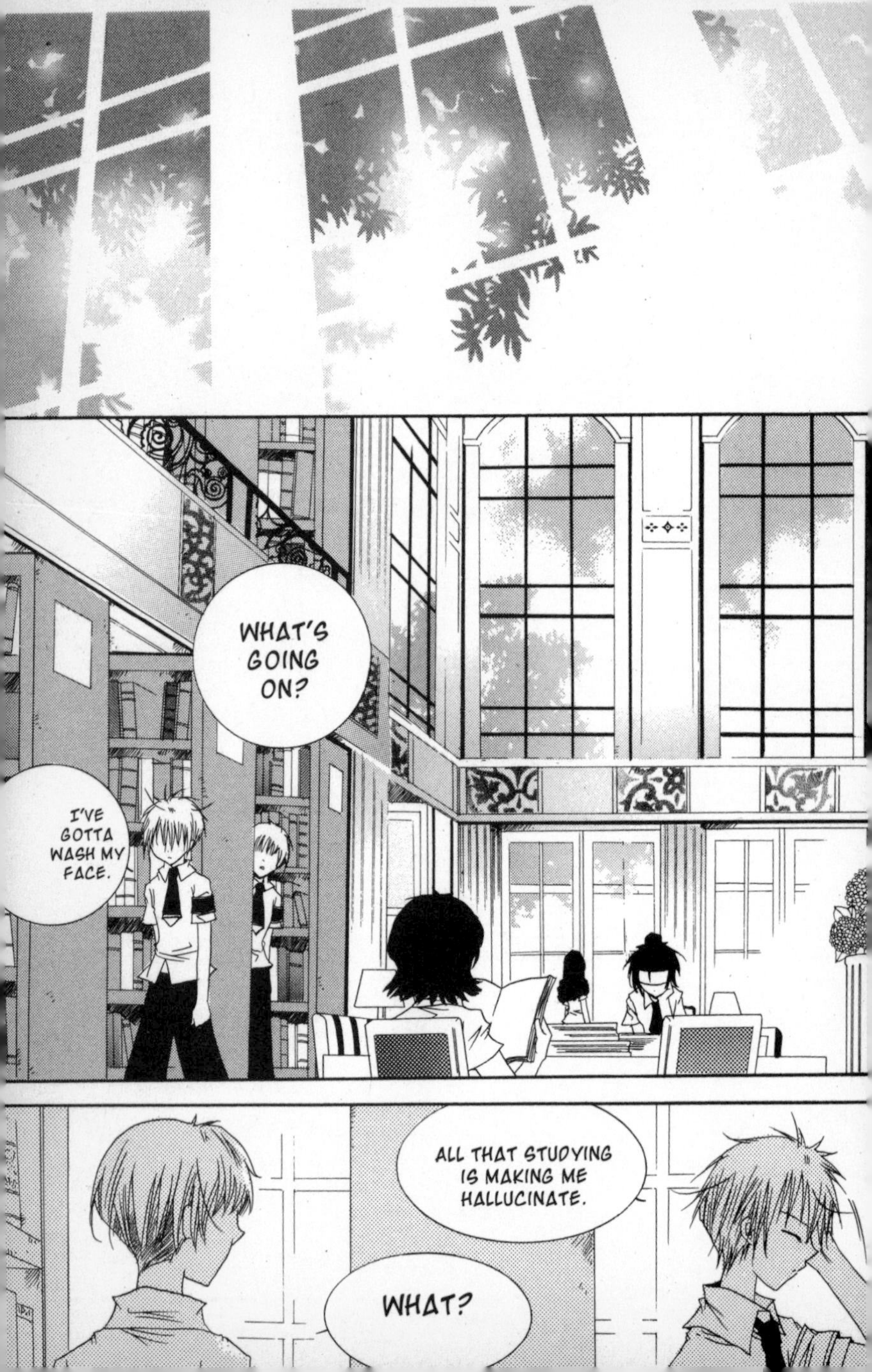
WHAT'S GOING ON?
I'VE GOTTA WASH MY FACE.
ALL THAT STUDYING IS MAKING ME HALLUCINATE.
WHAT?

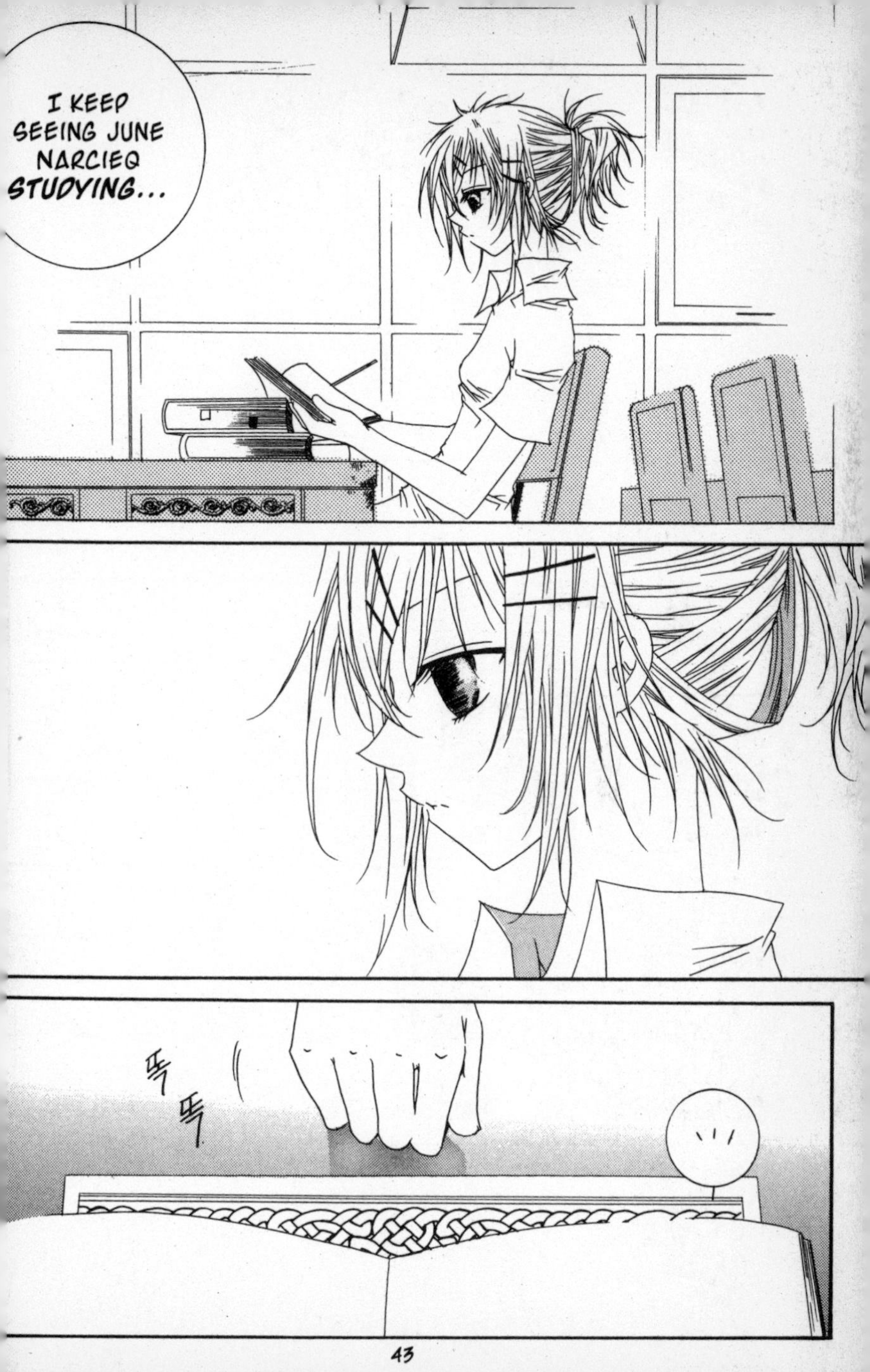
I KEEP SEEING JUNE NARCIEQ STUDYING...
똑
똑

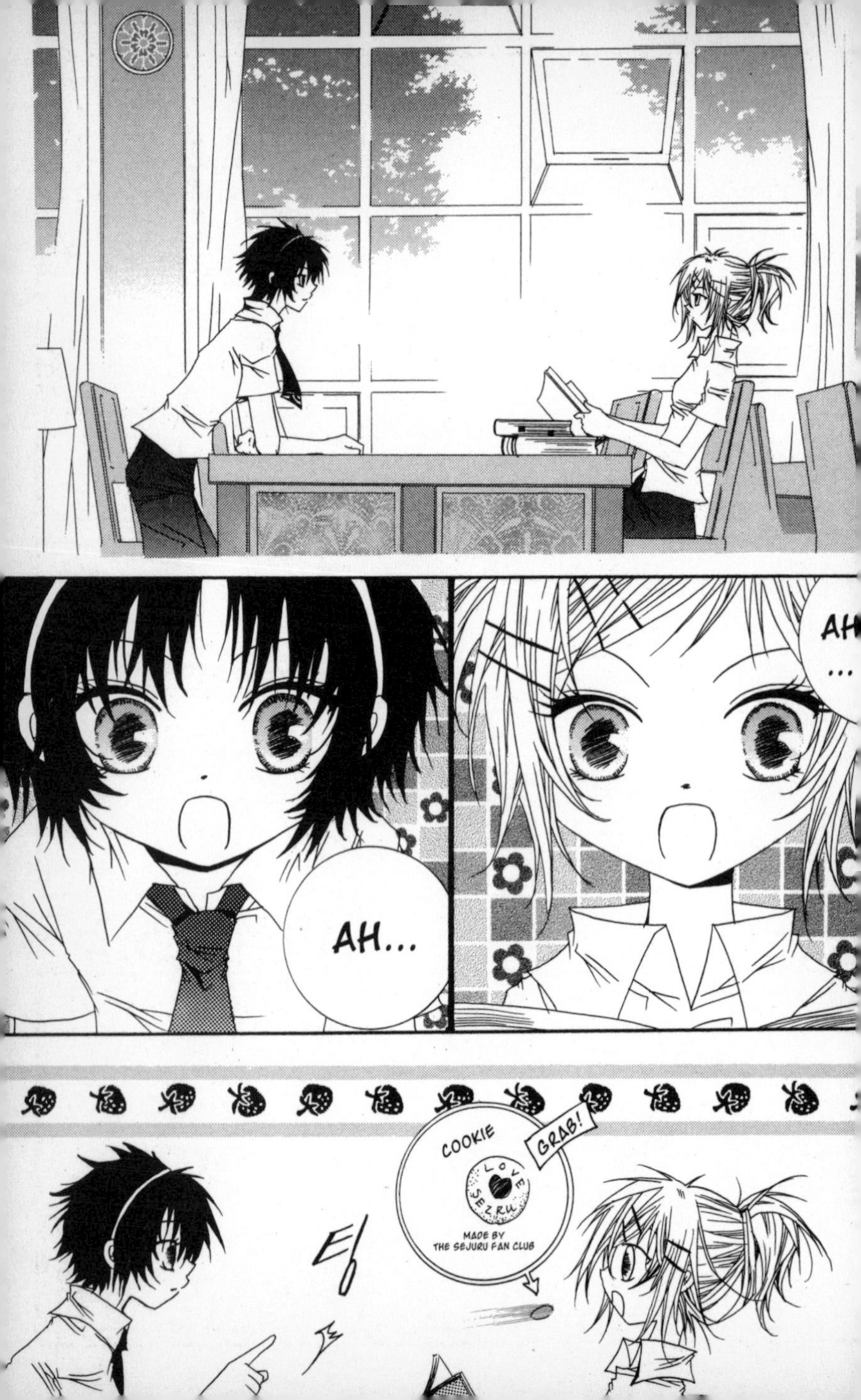
AH...
AH
...
COOKIE
GRAB!
LOVE SEZRU
MADE BY
THE SEJURU FAN CLUB

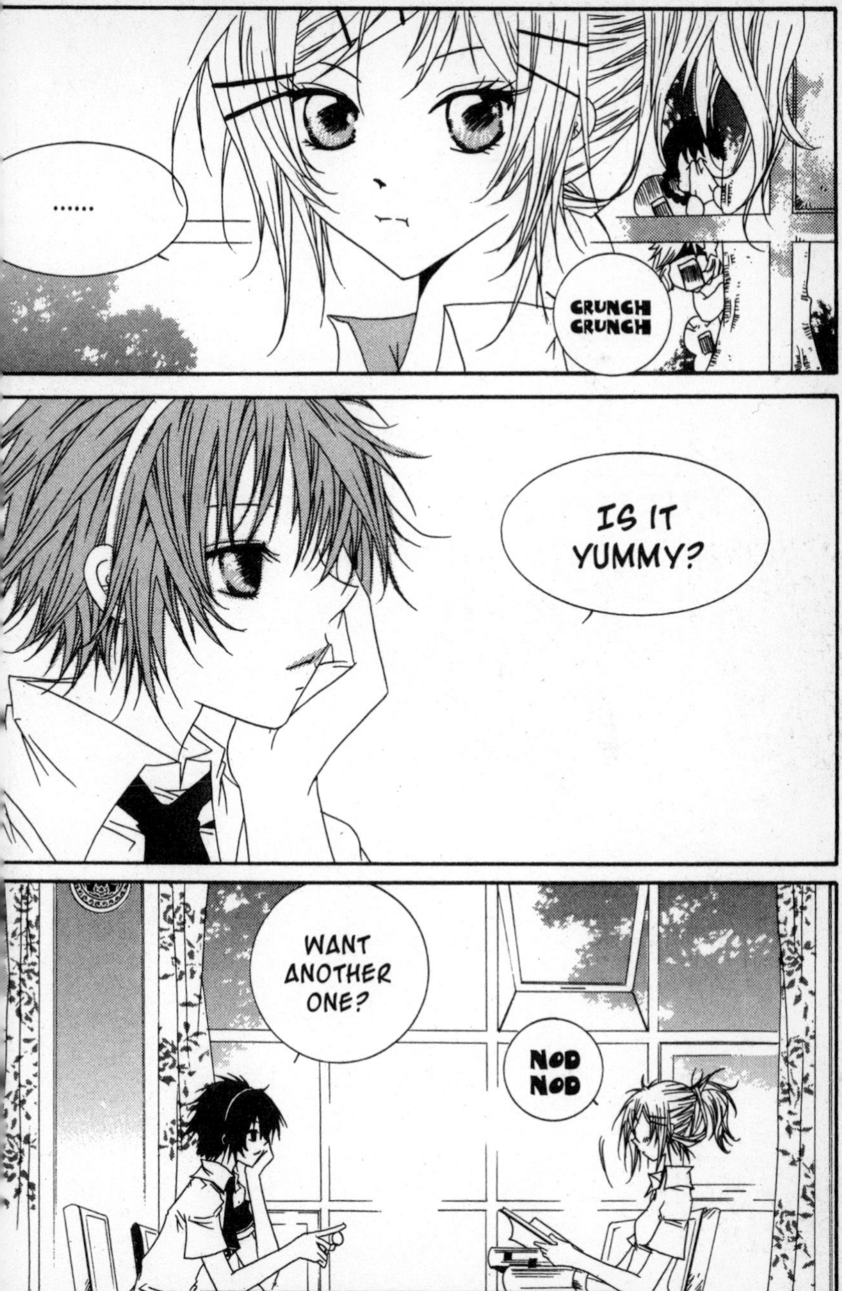
......
CRUNCH CRUNCH
IS IT YUMMY?
WANT ANOTHER ONE?
NOD NOD

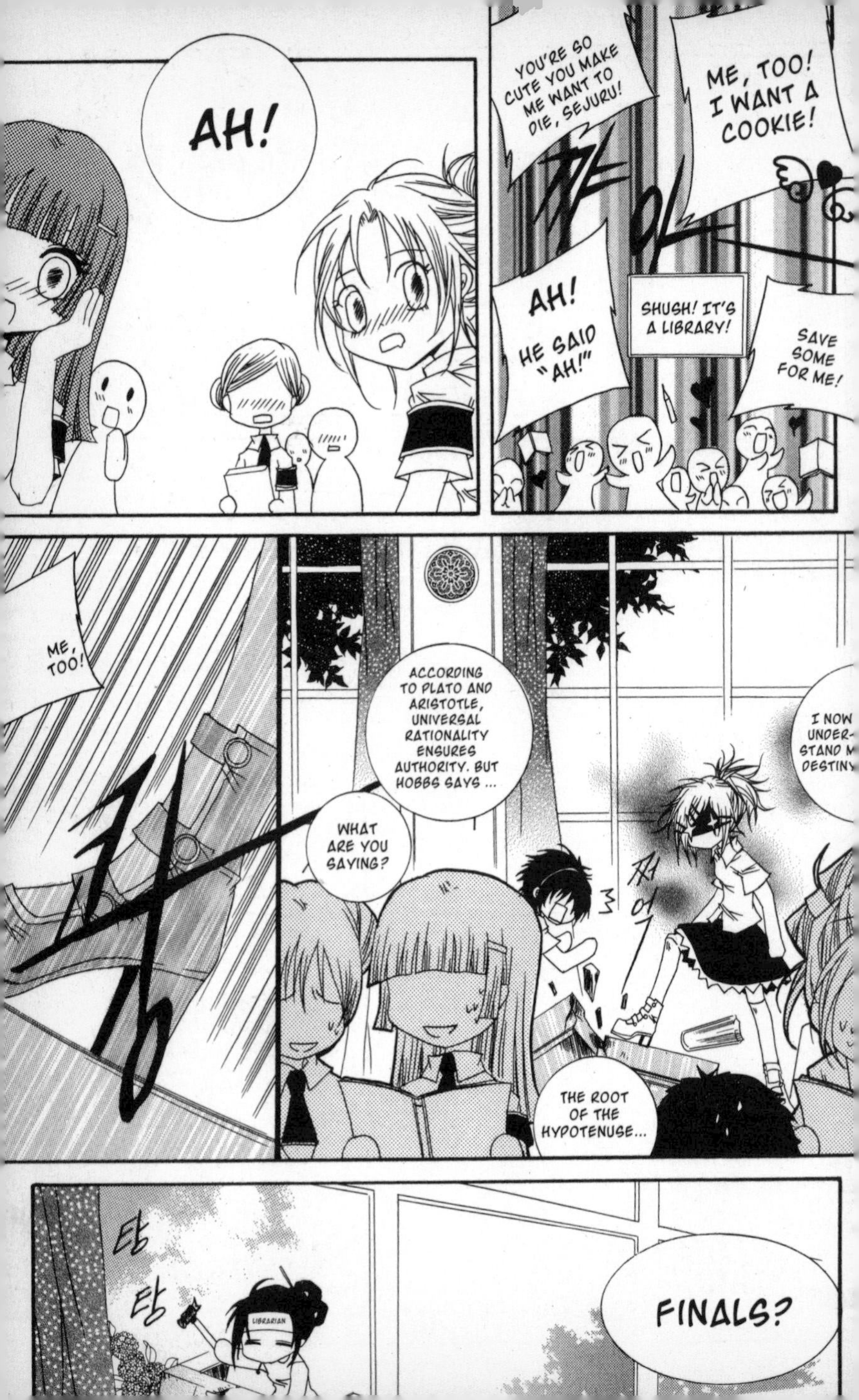
AH!
YOU'RE SO CUTE YOU MAKE ME WANT TO DIE, SEJURU!
ME, TOO! I WANT A COOKIE!
AH! HE SAID "AH!"
SHUSH! IT'S A LIBRARY!
SAVE SOME FOR ME!
ME, TOO!
ACCORDING TO PLATO AND ARISTOTLE, UNIVERSAL RATIONALITY ENSURES AUTHORITY. BUT HOBBS SAYS ...
WHAT ARE YOU SAYING?
I NOW UNDER- STAND M DESTIN
THE ROOT OF THE HYPOTENUSE...
탕
탕
LIBRARIAN
FINALS?

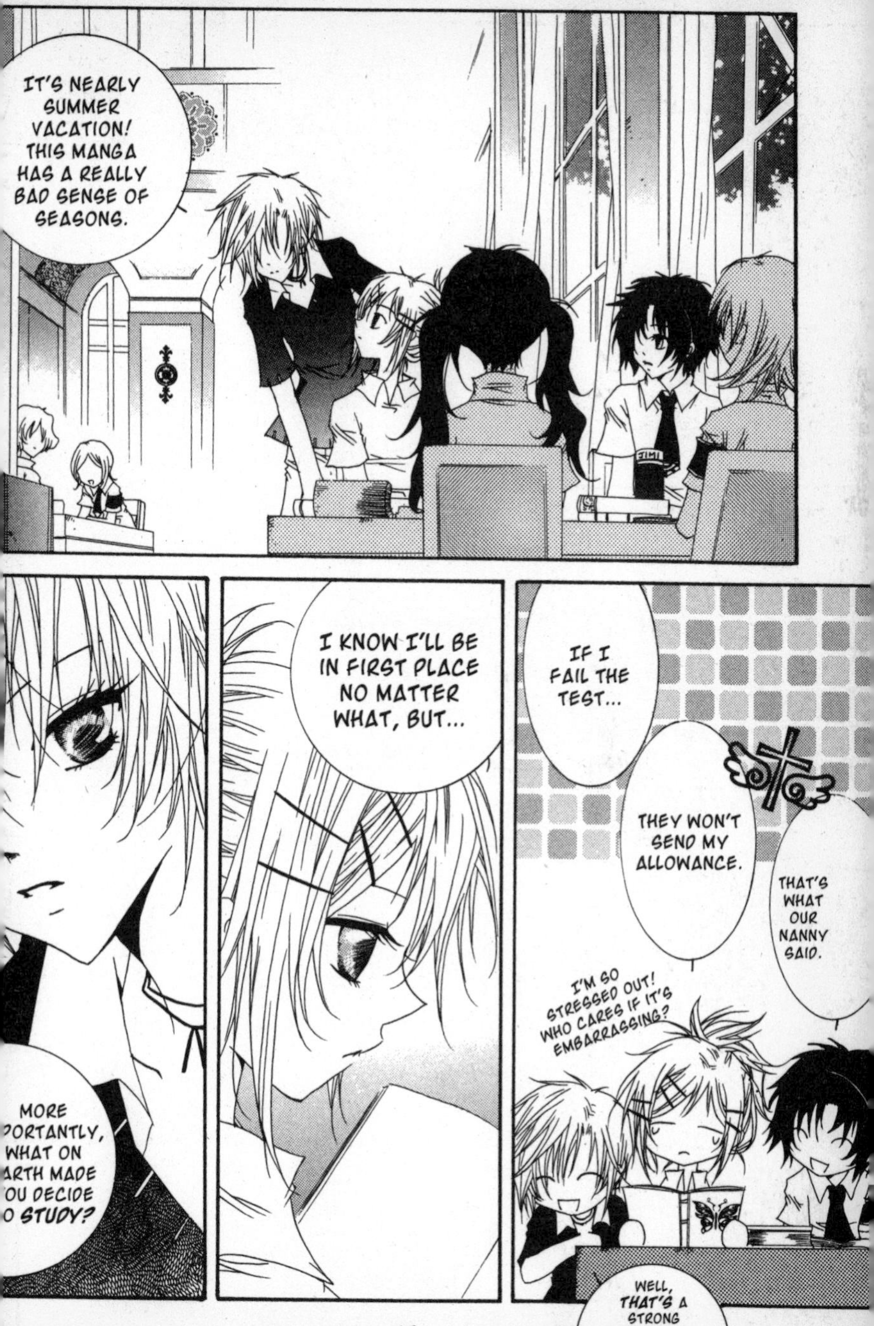

IT'S NEARLY SUMMER VACATION! THIS MANGA HAS A REALLY BAD SENSE OF SEASONS.
MORE PORTANTLY, WHAT ON ARTH MADE OU DECIDE O STUDY?
I KNOW I'LL BE IN FIRST PLACE NO MATTER WHAT, BUT...
IF I FAIL THE TEST...
THEY WON'T SEND MY ALLOWANCE.
THAT'S WHAT OUR NANNY SAID.
I'M SO STRESSED OUT! WHO CARES IF IT'S EMBARRASSING?
WELL, THAT'S A STRONG INCENTIVE.

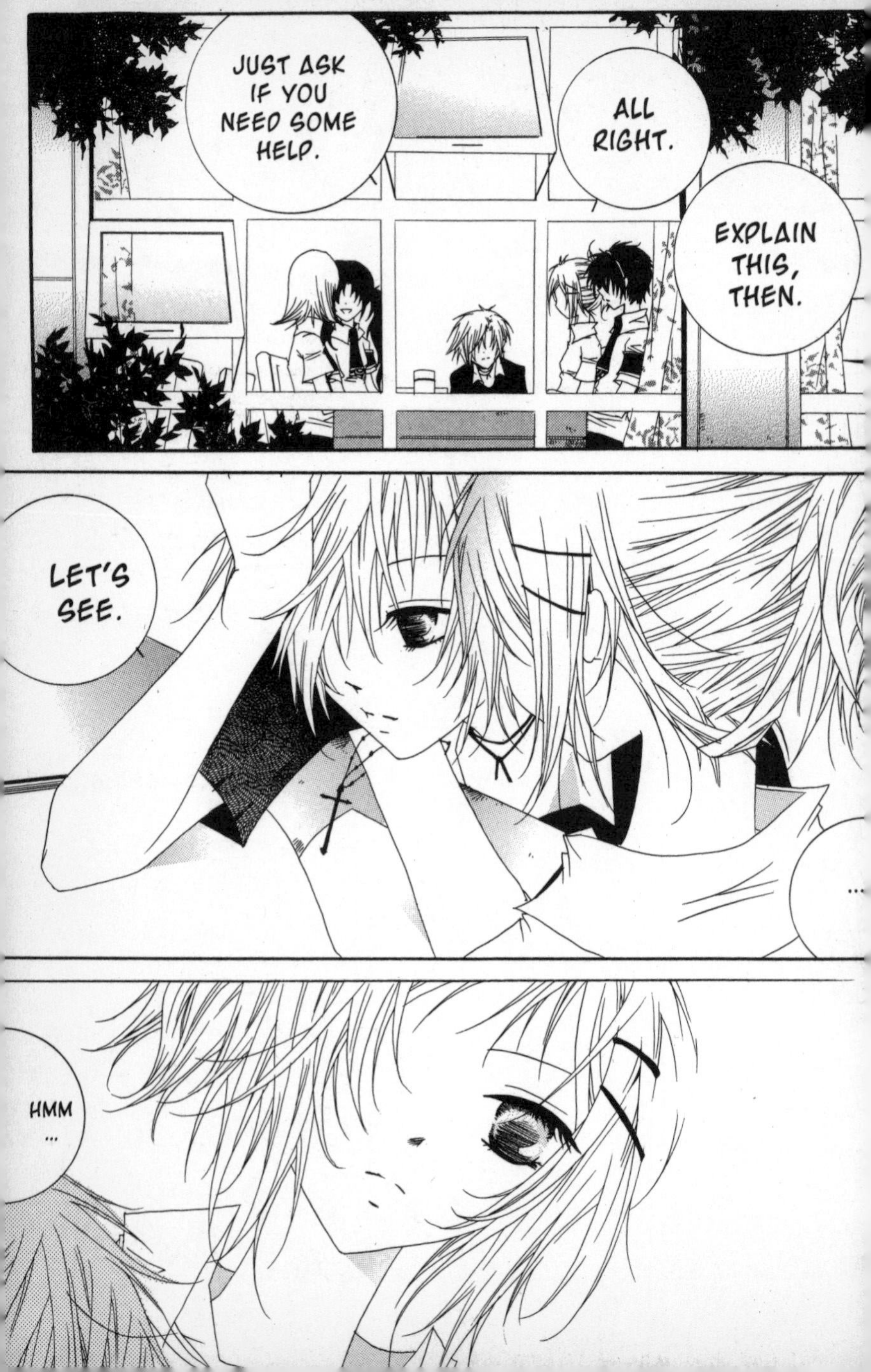
JUST ASK IF YOU NEED SOME HELP.
ALL RIGHT.
EXPLAIN THIS, THEN.
LET'S SEE.
...
HMM ...

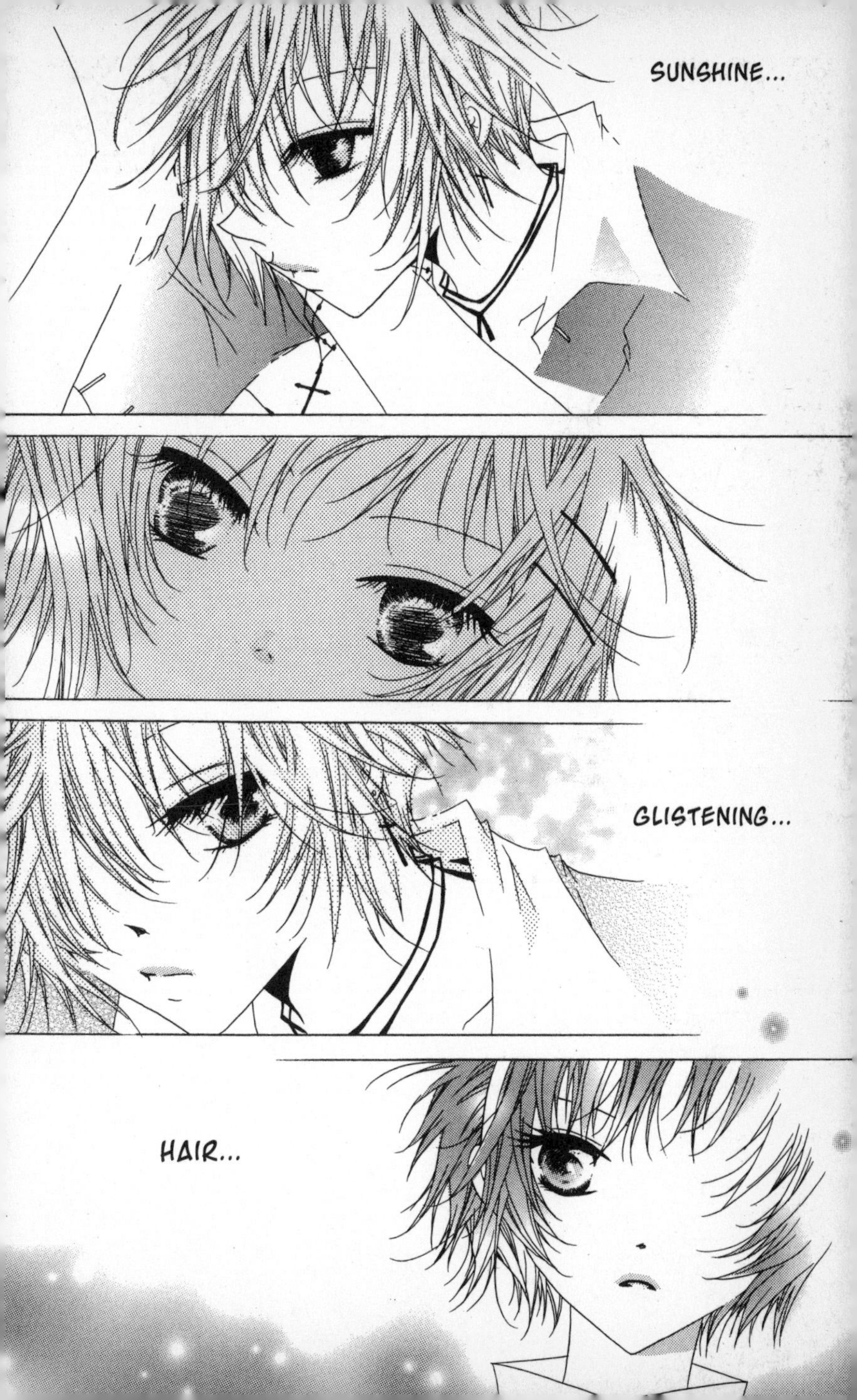
SUNSHINE...
GLISTENING...
HAIR...

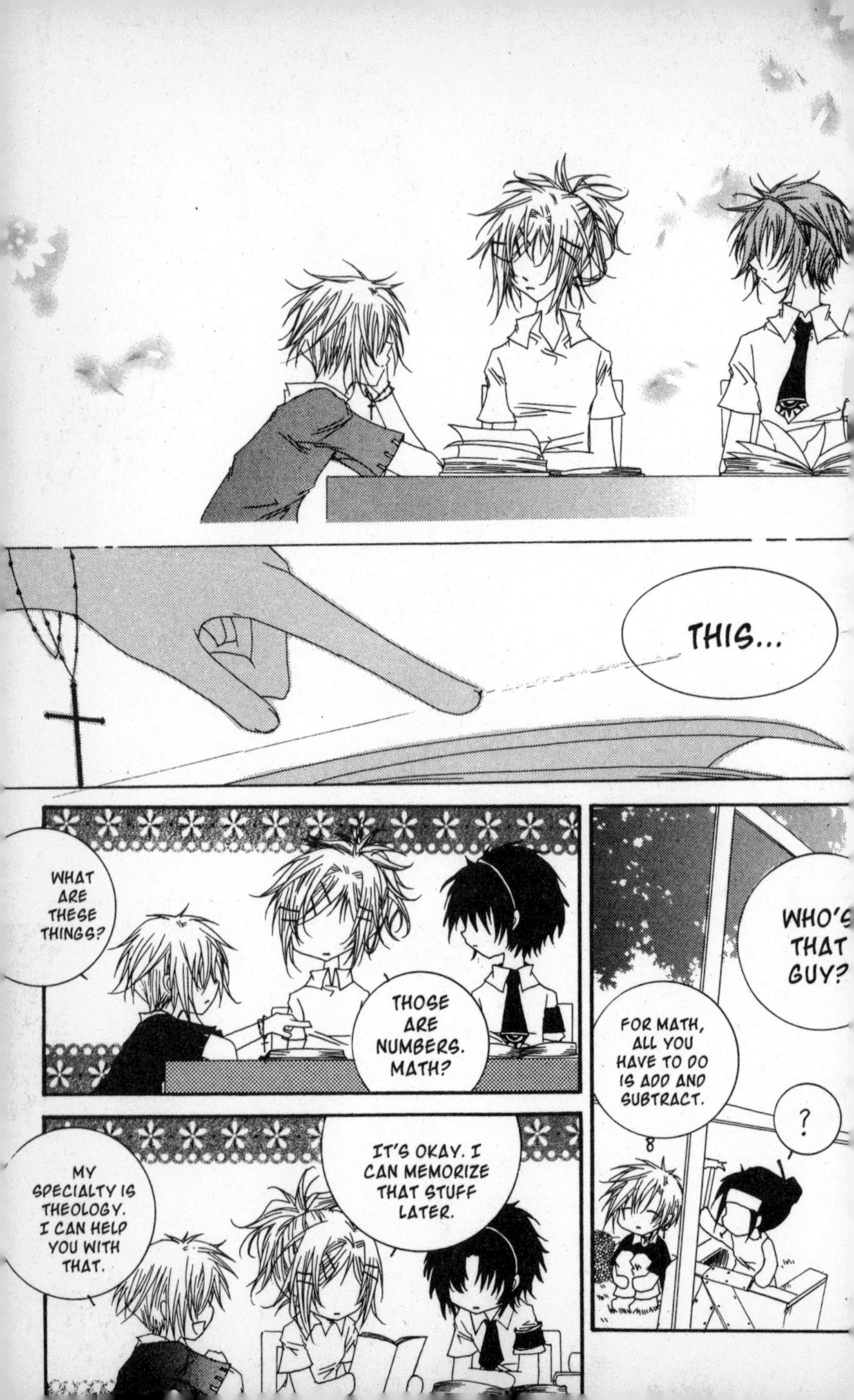
THIS...
WHAT ARE THESE THINGS?
THOSE ARE NUMBERS. MATH?
MY SPECIALTY IS THEOLOGY. I CAN HELP YOU WITH THAT.
IT'S OKAY. I CAN MEMORIZE THAT STUFF LATER.
WHO'S THAT GUY?
FOR MATH, ALL YOU HAVE TO DO IS ADD AND SUBTRACT.
?

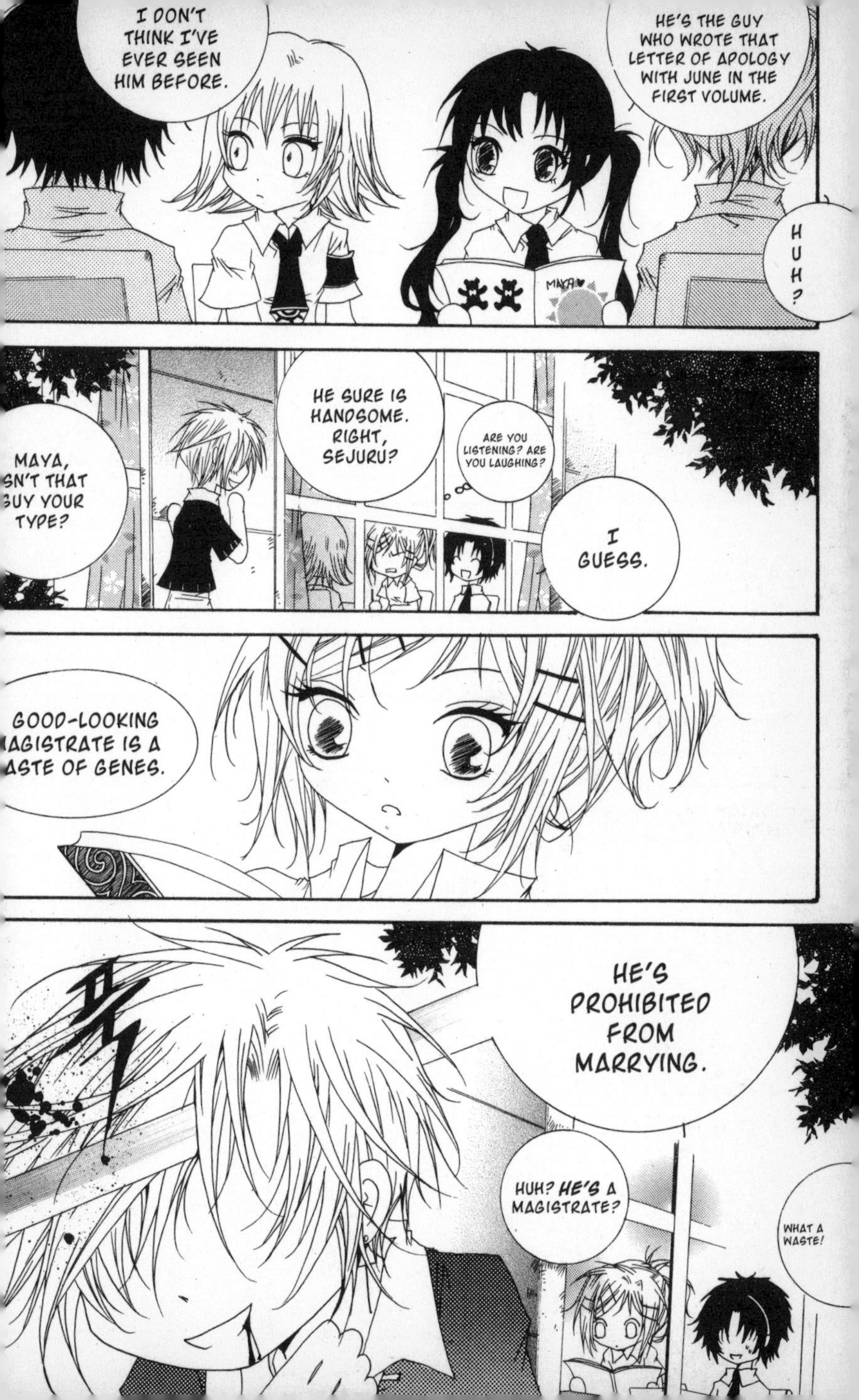
I DON'T THINK I'VE EVER SEEN HIM BEFORE.
HE'S THE GUY WHO WROTE THAT LETTER OF APOLOGY WITH JUNE IN THE FIRST VOLUME.
HUH?
MAYA♥
MAYA, SN'T THAT UY YOUR TYPE?
HE SURE IS HANDSOME. RIGHT, SEJURU?
ARE YOU LISTENING? ARE YOU LAUGHING?
I GUESS.
GOOD-LOOKING AGISTRATE IS A ASTE OF GENES.
HE'S PROHIBITED FROM MARRYING.
HUH? HE'S A MAGISTRATE?
WHAT A WASTE!

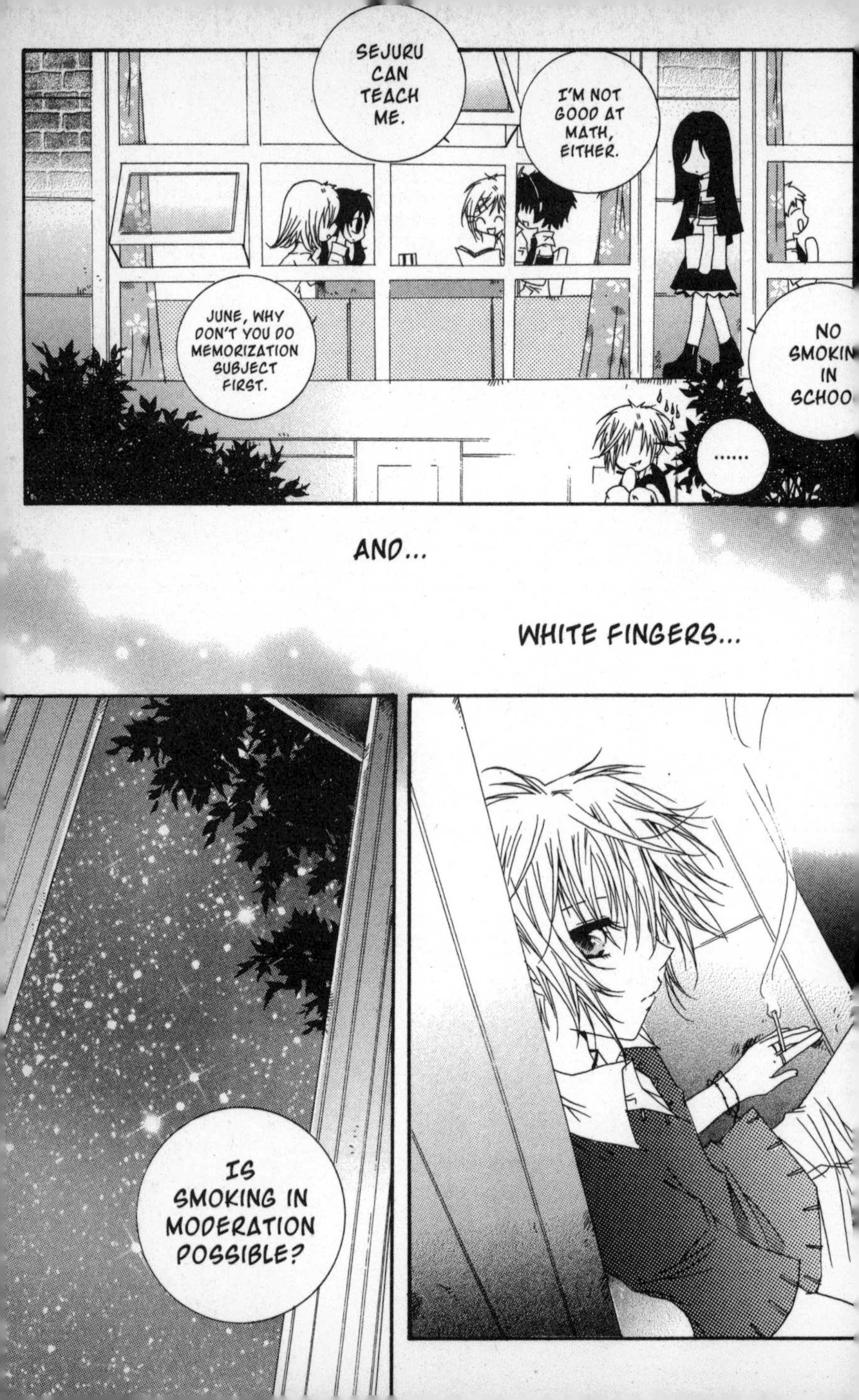
SEJURU CAN TEACH ME.
I'M NOT GOOD AT MATH, EITHER.
JUNE, WHY DON'T YOU DO MEMORIZATION SUBJECT FIRST.
NO SMOKIN IN SCHOO
......
AND...
WHITE FINGERS...
IS SMOKING IN MODERATION POSSIBLE?

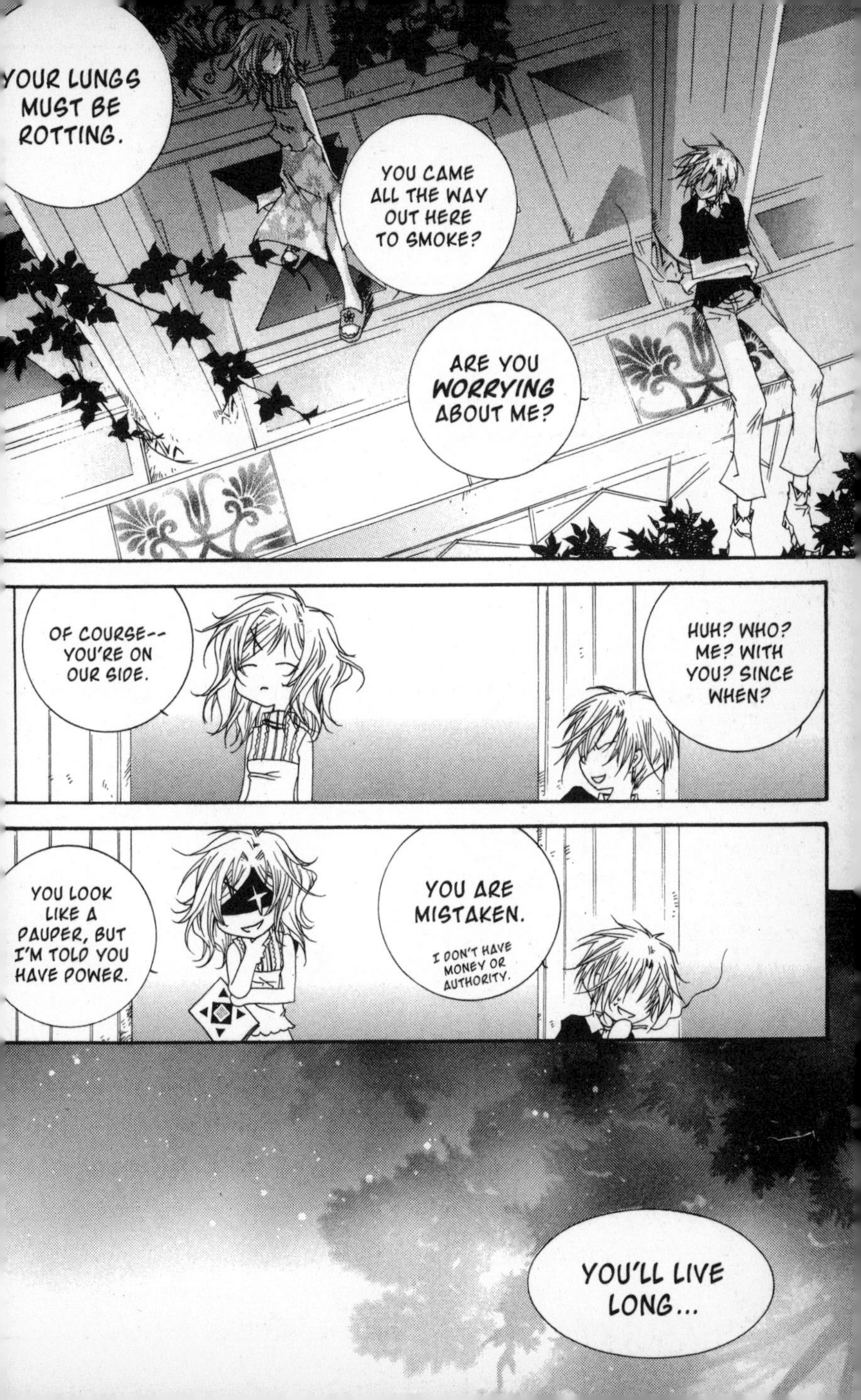
YOUR LUNGS MUST BE ROTTING.
YOU CAME ALL THE WAY OUT HERE TO SMOKE?
ARE YOU **WORRYING** ABOUT ME?
OF COURSE--YOU'RE ON OUR SIDE.
HUH? WHO? ME? WITH YOU? SINCE WHEN?
YOU LOOK LIKE A PAUPER, BUT I'M TOLD YOU HAVE POWER.
YOU ARE MISTAKEN.
I DON'T HAVE MONEY OR AUTHORITY.
YOU'LL LIVE LONG...

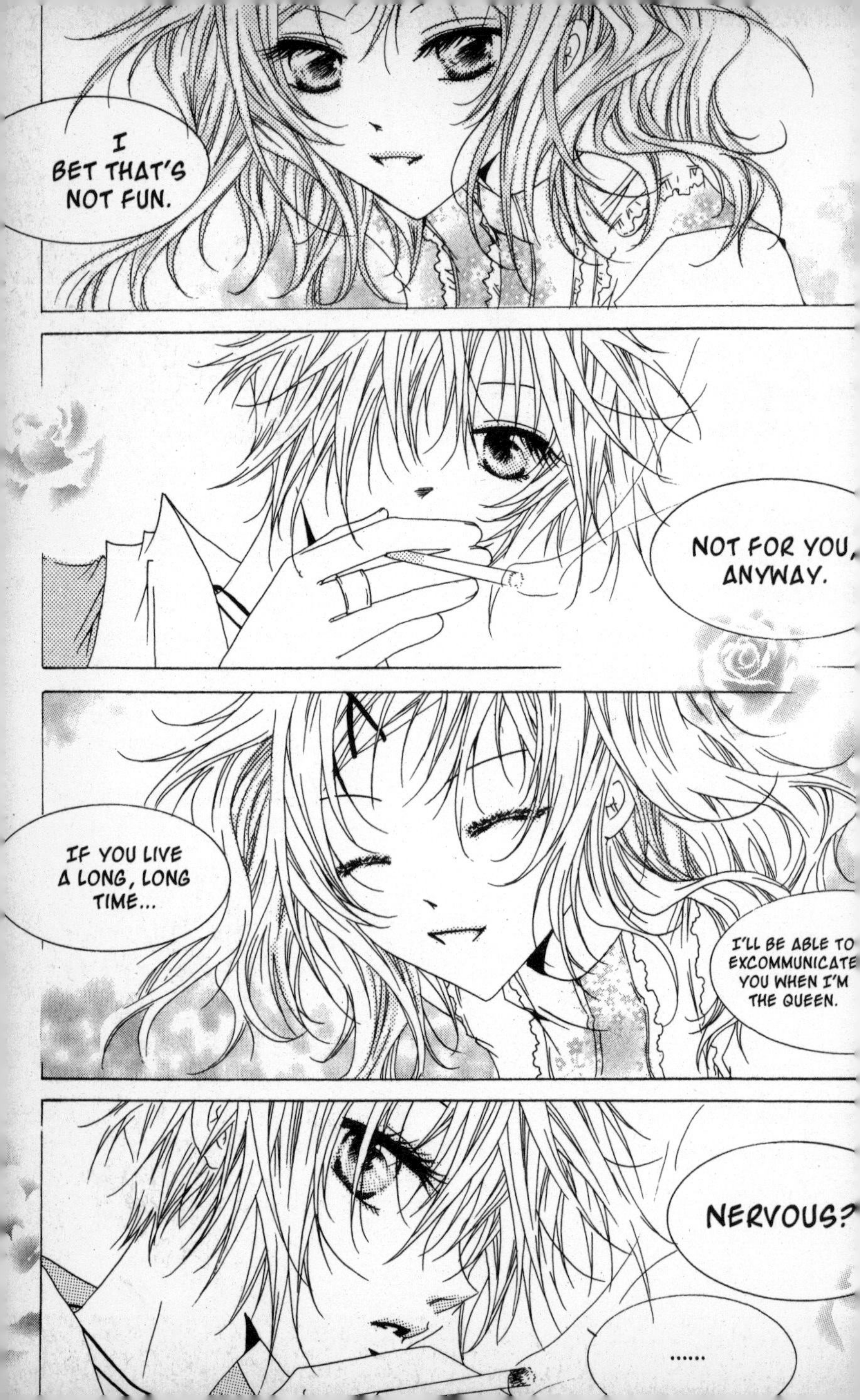
I BET THAT'S NOT FUN.
NOT FOR YOU, ANYWAY.
IF YOU LIVE A LONG, LONG TIME...
I'LL BE ABLE TO EXCOMMUNICATE YOU WHEN I'M THE QUEEN.
NERVOUS?
......

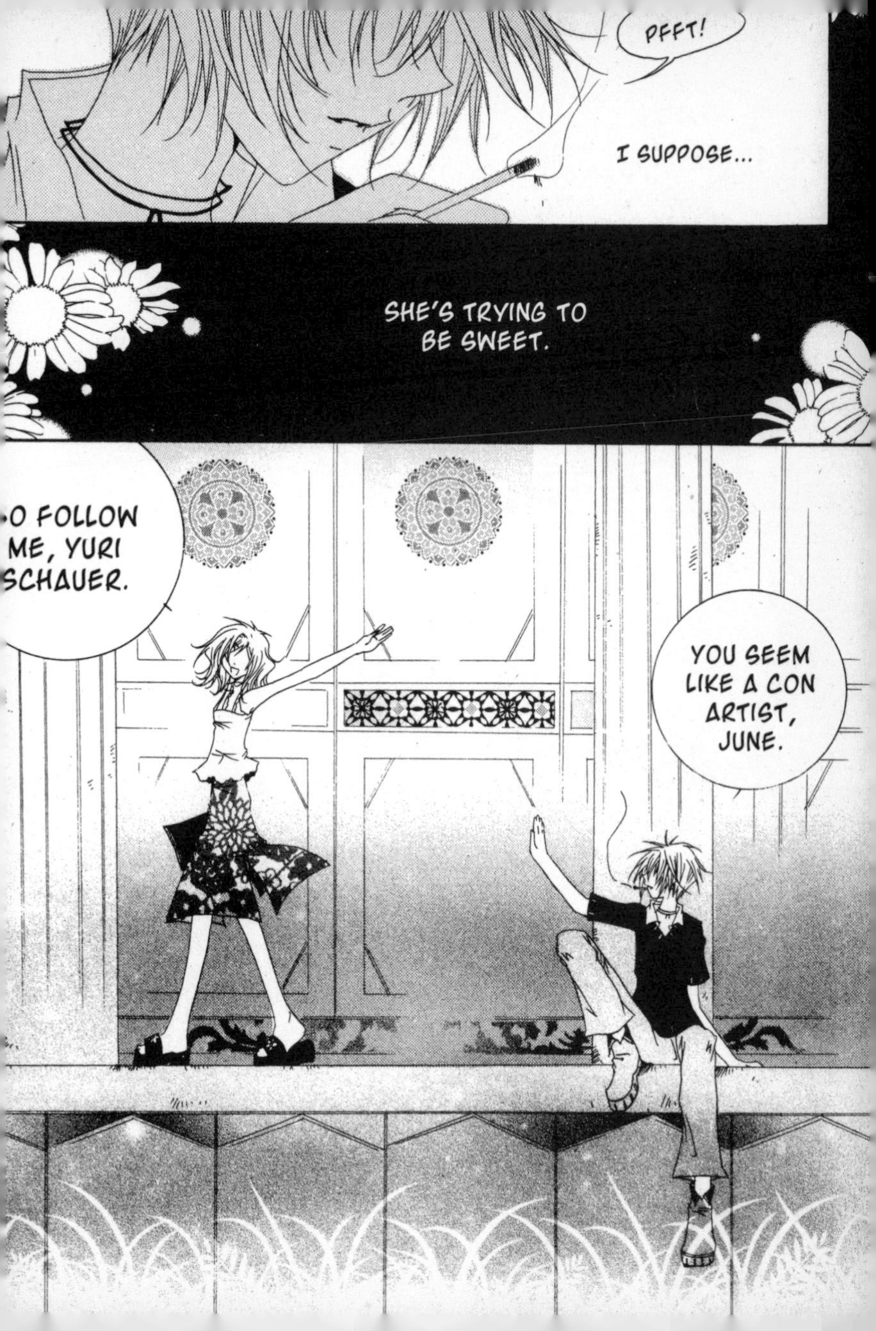
PFFT!
I SUPPOSE...
SHE'S TRYING TO BE SWEET.
-O FOLLOW ME, YURI SCHAUER.
YOU SEEM LIKE A CON ARTIST, JUNE.

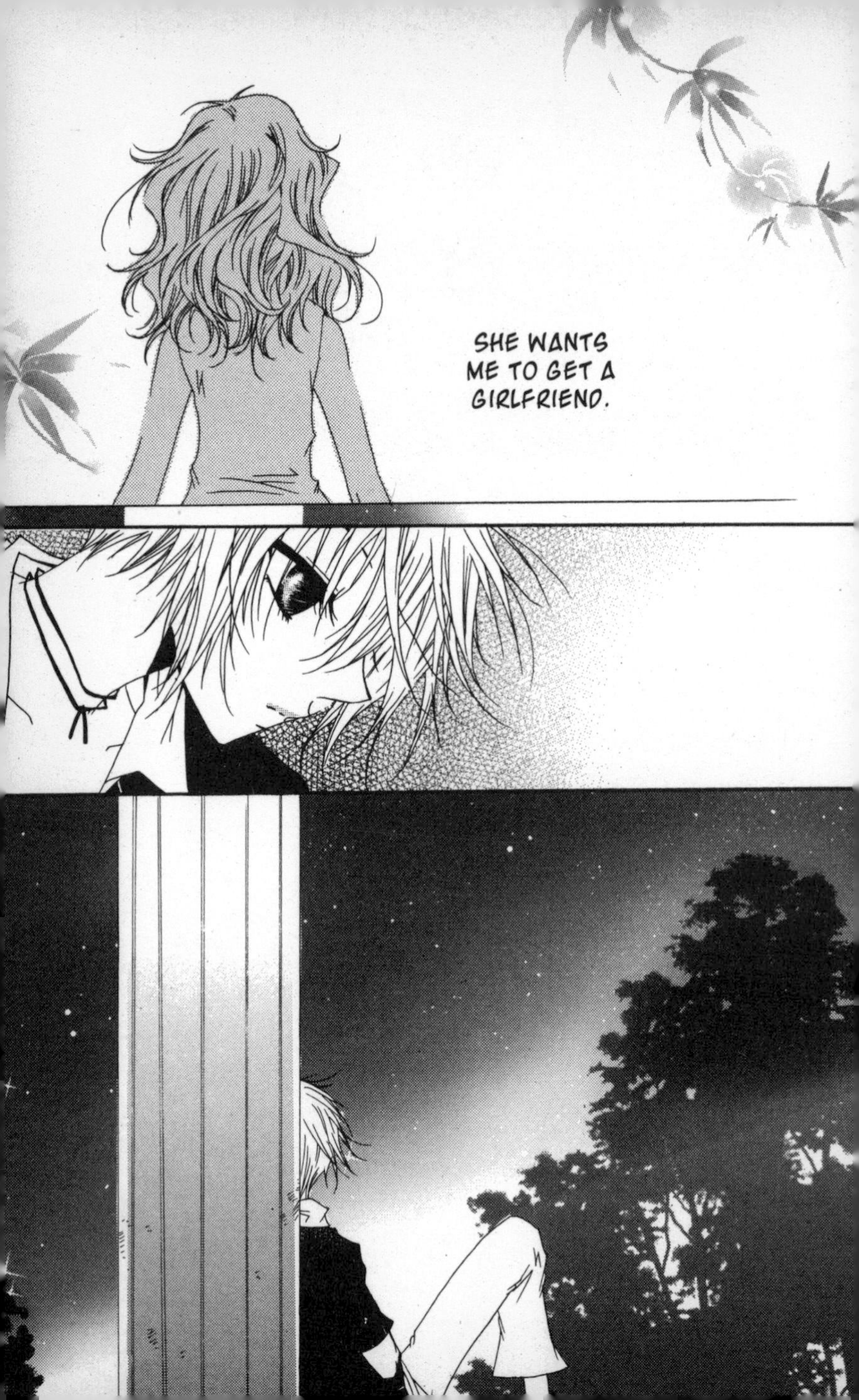
SHE WANTS ME TO GET A GIRLFRIEND.

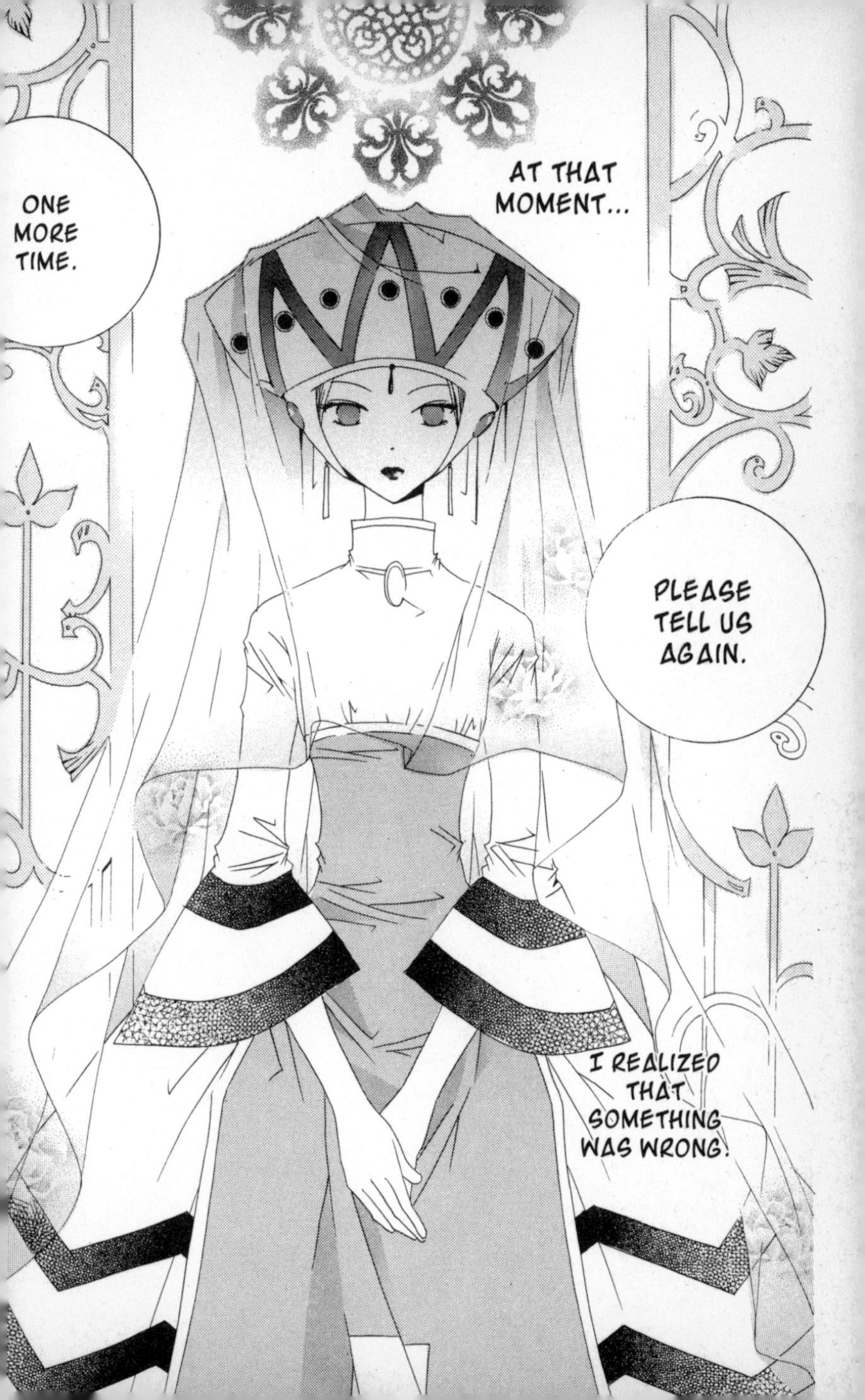
ONE MORE TIME.
AT THAT MOMENT...
PLEASE TELL US AGAIN.
I REALIZED THAT SOMETHING WAS WRONG.

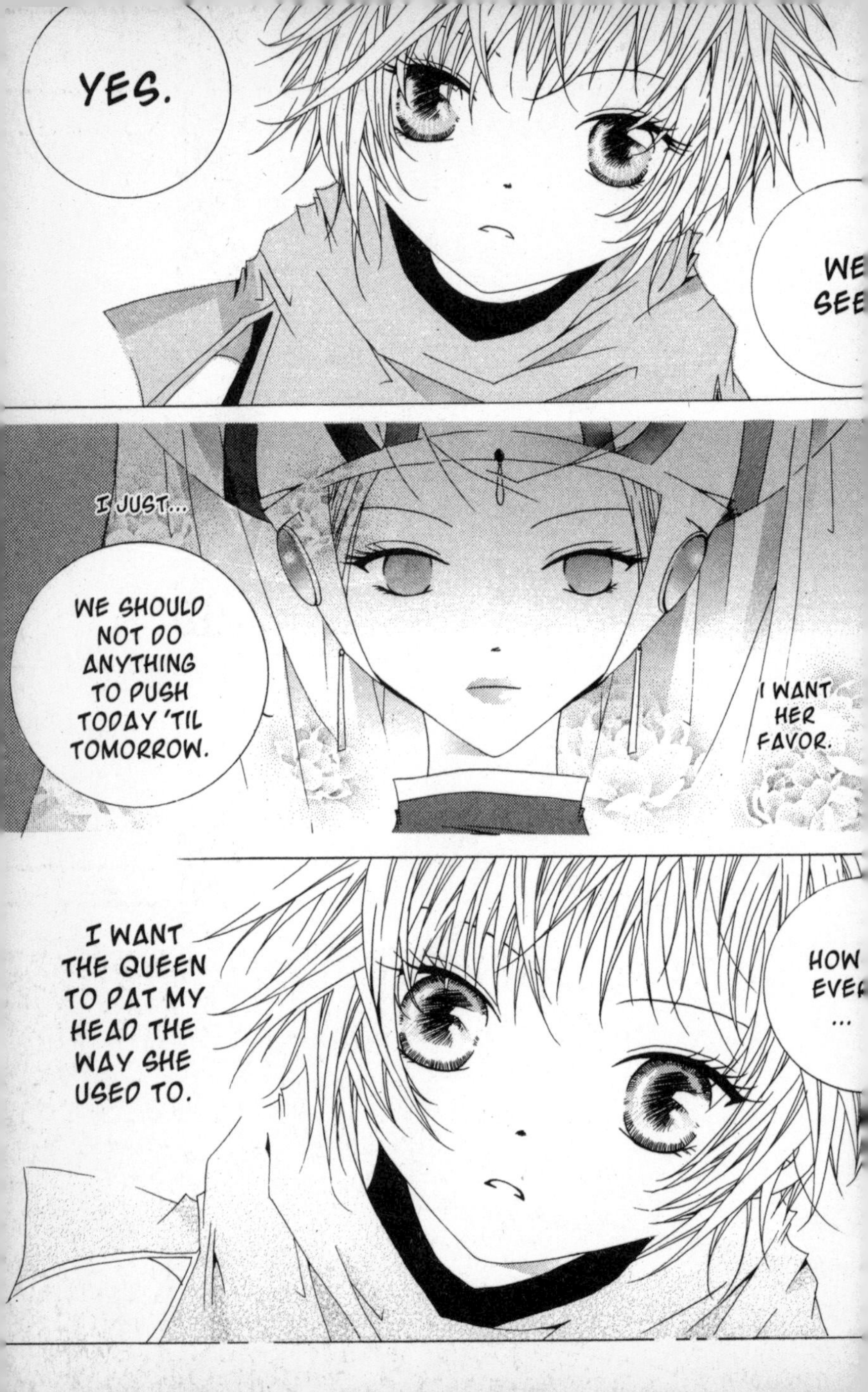
YES.
WE SEE
I JUST...
WE SHOULD NOT DO ANYTHING TO PUSH TODAY 'TIL TOMORROW.
I WANT HER FAVOR.
I WANT THE QUEEN TO PAT MY HEAD THE WAY SHE USED TO.
HOW EVE ...

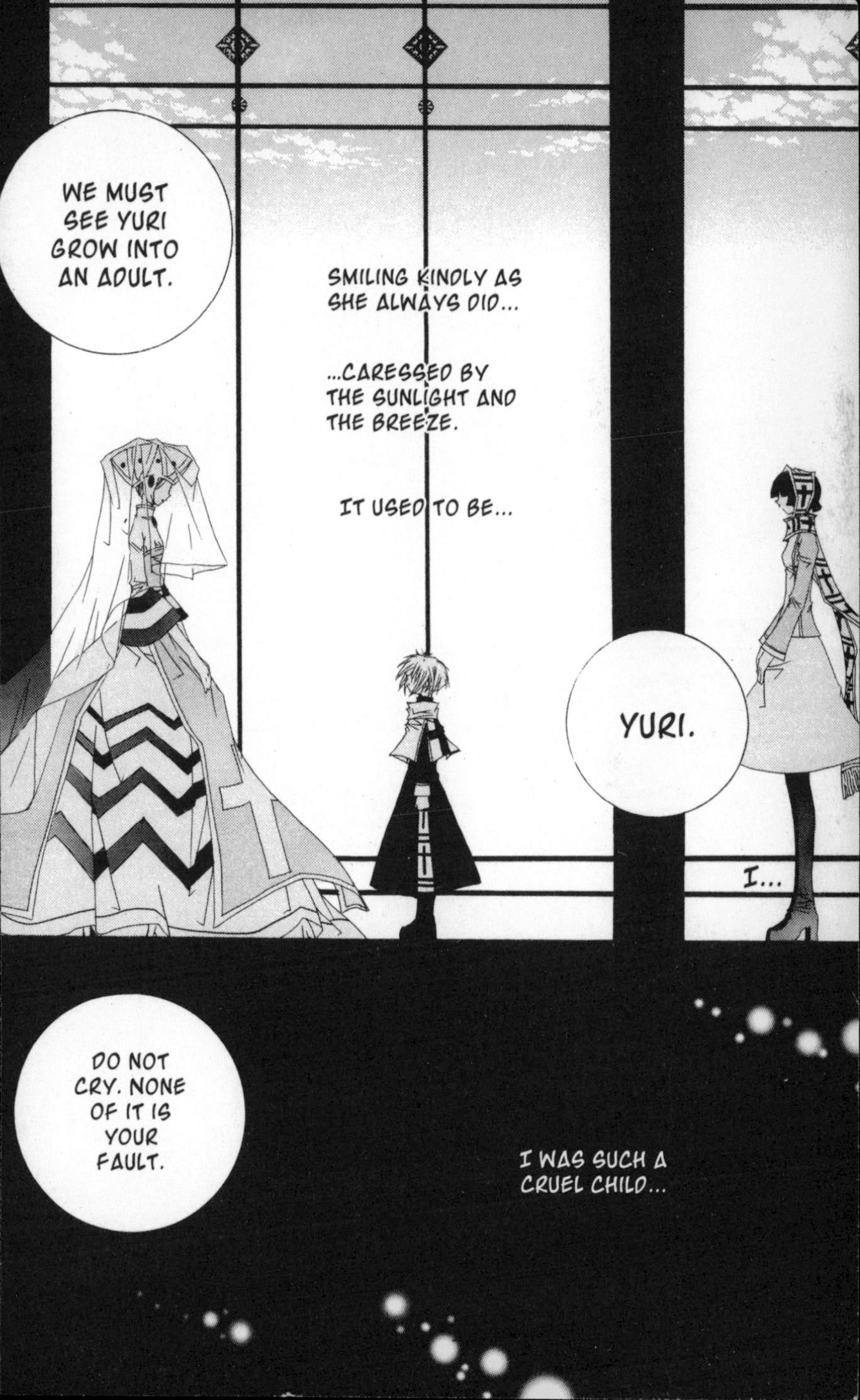
WE MUST SEE YURI GROW INTO AN ADULT.
SMILING KINDLY AS SHE ALWAYS DID...
...CARESSED BY THE SUNLIGHT AND THE BREEZE.
IT USED TO BE...
YURI.
I...
DO NOT CRY. NONE OF IT IS YOUR FAULT.
I WAS SUCH A CRUEL CHILD...

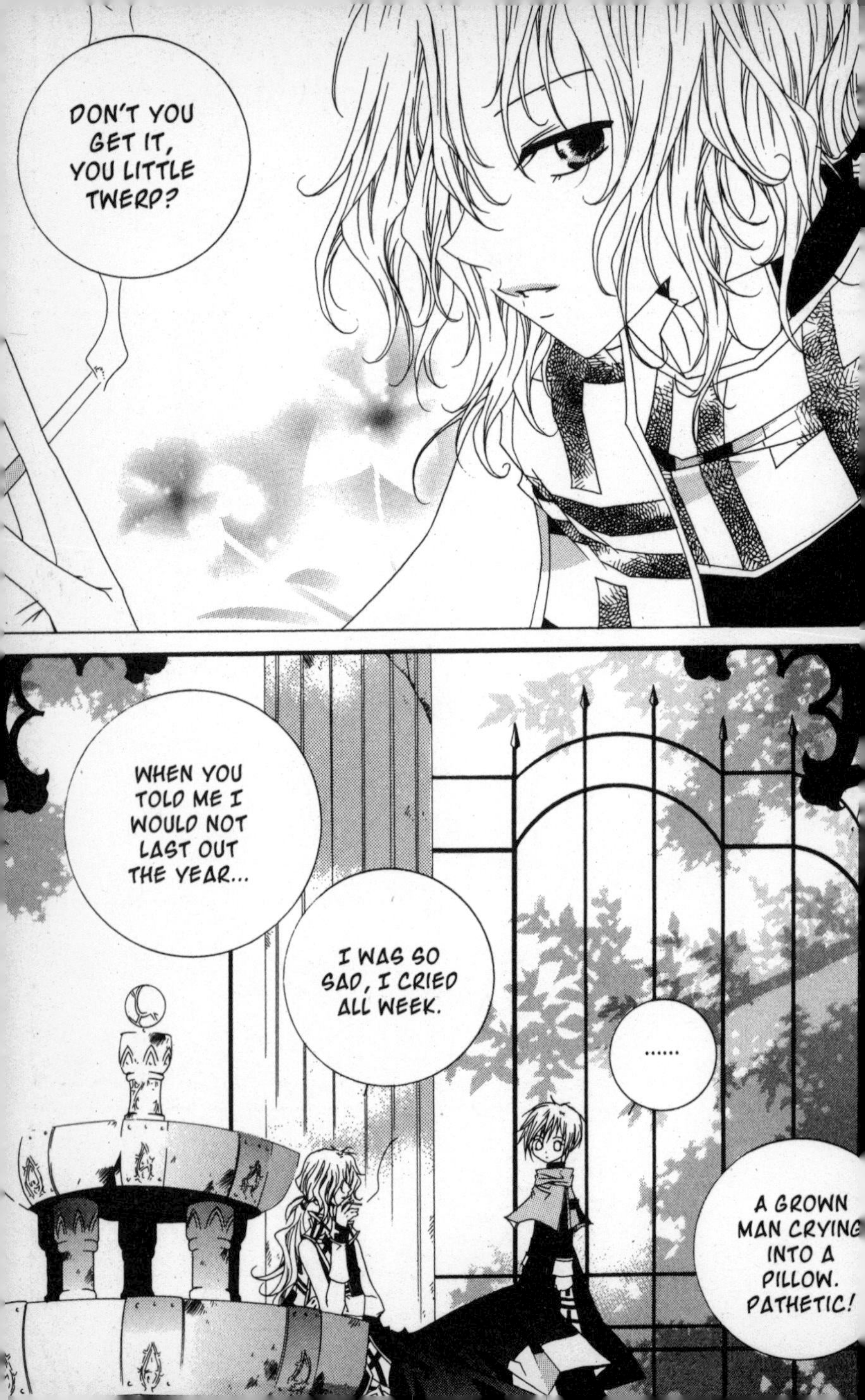
DON'T YOU GET IT, YOU LITTLE TWERP?
WHEN YOU TOLD ME I WOULD NOT LAST OUT THE YEAR...
I WAS SO SAD, I CRIED ALL WEEK.
......
A GROWN MAN CRYING INTO A PILLOW. PATHETIC!

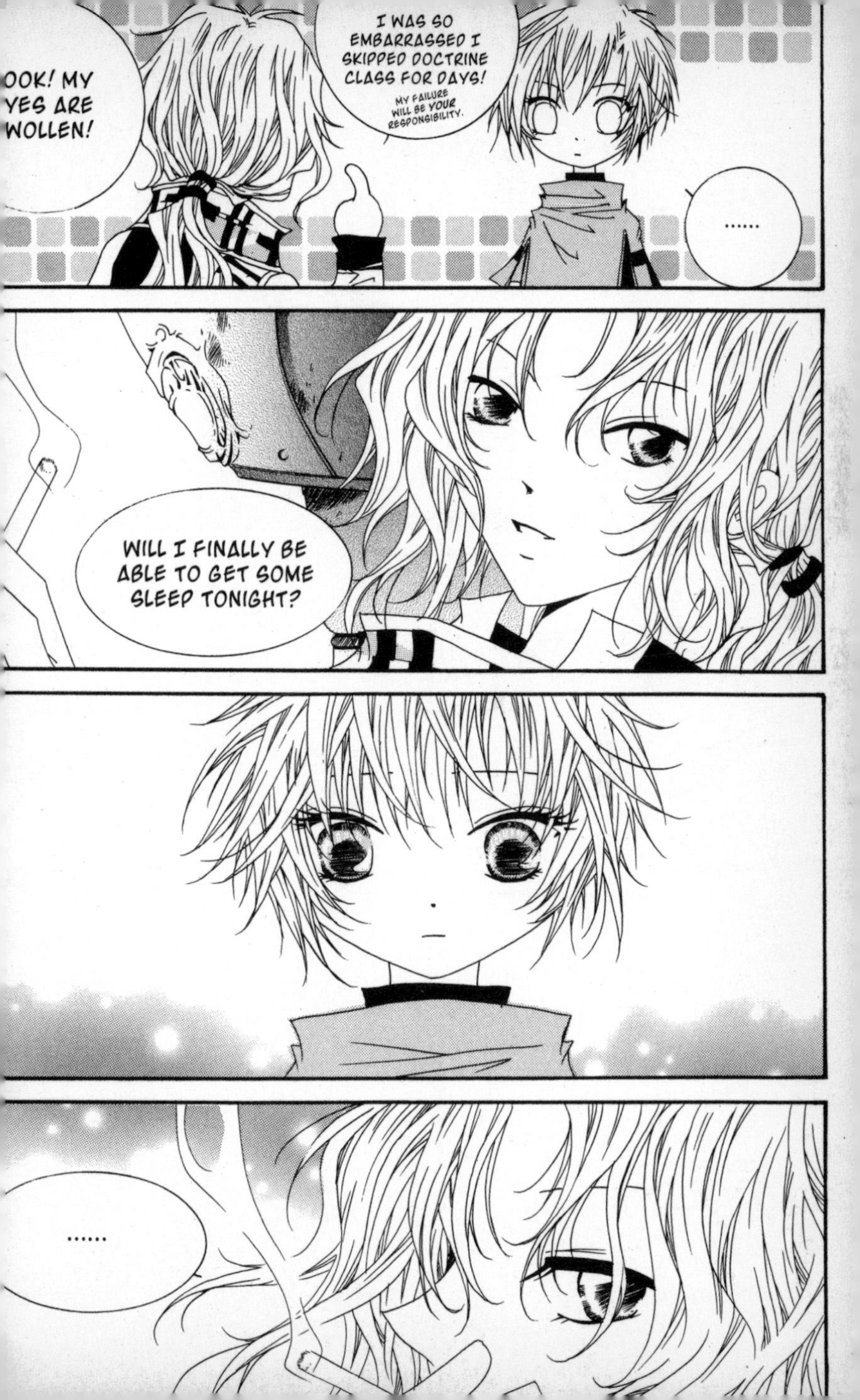
OOK! MY
YES ARE
WOLLEN!
I WAS SO EMBARRASSED I SKIPPED DOCTRINE CLASS FOR DAYS!
MY FAILURE WILL BE YOUR RESPONSIBILITY.
......
WILL I FINALLY BE ABLE TO GET SOME SLEEP TONIGHT?
......

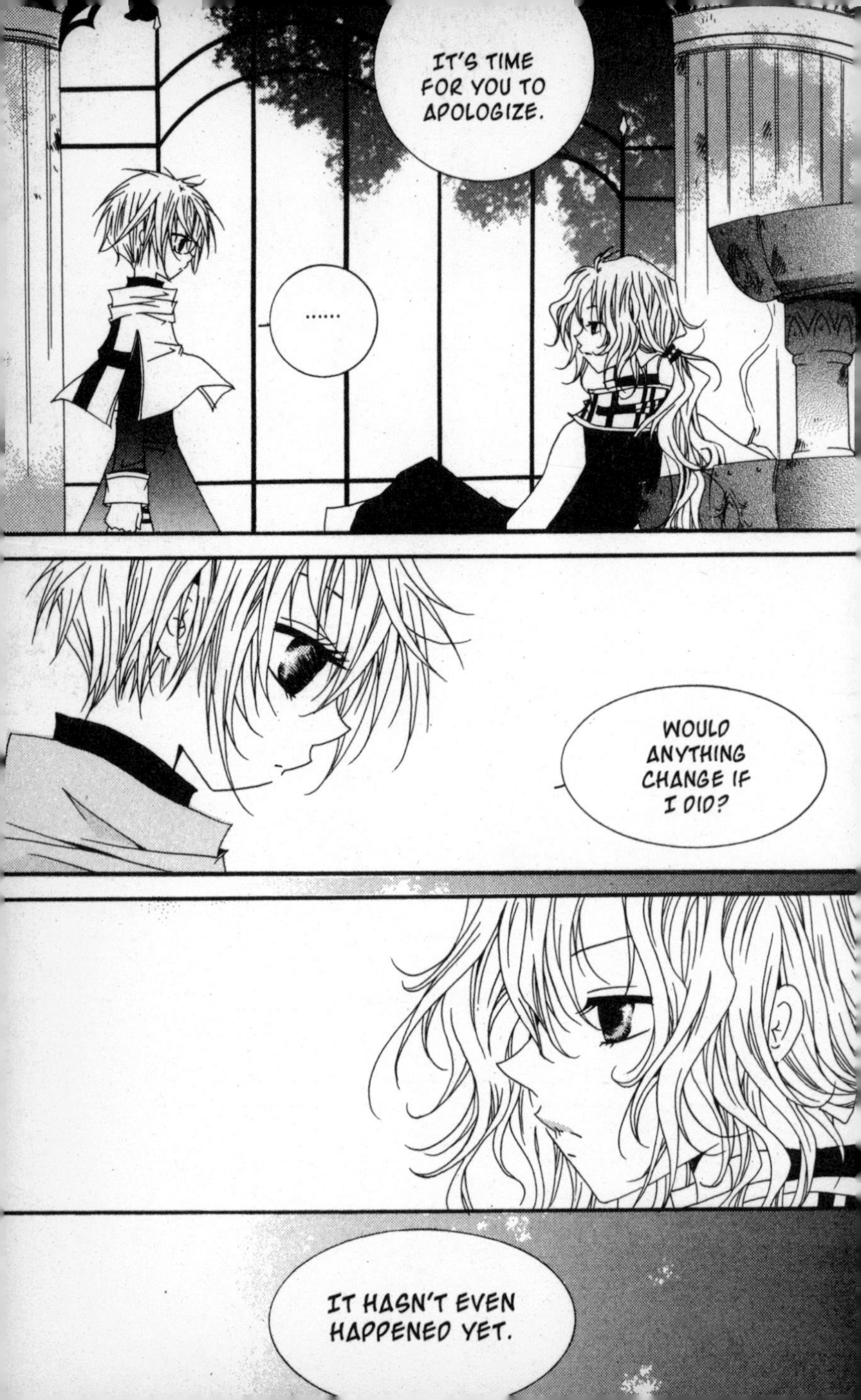
IT'S TIME FOR YOU TO APOLOGIZE.
......
WOULD ANYTHING CHANGE IF I DID?
IT HASN'T EVEN HAPPENED YET.

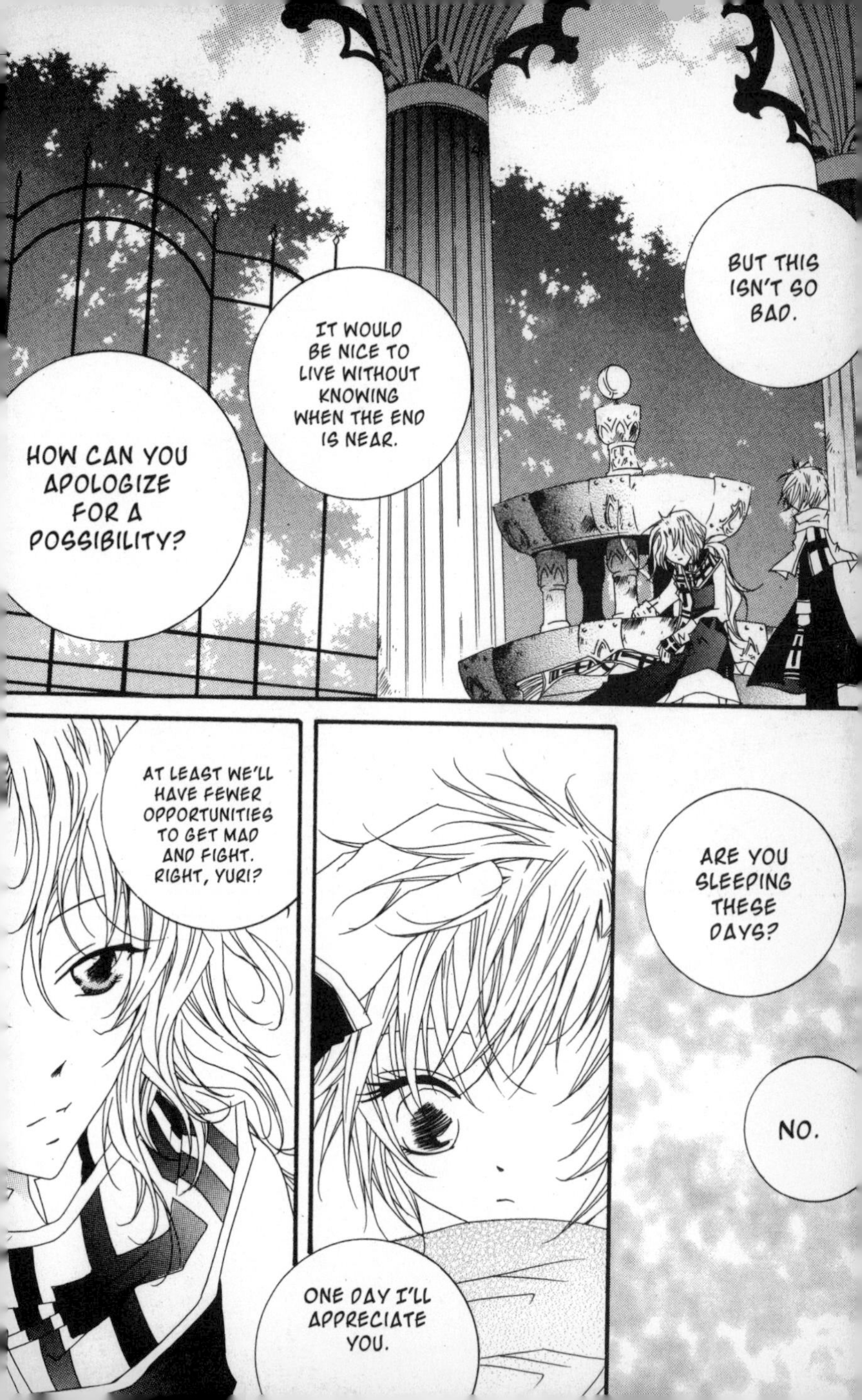
HOW CAN YOU APOLOGIZE FOR A POSSIBILITY?
IT WOULD BE NICE TO LIVE WITHOUT KNOWING WHEN THE END IS NEAR.
BUT THIS ISN'T SO BAD.
AT LEAST WE'LL HAVE FEWER OPPORTUNITIES TO GET MAD AND FIGHT. RIGHT, YURI?
ONE DAY I'LL APPRECIATE YOU.
ARE YOU SLEEPING THESE DAYS?
NO.

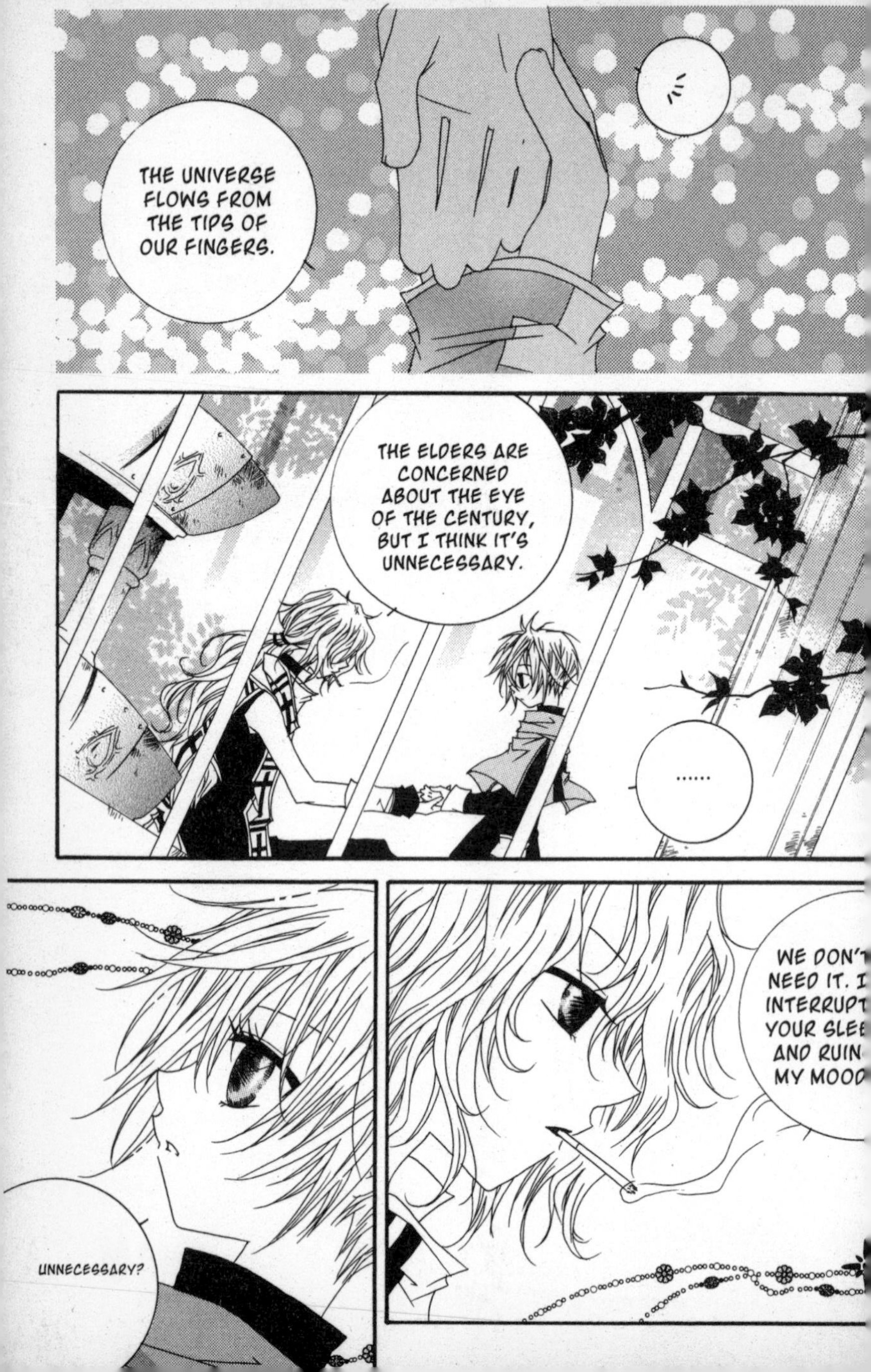
THE UNIVERSE FLOWS FROM THE TIPS OF OUR FINGERS.
...
THE ELDERS ARE CONCERNED ABOUT THE EYE OF THE CENTURY, BUT I THINK IT'S UNNECESSARY.
......
UNNECESSARY?
WE DON'T NEED IT. I INTERRUPT YOUR SLEE AND RUIN MY MOOD

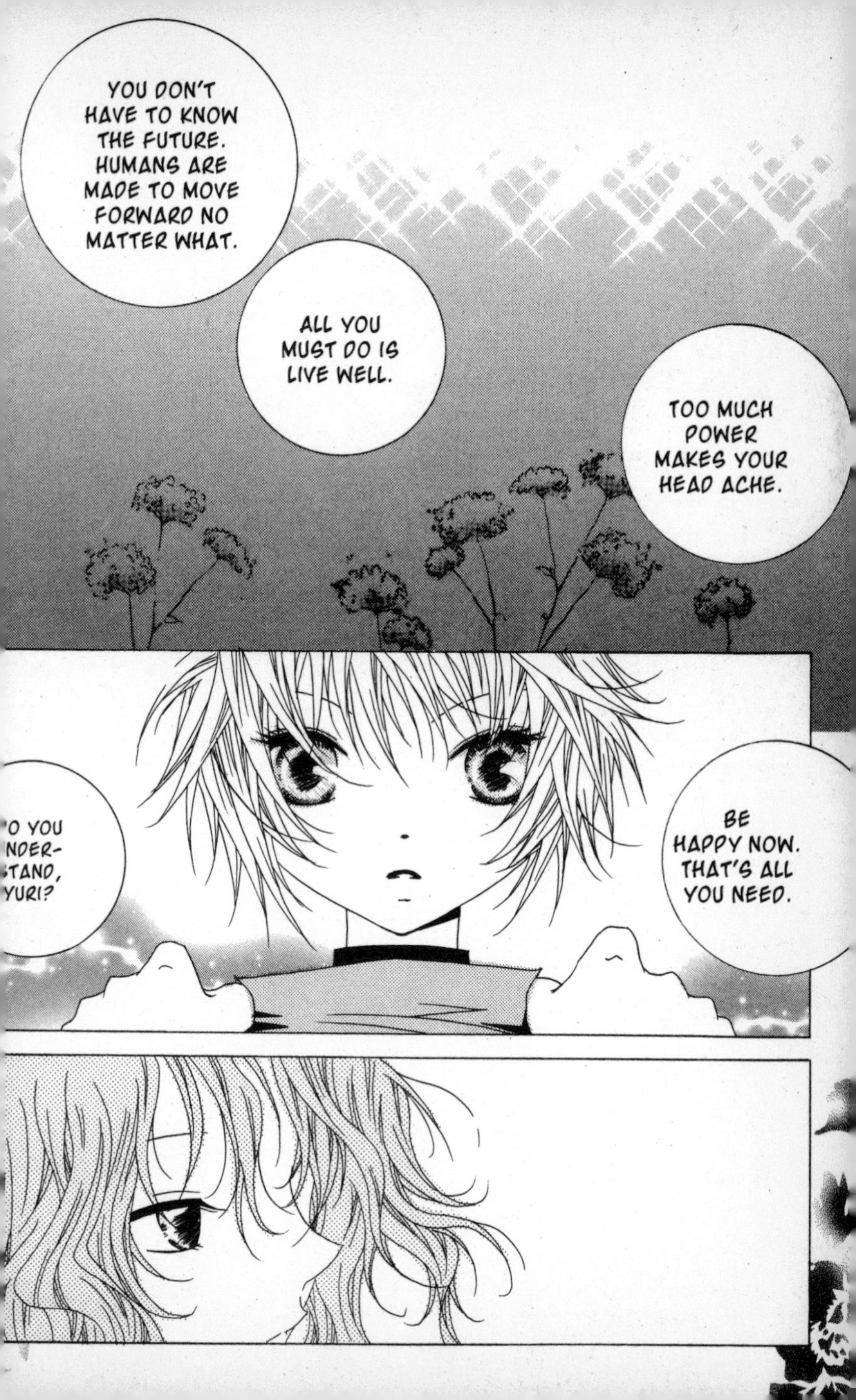
YOU DON'T HAVE TO KNOW THE FUTURE. HUMANS ARE MADE TO MOVE FORWARD NO MATTER WHAT.
ALL YOU MUST DO IS LIVE WELL.
TOO MUCH POWER MAKES YOUR HEAD ACHE.
'O YOU NDER-STAND, YURI?
BE HAPPY NOW. THAT'S ALL YOU NEED.

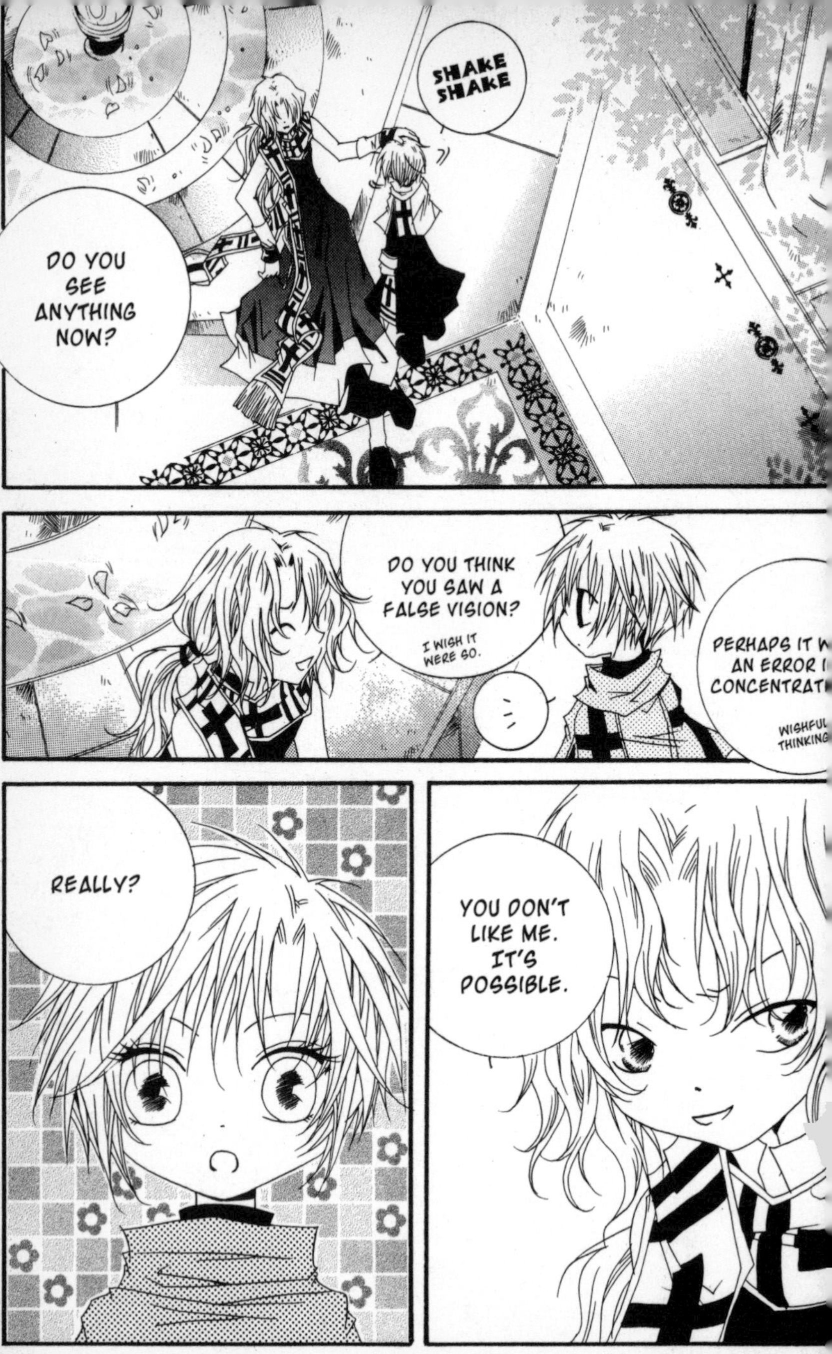
SHAKE SHAKE
DO YOU SEE ANYTHING NOW?
DO YOU THINK YOU SAW A FALSE VISION?
I WISH IT WERE SO.
PERHAPS IT W
AN ERROR I
CONCENTRAT
WISHFUL
THINKING
REALLY?
YOU DON'T LIKE ME. IT'S POSSIBLE.

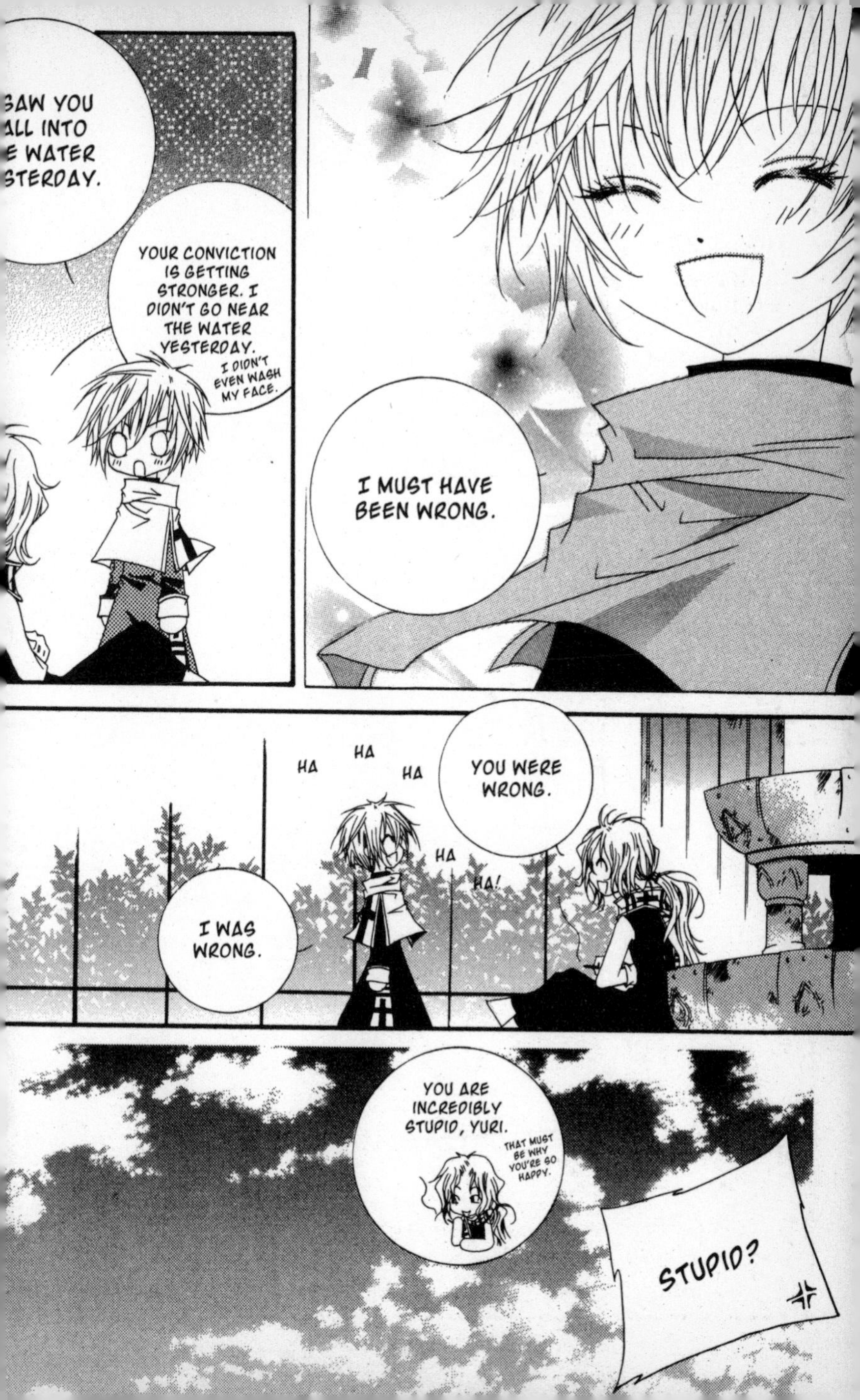
SAW YOU
ALL INTO
E WATER
STERDAY.
YOUR CONVICTION IS GETTING STRONGER. I DIDN'T GO NEAR THE WATER YESTERDAY.
I DIDN'T EVEN WASH MY FACE.
I MUST HAVE BEEN WRONG.
I WAS WRONG.
HA
HA
HA
HA
HA!
YOU WERE WRONG.
YOU ARE INCREDIBLY STUPID, YURI.
THAT MUST BE WHY YOU'RE SO HAPPY.
STUPID?

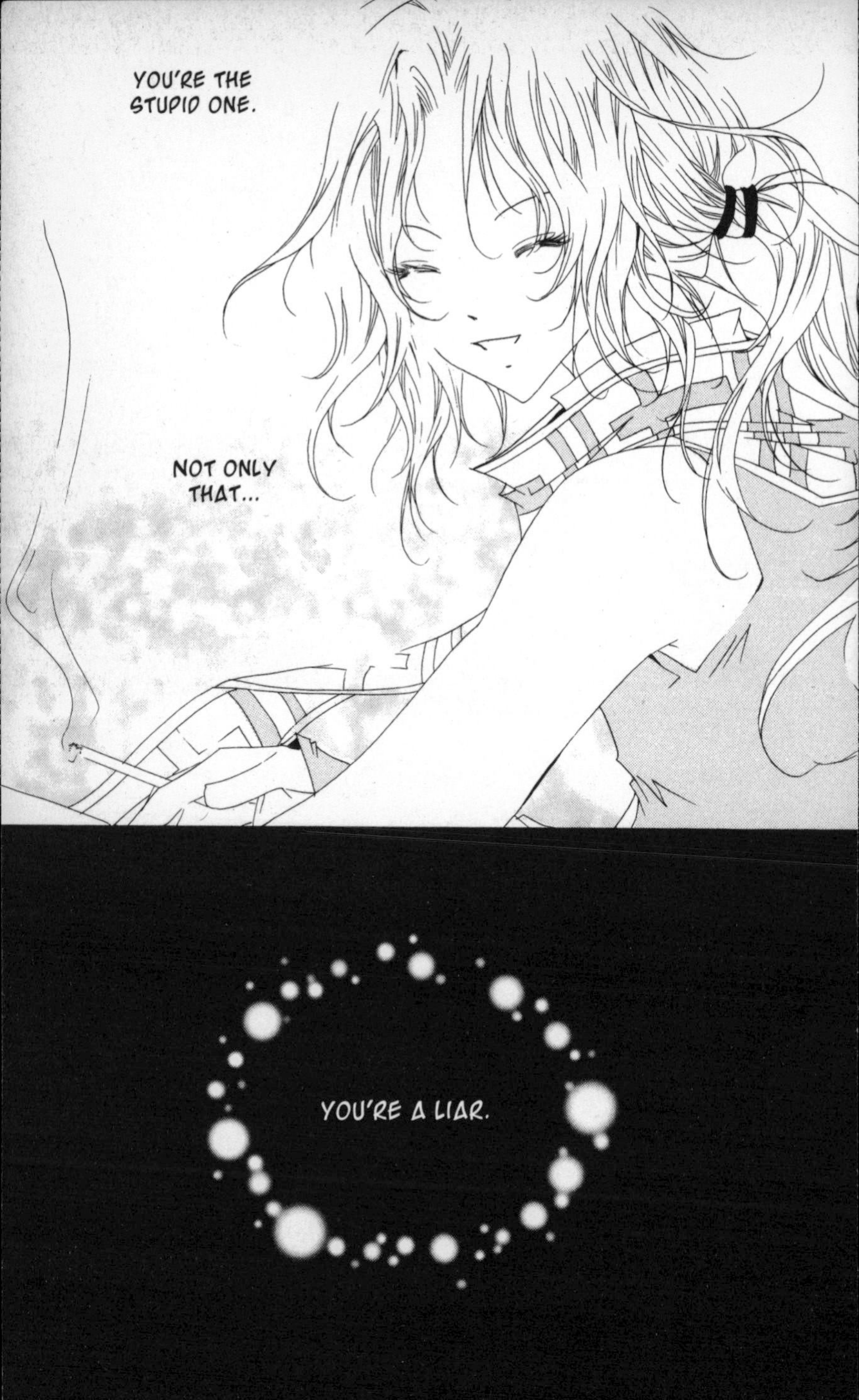
YOU'RE THE STUPID ONE.
NOT ONLY THAT...
YOU'RE A LIAR.

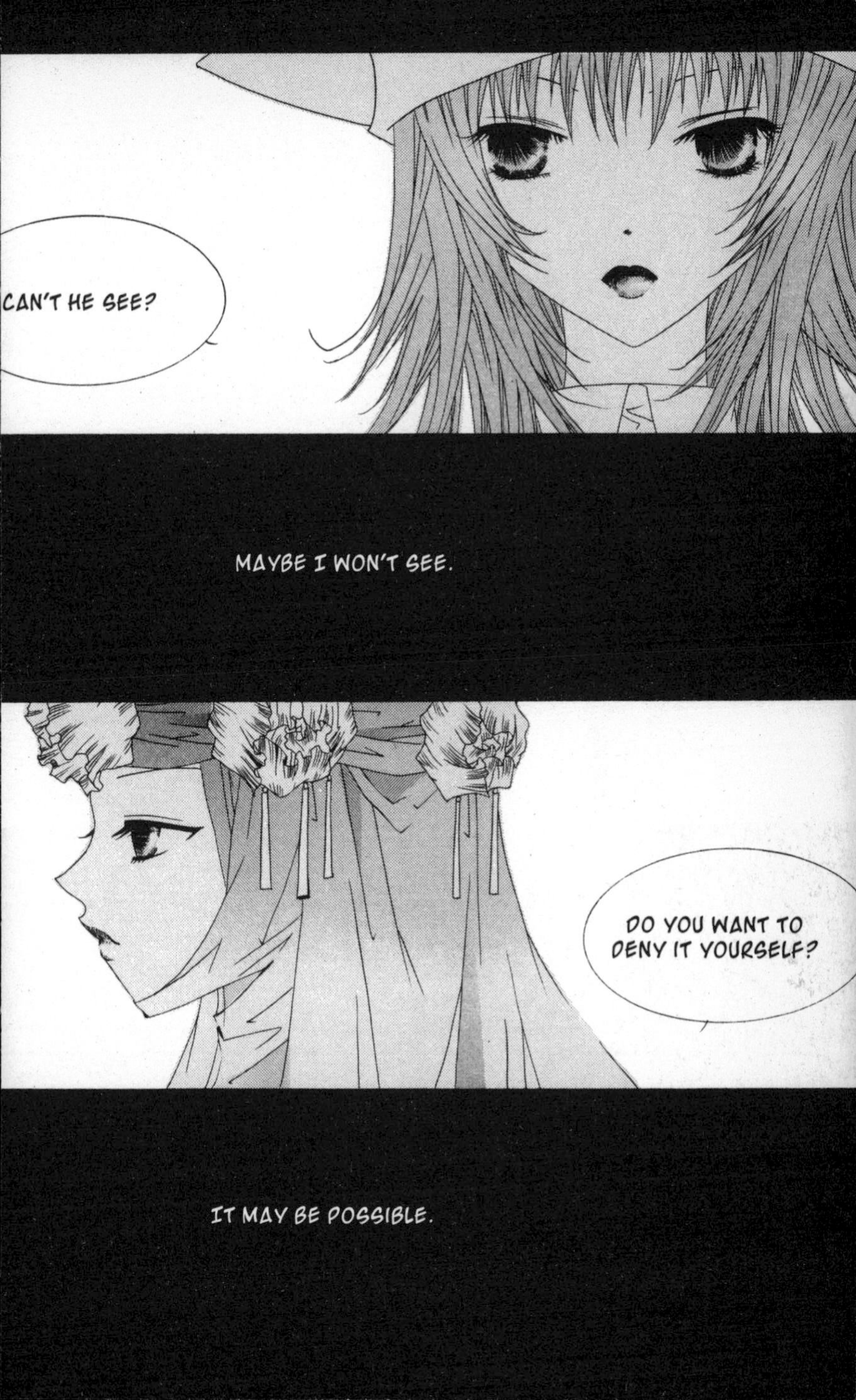
CAN'T HE SEE?
MAYBE I WON'T SEE.
DO YOU WANT TO DENY IT YOURSELF?
IT MAY BE POSSIBLE.

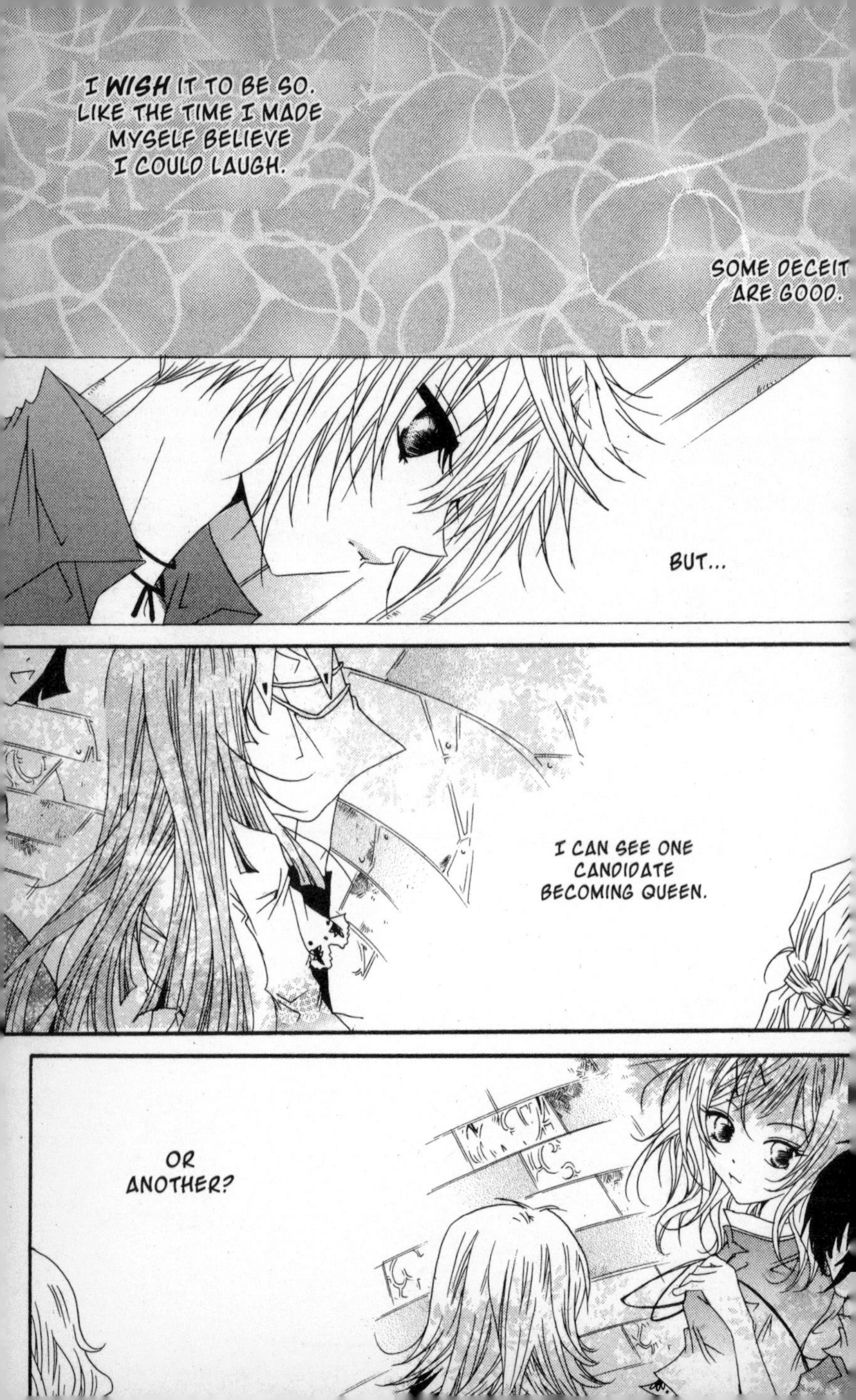
I WISH IT TO BE SO. LIKE THE TIME I MADE MYSELF BELIEVE I COULD LAUGH.
SOME DECEIT ARE GOOD.
BUT...
I CAN SEE ONE CANDIDATE BECOMING QUEEN.
OR ANOTHER?

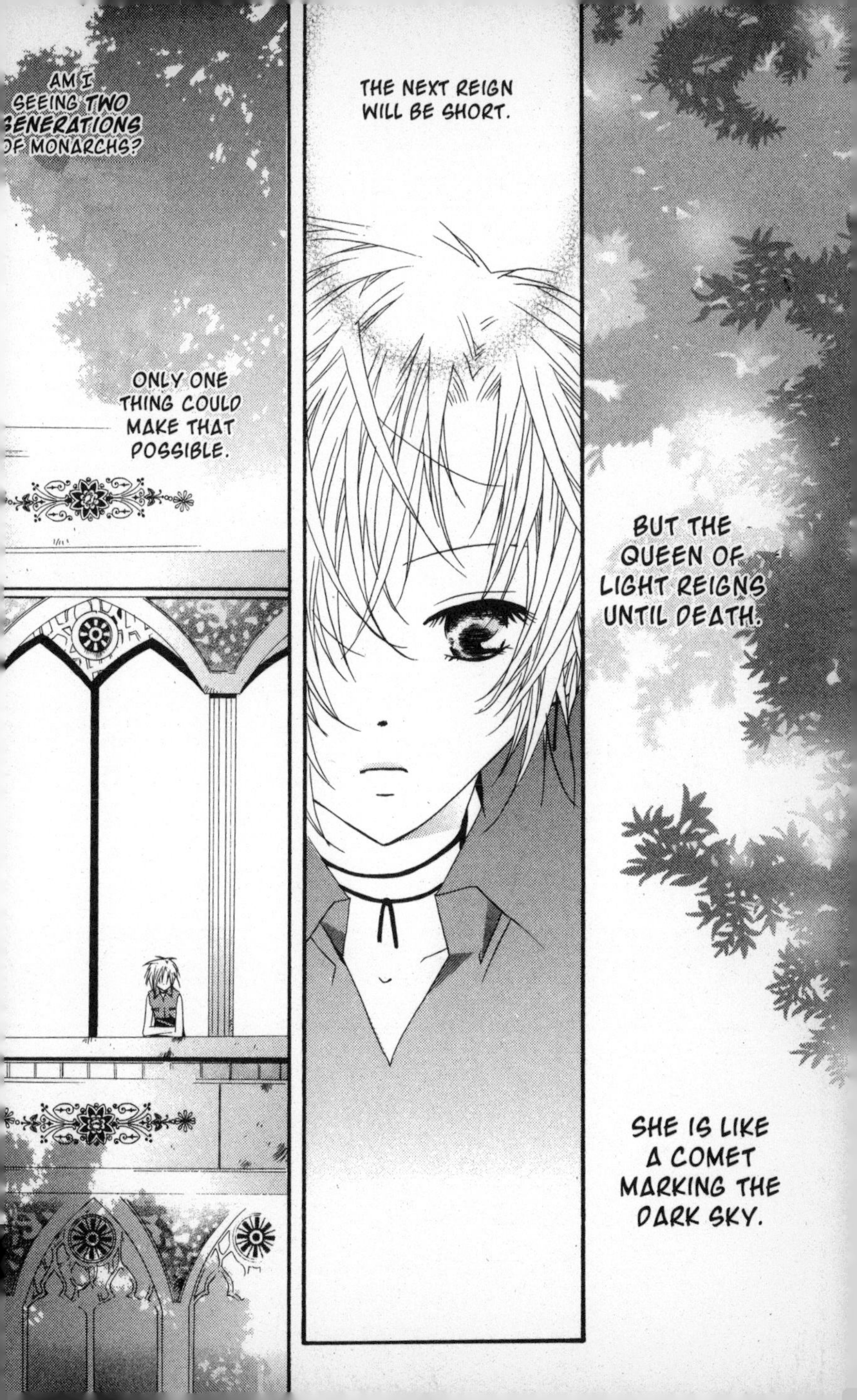
AM I SEEING TWO GENERATIONS OF MONARCHS?
ONLY ONE THING COULD MAKE THAT POSSIBLE.
THE NEXT REIGN WILL BE SHORT.
BUT THE QUEEN OF LIGHT REIGNS UNTIL DEATH.
SHE IS LIKE A COMET MARKING THE DARK SKY.

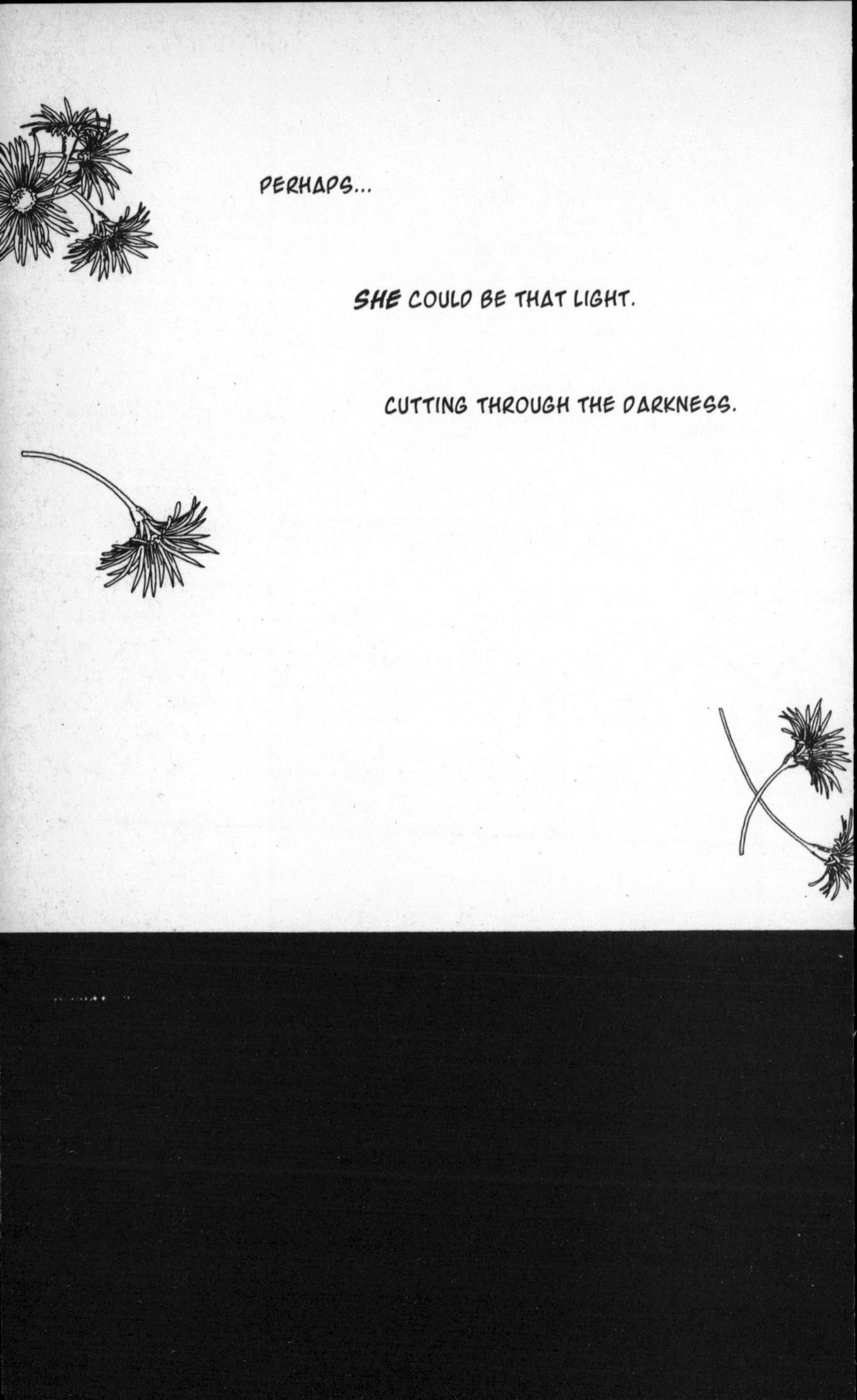
PERHAPS...
SHE COULD BE THAT LIGHT.
CUTTING THROUGH THE DARKNESS.

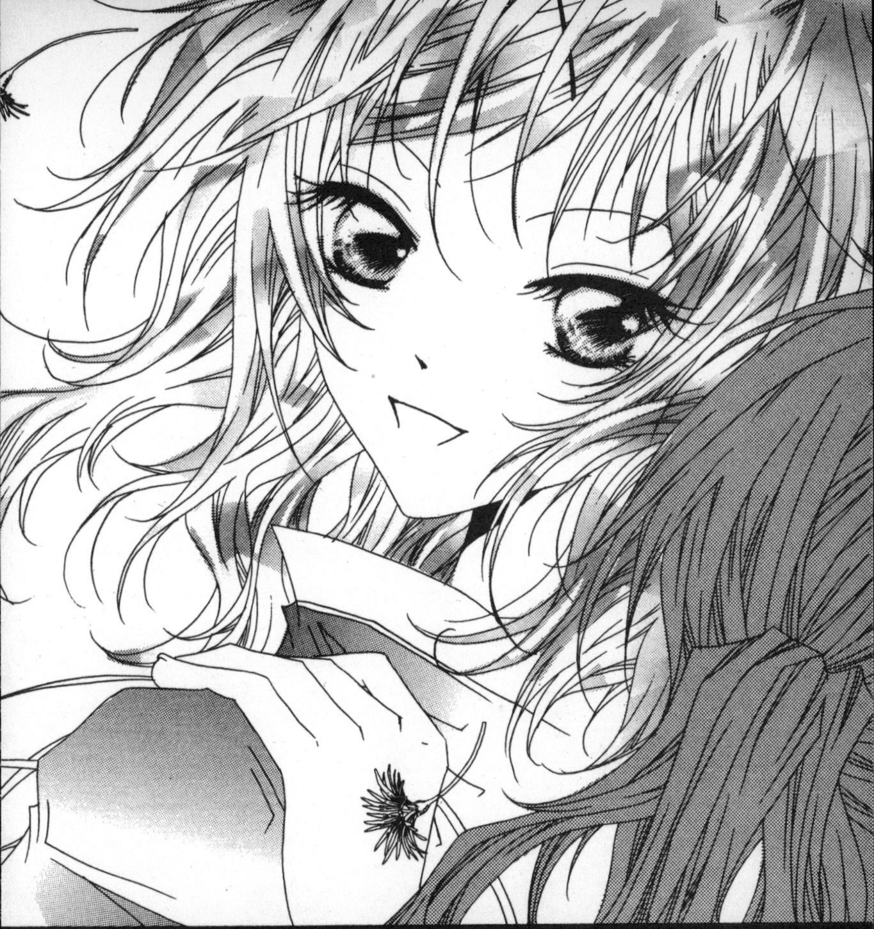

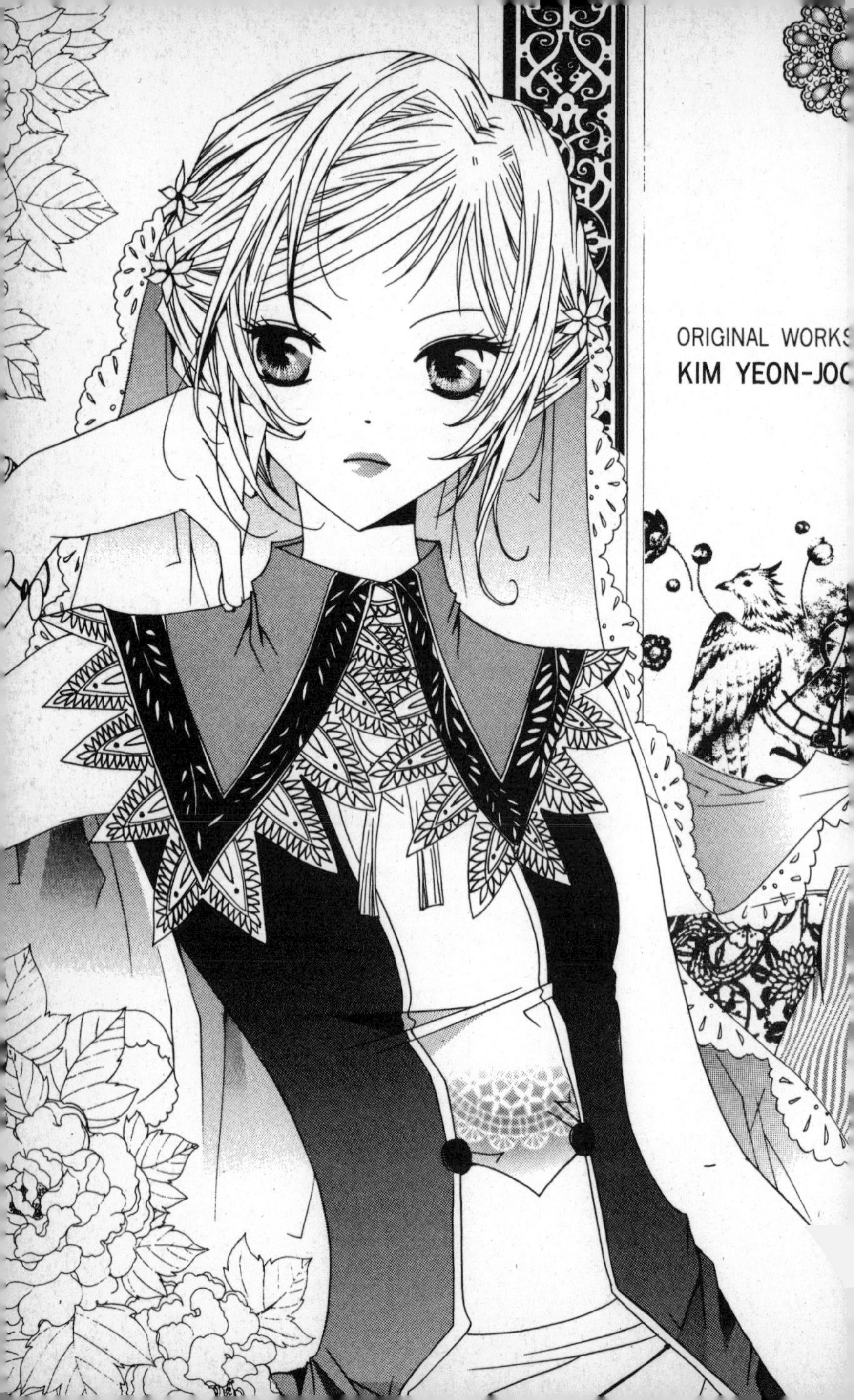
ORIGINAL WORKS
KIM YEON-JO

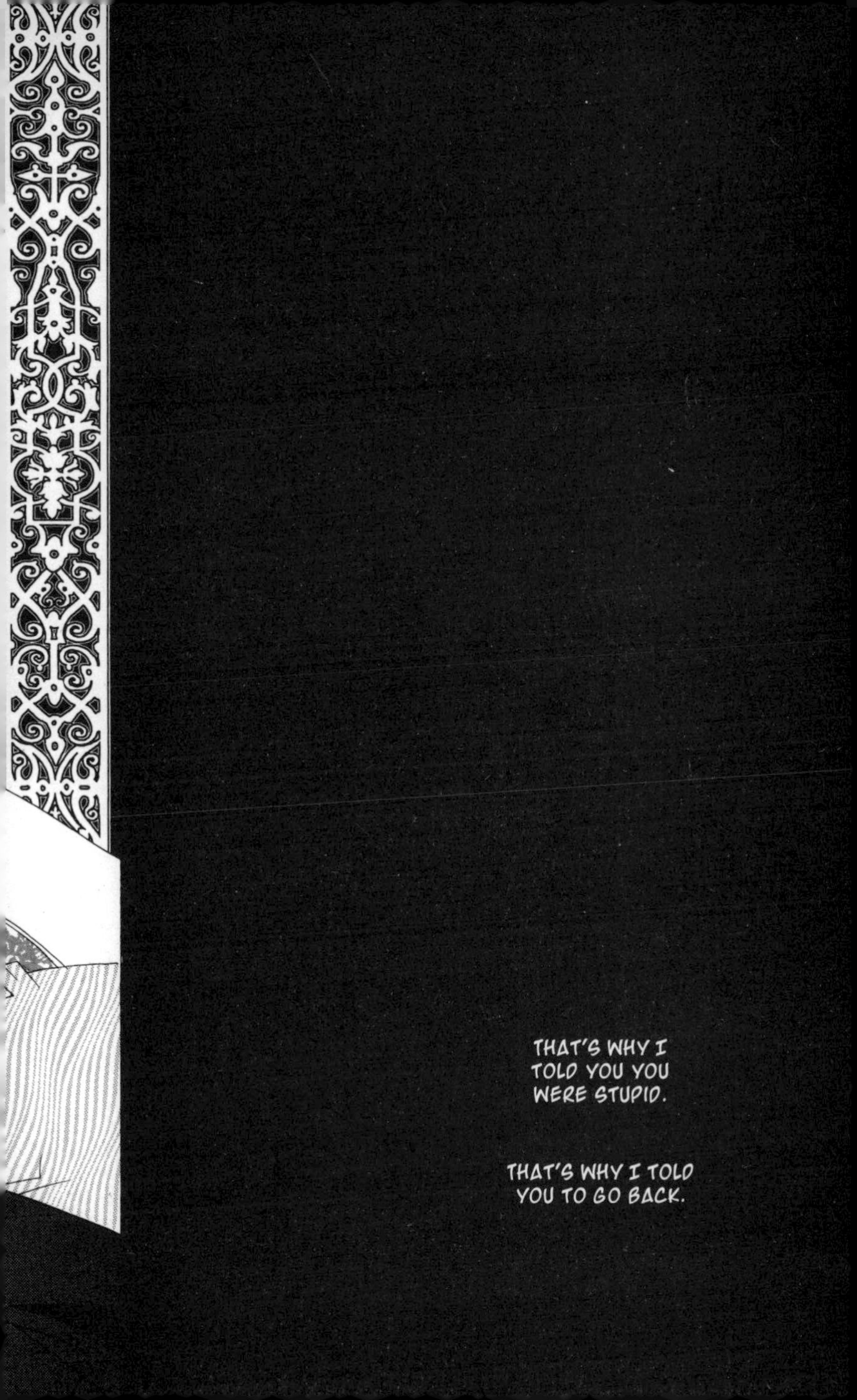
THAT'S WHY I TOLD YOU YOU WERE STUPID.
THAT'S WHY I TOLD YOU TO GO BACK.

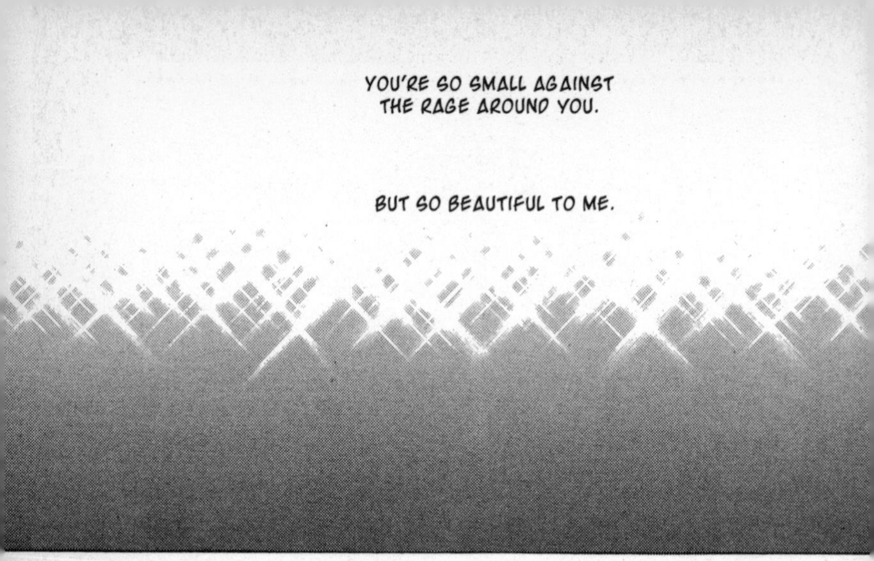
YOU'RE SO SMALL AGAINST THE RAGE AROUND YOU.
BUT SO BEAUTIFUL TO ME.

Transparent, Sharp and Piercing the Heart

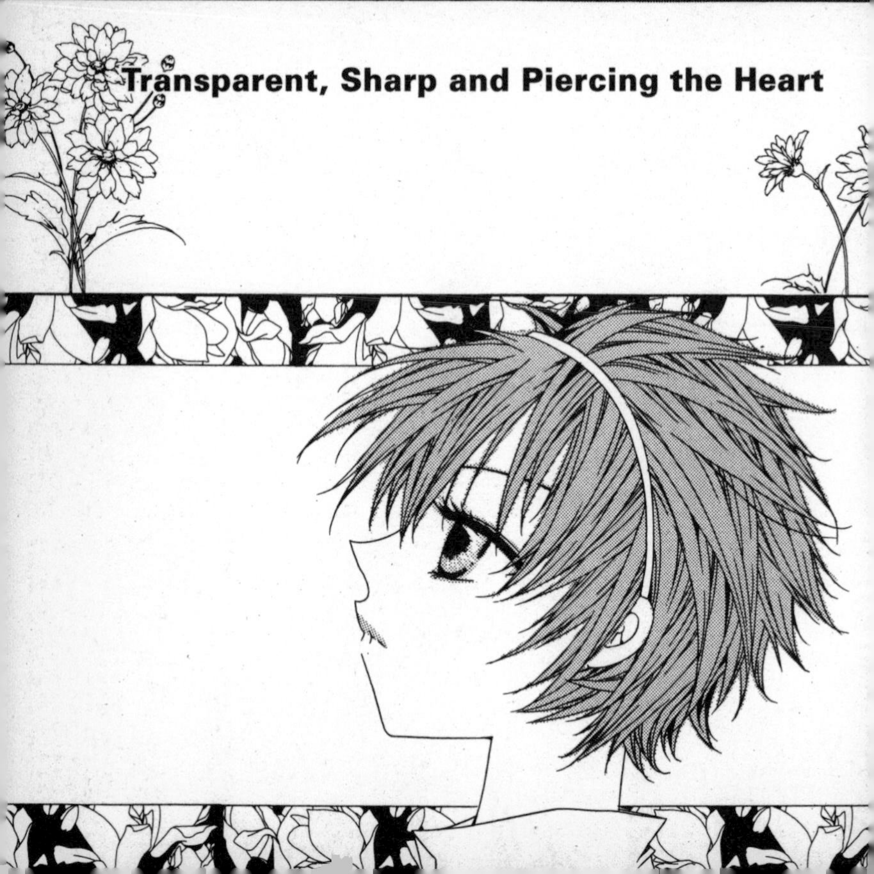

FIRST TERM		RANK TOP 50	
1	LUCIA LUFERR		✦
2	GENEVIEVE BELL		✦

22	ARTIR LEGER ERNICA	✦
23	MAYA LYNN KIM	✦
24	ROSEN PAVRONIA	●
25	ANA SHAY COPRISS	✦
26	PHYLLIAS WINOBLE	✦
27		

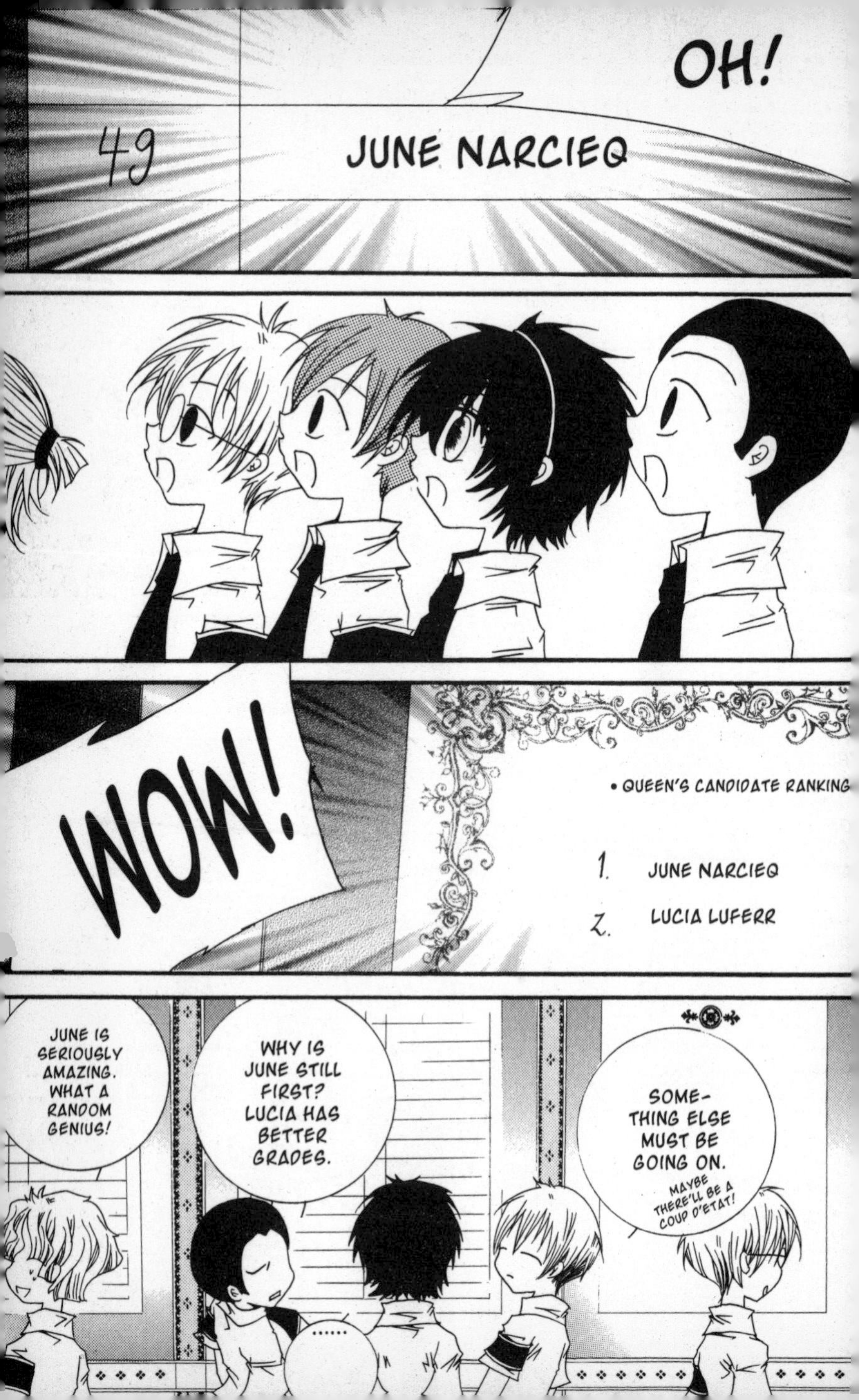
OH!
49
JUNE NARCIEQ
WOW!
• QUEEN'S CANDIDATE RANKING
1. JUNE NARCIEQ
2. LUCIA LUFERR
JUNE IS SERIOUSLY AMAZING. WHAT A RANDOM GENIUS!
WHY IS JUNE STILL FIRST? LUCIA HAS BETTER GRADES.
SOME-THING ELSE MUST BE GOING ON.
MAYBE THERE'LL BE A COUP D'ETAT!
......

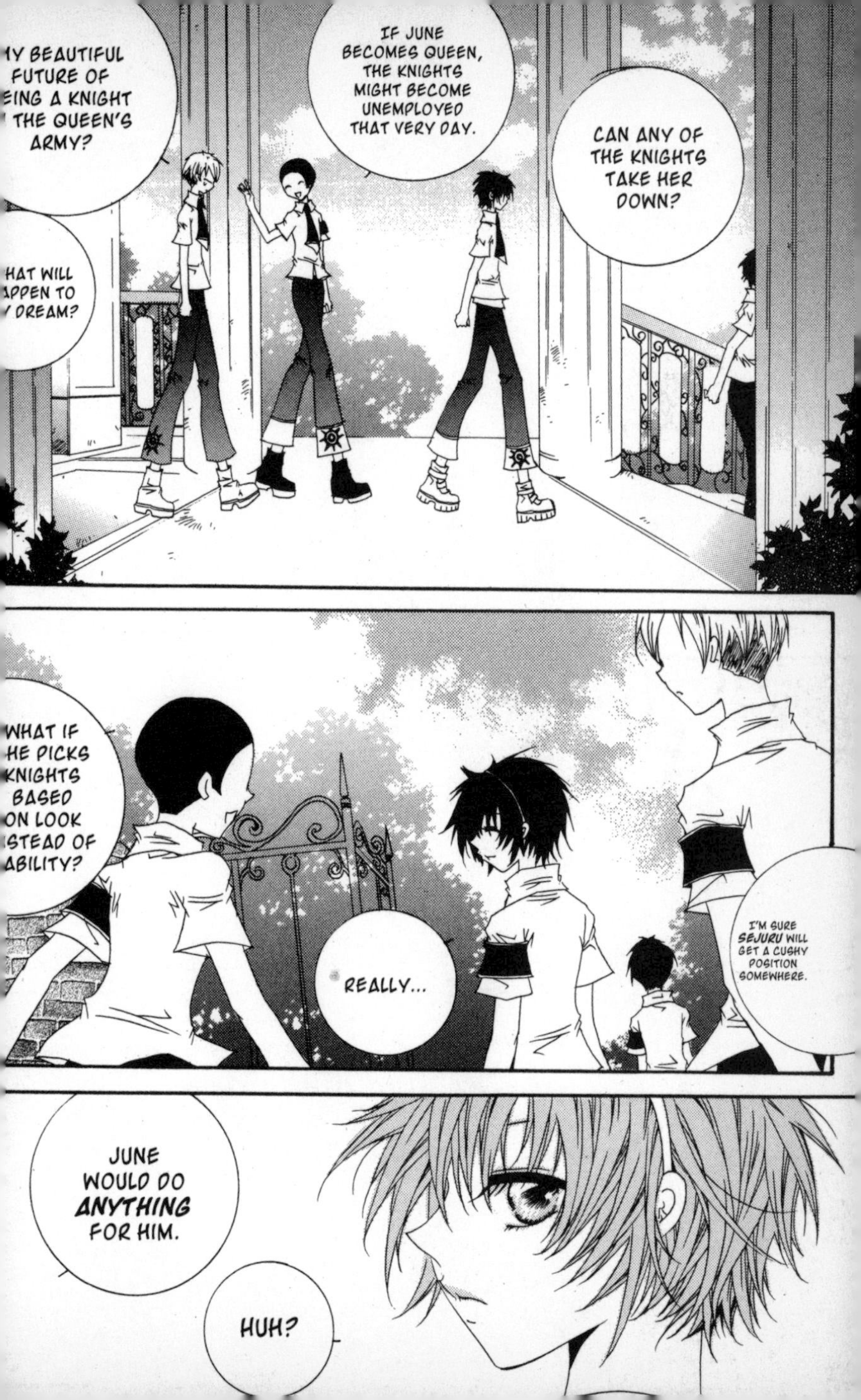
Y BEAUTIFUL FUTURE OF EING A KNIGHT THE QUEEN'S ARMY?
HAT WILL APPEN TO DREAM?
IF JUNE BECOMES QUEEN, THE KNIGHTS MIGHT BECOME UNEMPLOYED THAT VERY DAY.
CAN ANY OF THE KNIGHTS TAKE HER DOWN?
WHAT IF HE PICKS KNIGHTS BASED ON LOOK STEAD OF ABILITY?
REALLY...
I'M SURE SEJURU WILL GET A CUSHY POSITION SOMEWHERE.
JUNE WOULD DO ANYTHING FOR HIM.
HUH?

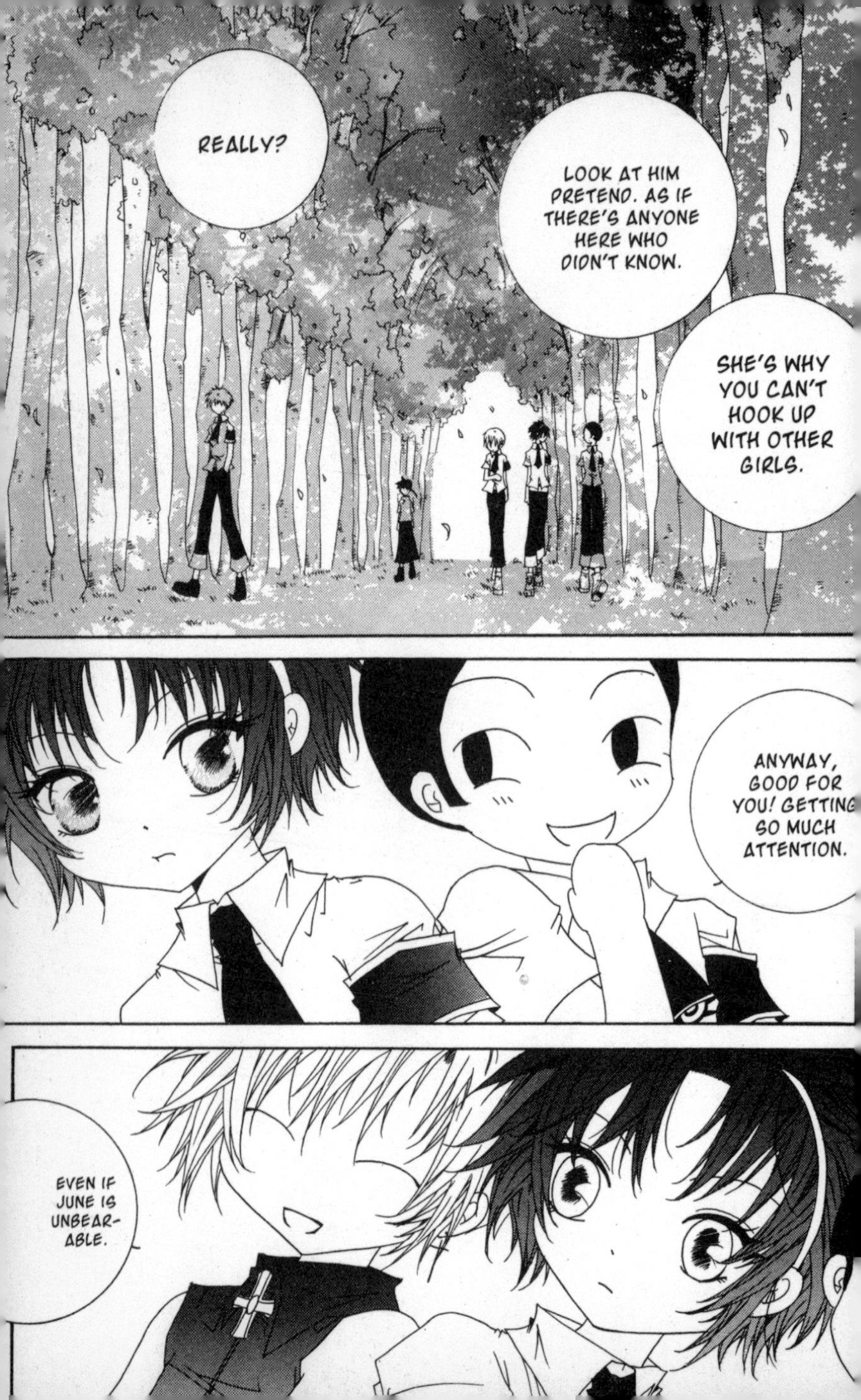
REALLY?
LOOK AT HIM PRETEND. AS IF THERE'S ANYONE HERE WHO DIDN'T KNOW.
SHE'S WHY YOU CAN'T HOOK UP WITH OTHER GIRLS.
ANYWAY, GOOD FOR YOU! GETTING SO MUCH ATTENTION.
EVEN IF JUNE IS UNBEAR-ABLE.

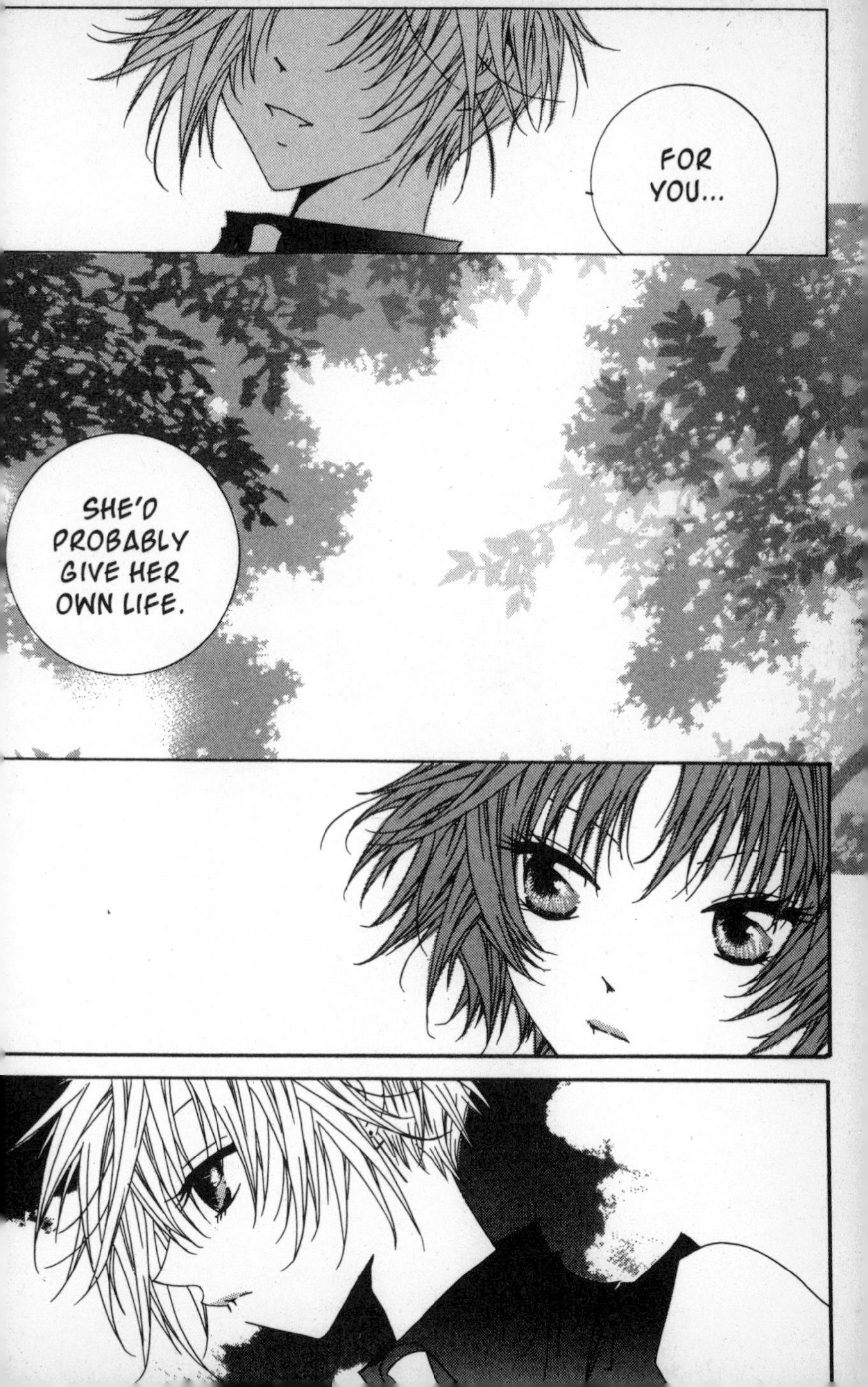
FOR YOU...
SHE'D PROBABLY GIVE HER OWN LIFE.

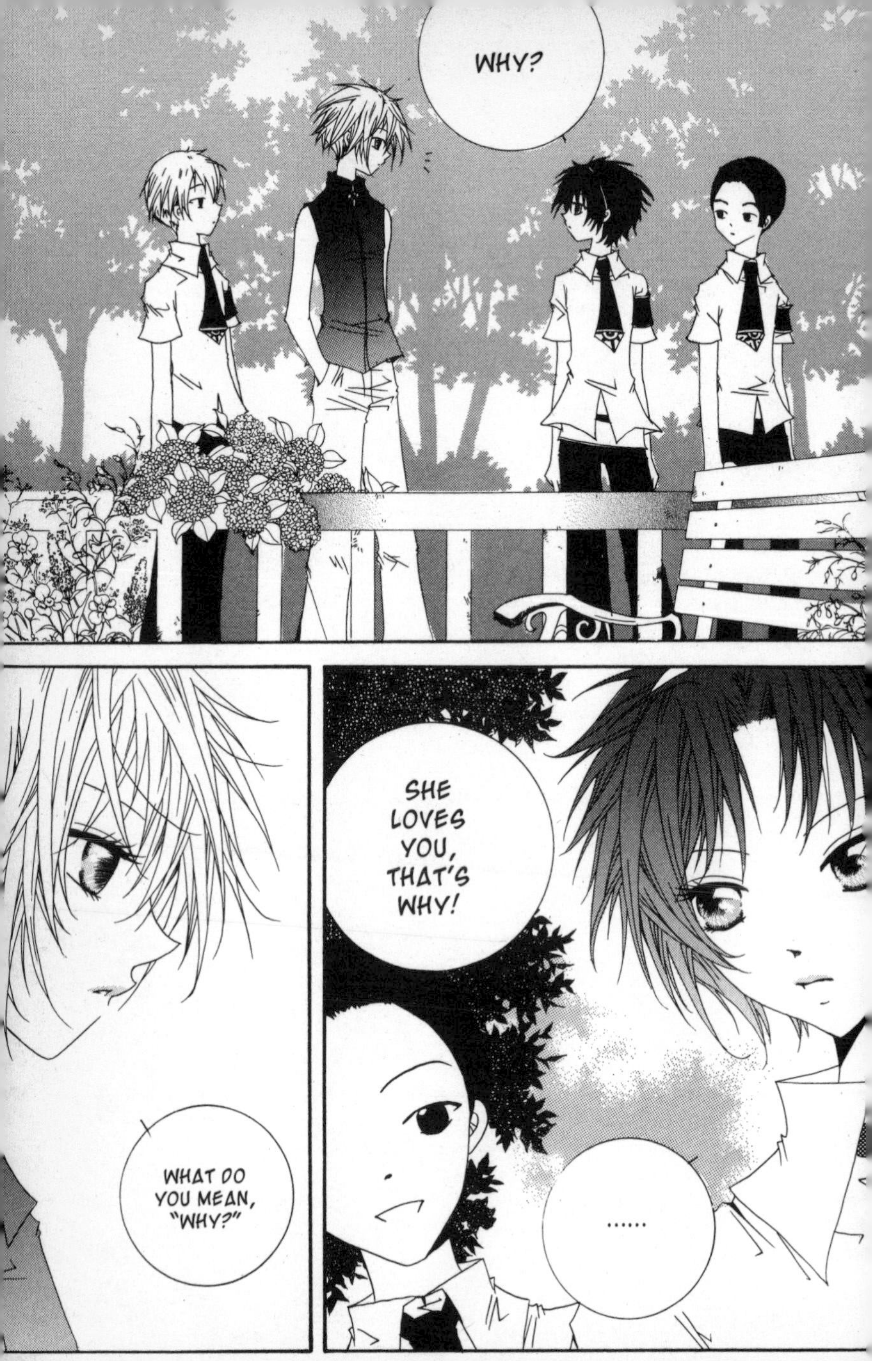
WHY?
WHAT DO YOU MEAN, "WHY?"
SHE LOVES YOU, THAT'S WHY!
......

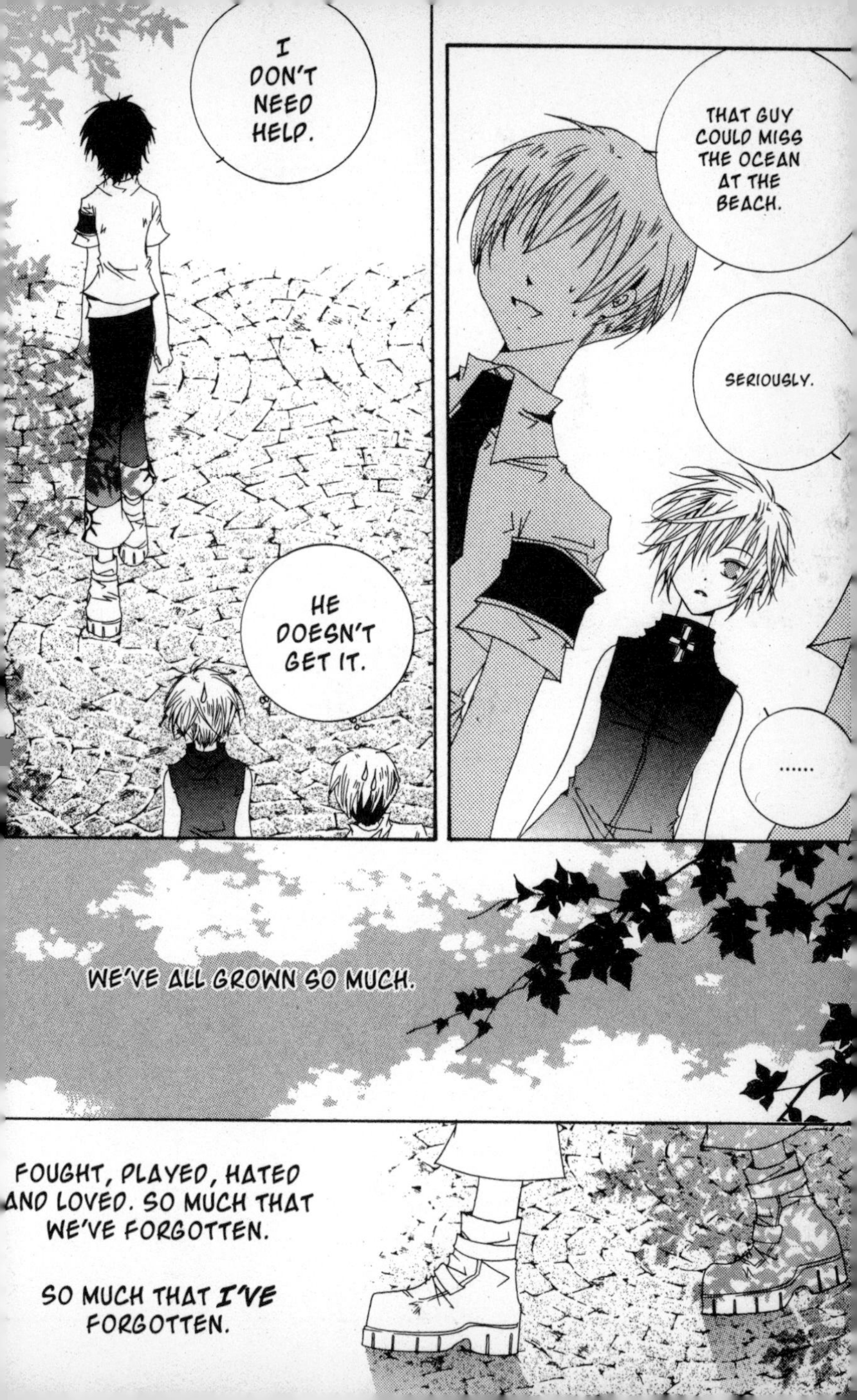
I DON'T NEED HELP.
HE DOESN'T GET IT.
THAT GUY COULD MISS THE OCEAN AT THE BEACH.
SERIOUSLY.
......
WE'VE ALL GROWN SO MUCH.
FOUGHT, PLAYED, HATED AND LOVED. SO MUCH THAT WE'VE FORGOTTEN.
SO MUCH THAT *I'VE* FORGOTTEN.

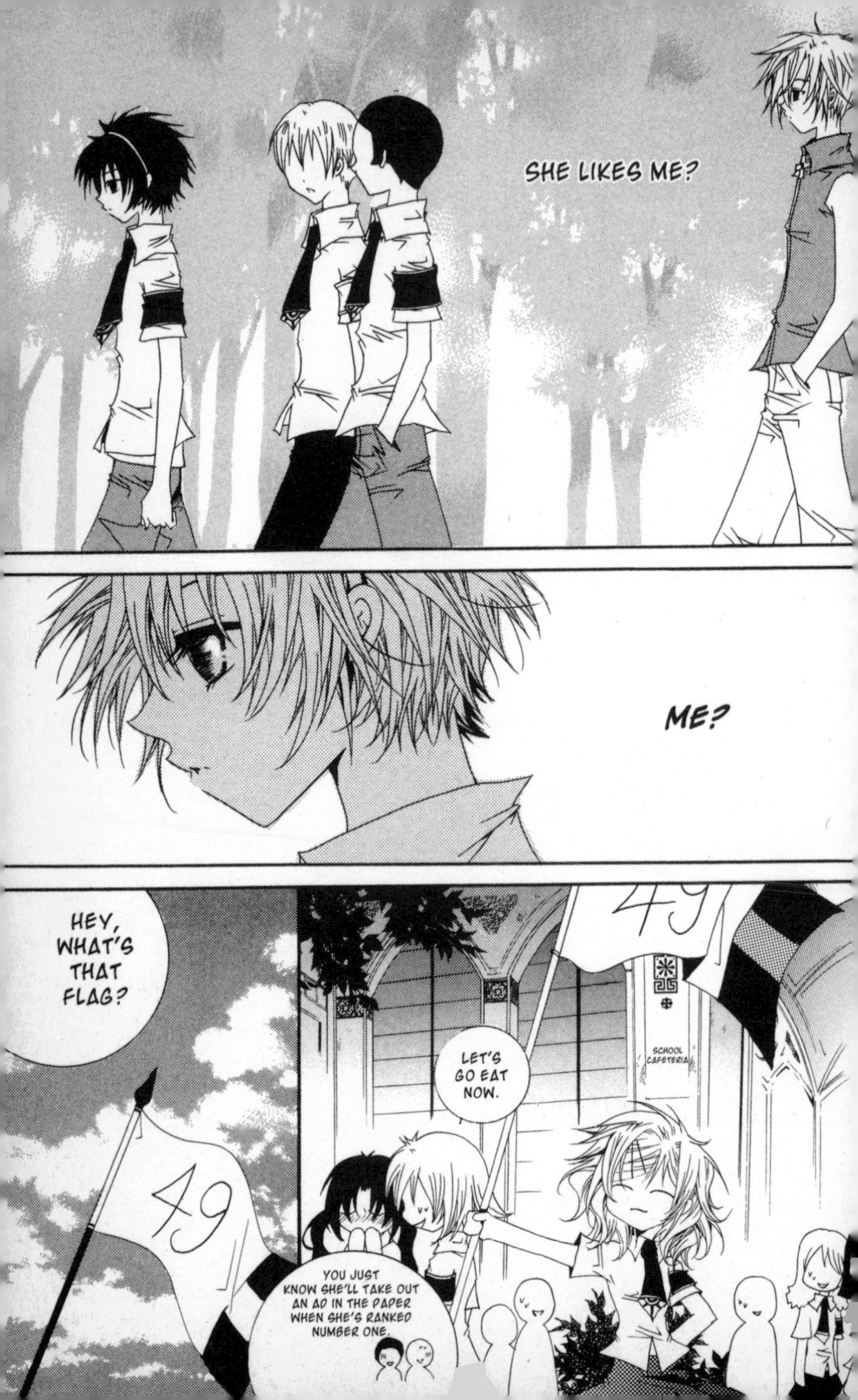
SHE LIKES ME?
ME?
HEY, WHAT'S THAT FLAG?
LET'S GO EAT NOW.
SCHOOL CAFETERIA
49
YOU JUST KNOW SHE'LL TAKE OUT AN AD IN THE PAPER WHEN SHE'S RANKED NUMBER ONE.

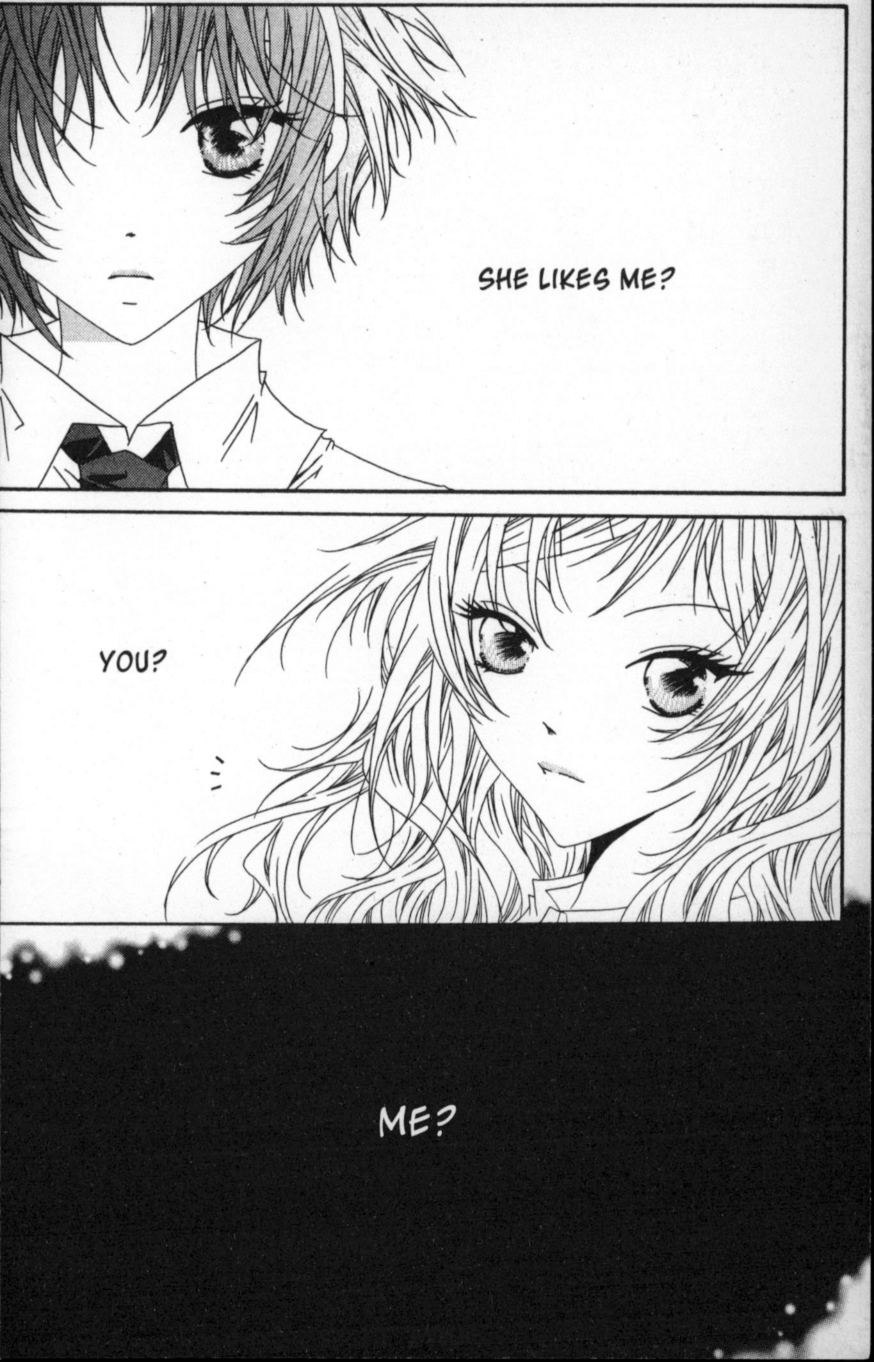
SHE LIKES ME?
YOU?
ME?

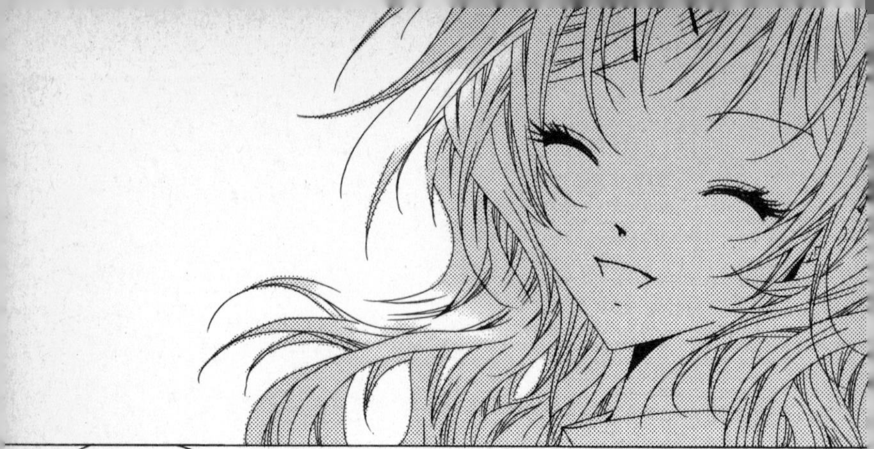

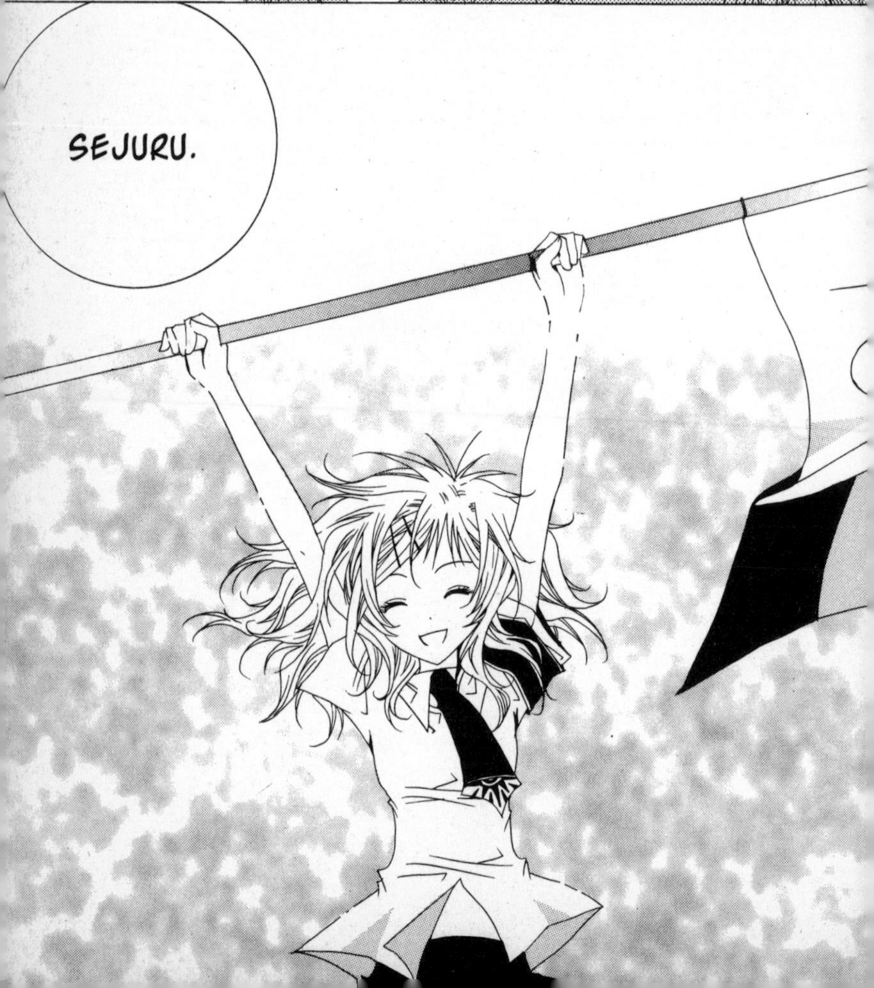
SEJURU.

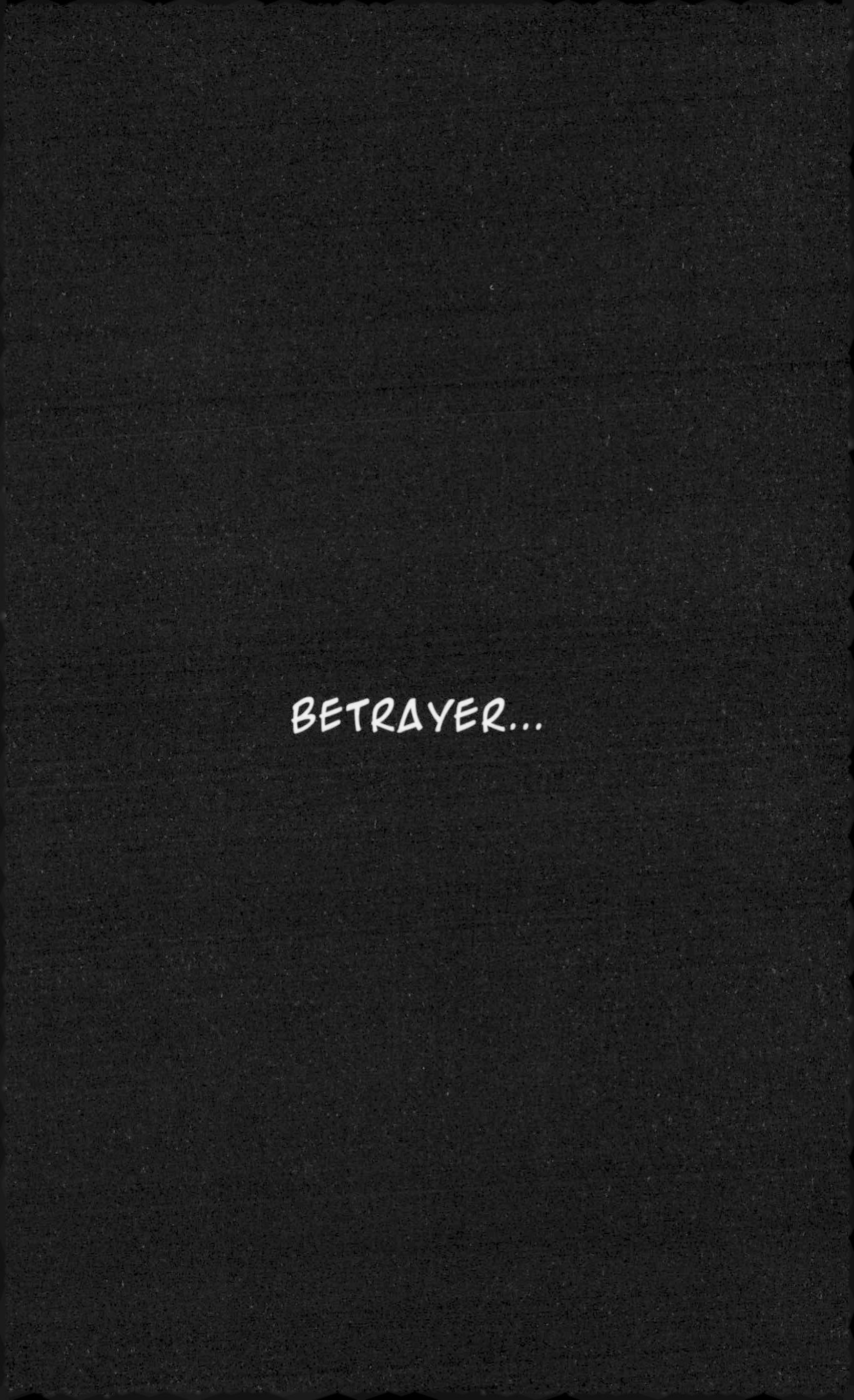
BETRAYER...

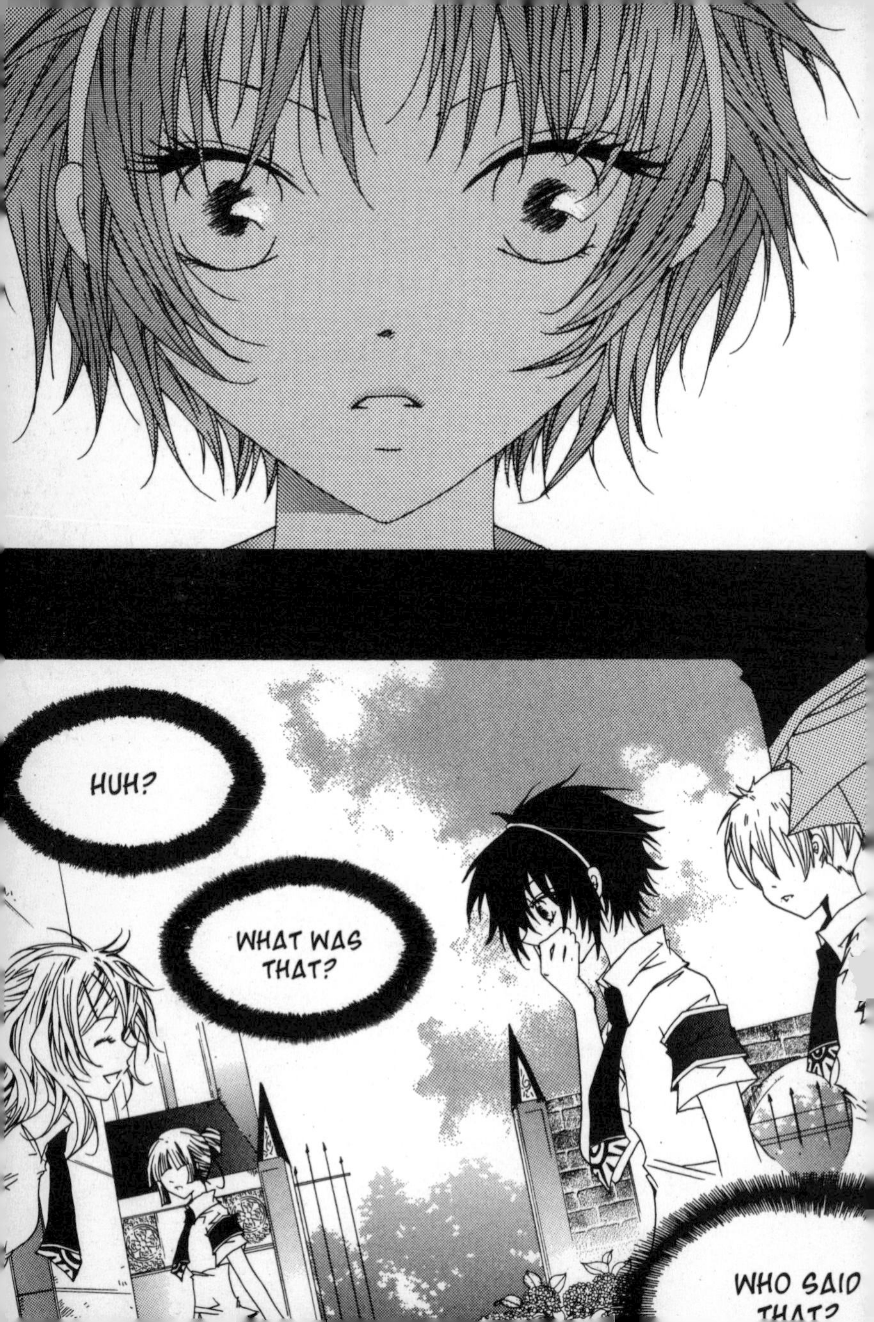
HUH?
WHAT WAS THAT?
WHO SAID

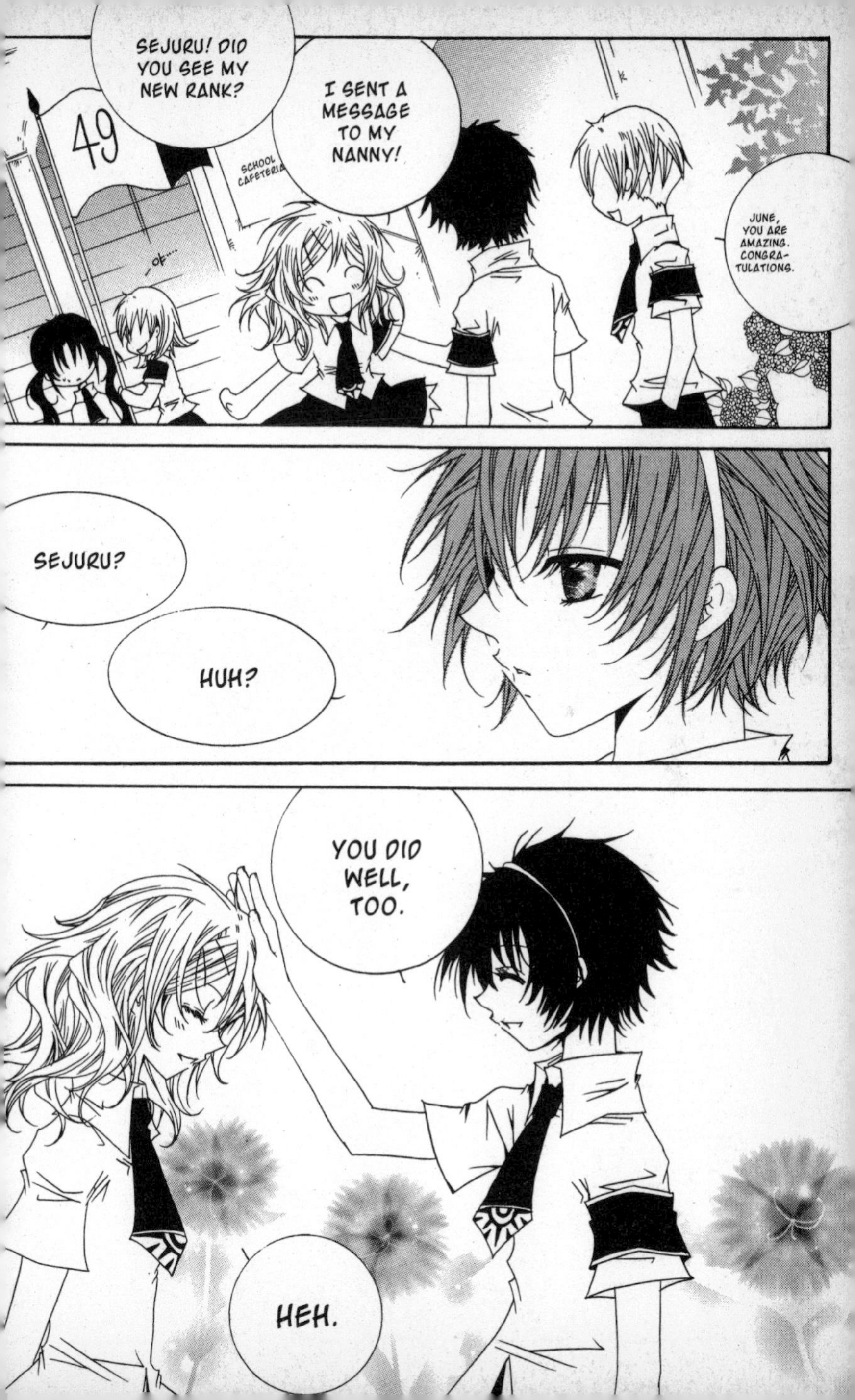
JUNE, YOU ARE AMAZING. CONGRATULATIONS.
I SENT A MESSAGE TO MY NANNY!
SEJURU! DID YOU SEE MY NEW RANK?
SCHOOL CAFETERIA
49
SEJURU?
HUH?
YOU DID WELL, TOO.
HEH.

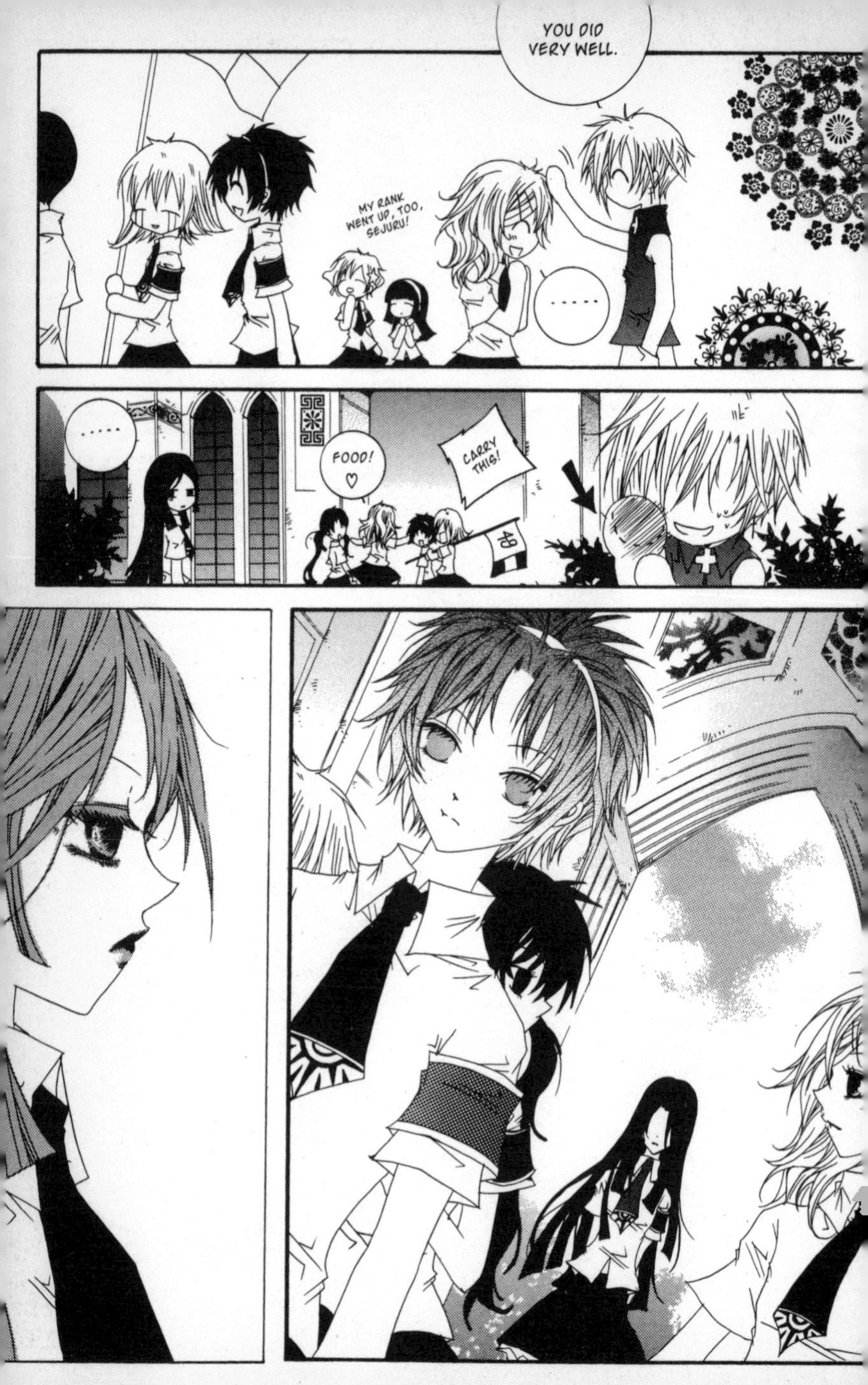
MY RANK WENT UP, TOO, SEJURU!
YOU DID VERY WELL.
.....
.....
FOOD! ♡
CARRY THIS!

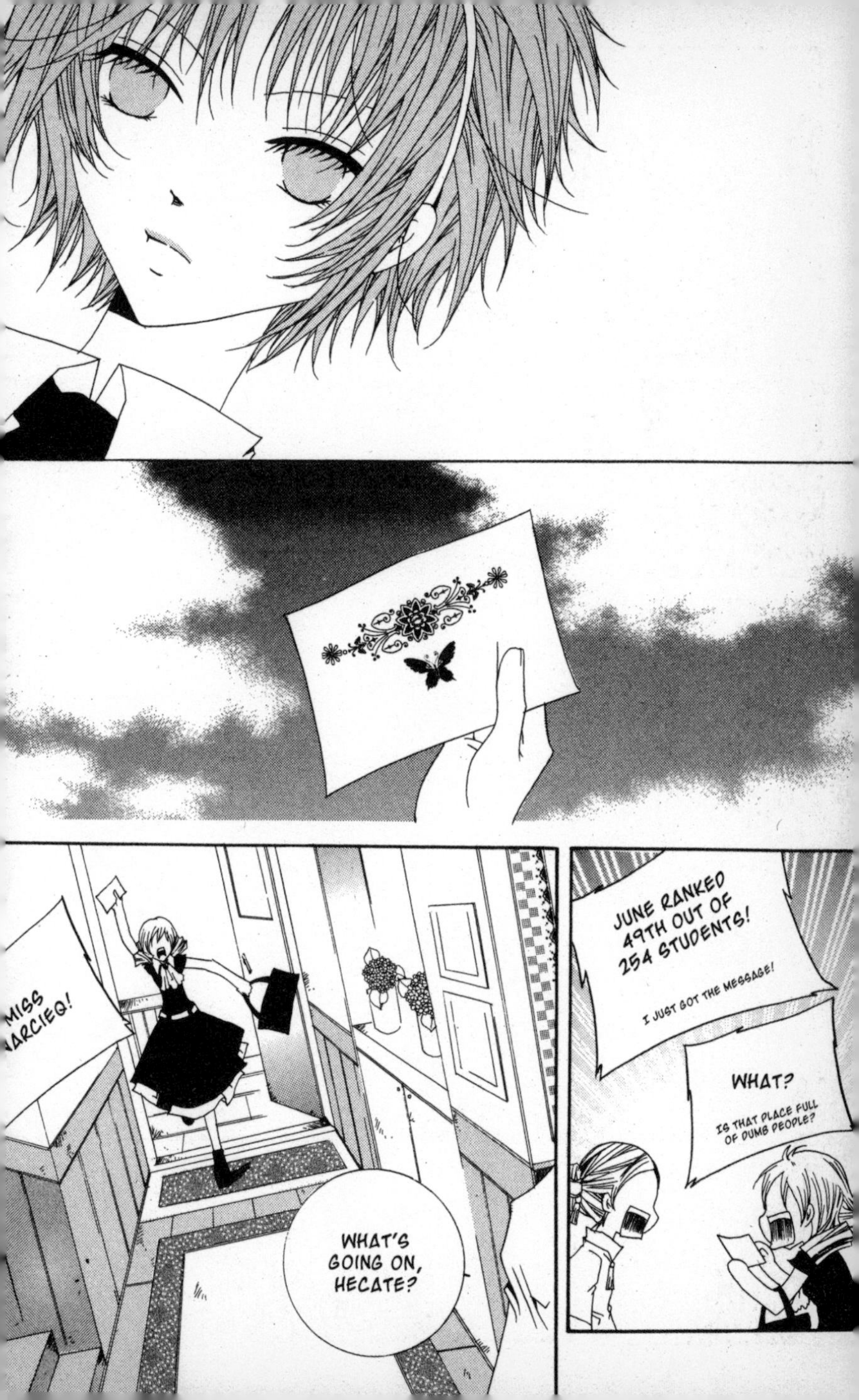
MISS ARCIEQ!
WHAT'S GOING ON, HECATE?
JUNE RANKED 49TH OUT OF 254 STUDENTS!
I JUST GOT THE MESSAGE!
WHAT?
IS THAT PLACE FULL OF DUMB PEOPLE?

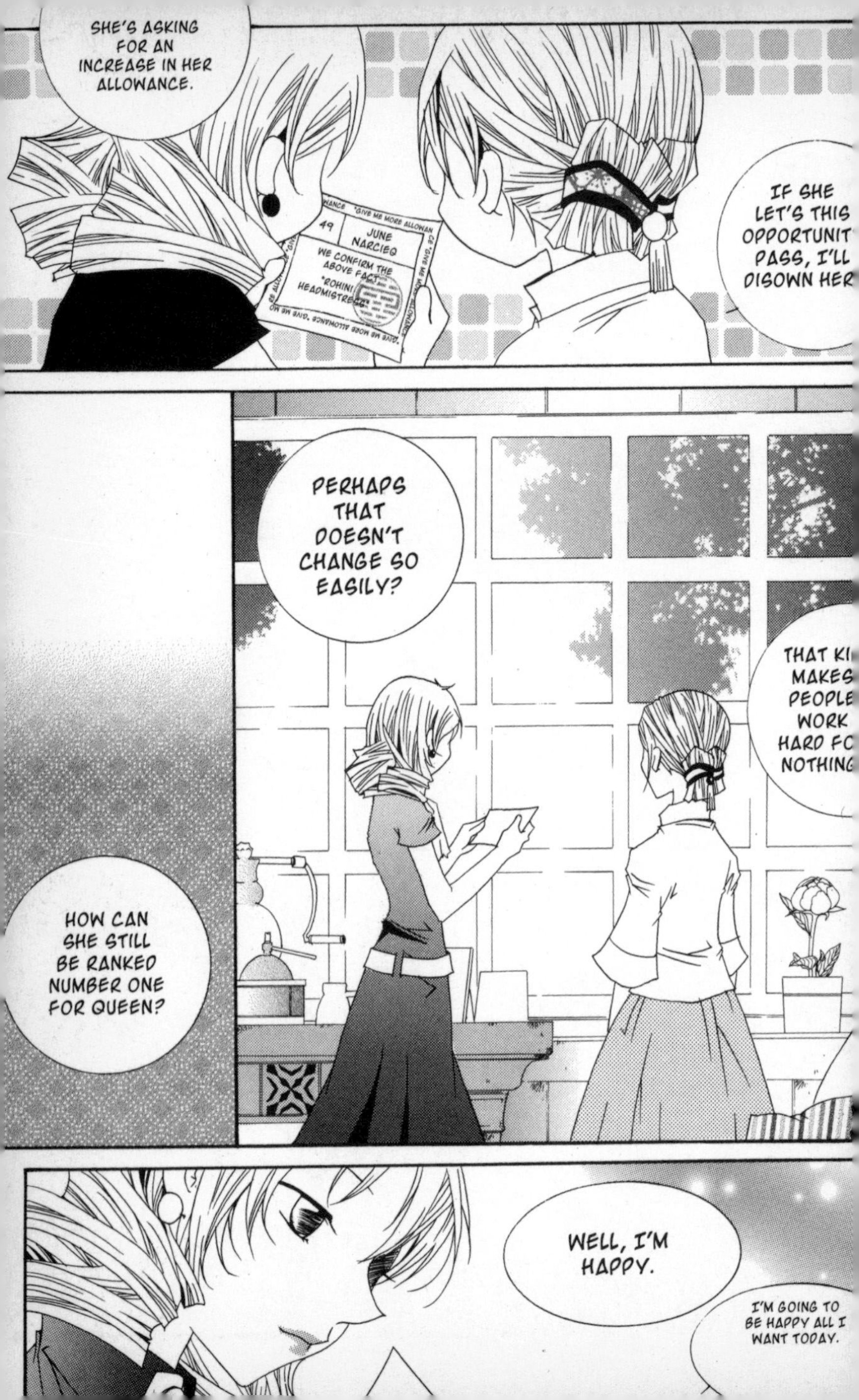
SHE'S ASKING FOR AN INCREASE IN HER ALLOWANCE.
49
JUNE NARCIEQ
WE CONFIRM THE ABOVE FACT. *ROHINI HEADMISTRESS
IF SHE LET'S THIS OPPORTUNIT PASS, I'LL DISOWN HER
HOW CAN SHE STILL BE RANKED NUMBER ONE FOR QUEEN?
PERHAPS THAT DOESN'T CHANGE SO EASILY?
THAT KI MAKES PEOPLE WORK HARD FO NOTHING
WELL, I'M HAPPY.
I'M GOING TO BE HAPPY ALL I WANT TODAY.

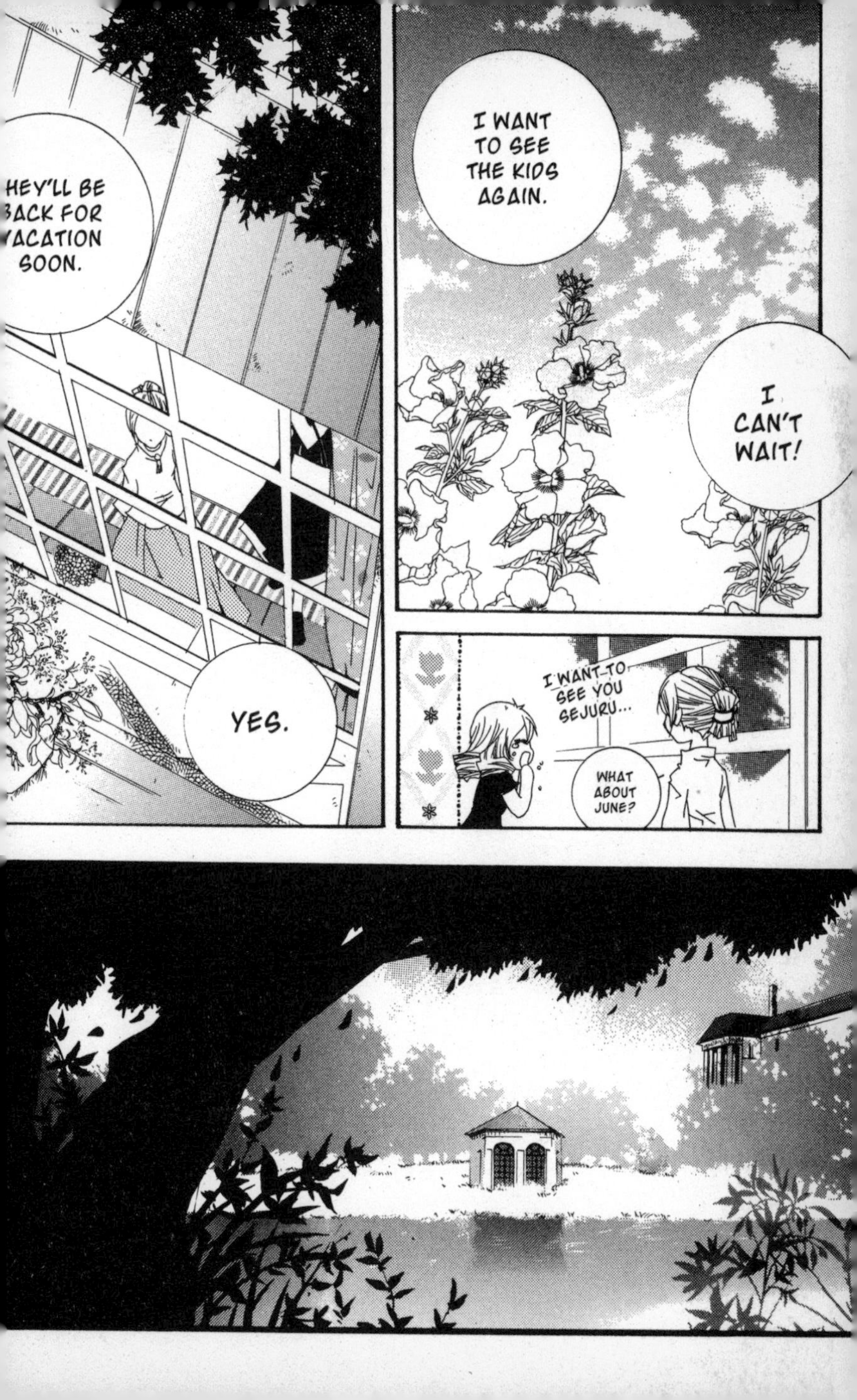
HEY'LL BE
BACK FOR
VACATION
SOON.
YES.
I WANT
TO SEE
THE KIDS
AGAIN.
I
CAN'T
WAIT!
I WANT TO
SEE YOU
SEJURU...
WHAT
ABOUT
JUNE?

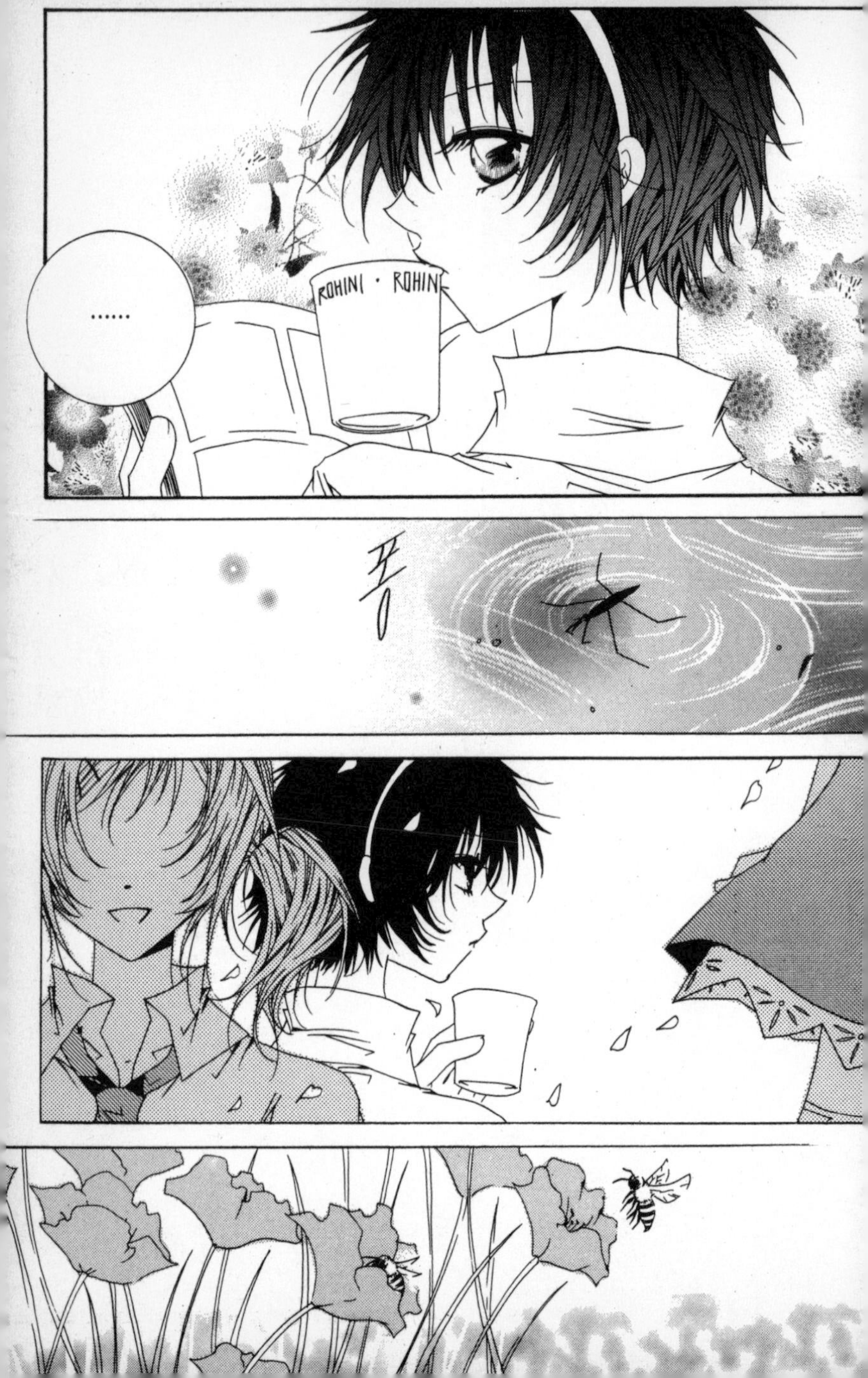

......
ROHINI · ROHIN

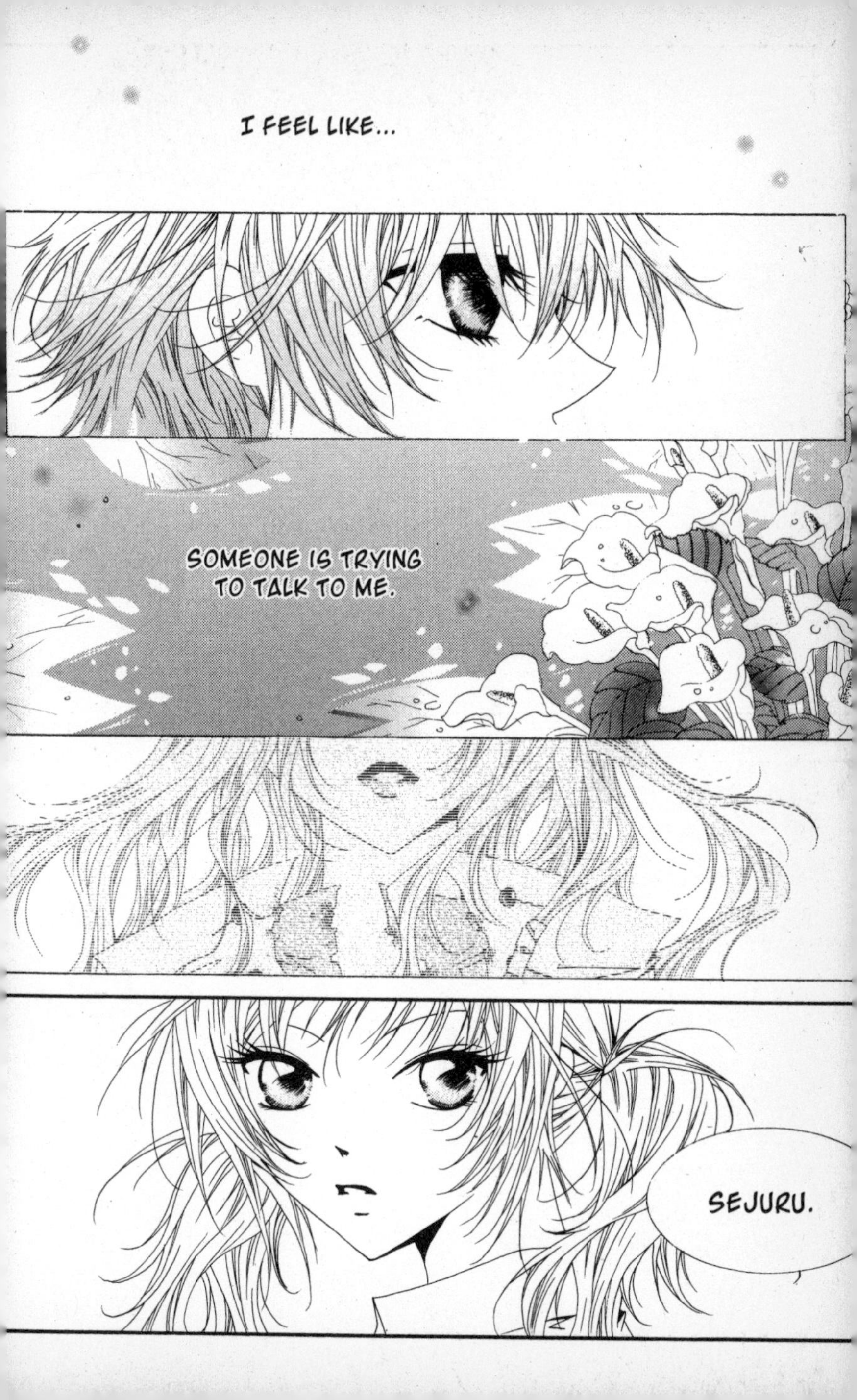
I FEEL LIKE...
SOMEONE IS TRYING TO TALK TO ME.
SEJURU.

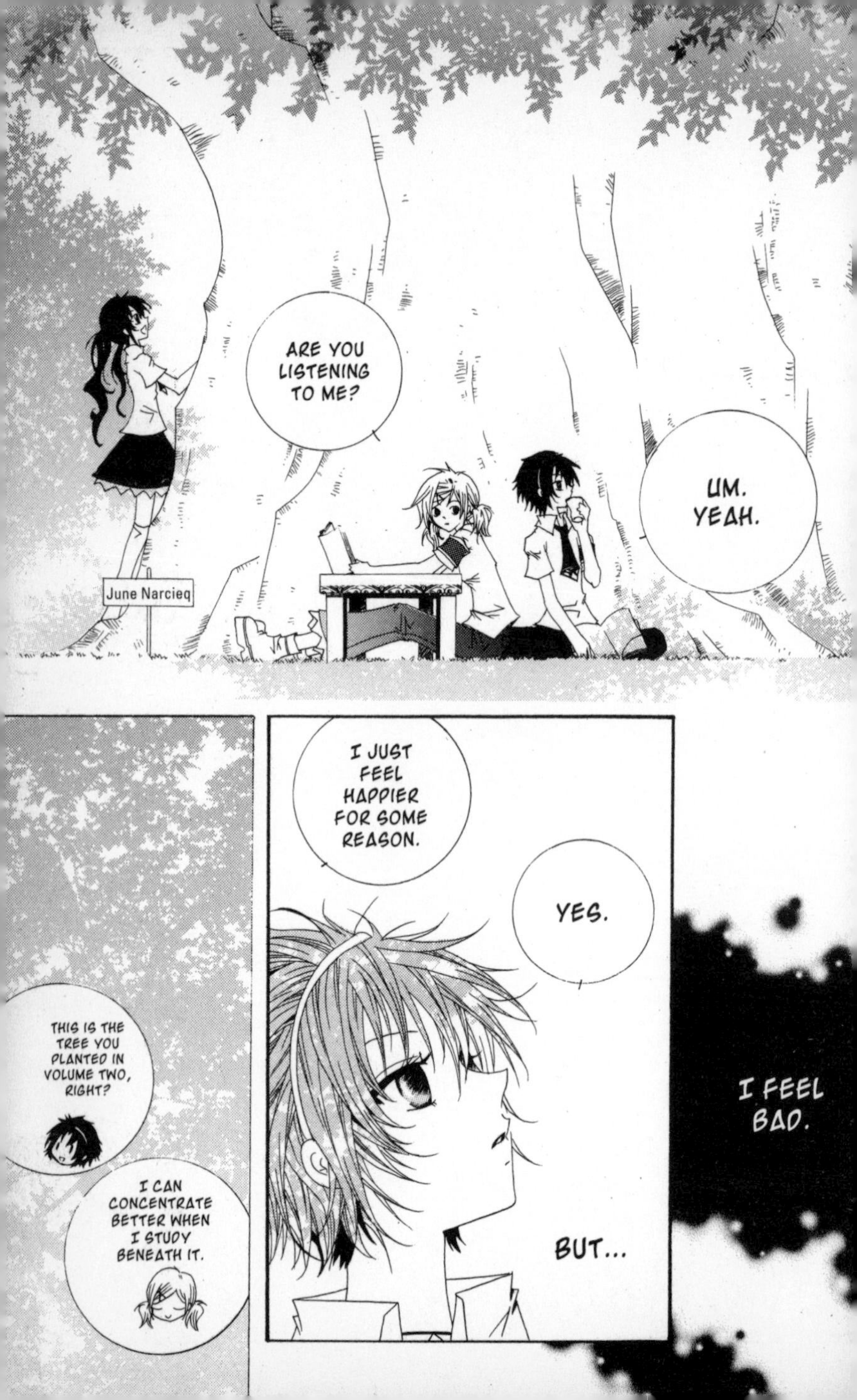
June Narcieq
ARE YOU LISTENING TO ME?
UM. YEAH.
THIS IS THE TREE YOU PLANTED IN VOLUME TWO, RIGHT?
I CAN CONCENTRATE BETTER WHEN I STUDY BENEATH IT.
I JUST FEEL HAPPIER FOR SOME REASON.
YES.
BUT...
I FEEL BAD.

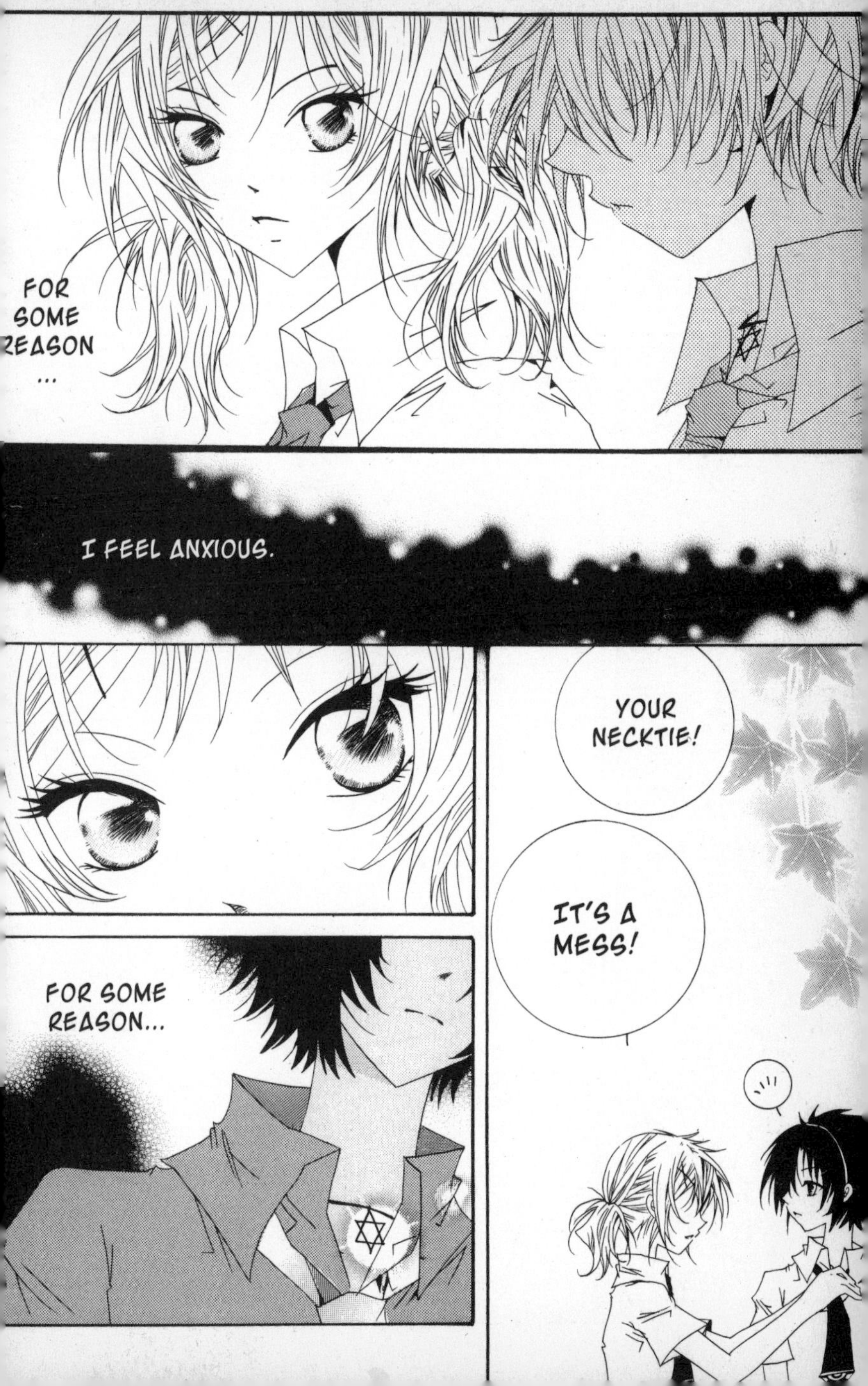
FOR SOME REASON ...
I FEEL ANXIOUS.
FOR SOME REASON...
YOUR NECKTIE!
IT'S A MESS!

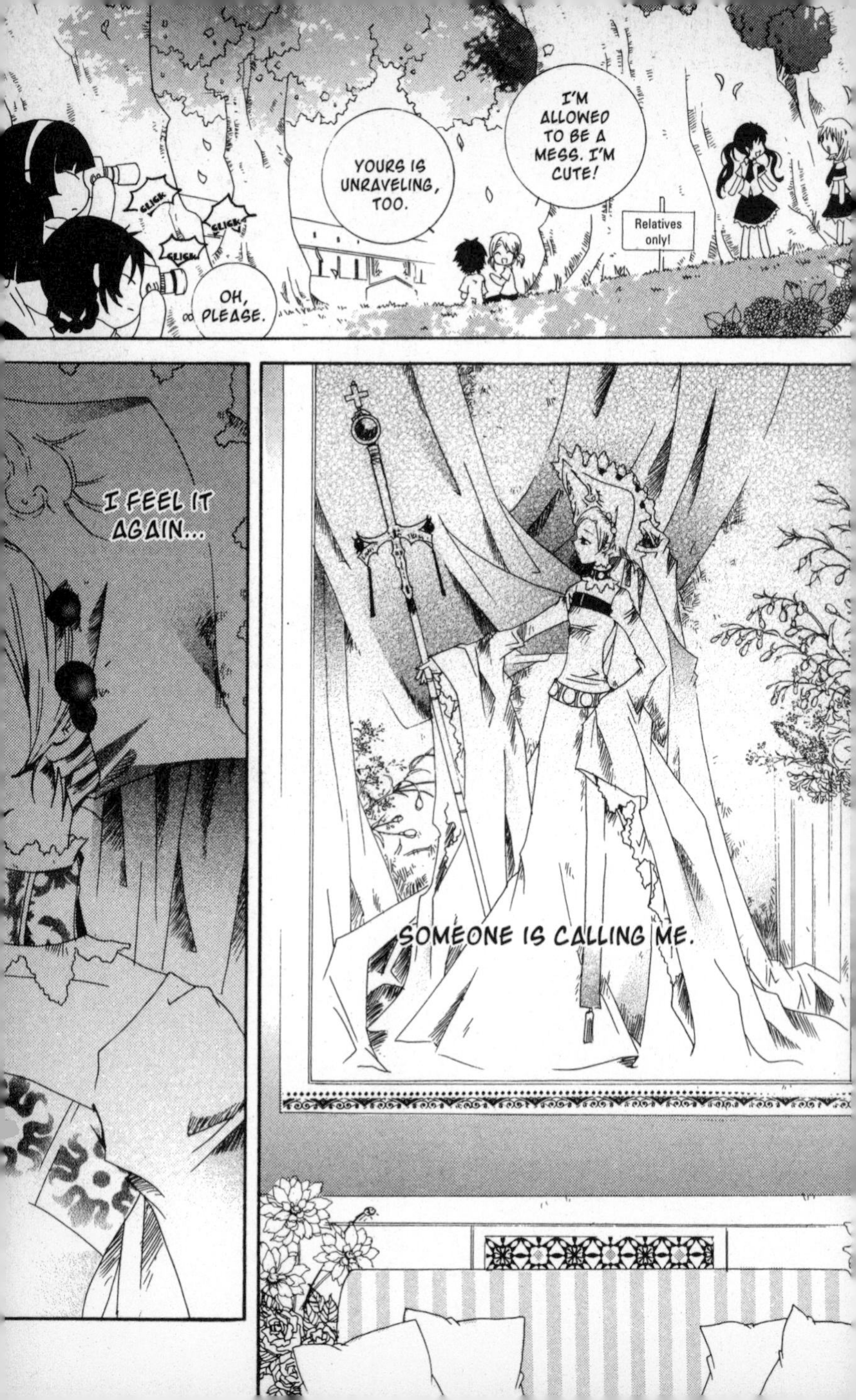
CLICK
CLICK
CLICK
YOURS IS UNRAVELING, TOO.
I'M ALLOWED TO BE A MESS. I'M CUTE!
OH, PLEASE.
Relatives only!
I FEEL IT AGAIN...
SOMEONE IS CALLING ME.

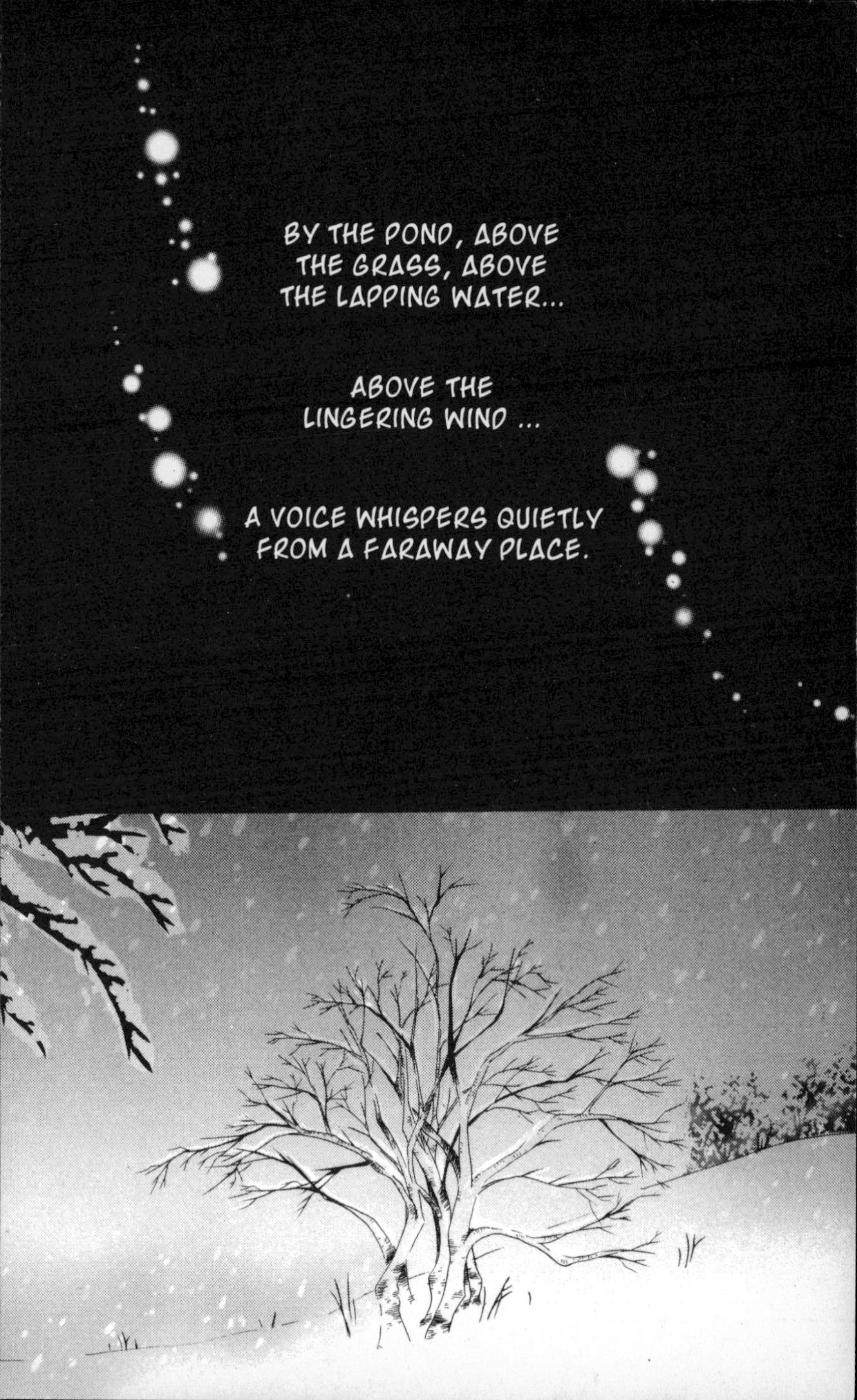
BY THE POND, ABOVE THE GRASS, ABOVE THE LAPPING WATER...
ABOVE THE LINGERING WIND ...
A VOICE WHISPERS QUIETLY FROM A FARAWAY PLACE.

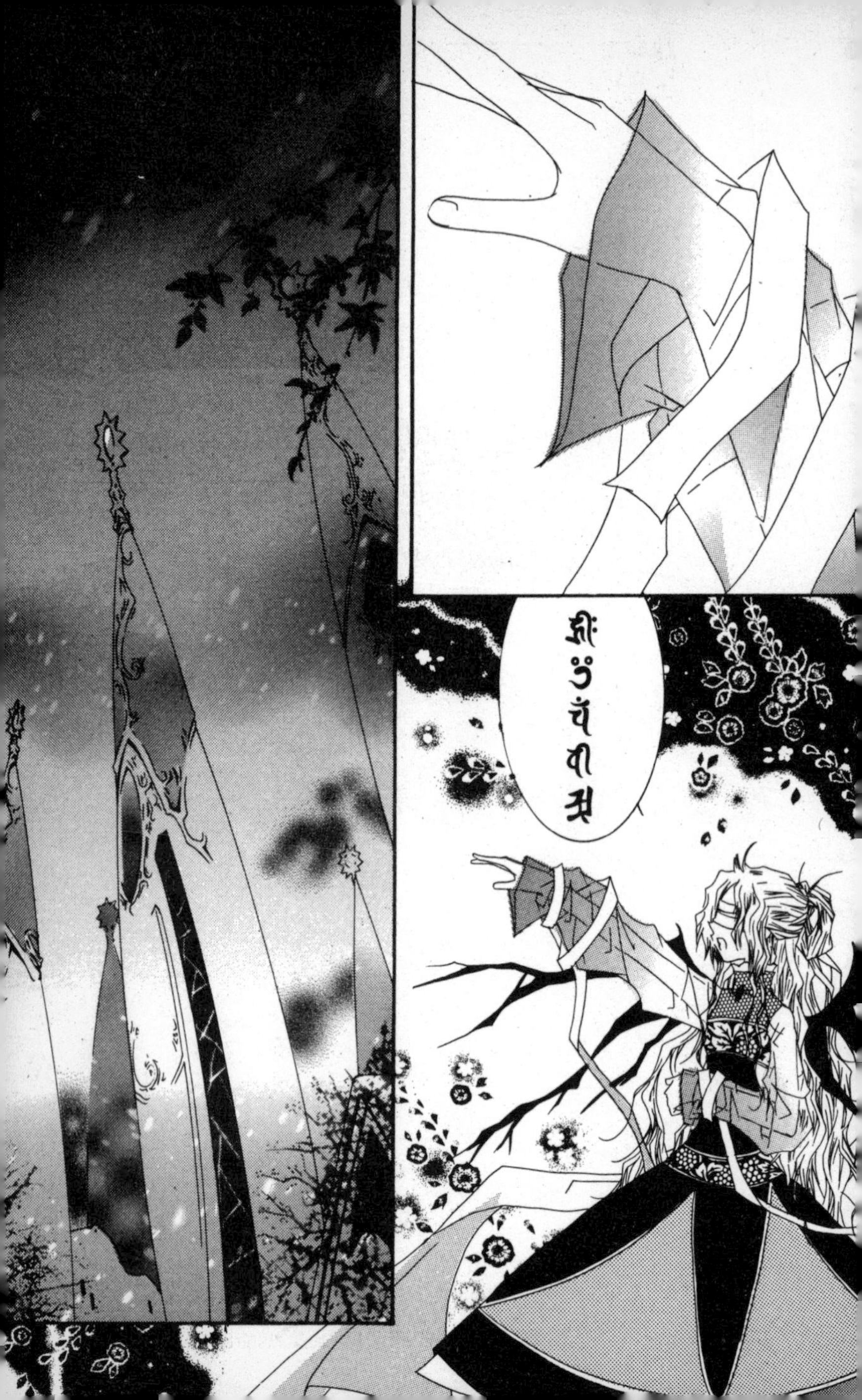

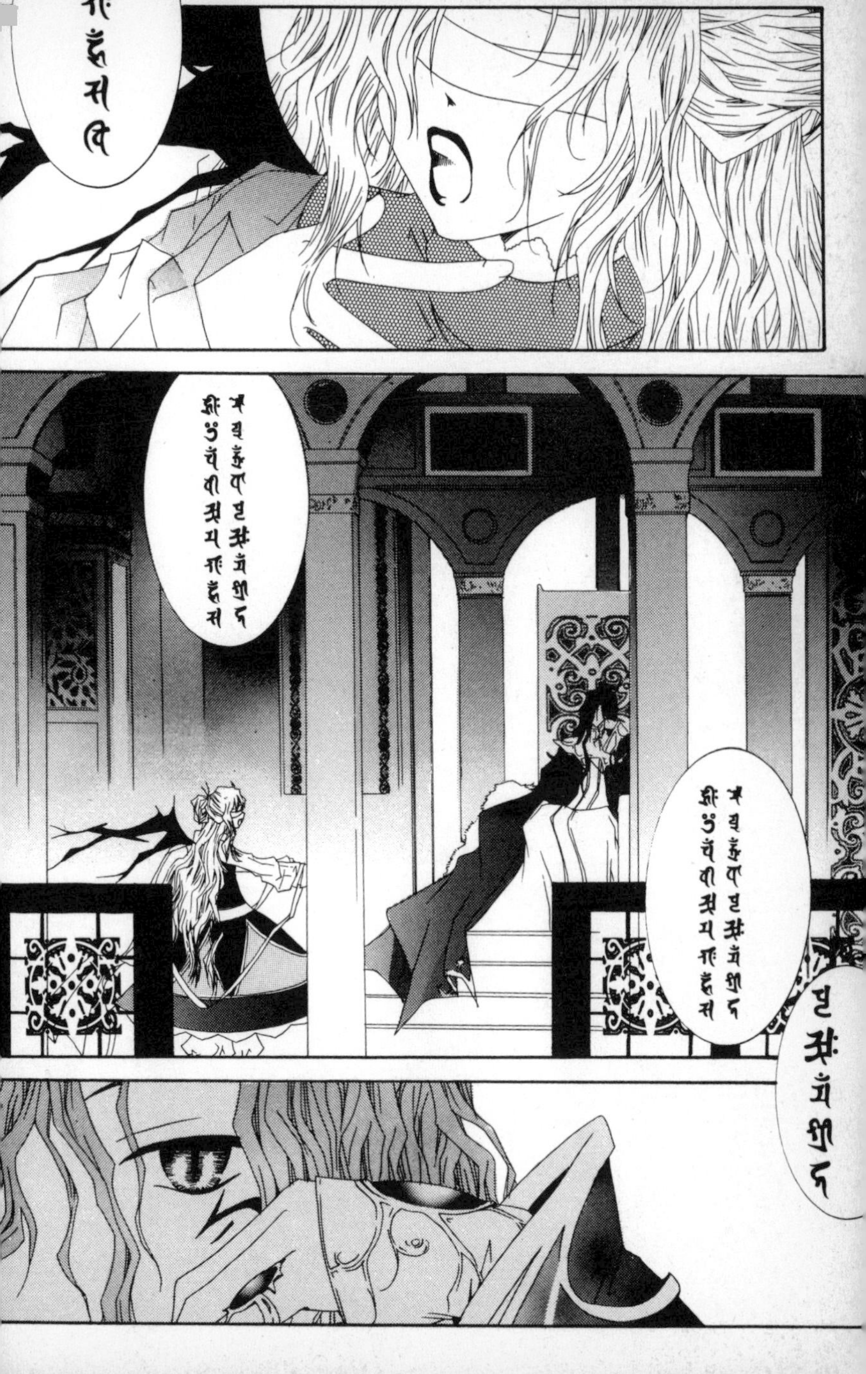

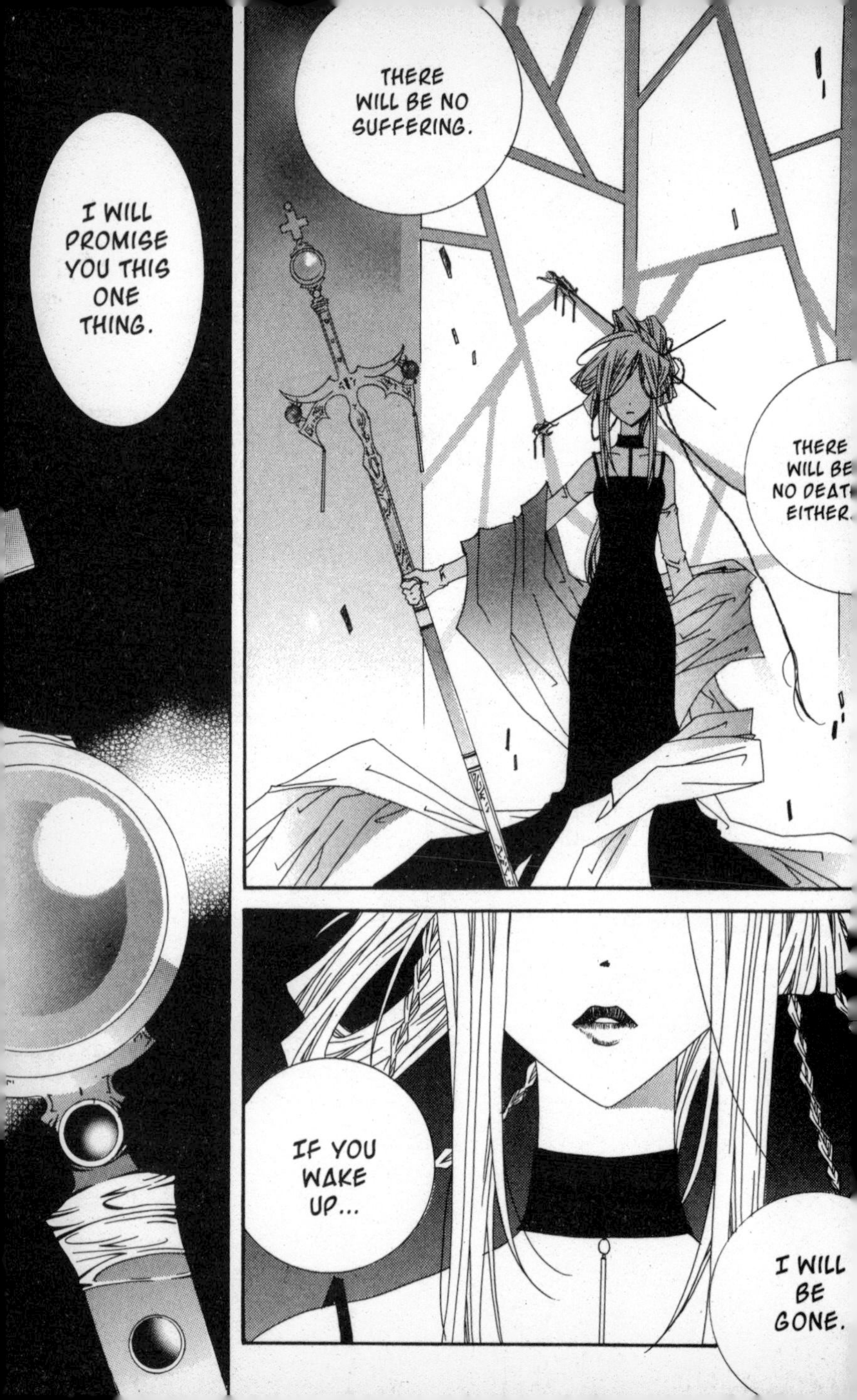
I WILL PROMISE YOU THIS ONE THING.
THERE WILL BE NO SUFFERING.
THERE WILL BE NO DEAT EITHER.
IF YOU WAKE UP...
I WILL BE GONE.

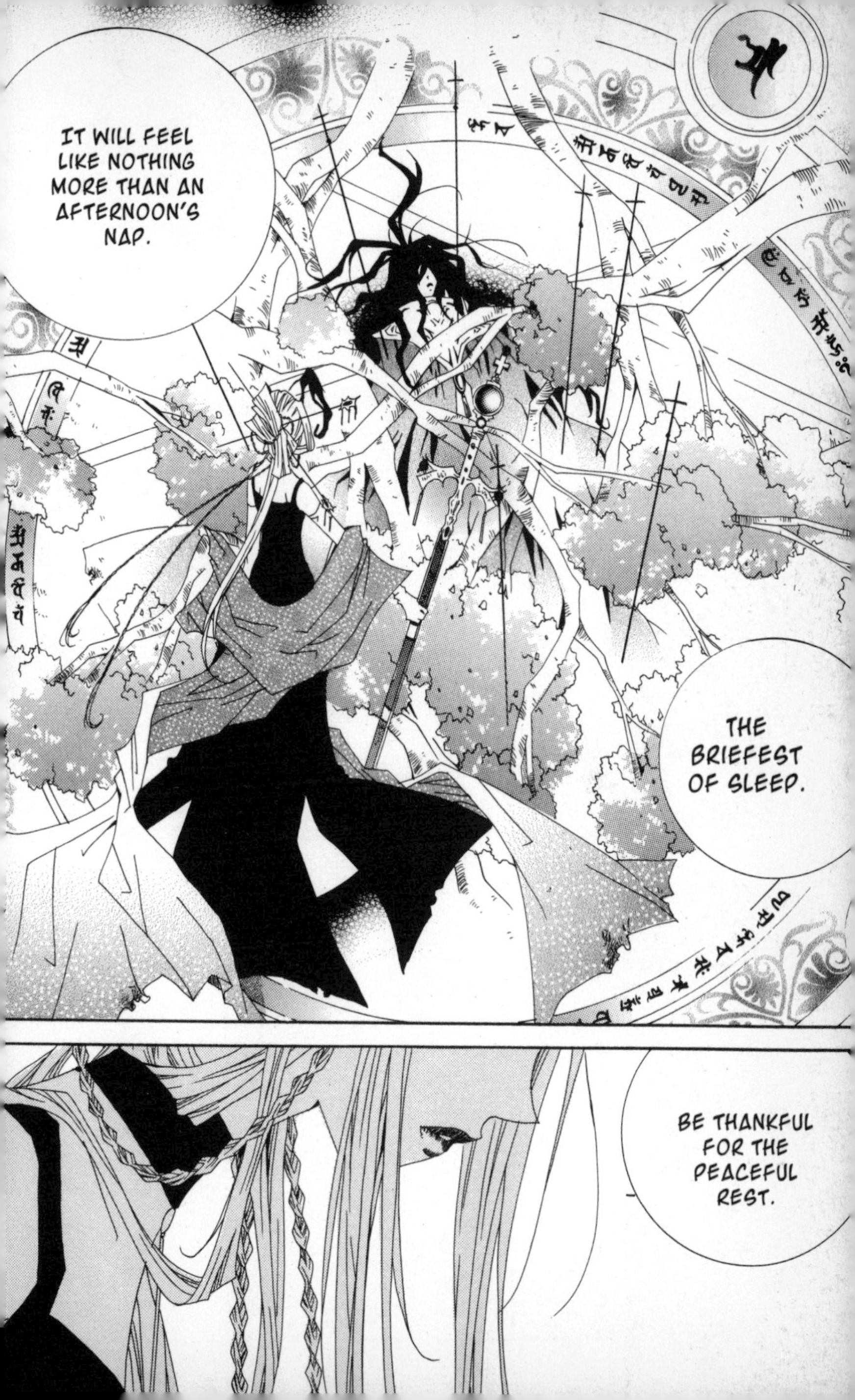
IT WILL FEEL LIKE NOTHING MORE THAN AN AFTERNOON'S NAP.
THE BRIEFEST OF SLEEP.
BE THANKFUL FOR THE PEACEFUL REST.

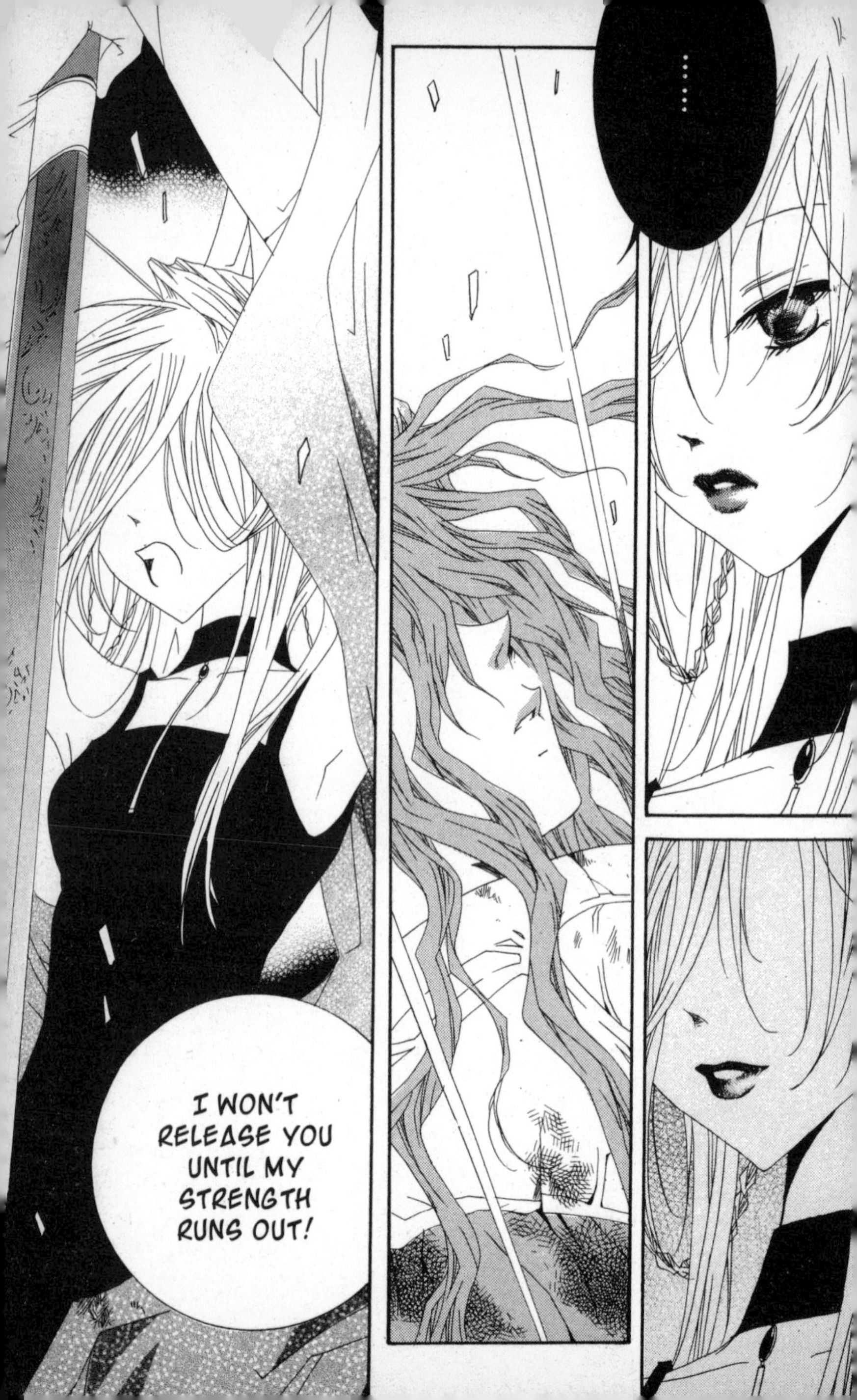
......
I WON'T RELEASE YOU UNTIL MY STRENGTH RUNS OUT!

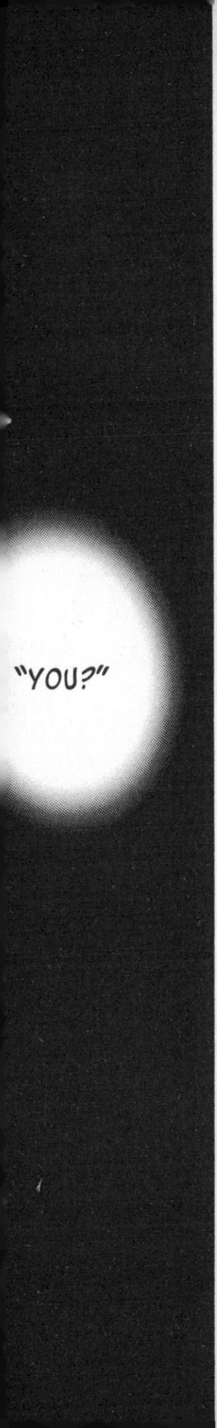
"YOU?"
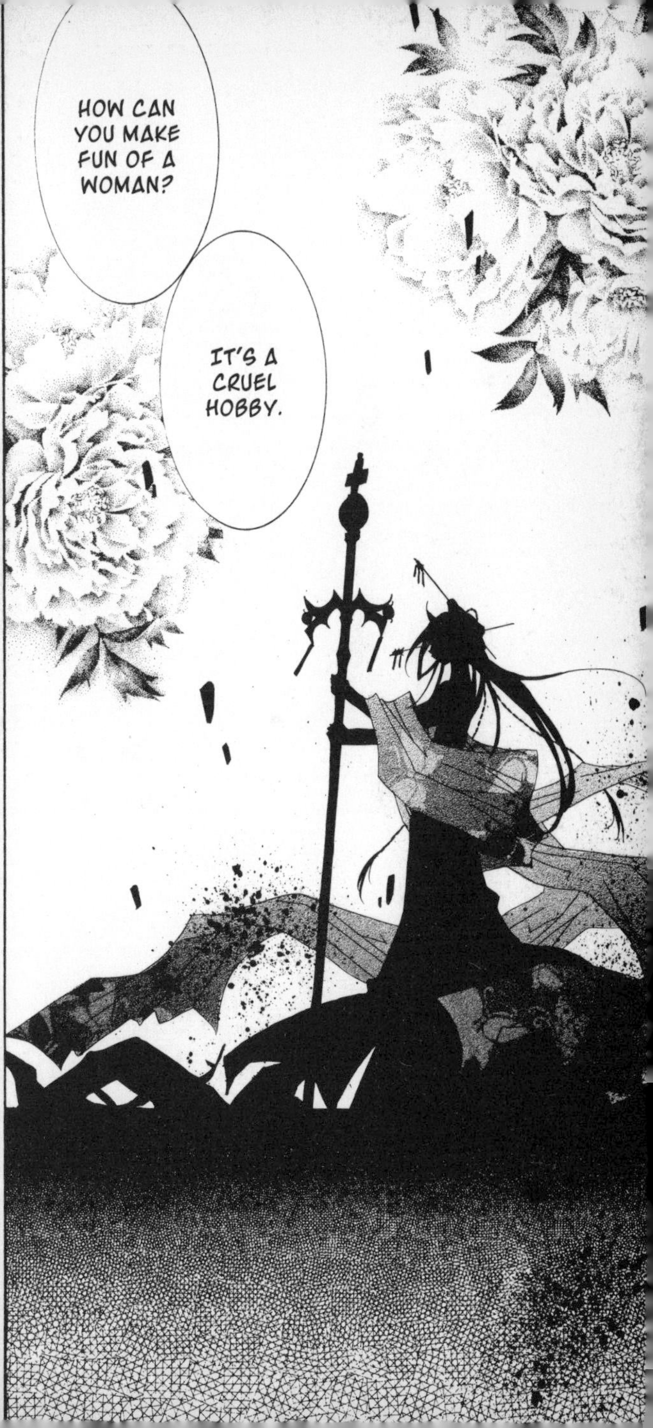
HOW CAN YOU MAKE FUN OF A WOMAN?
IT'S A CRUEL HOBBY.

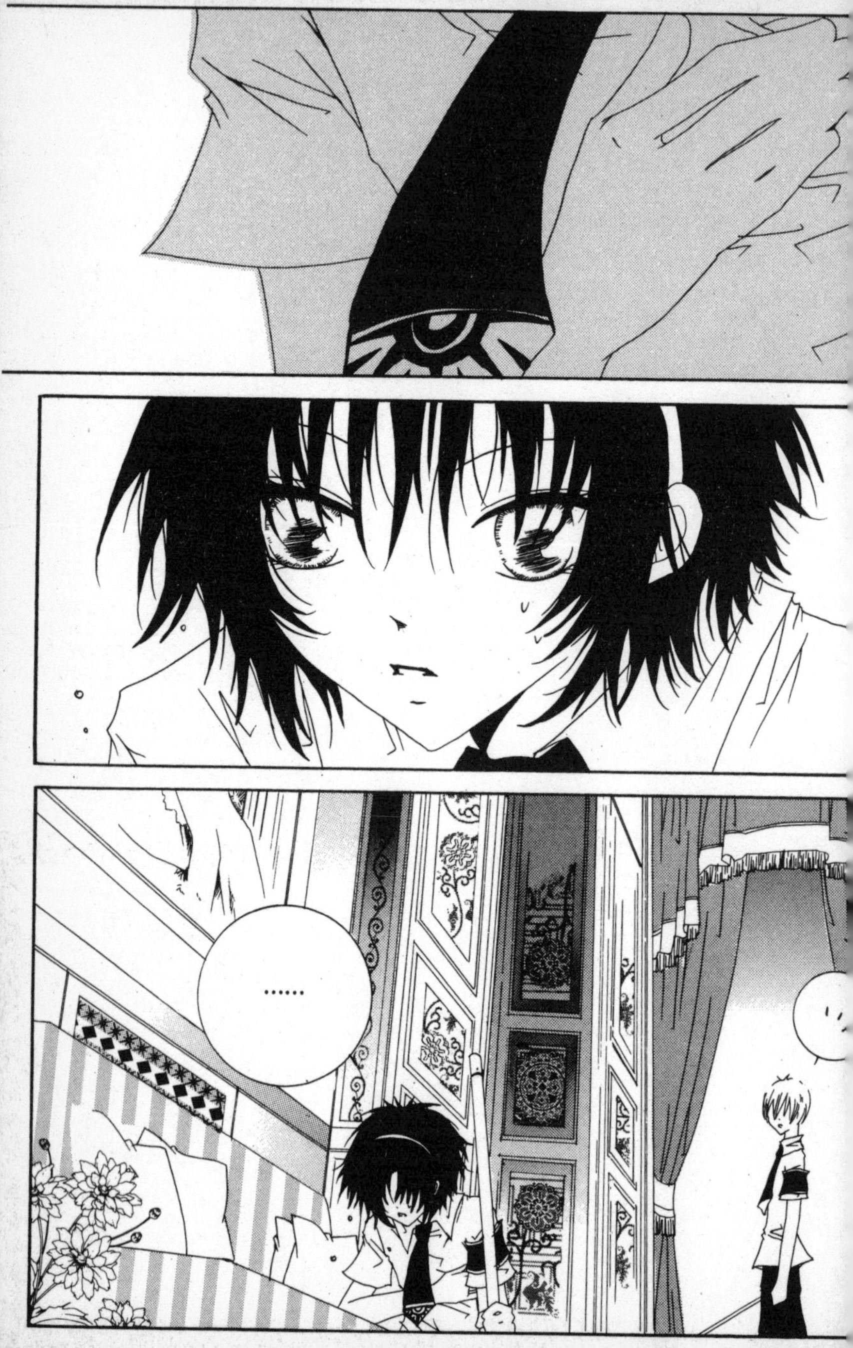
......

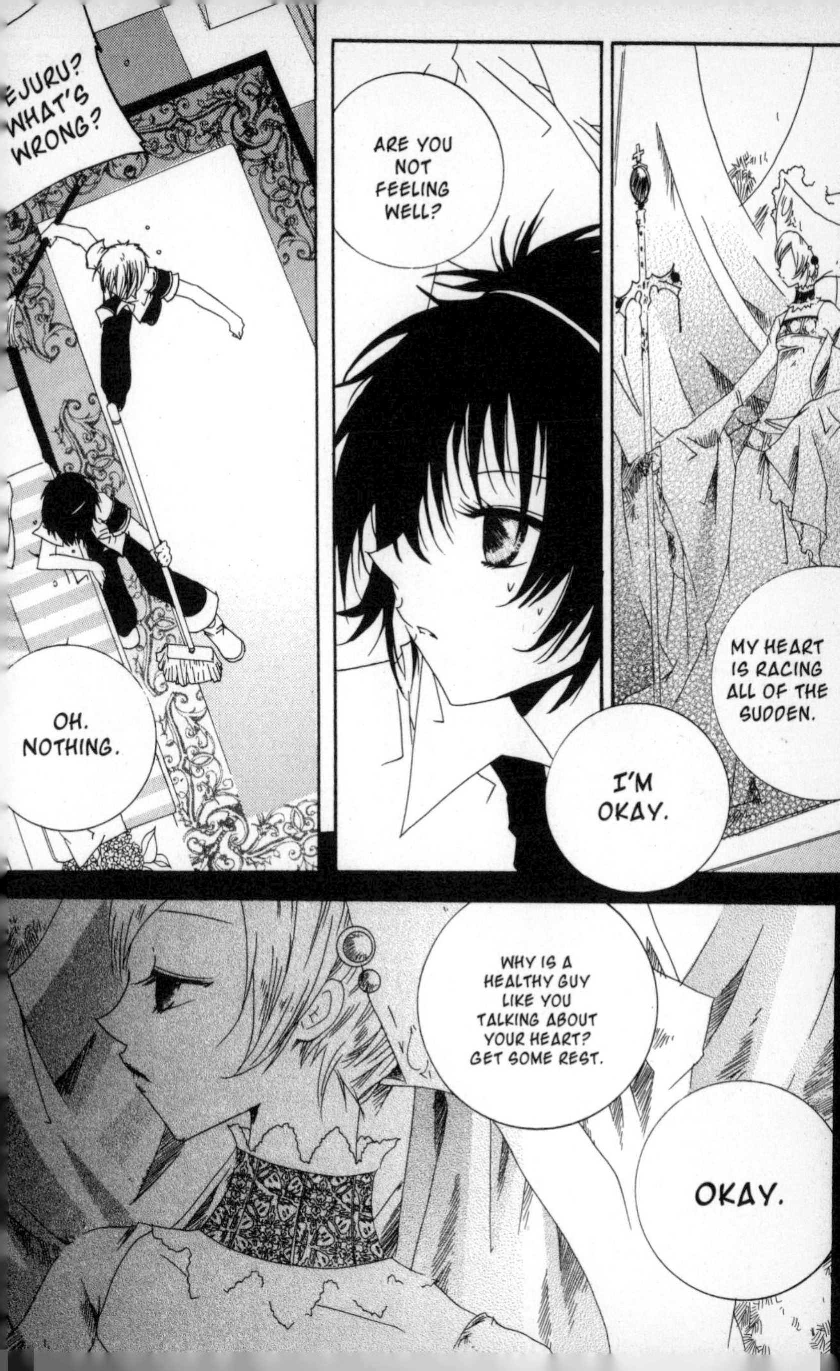
EJURU? WHAT'S WRONG?
OH. NOTHING.
ARE YOU NOT FEELING WELL?
I'M OKAY.
MY HEART IS RACING ALL OF THE SUDDEN.
WHY IS A HEALTHY GUY LIKE YOU TALKING ABOUT YOUR HEART? GET SOME REST.
OKAY.

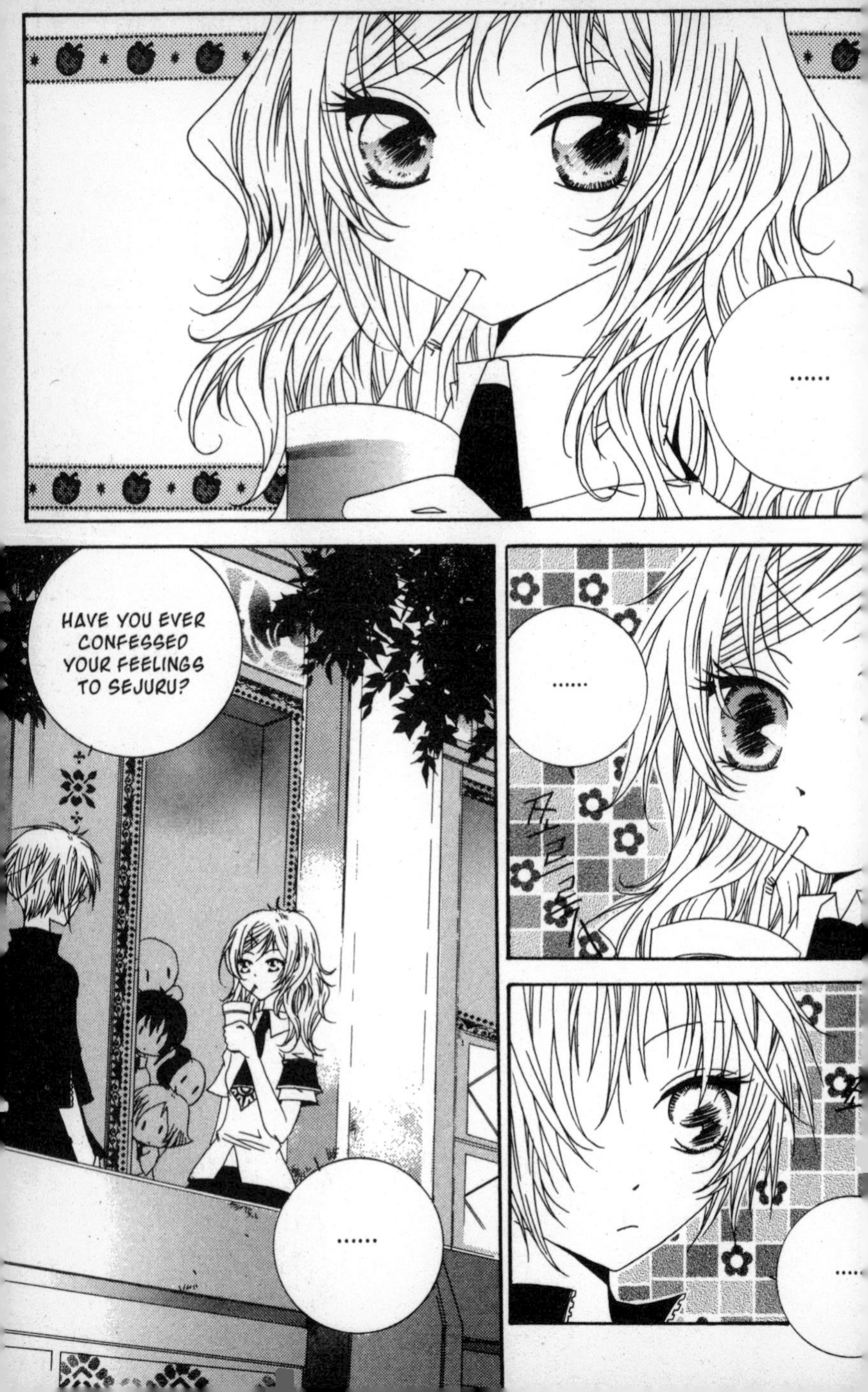

......
HAVE YOU EVER CONFESSED YOUR FEELINGS TO SEJURU?
......
......
....

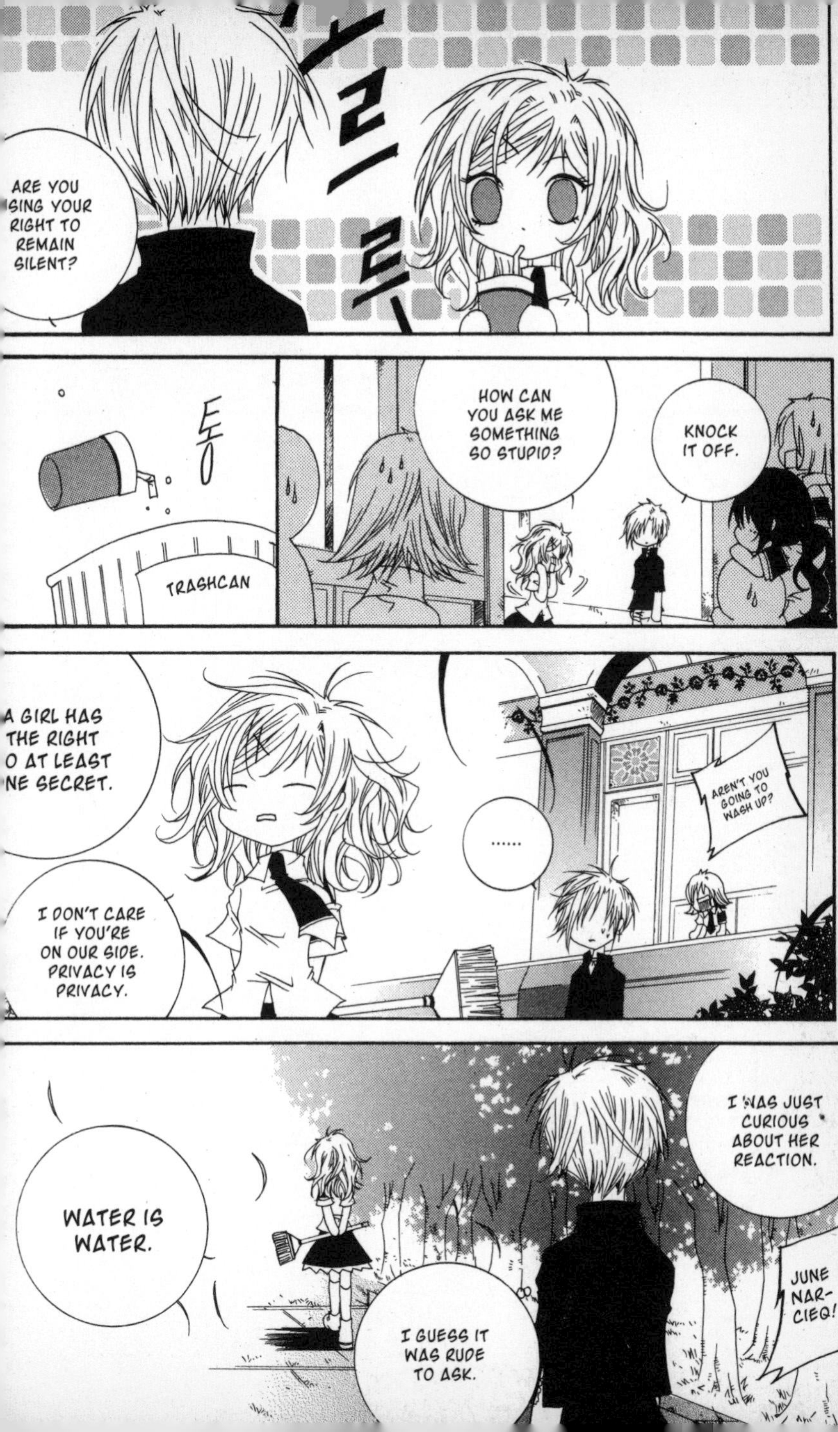
ARE YOU SING YOUR RIGHT TO REMAIN SILENT?
통
TRASHCAN
HOW CAN YOU ASK ME SOMETHING SO STUPID?
KNOCK IT OFF.
A GIRL HAS THE RIGHT O AT LEAST NE SECRET.
I DON'T CARE IF YOU'RE ON OUR SIDE. PRIVACY IS PRIVACY.
......
AREN'T YOU GOING TO WASH UP?
WATER IS WATER.
I GUESS IT WAS RUDE TO ASK.
I WAS JUST CURIOUS ABOUT HER REACTION.
JUNE NAR-CIEQ!

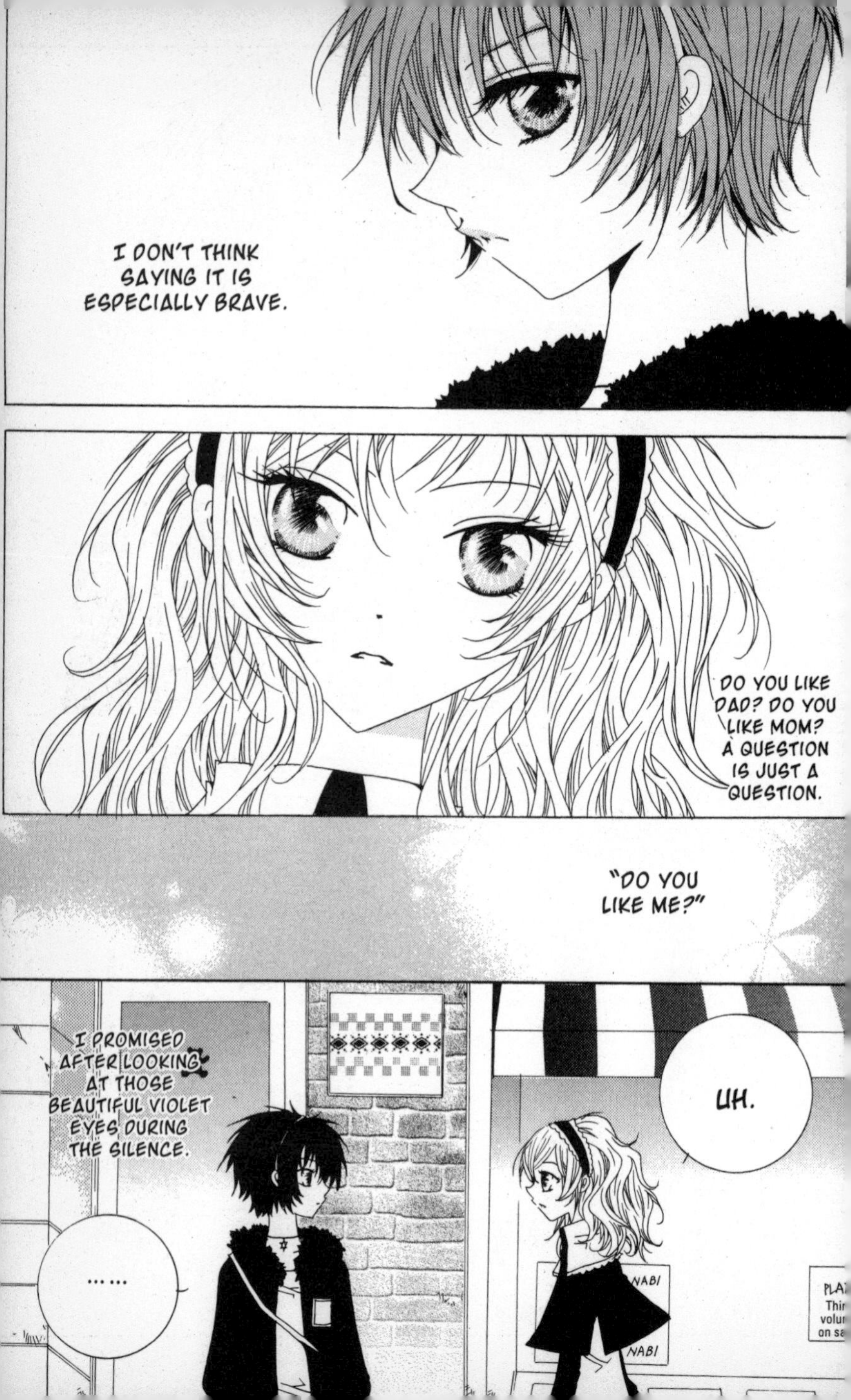
I DON'T THINK SAYING IT IS ESPECIALLY BRAVE.
DO YOU LIKE DAD? DO YOU LIKE MOM? A QUESTION IS JUST A QUESTION.
"DO YOU LIKE ME?"
I PROMISED AFTER LOOKING AT THOSE BEAUTIFUL VIOLET EYES DURING THE SILENCE.
......
UH.
NABI
NABI

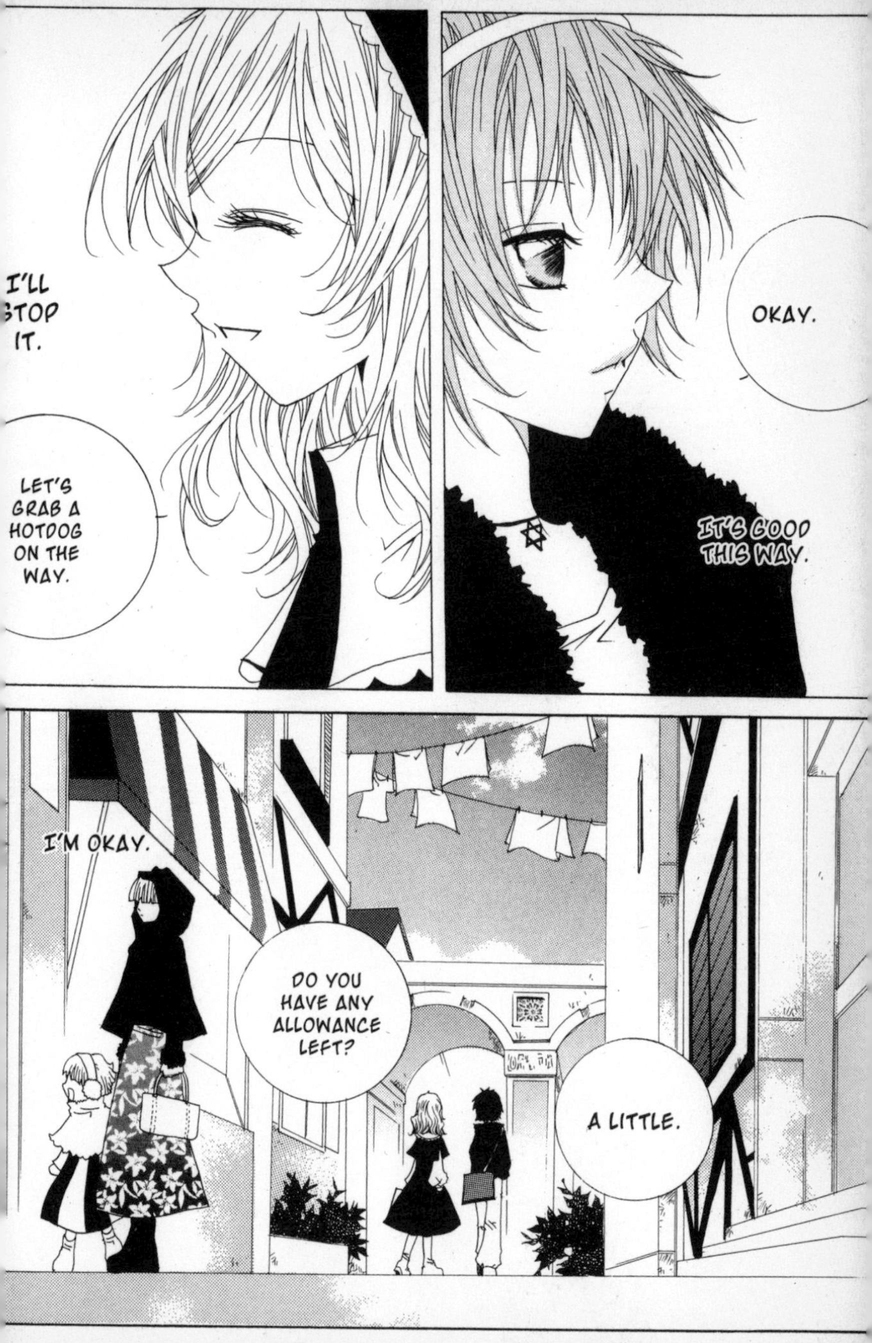
I'LL STOP IT.
LET'S GRAB A HOTDOG ON THE WAY.
OKAY.
IT'S GOOD THIS WAY.
I'M OKAY.
DO YOU HAVE ANY ALLOWANCE LEFT?
A LITTLE.

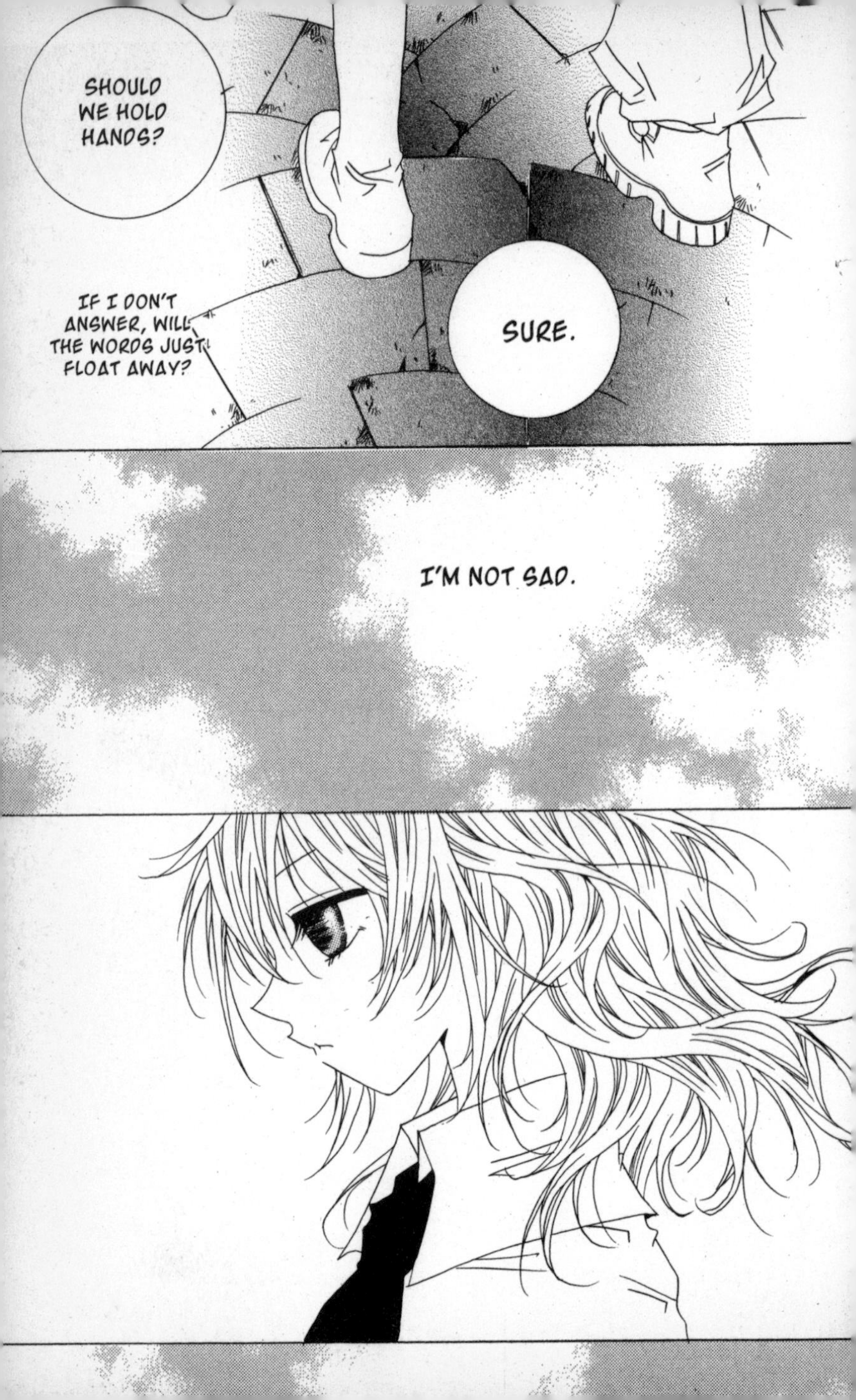
SHOULD WE HOLD HANDS?
IF I DON'T ANSWER, WILL THE WORDS JUST FLOAT AWAY?
SURE.
I'M NOT SAD.

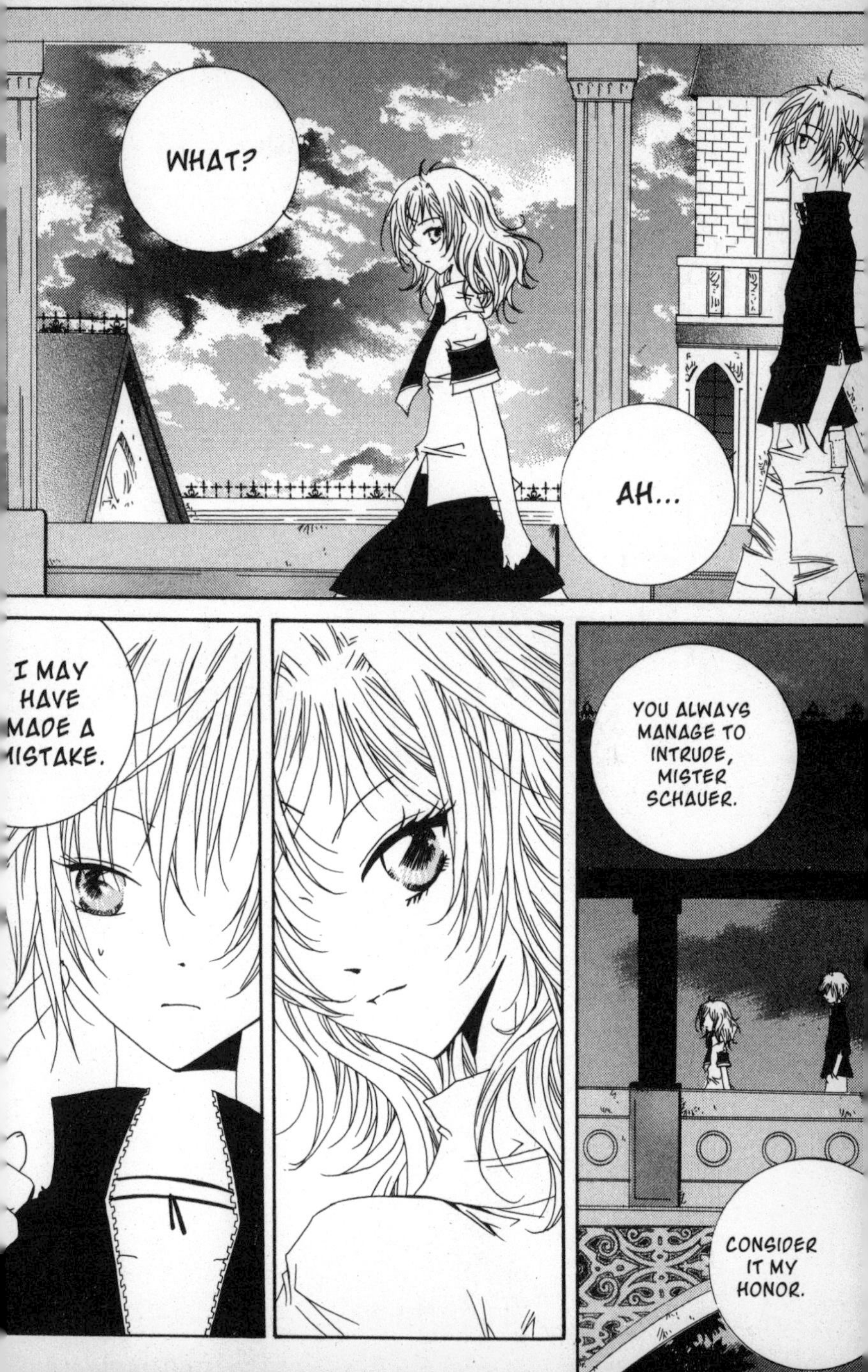
WHAT?
AH...
I MAY HAVE MADE A MISTAKE.
YOU ALWAYS MANAGE TO INTRUDE, MISTER SCHAUER.
CONSIDER IT MY HONOR.

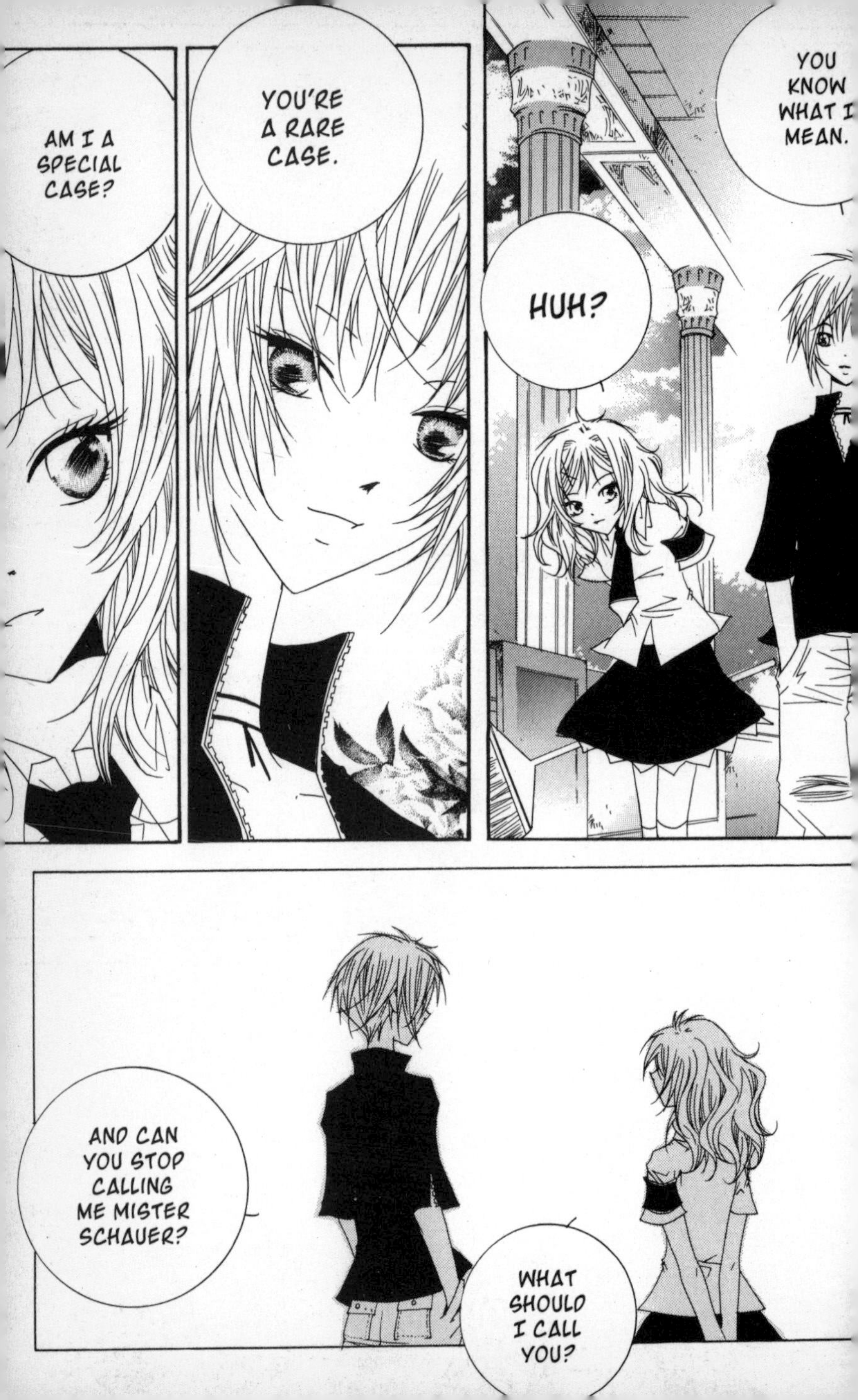
AM I A SPECIAL CASE?
YOU'RE A RARE CASE.
YOU KNOW WHAT I MEAN.
HUH?
AND CAN YOU STOP CALLING ME MISTER SCHAUER?
WHAT SHOULD I CALL YOU?

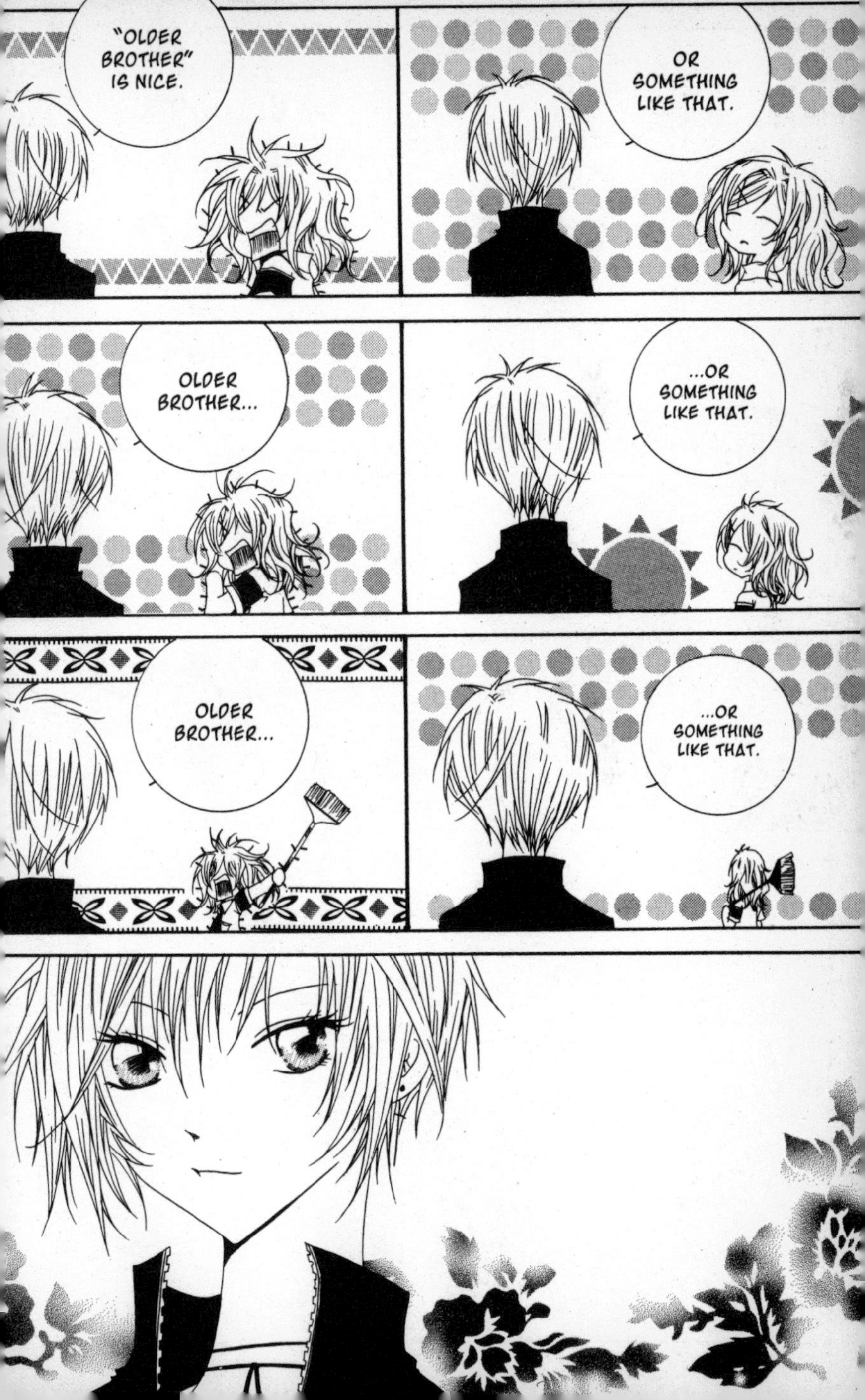
"OLDER BROTHER" IS NICE.
OR SOMETHING LIKE THAT.
OLDER BROTHER...
...OR SOMETHING LIKE THAT.
OLDER BROTHER...
...OR SOMETHING LIKE THAT.

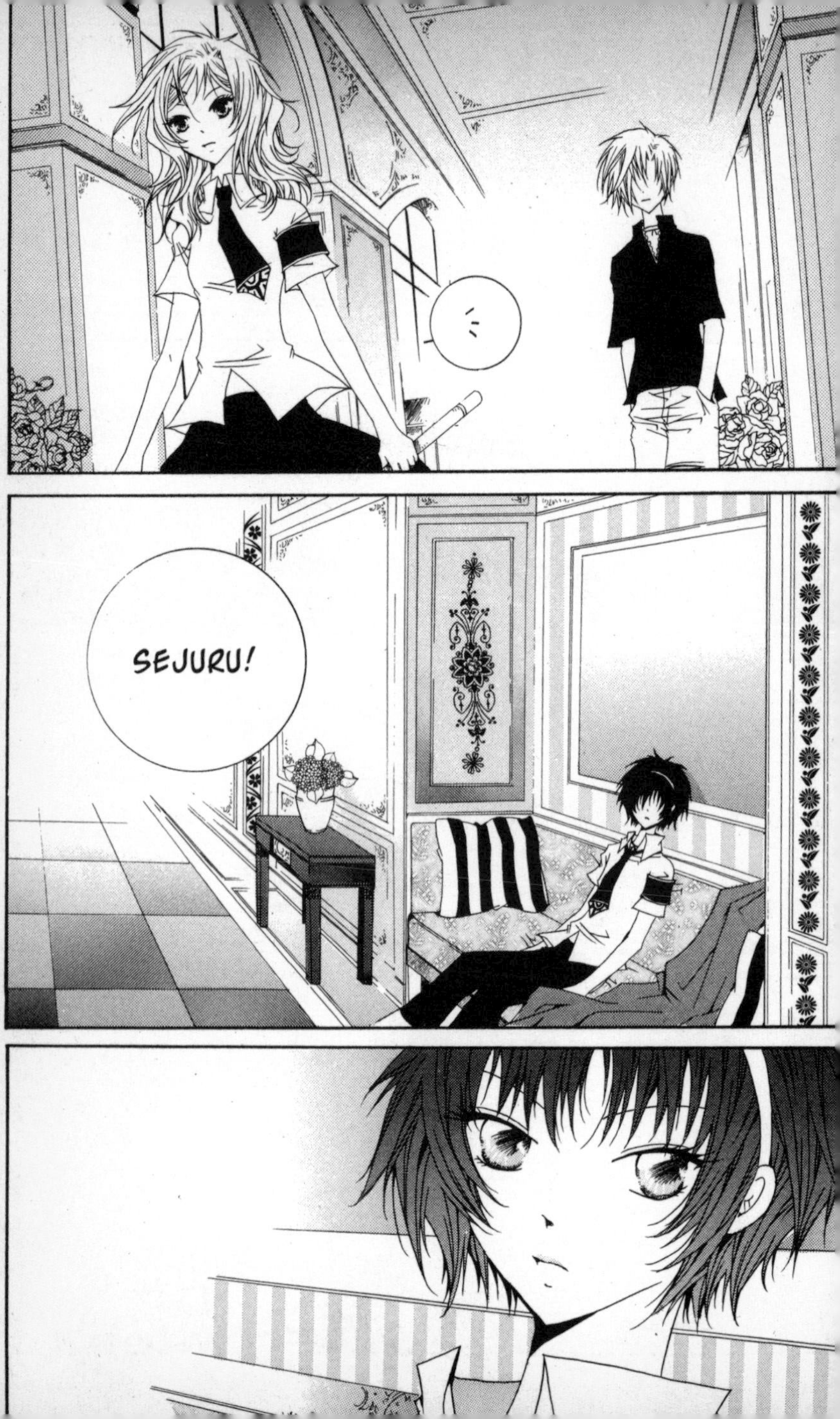
SEJURU!

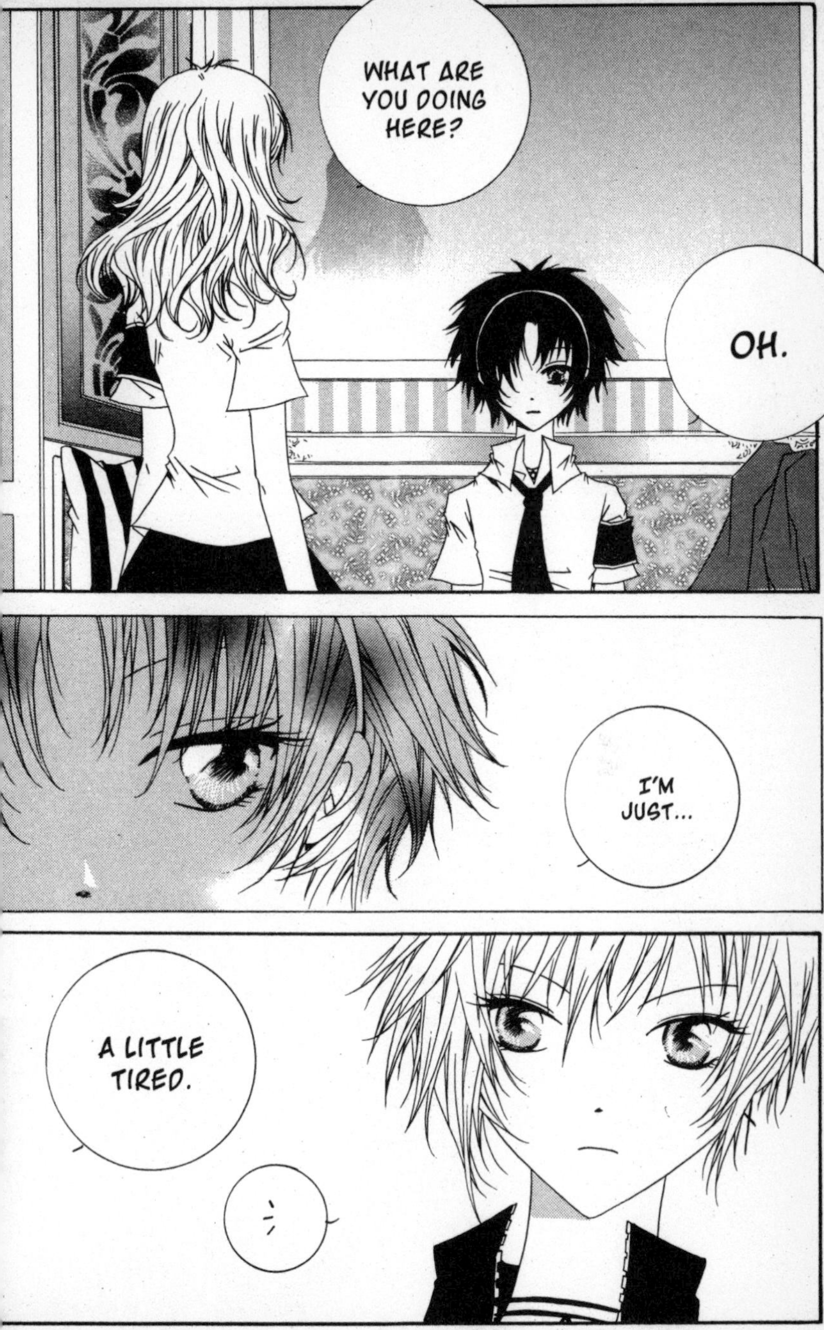
WHAT ARE YOU DOING HERE?
OH.
I'M JUST...
A LITTLE TIRED.
...

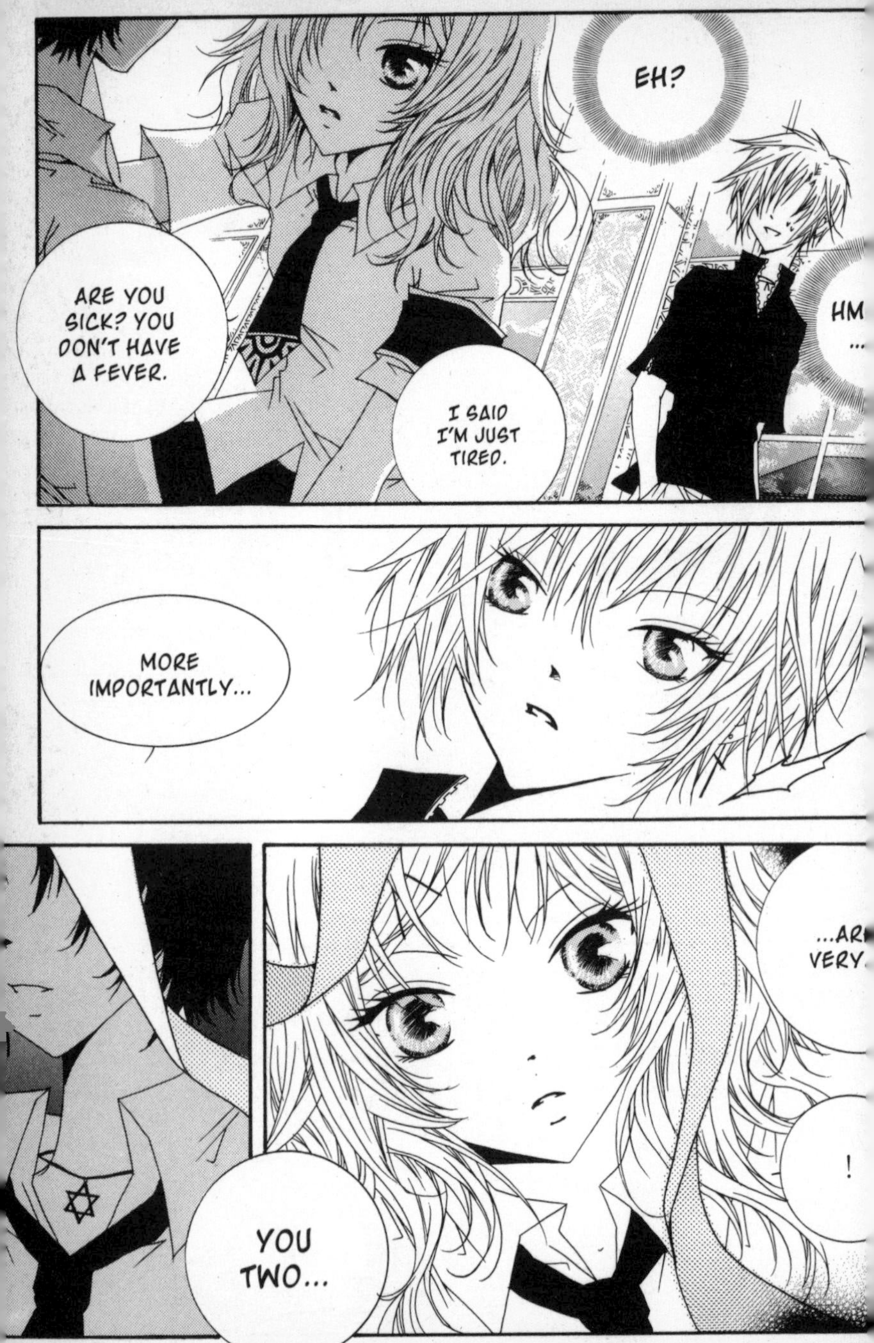
ARE YOU SICK? YOU DON'T HAVE A FEVER.
I SAID I'M JUST TIRED.
EH?
HM ...
MORE IMPORTANTLY...
YOU TWO...
...AR VERY
!

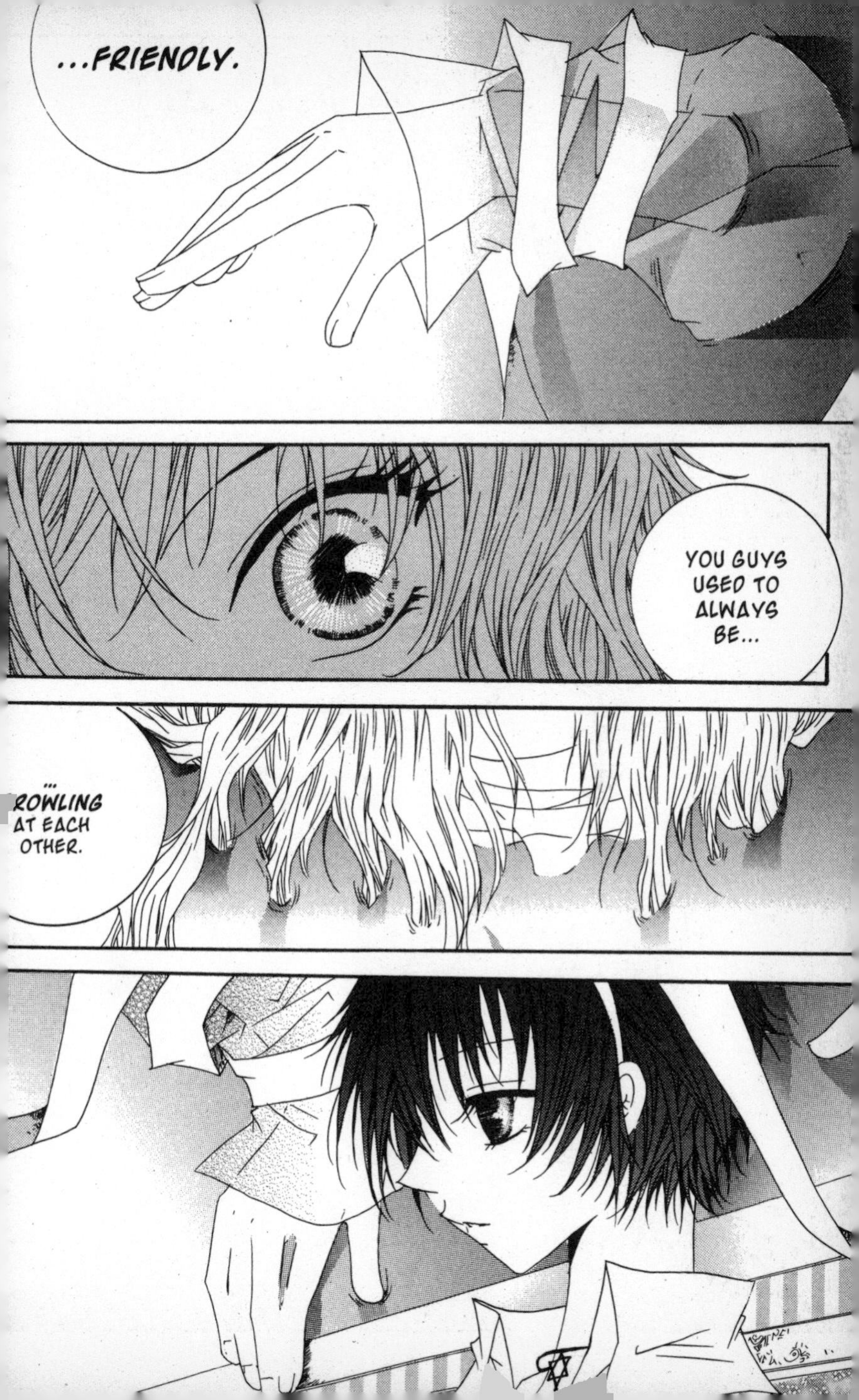
...FRIENDLY.
YOU GUYS USED TO ALWAYS BE...
...
ROWLING AT EACH OTHER.

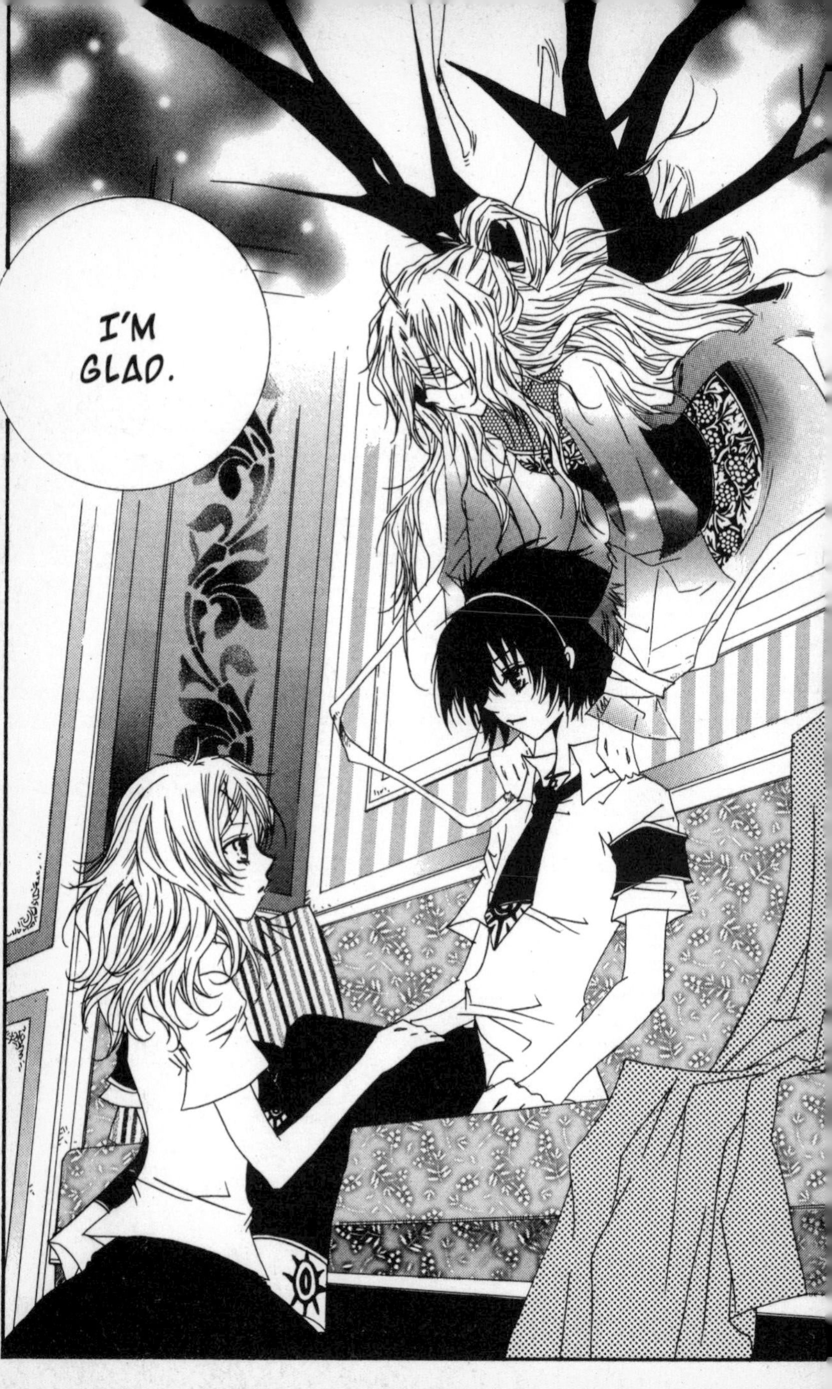
I'M GLAD.

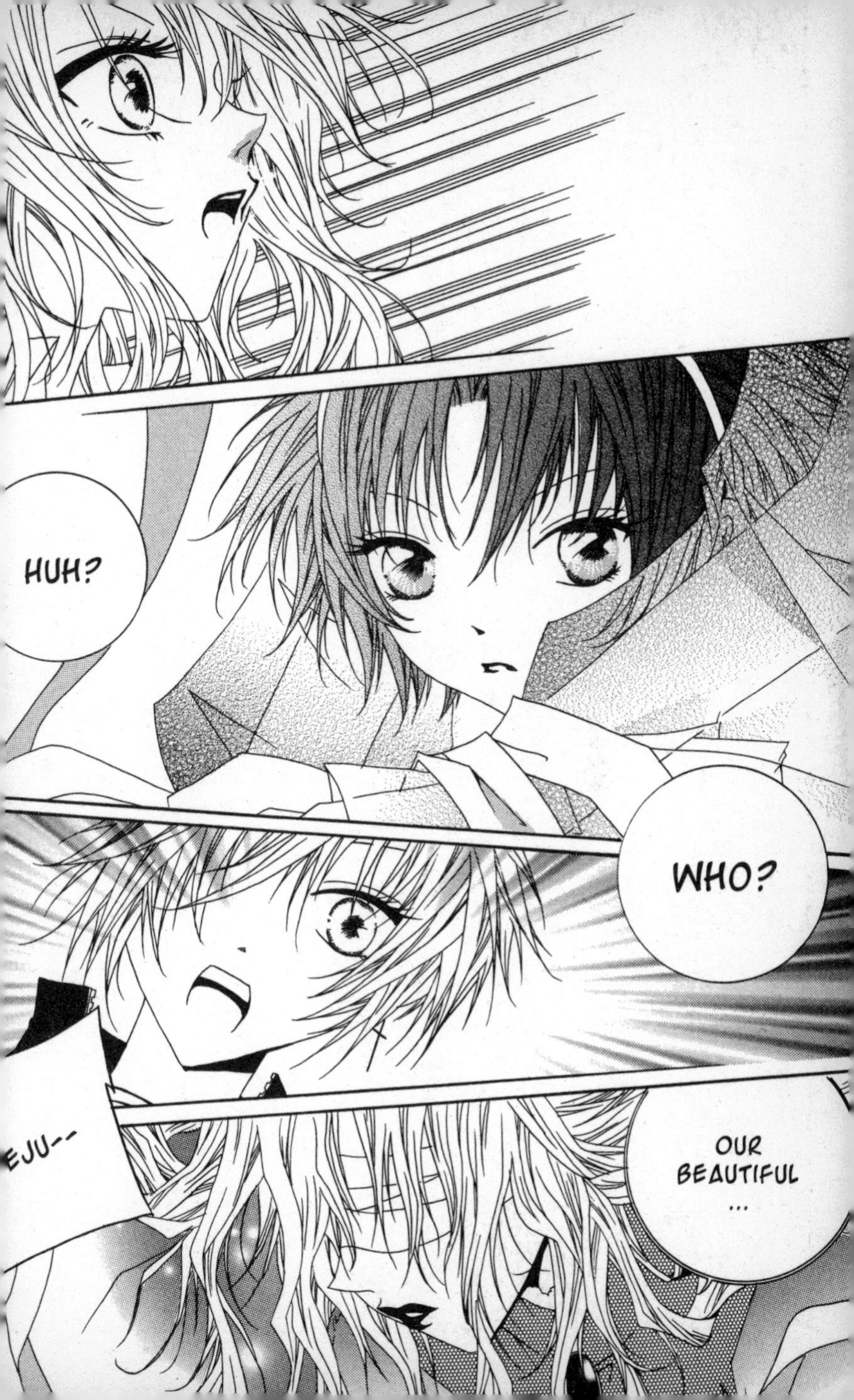
HUH?
WHO?
EJU--
OUR BEAUTIFUL ...

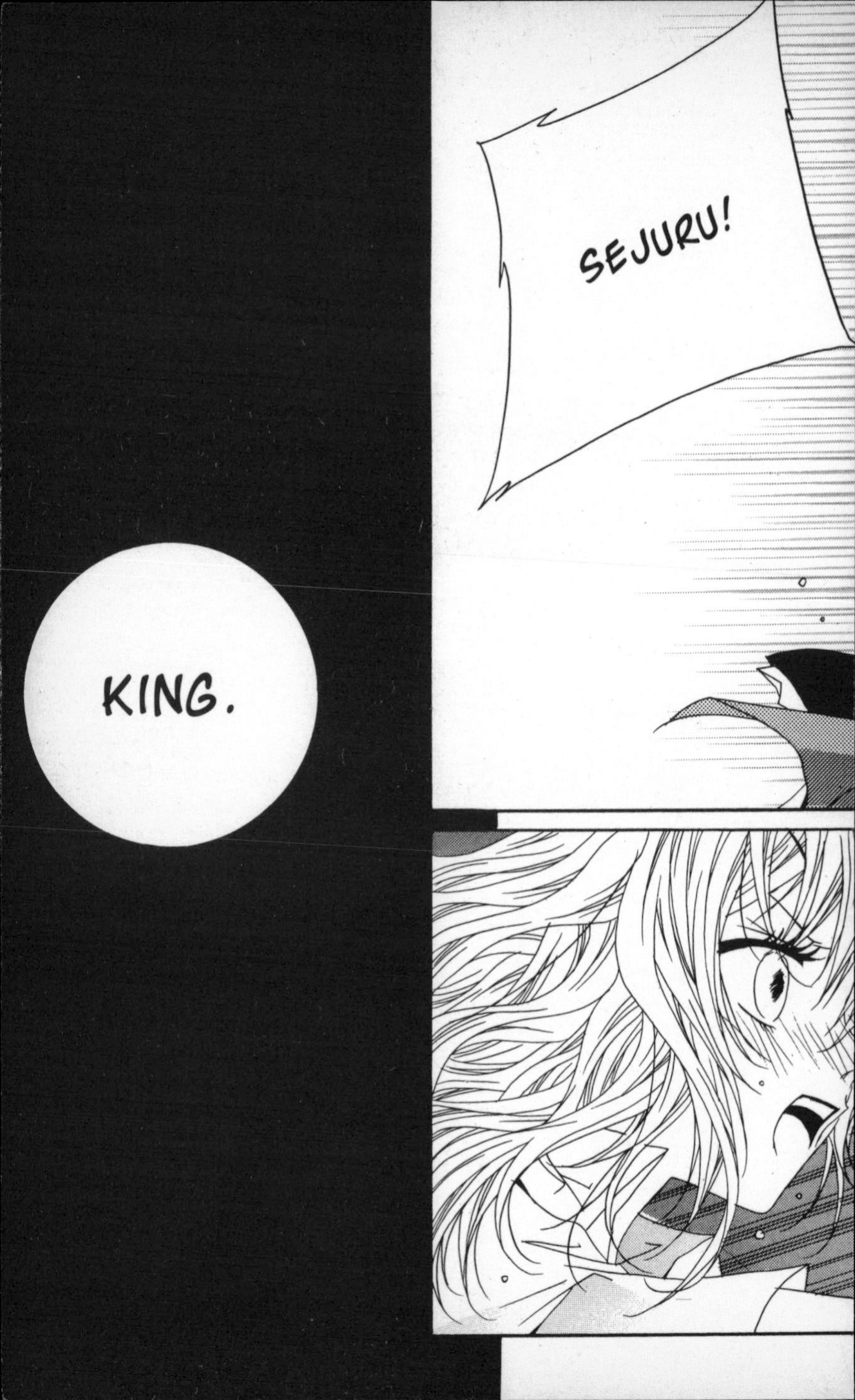
KING.
SEJURU!

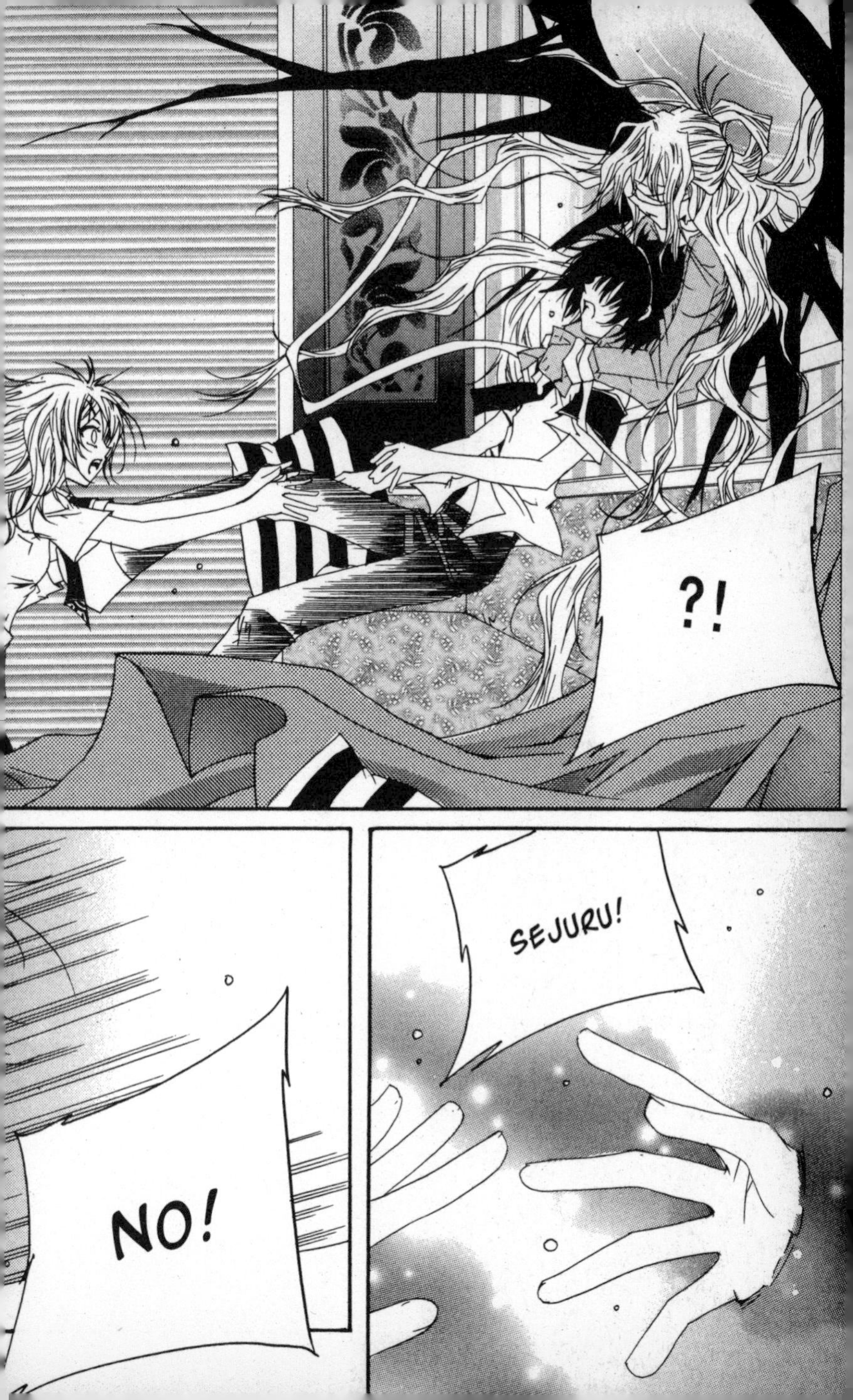
?!
NO!
SEJURU!

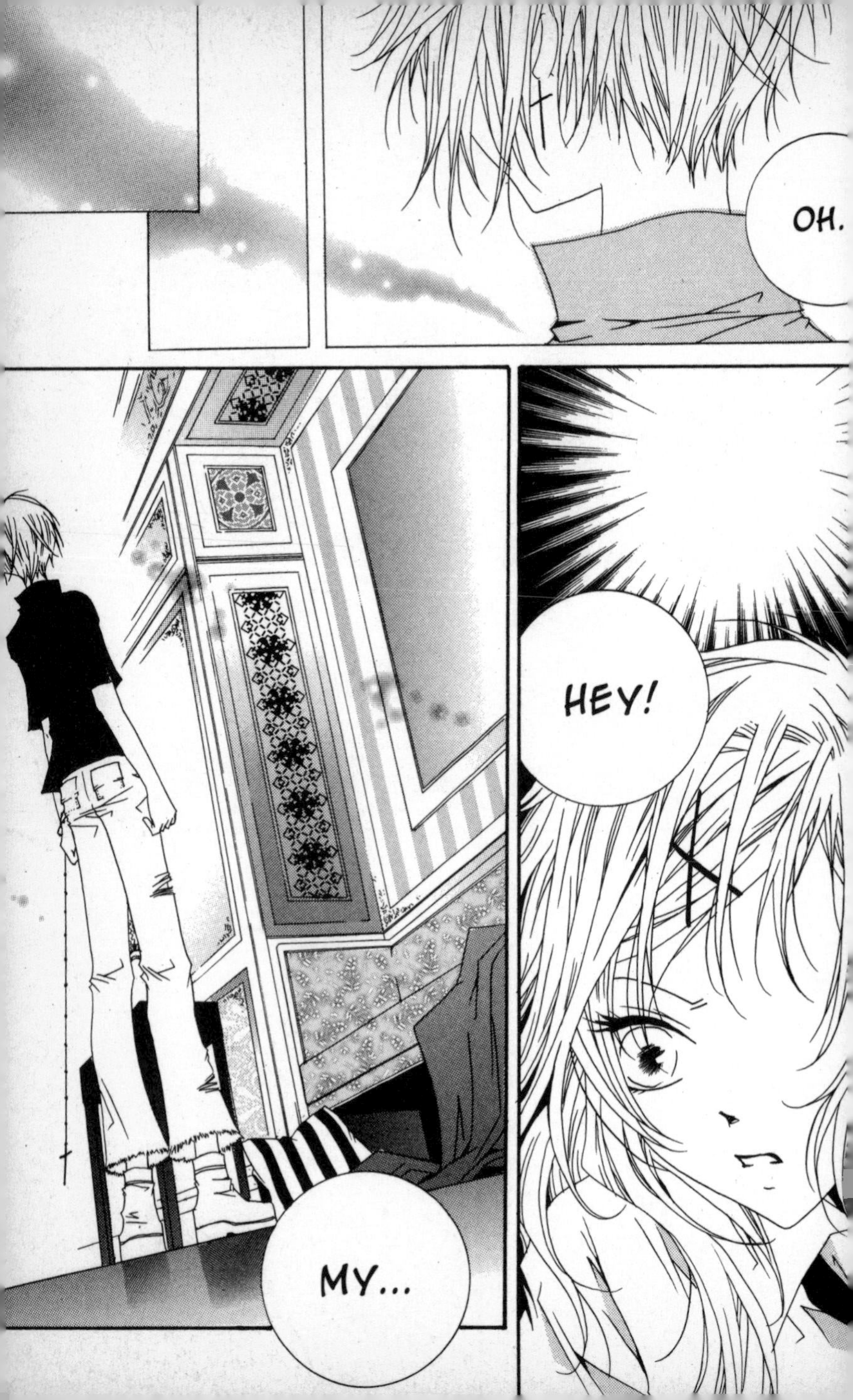
OH.
MY...
HEY!

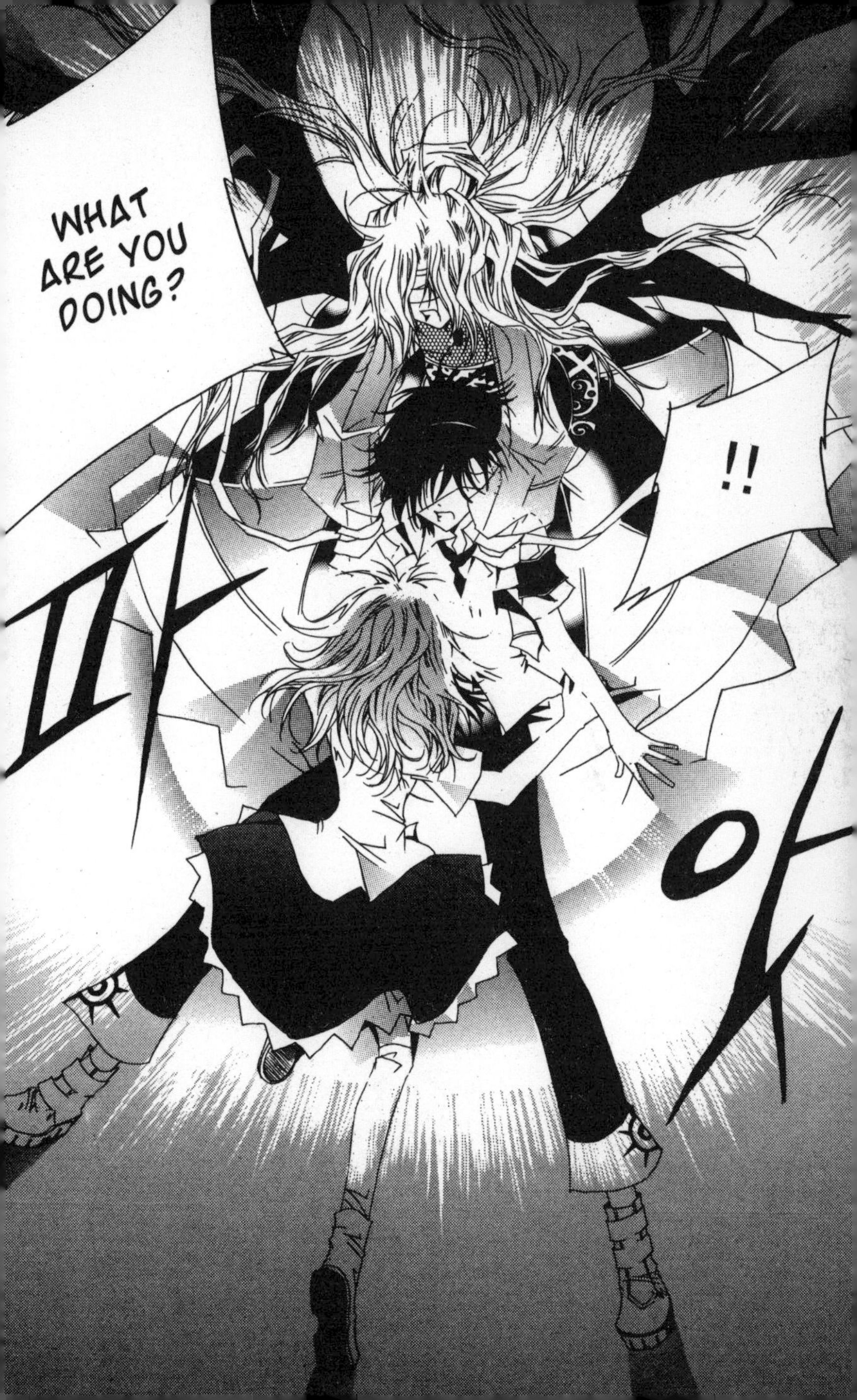
WHAT ARE YOU DOING?
!!

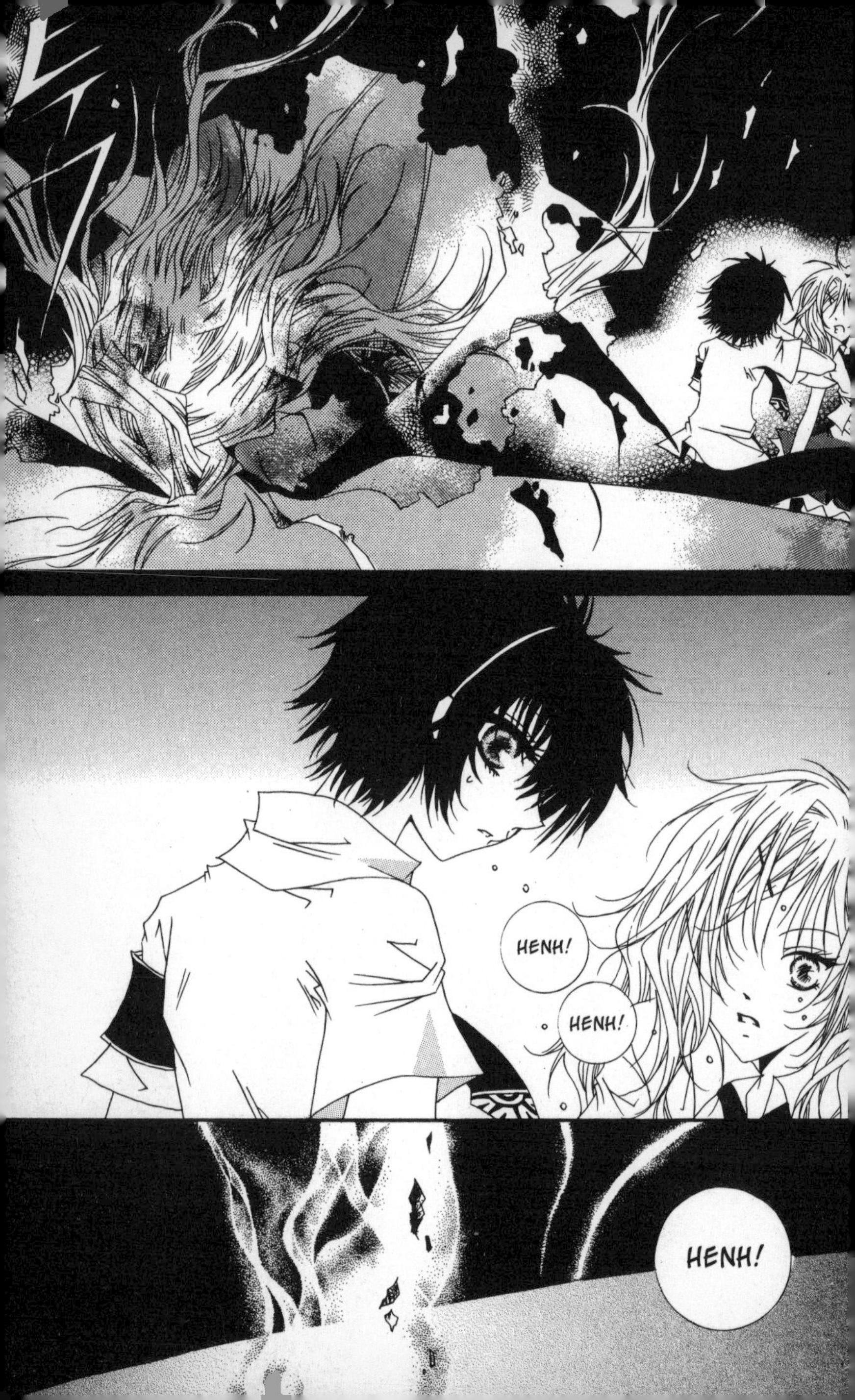
HENH!
HENH!
HENH!

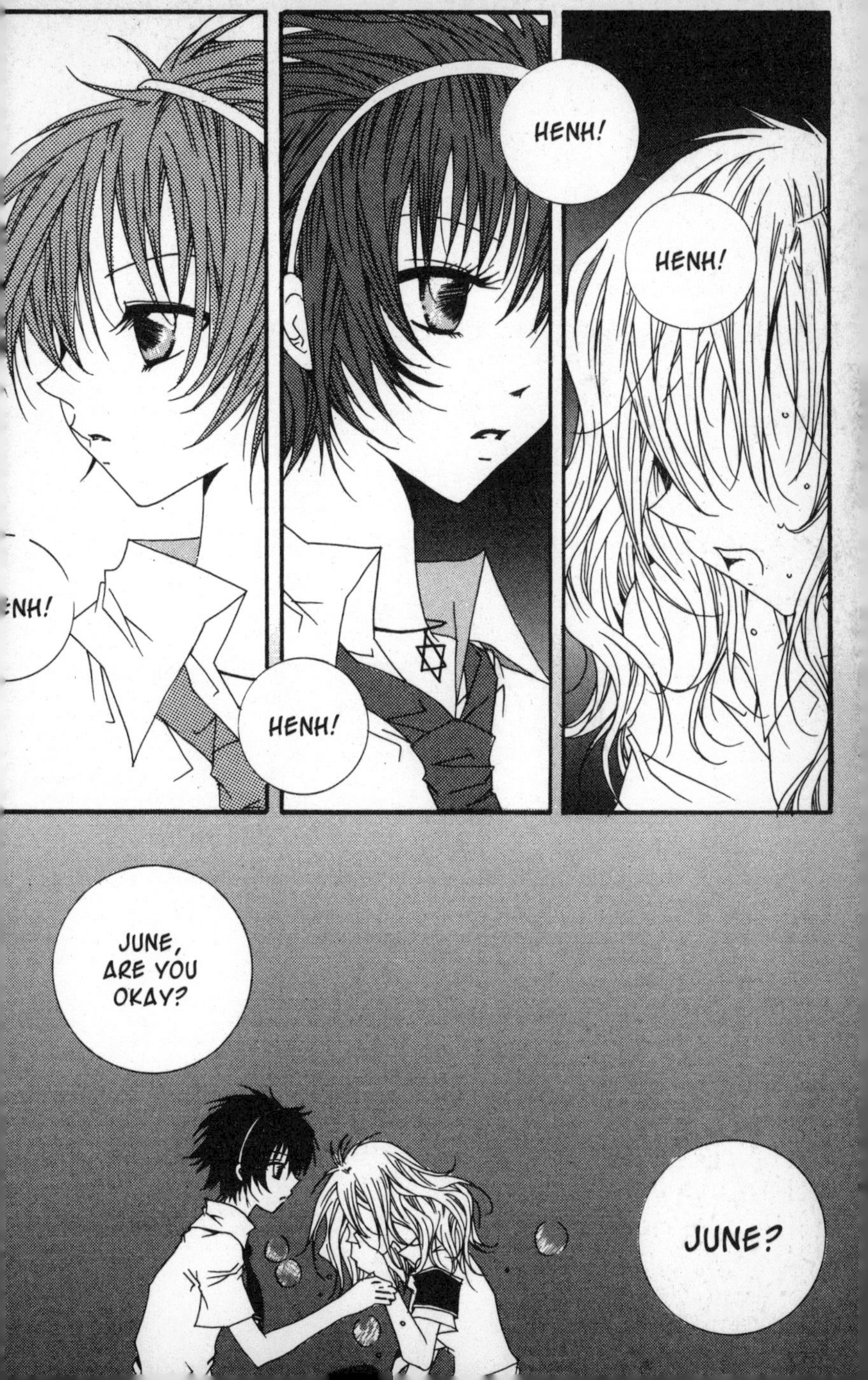
NH!
HENH!
HENH!
HENH!
JUNE, ARE YOU OKAY?
JUNE?

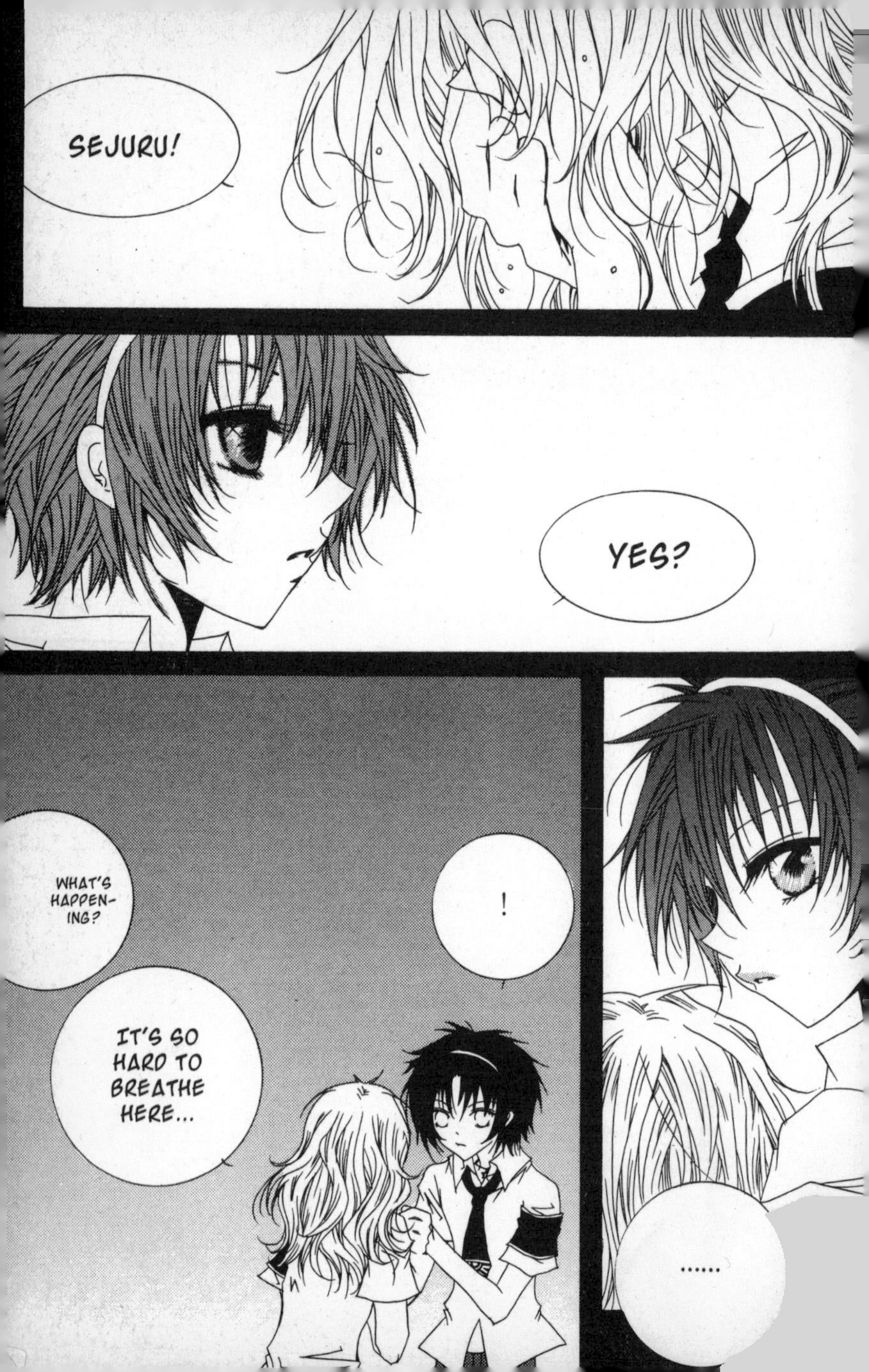
SEJURU!
YES?
WHAT'S HAPPENING?
IT'S SO HARD TO BREATHE HERE...
!
......

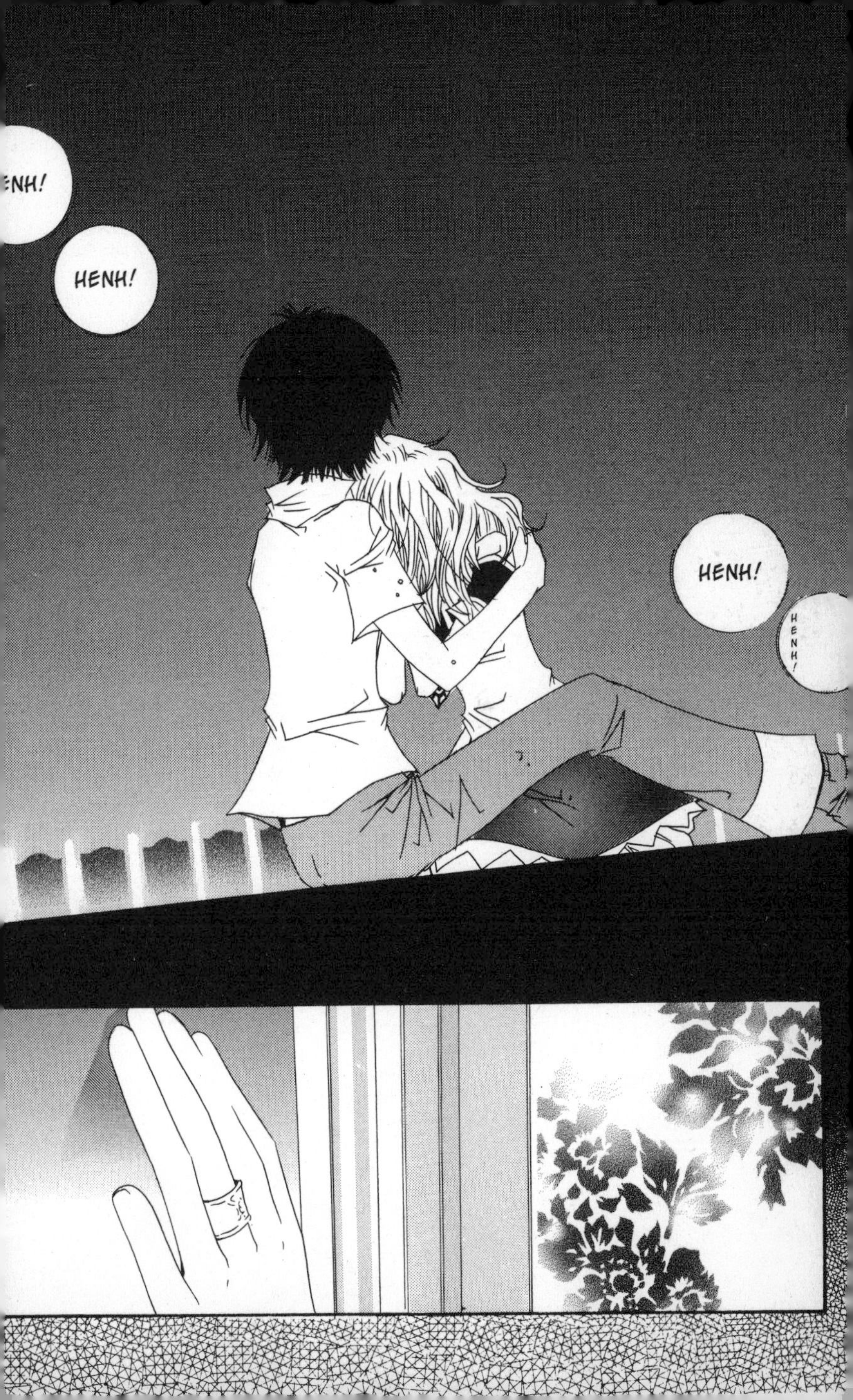
ENH!
HENH!
HENH!
HENH!

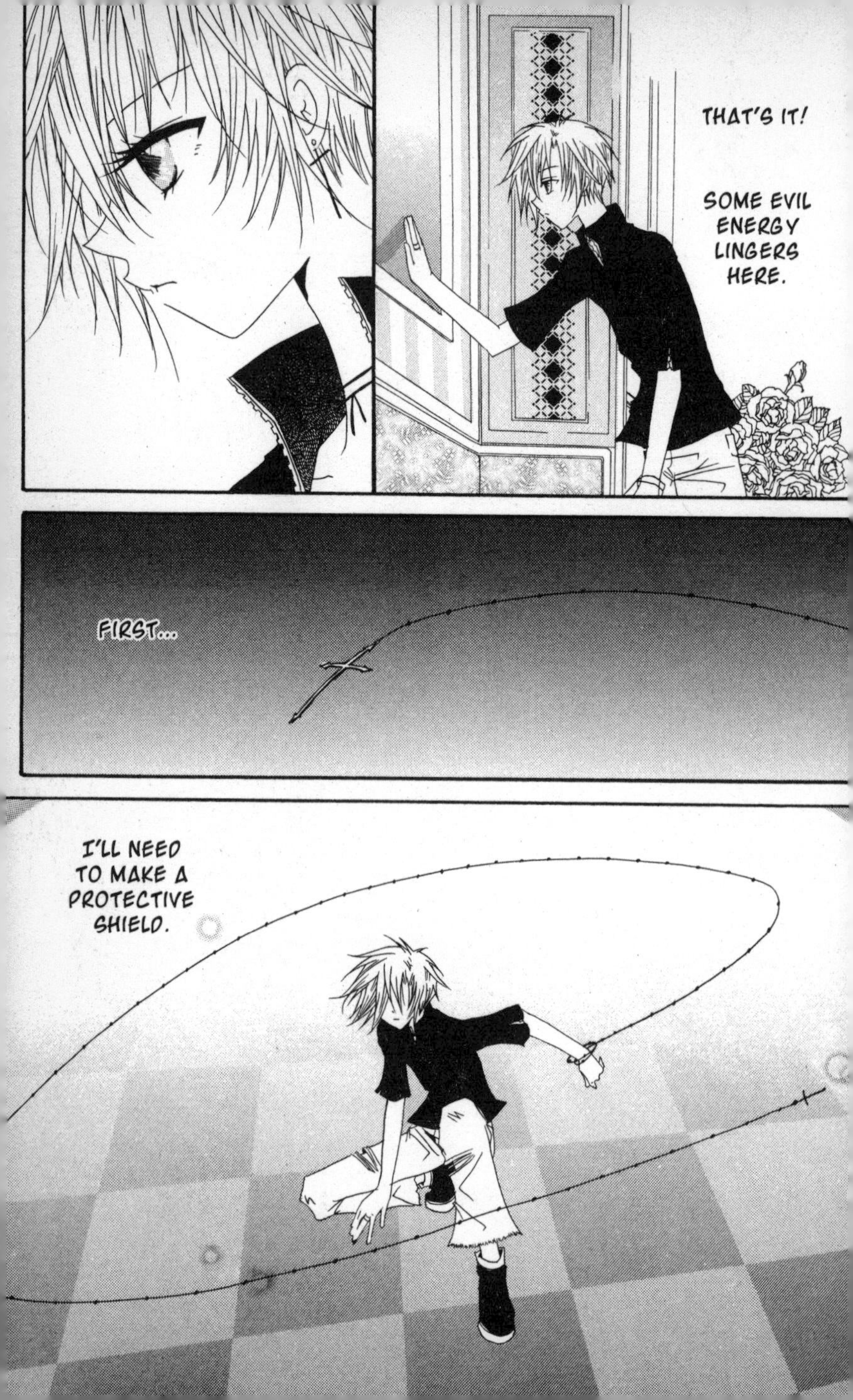
THAT'S IT!
SOME EVIL ENERGY LINGERS HERE.
FIRST...
I'LL NEED TO MAKE A PROTECTIVE SHIELD.

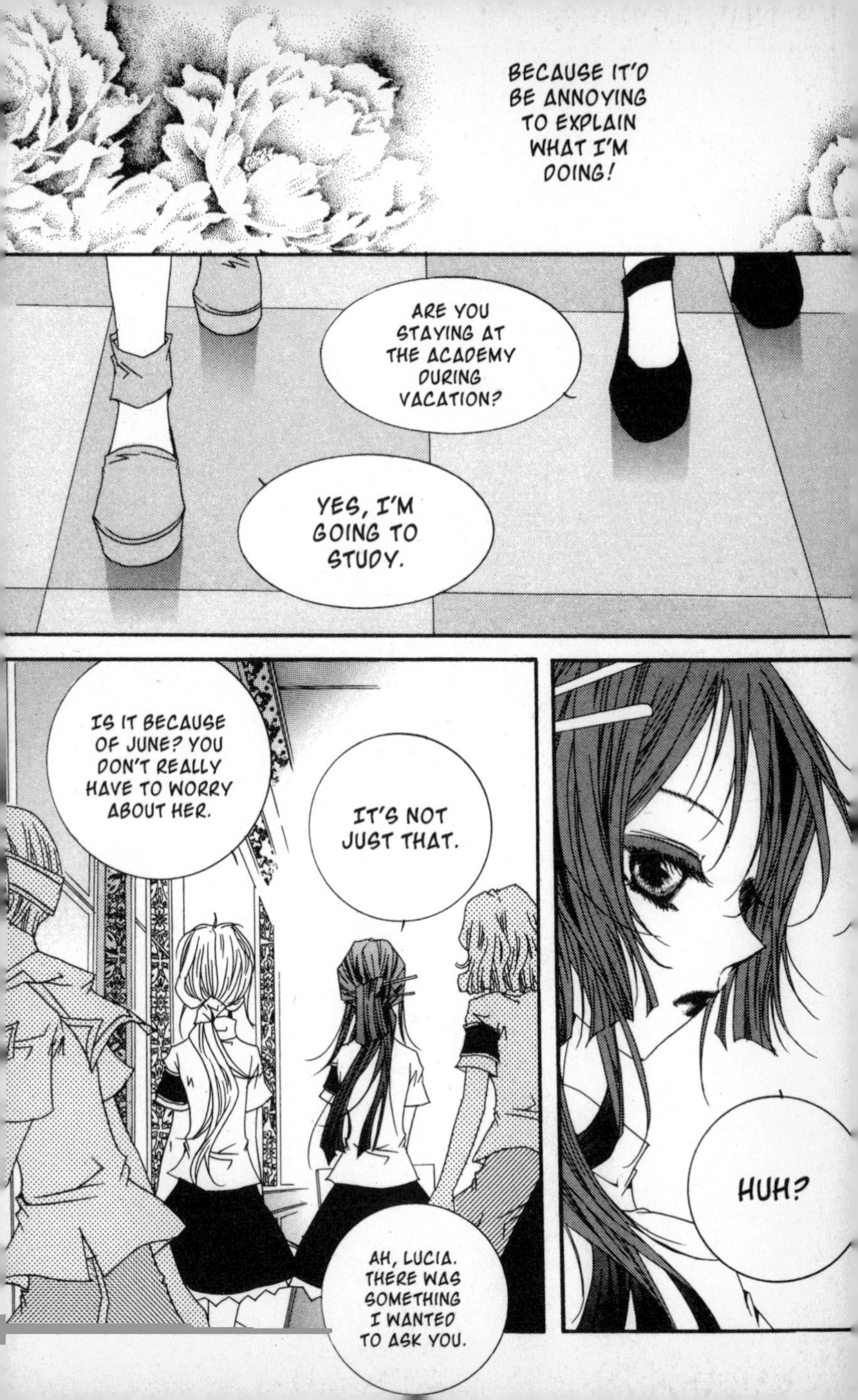
BECAUSE IT'D BE ANNOYING TO EXPLAIN WHAT I'M DOING!
ARE YOU STAYING AT THE ACADEMY DURING VACATION?
YES, I'M GOING TO STUDY.
IS IT BECAUSE OF JUNE? YOU DON'T REALLY HAVE TO WORRY ABOUT HER.
IT'S NOT JUST THAT.
AH, LUCIA. THERE WAS SOMETHING I WANTED TO ASK YOU.
HUH?

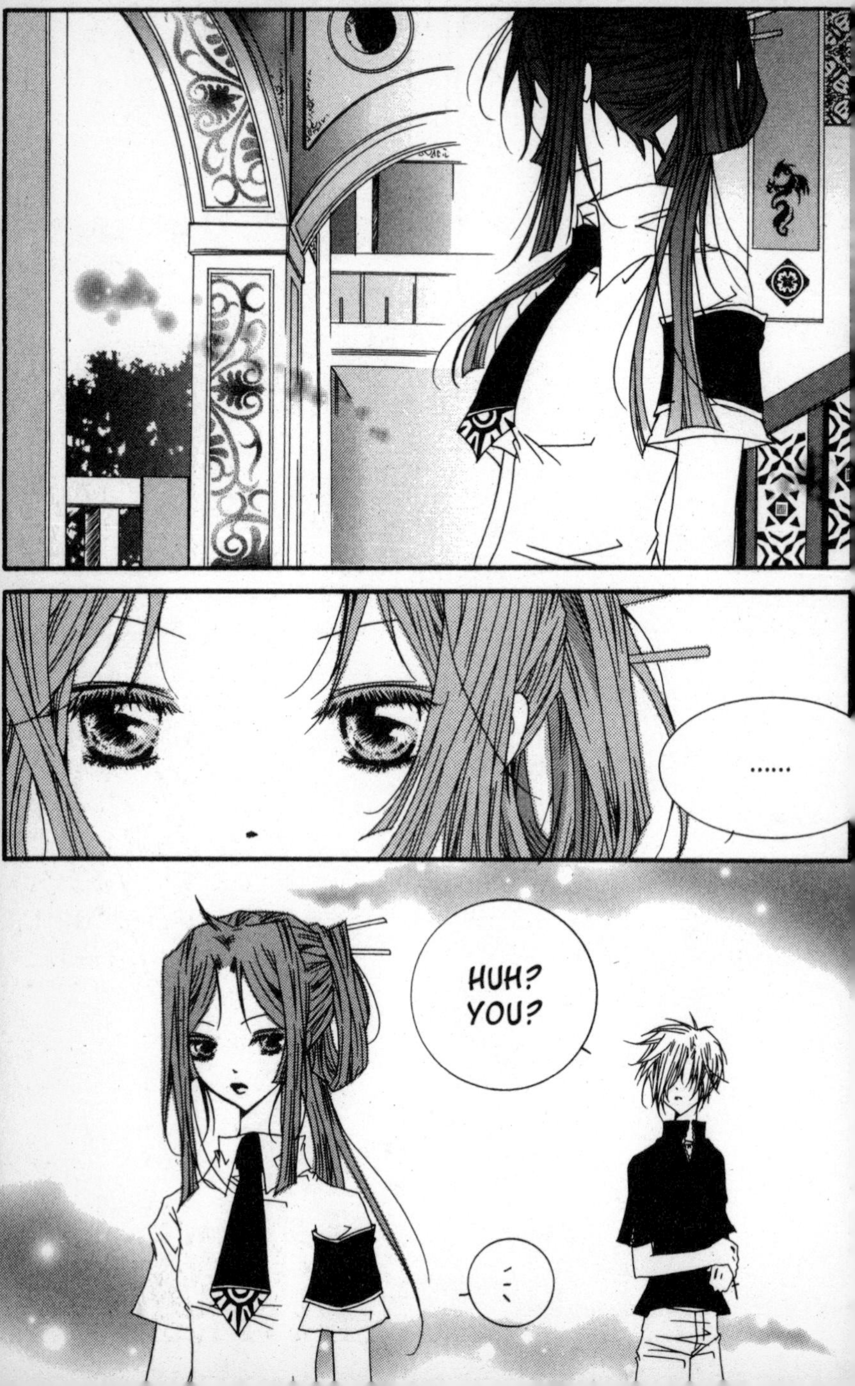
......
HUH?
YOU?

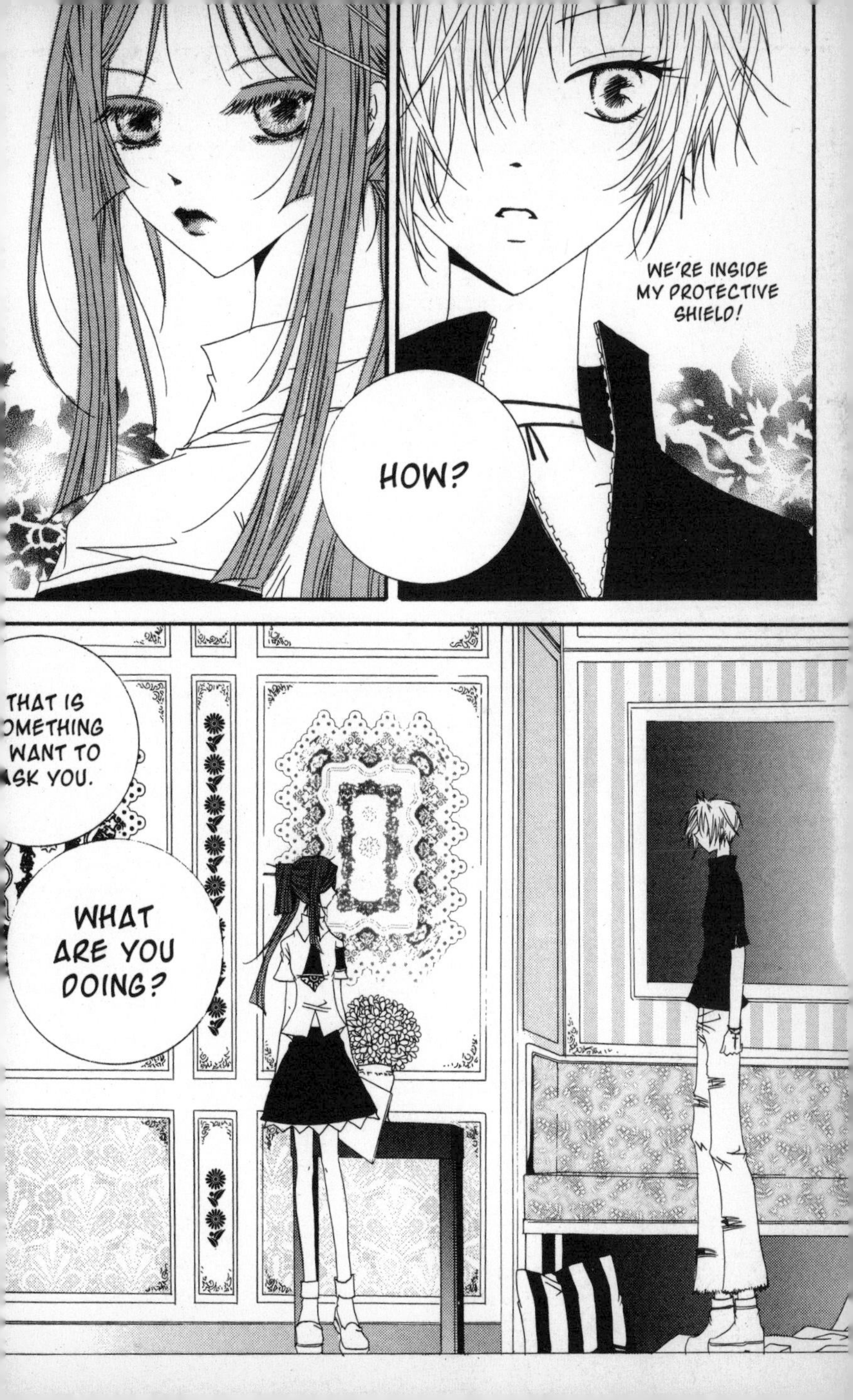
WE'RE INSIDE MY PROTECTIVE SHIELD!
HOW?
THAT IS OMETHING WANT TO SK YOU.
WHAT ARE YOU DOING?

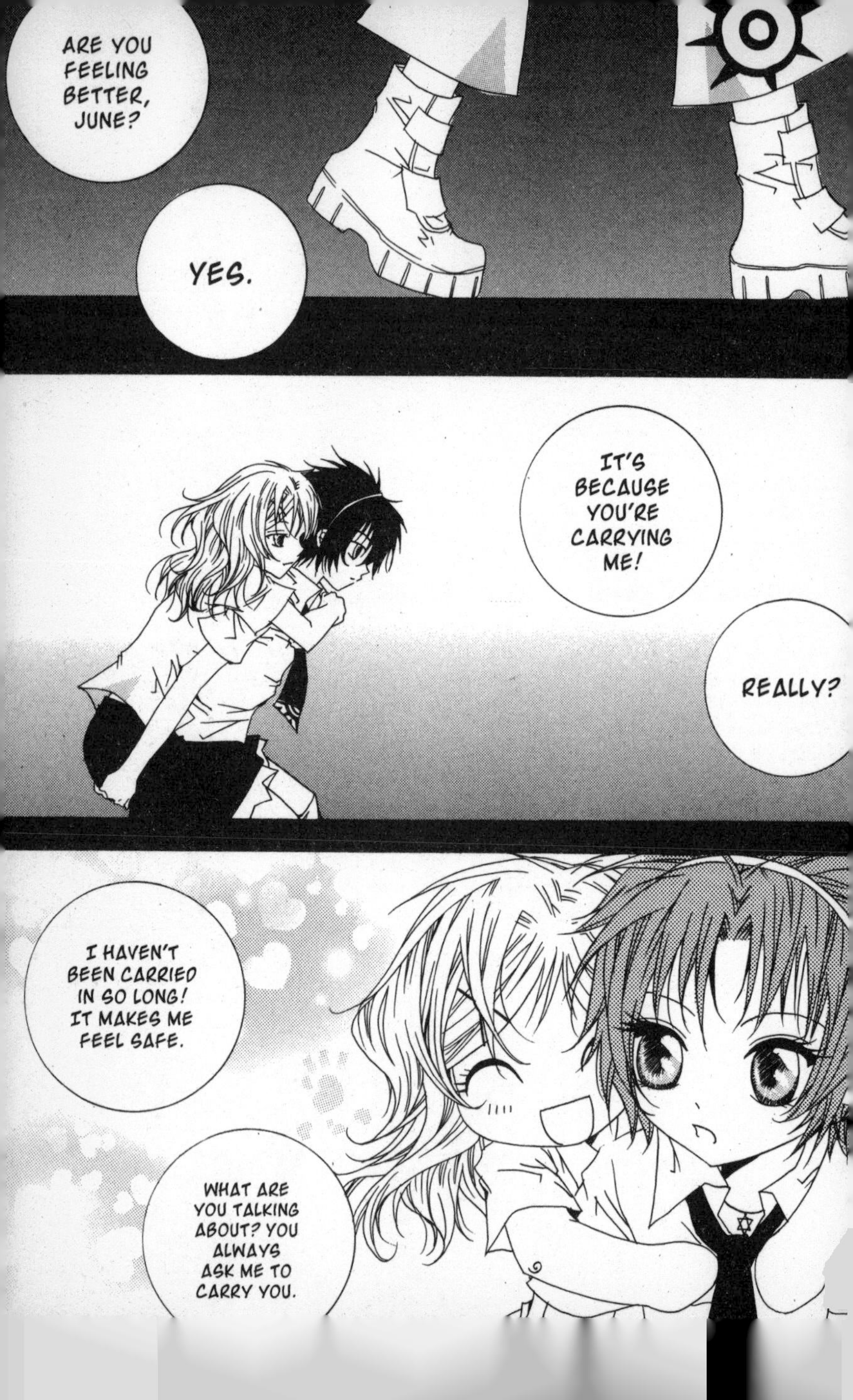
ARE YOU FEELING BETTER, JUNE?
YES.
IT'S BECAUSE YOU'RE CARRYING ME!
REALLY?
I HAVEN'T BEEN CARRIED IN SO LONG! IT MAKES ME FEEL SAFE.
WHAT ARE YOU TALKING ABOUT? YOU ALWAYS ASK ME TO CARRY YOU.

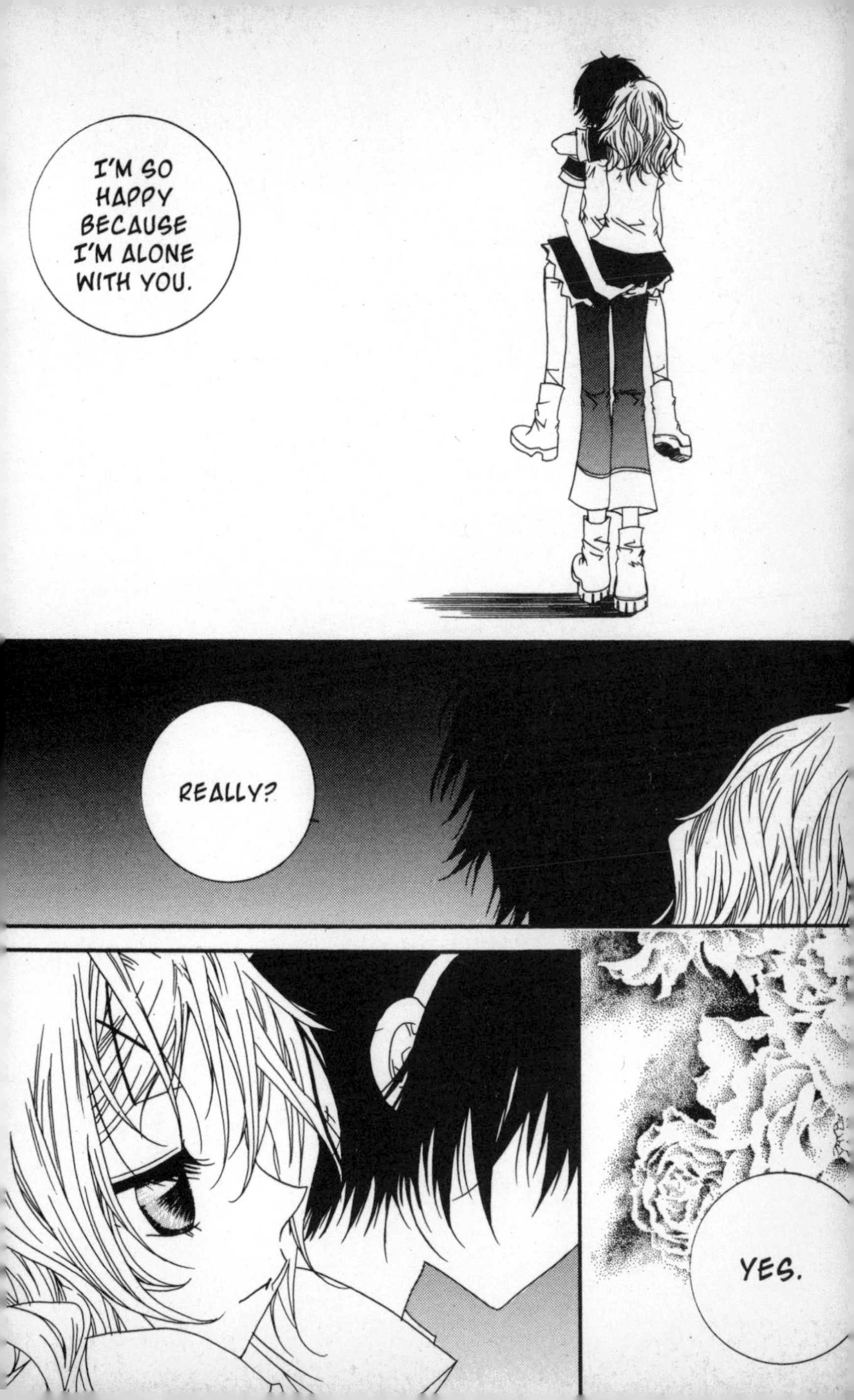
I'M SO HAPPY BECAUSE I'M ALONE WITH YOU.
REALLY?
YES.

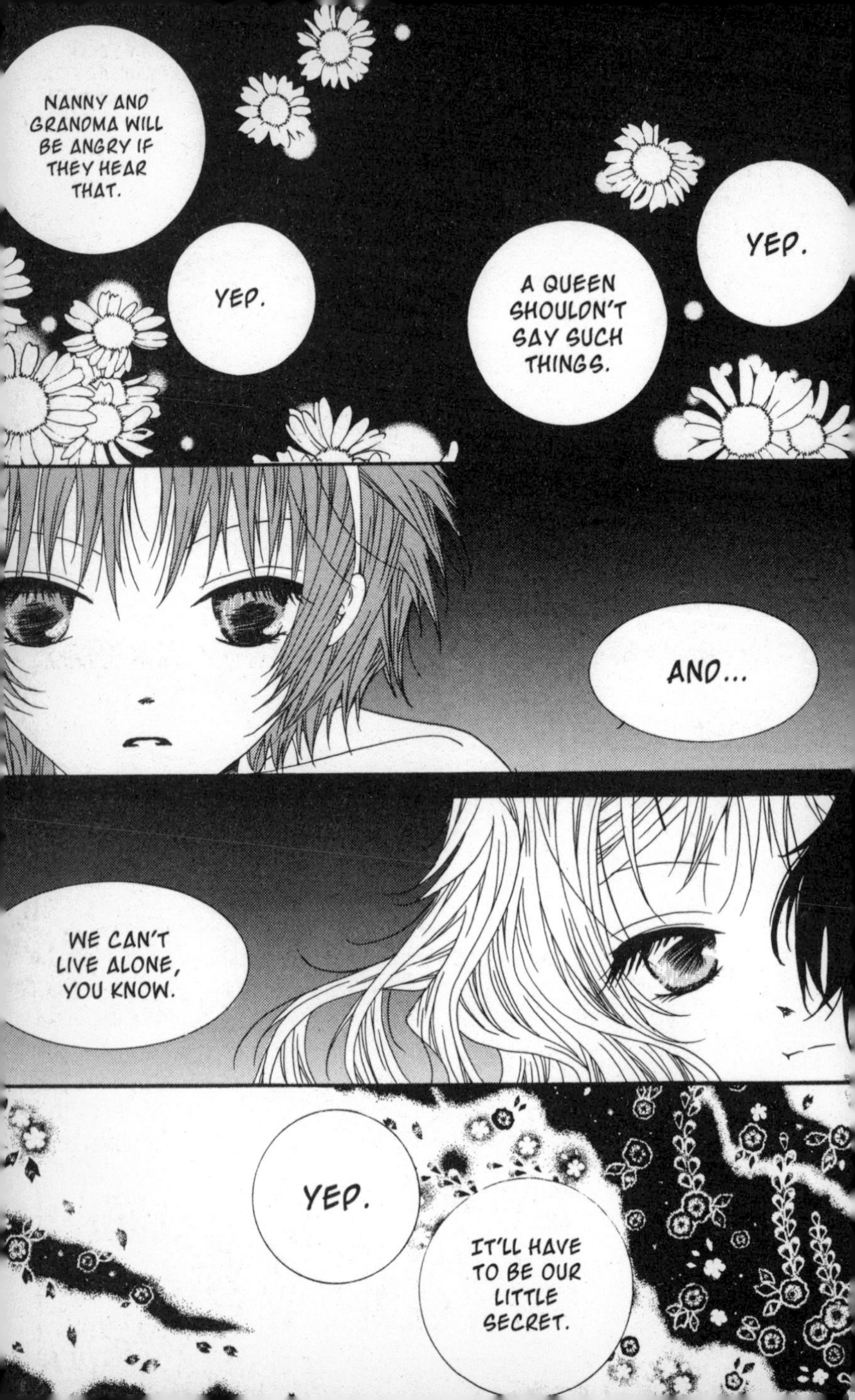
NANNY AND GRANDMA WILL BE ANGRY IF THEY HEAR THAT.
YEP.
A QUEEN SHOULDN'T SAY SUCH THINGS.
YEP.
AND...
WE CAN'T LIVE ALONE, YOU KNOW.
YEP.
IT'LL HAVE TO BE OUR LITTLE SECRET.

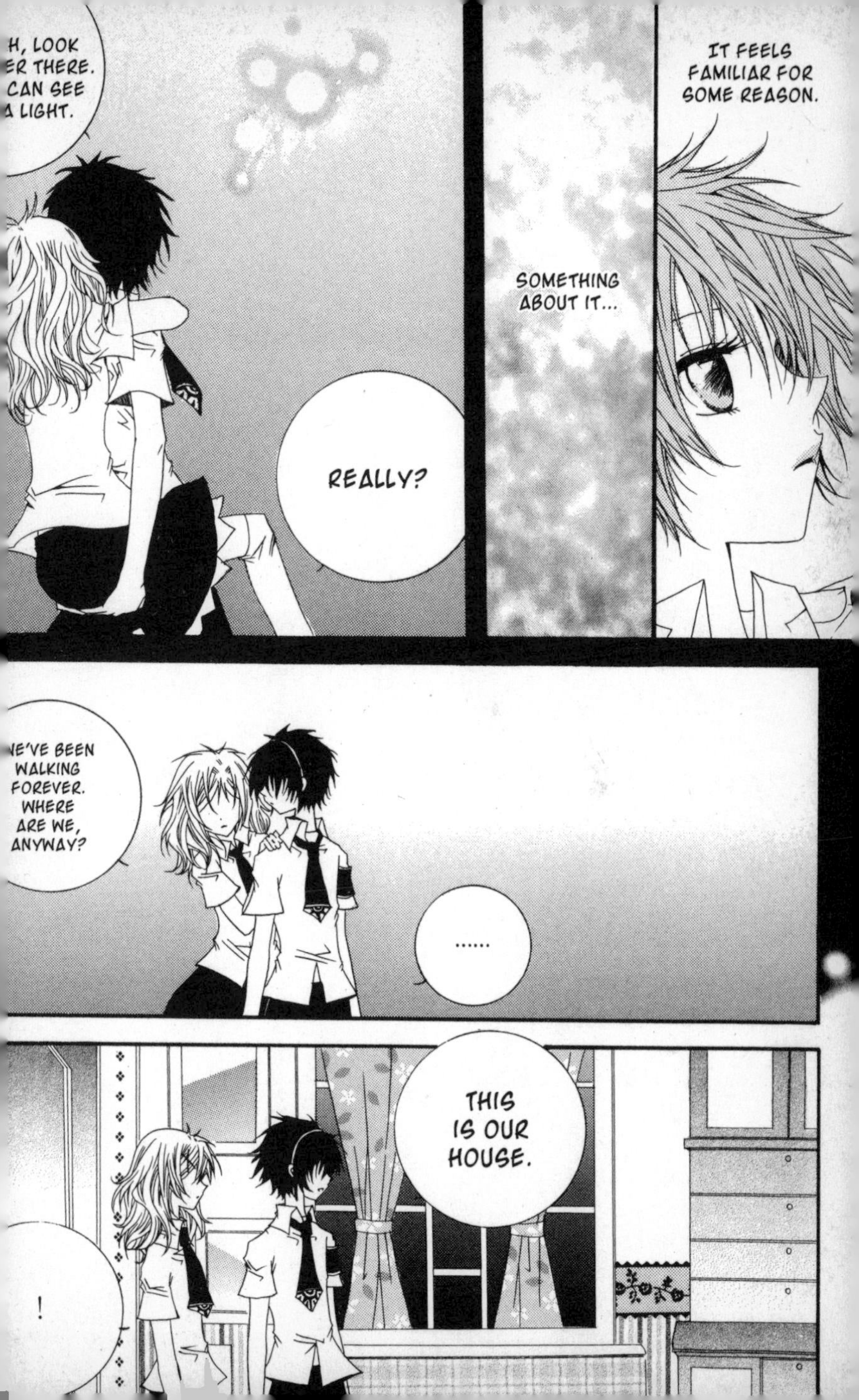

H, LOOK
ER THERE.
CAN SEE
A LIGHT.
REALLY?
SOMETHING ABOUT IT...
IT FEELS FAMILIAR FOR SOME REASON.
E'VE BEEN WALKING FOREVER. WHERE ARE WE, ANYWAY?
......
!
THIS IS OUR HOUSE.

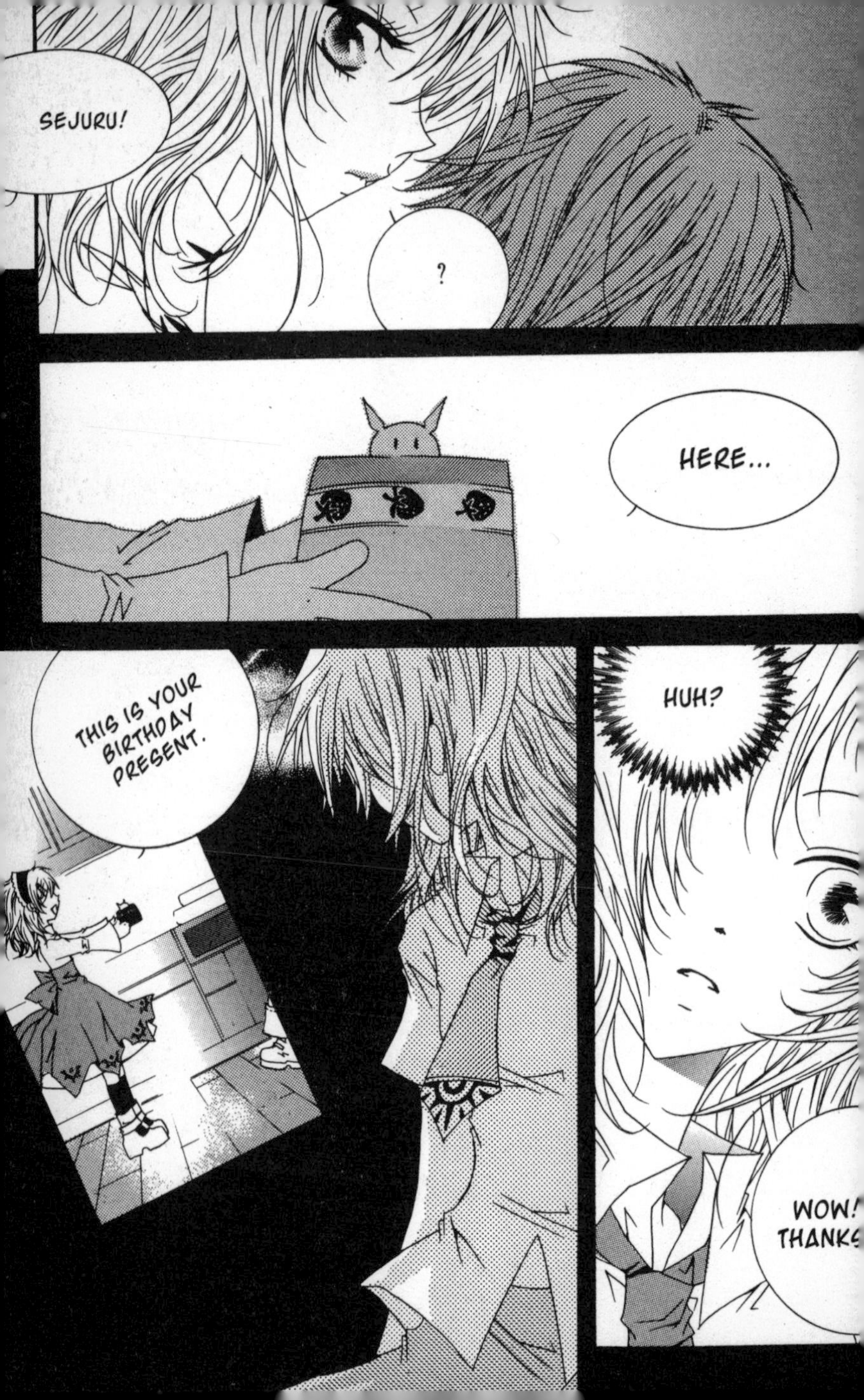
SEJURU!
?
HERE...
THIS IS YOUR BIRTHDAY PRESENT.
HUH?
WOW! THANKS

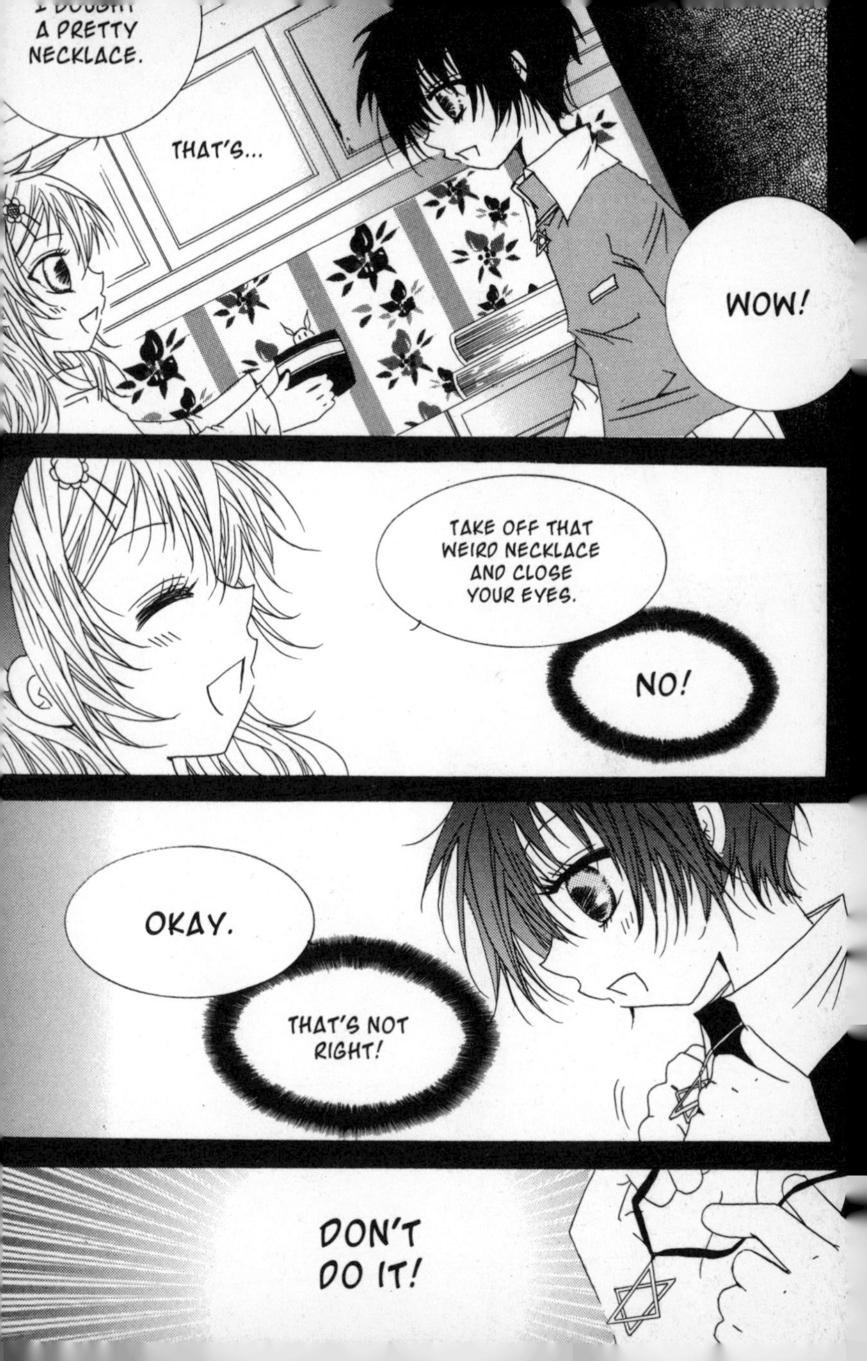
A PRETTY NECKLACE.
THAT'S...
WOW!
TAKE OFF THAT WEIRD NECKLACE AND CLOSE YOUR EYES.
NO!
OKAY.
THAT'S NOT RIGHT!
DON'T DO IT!

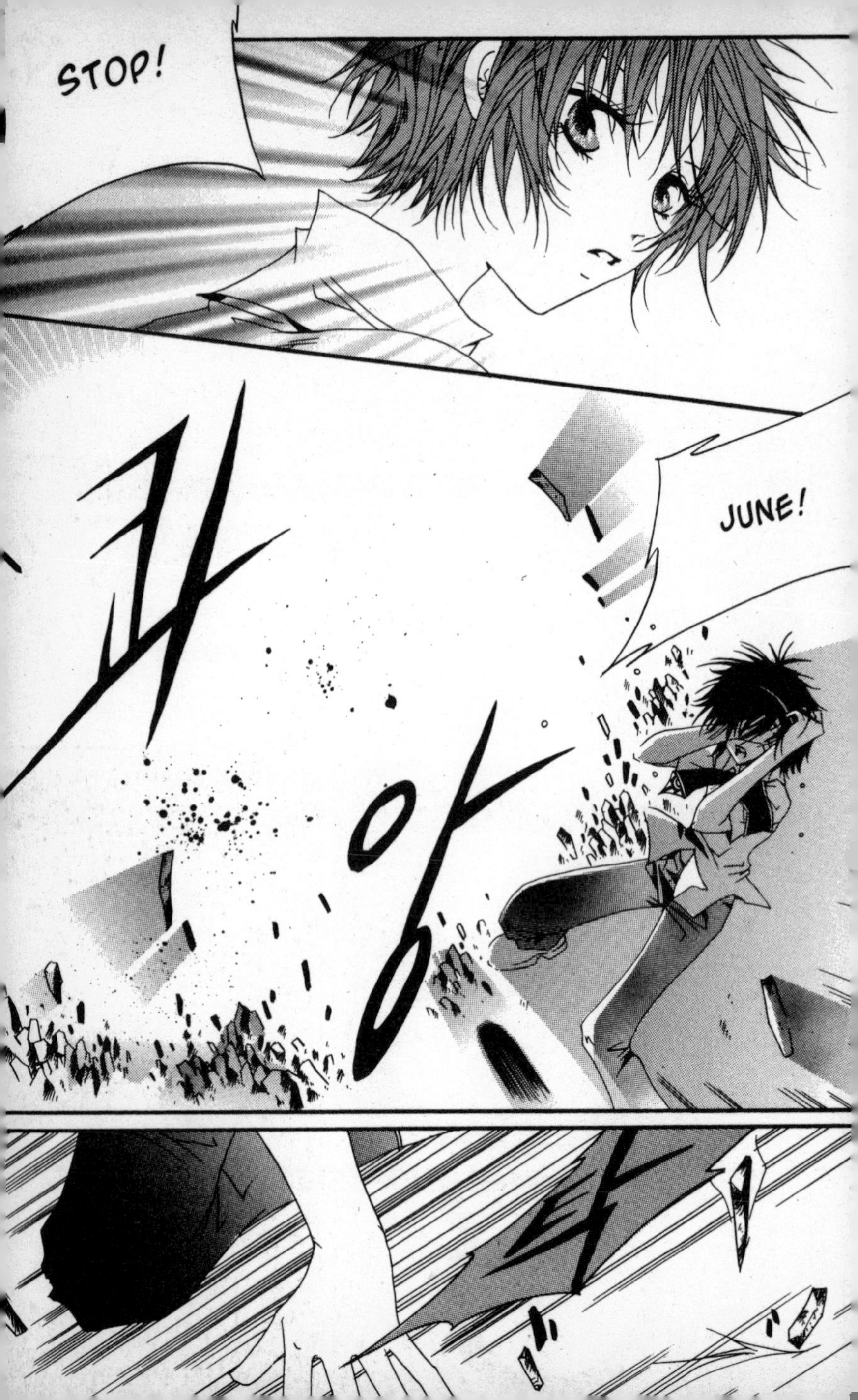
STOP!
콰앙
JUNE!

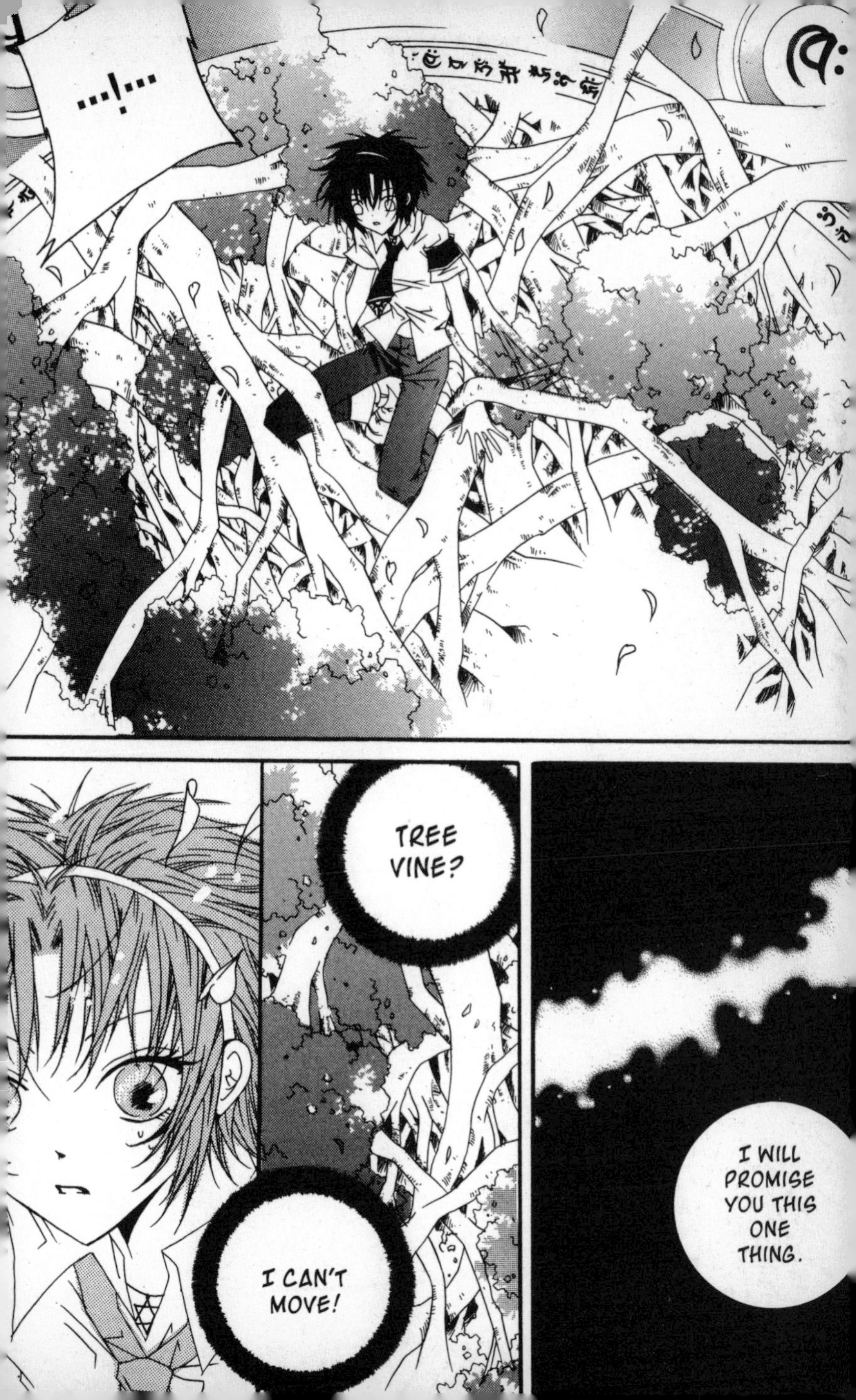
...!...
TREE VINE?
I CAN'T MOVE!
I WILL PROMISE YOU THIS ONE THING.

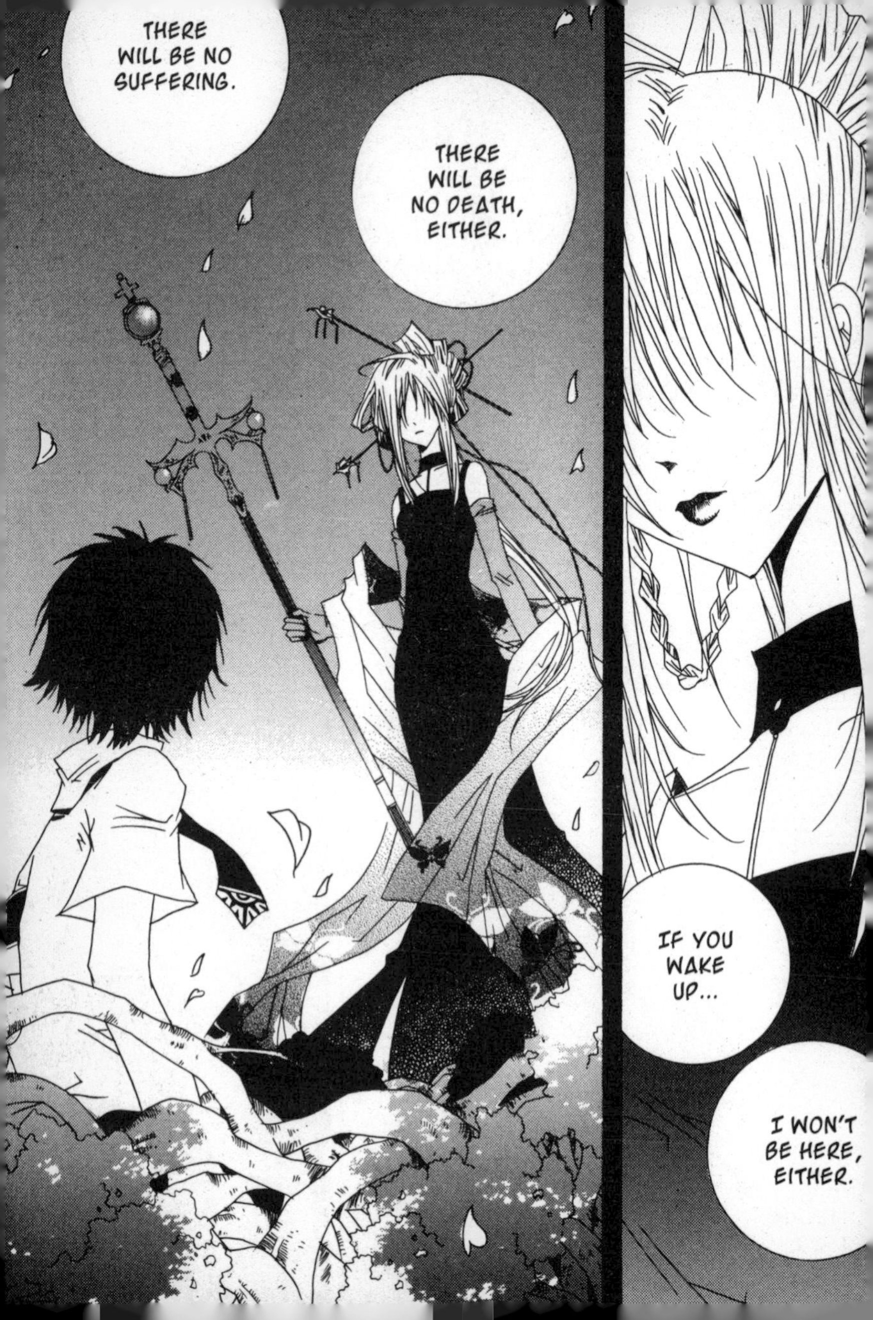
THERE WILL BE NO SUFFERING.
THERE WILL BE NO DEATH, EITHER.
IF YOU WAKE UP...
I WON'T BE HERE, EITHER.

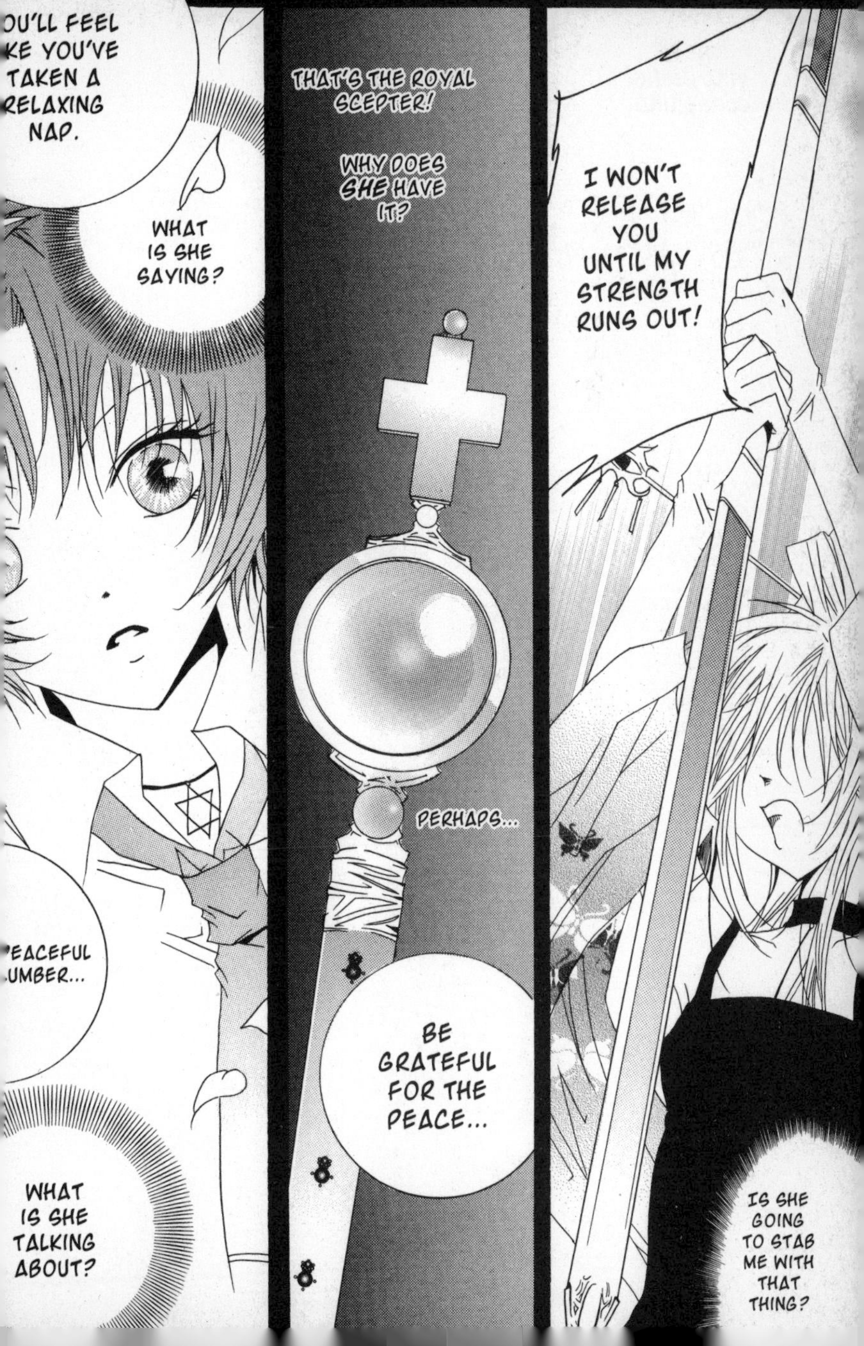
OU'LL FEEL
KE YOU'VE
TAKEN A
RELAXING
NAP.
WHAT IS SHE SAYING?
EACEFUL
UMBER...
WHAT IS SHE TALKING ABOUT?
THAT'S THE ROYAL SCEPTER!
WHY DOES SHE HAVE IT?
PERHAPS...
BE GRATEFUL FOR THE PEACE...
I WON'T RELEASE YOU UNTIL MY STRENGTH RUNS OUT!
IS SHE GOING TO STAB ME WITH THAT THING?

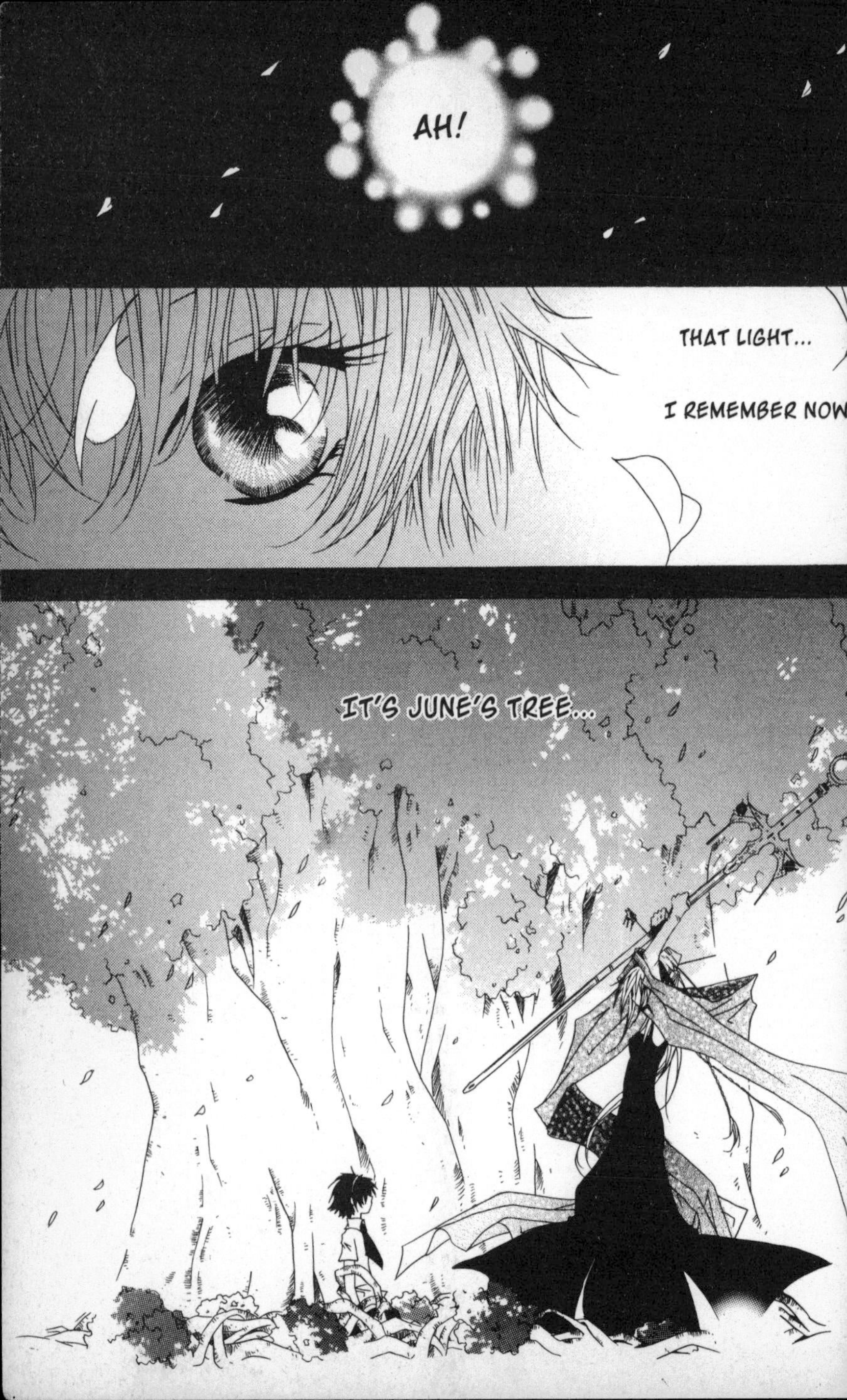
AH!
THAT LIGHT...
I REMEMBER NOW
IT'S JUNE'S TREE...

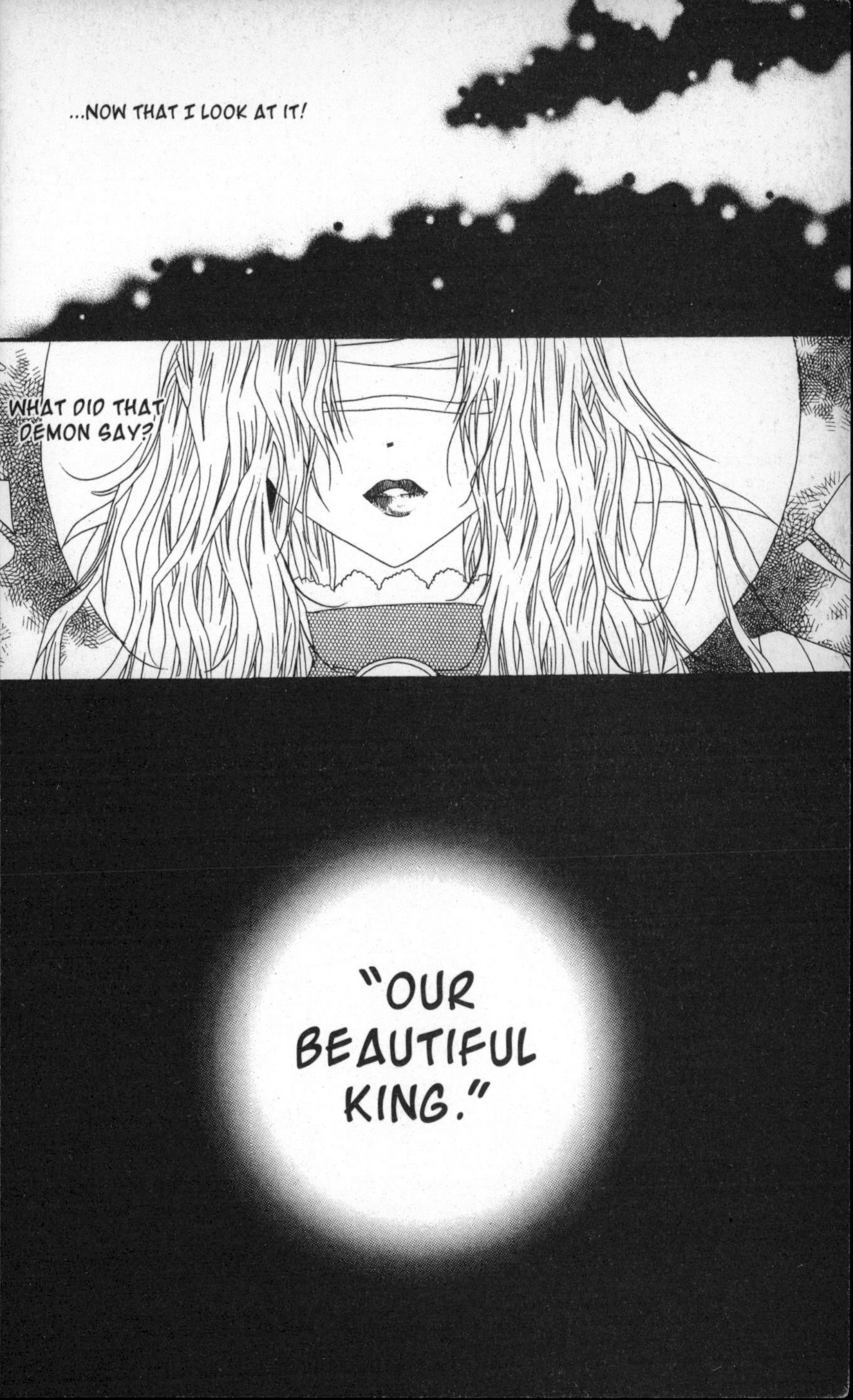
...NOW THAT I LOOK AT IT!
WHAT DID THAT DEMON SAY?
"OUR BEAUTIFUL KING."

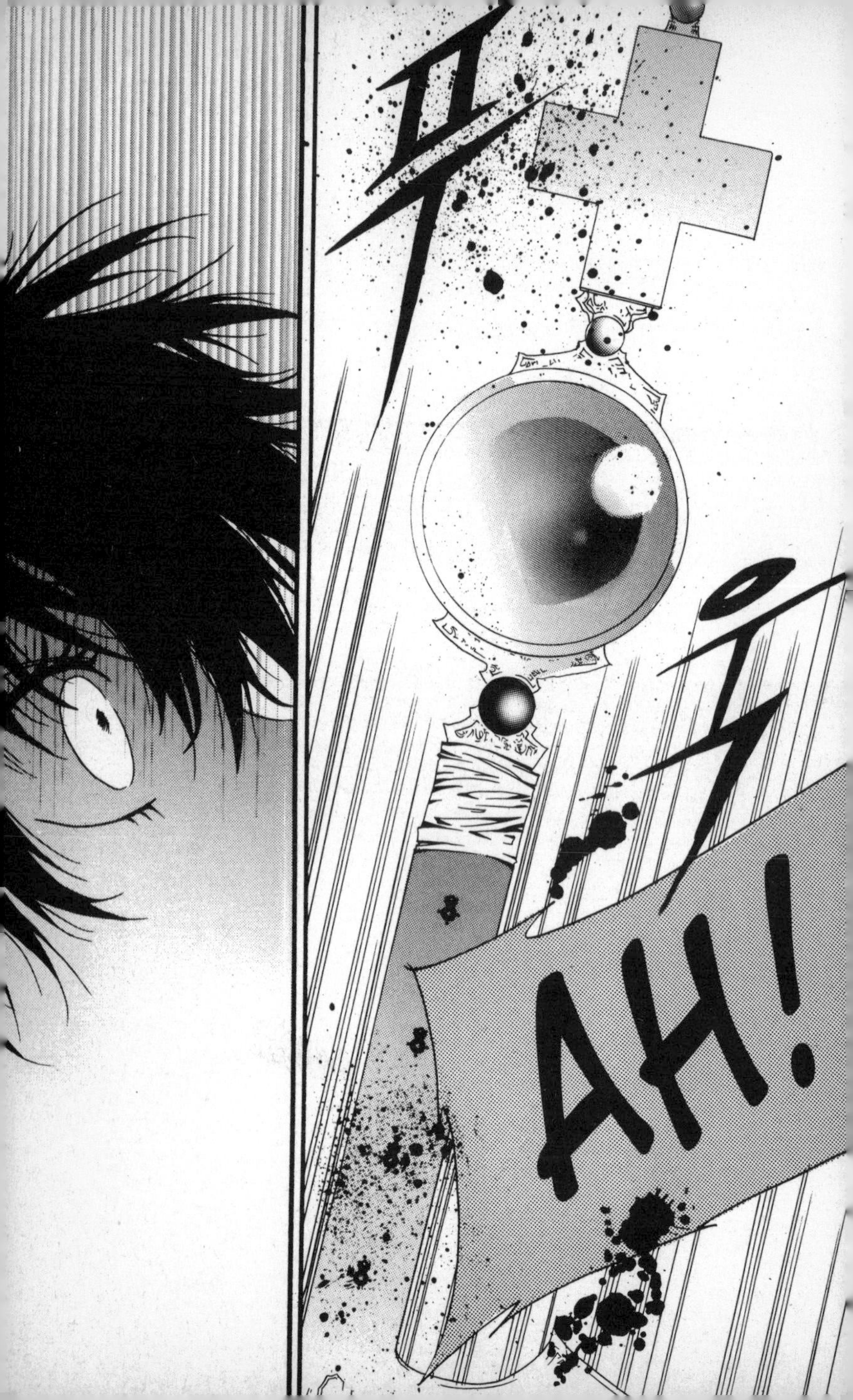
AH!

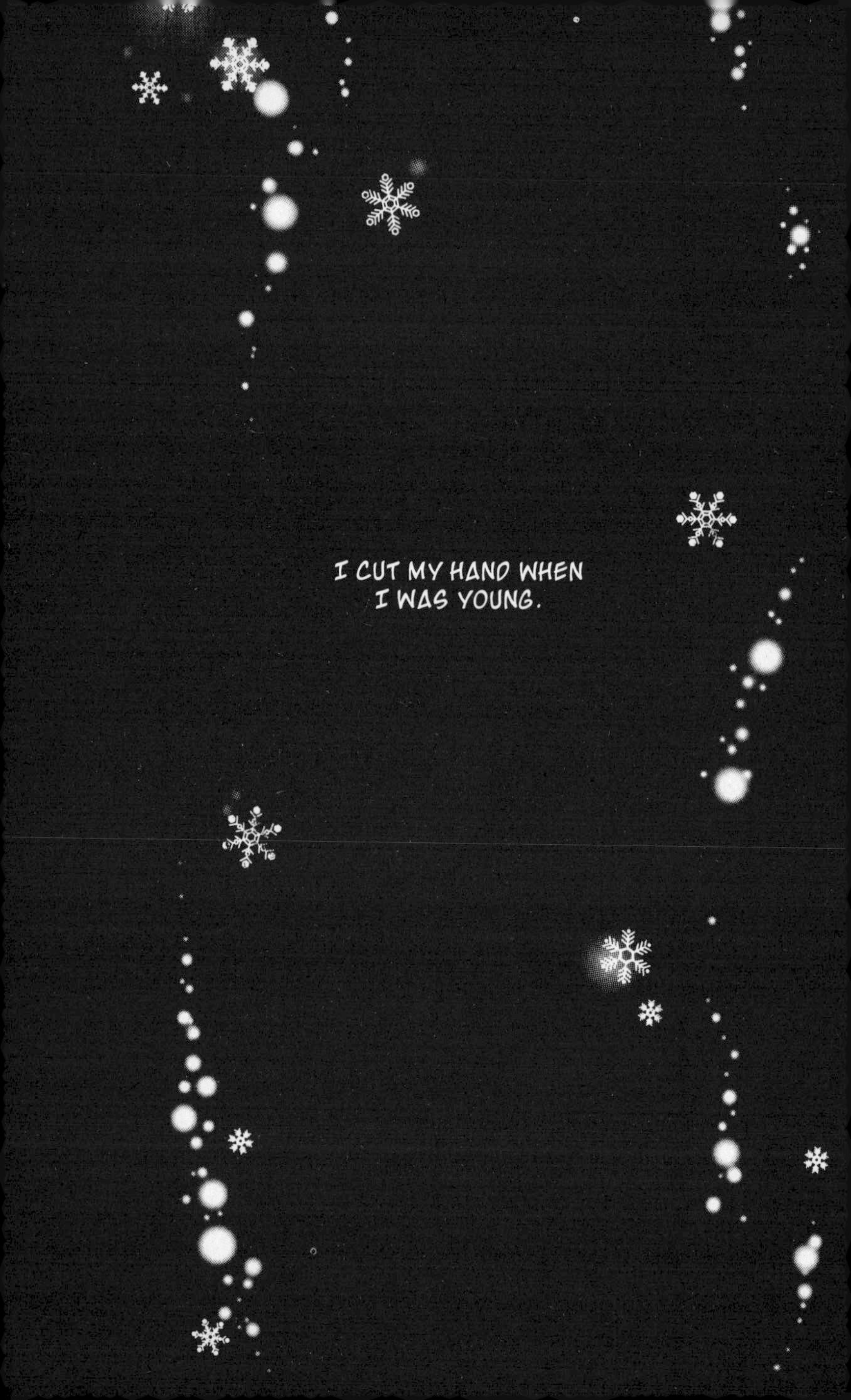
I CUT MY HAND WHEN I WAS YOUNG.

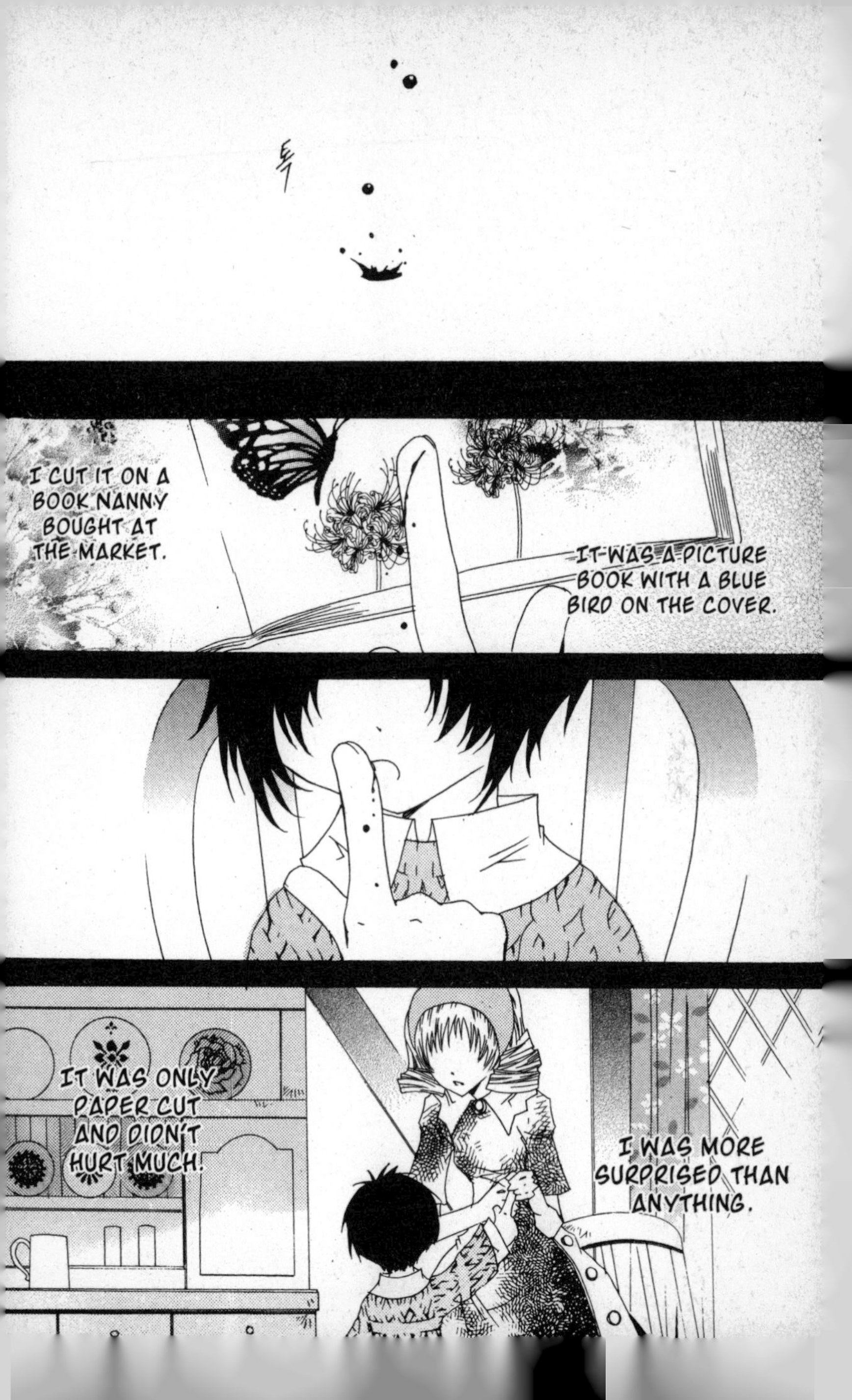
I CUT IT ON A BOOK NANNY BOUGHT AT THE MARKET.
IT WAS A PICTURE BOOK WITH A BLUE BIRD ON THE COVER.
IT WAS ONLY PAPER CUT AND DIDN'T HURT MUCH.
I WAS MORE SURPRISED THAN ANYTHING.

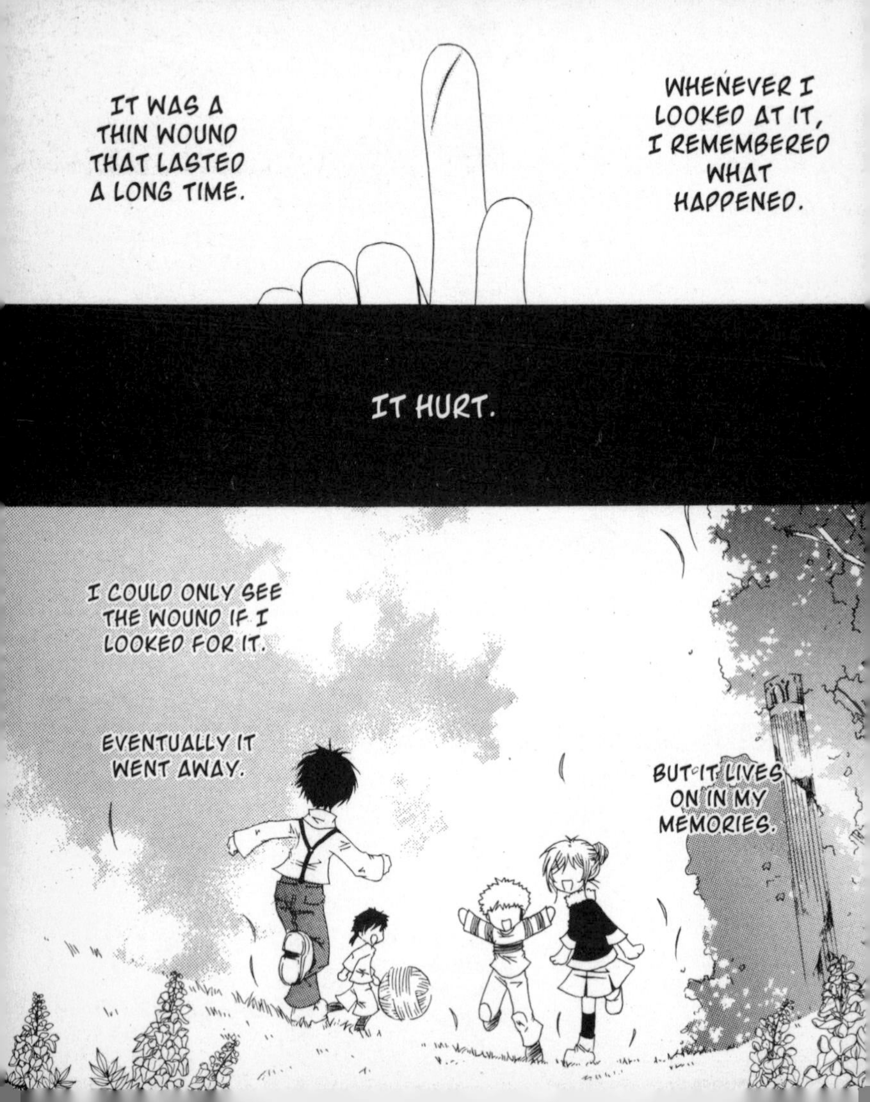
IT WAS A THIN WOUND THAT LASTED A LONG TIME.
WHENEVER I LOOKED AT IT, I REMEMBERED WHAT HAPPENED.
IT HURT.
I COULD ONLY SEE THE WOUND IF I LOOKED FOR IT.
EVENTUALLY IT WENT AWAY.
BUT IT LIVES ON IN MY MEMORIES.

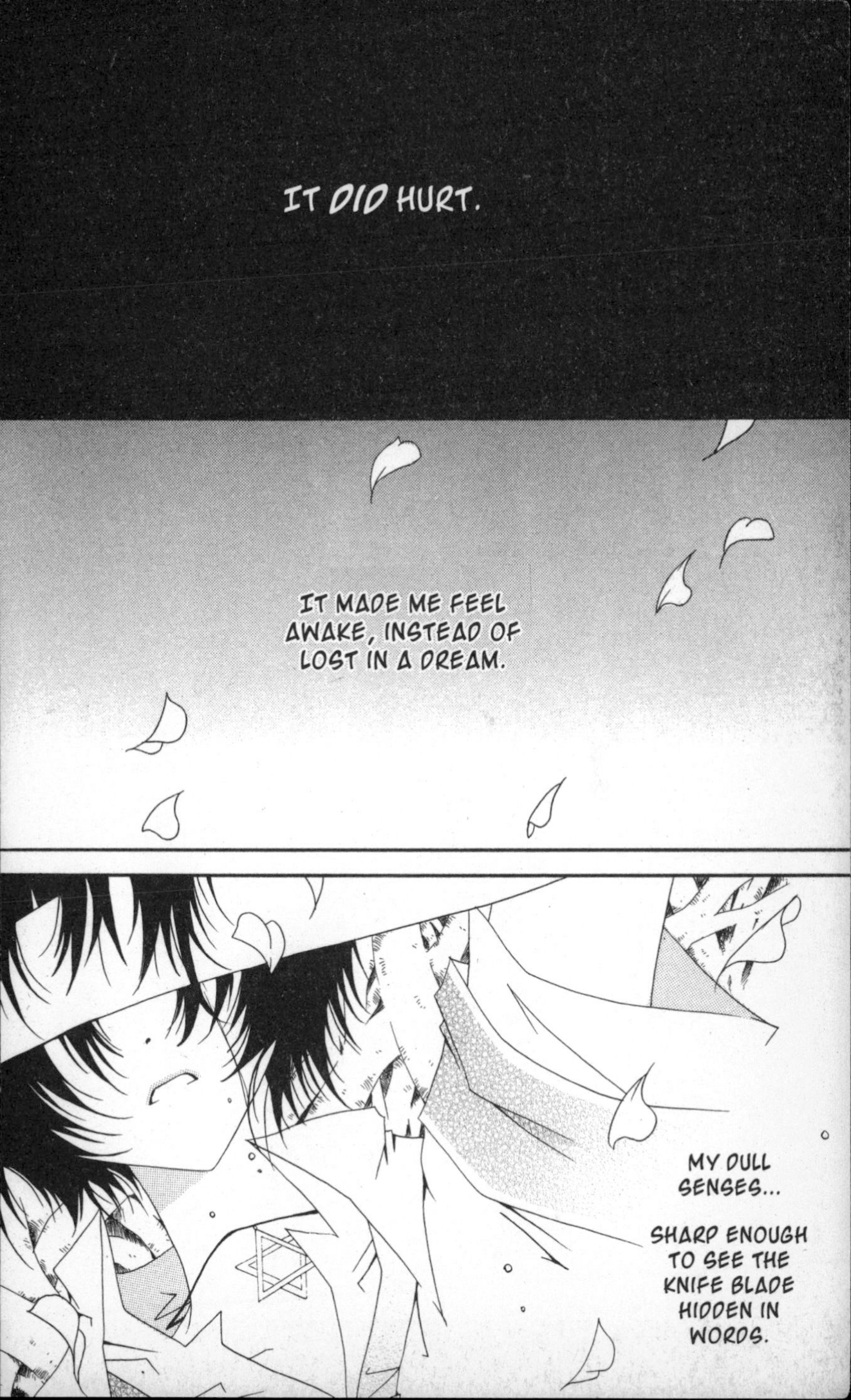
IT DID HURT.
IT MADE ME FEEL AWAKE, INSTEAD OF LOST IN A DREAM.
MY DULL SENSES...
SHARP ENOUGH TO SEE THE KNIFE BLADE HIDDEN IN WORDS.

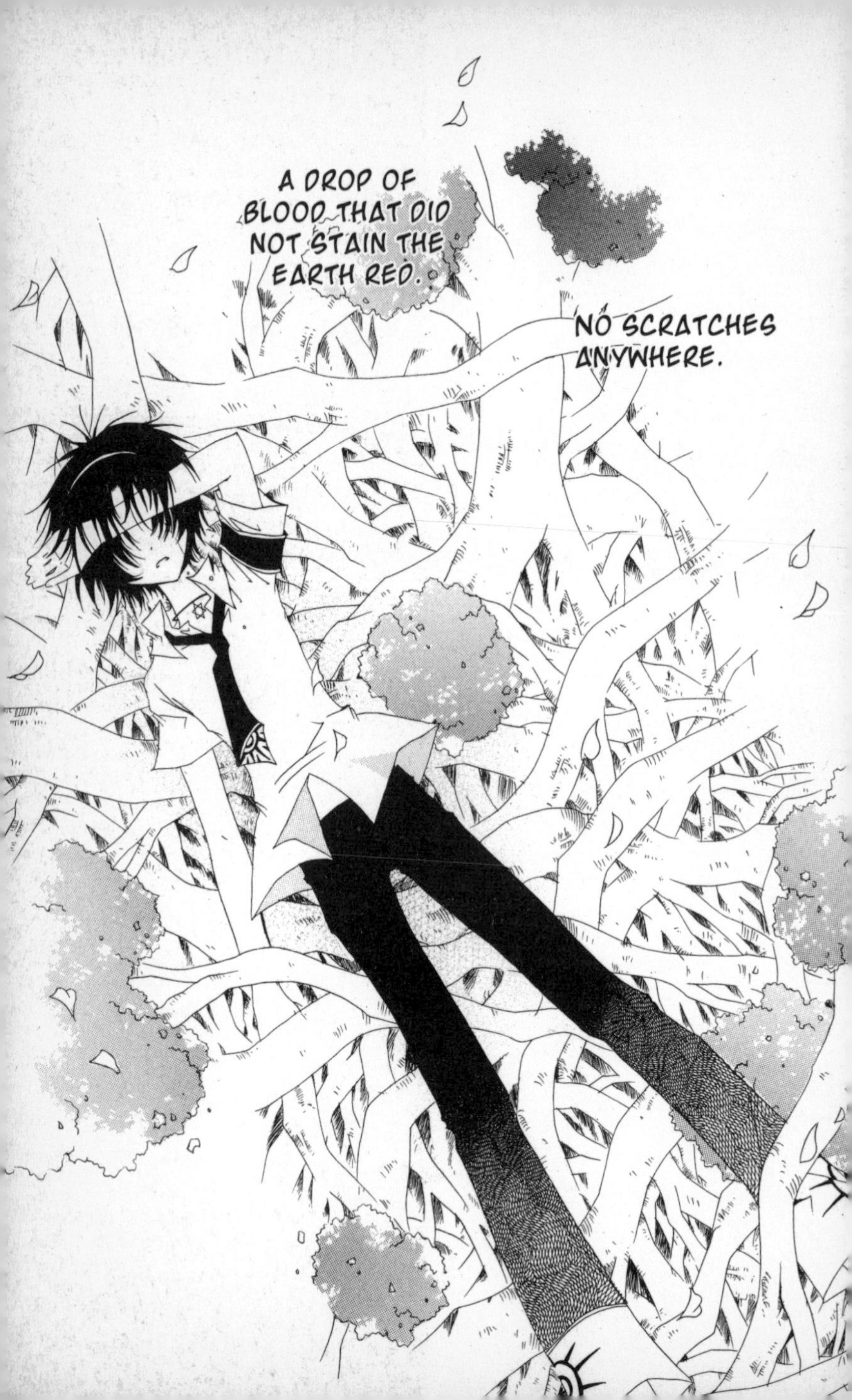
A DROP OF BLOOD THAT DID NOT STAIN THE EARTH RED.
NO SCRATCHES ANYWHERE.

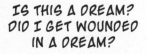

WHO AM I?

IS THIS A DREAM?
DID I GET WOUNDED
IN A DREAM?

NO.

IT HURT.

BUT I CAN'T FIND
THE WOUND!

WHAT
AM I?

I CAN'T STOP
CRYING ANYWAY.

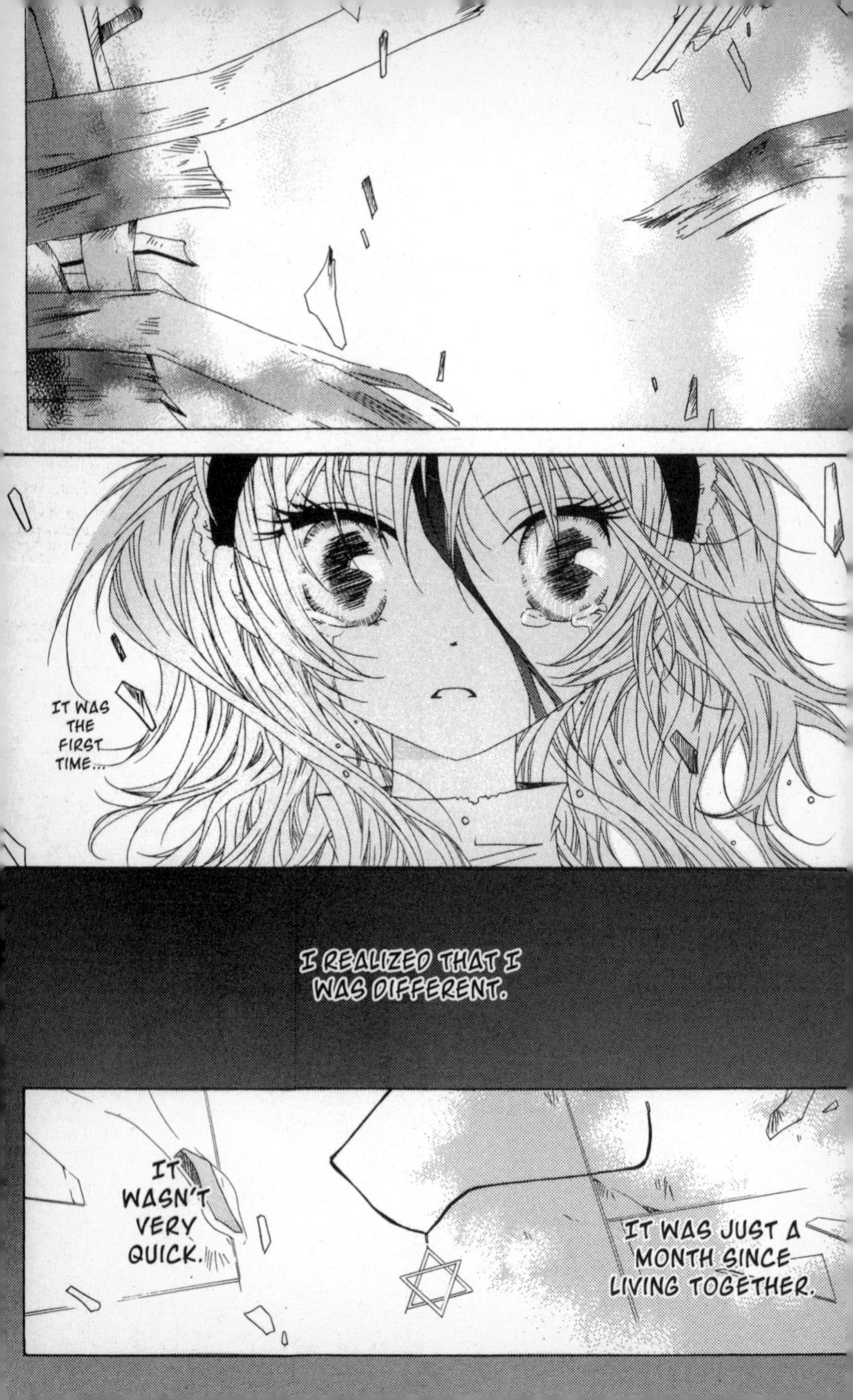
IT WAS THE FIRST TIME...
I REALIZED THAT I WAS DIFFERENT.
IT WASN'T VERY QUICK.
IT WAS JUST A MONTH SINCE LIVING TOGETHER.

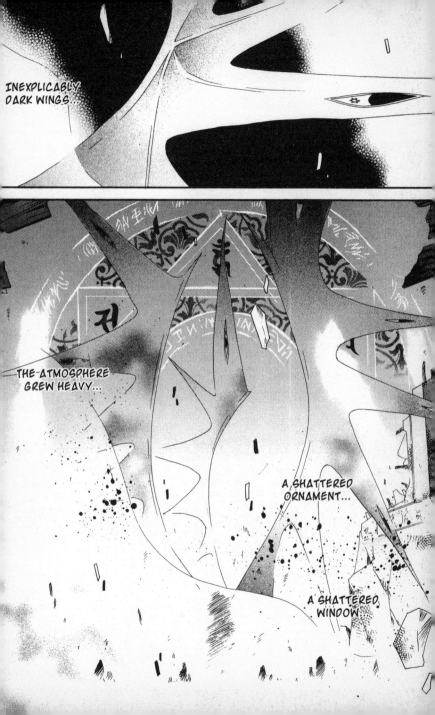

INEXPLICABLY DARK WINGS...

THE ATMOSPHERE GREW HEAVY...

A SHATTERED ORNAMENT...

A SHATTERED WINDOW

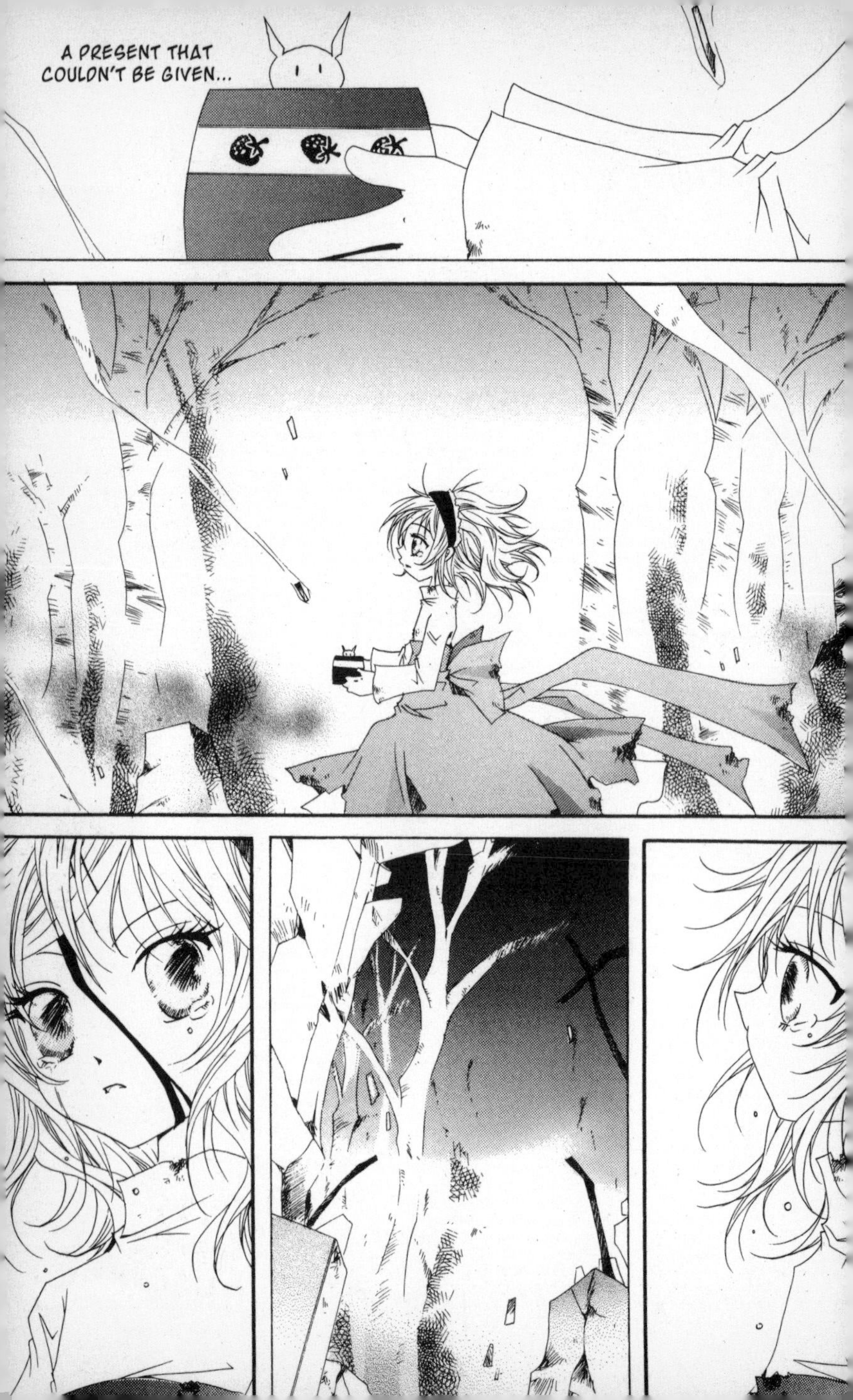
A PRESENT THAT COULDN'T BE GIVEN...

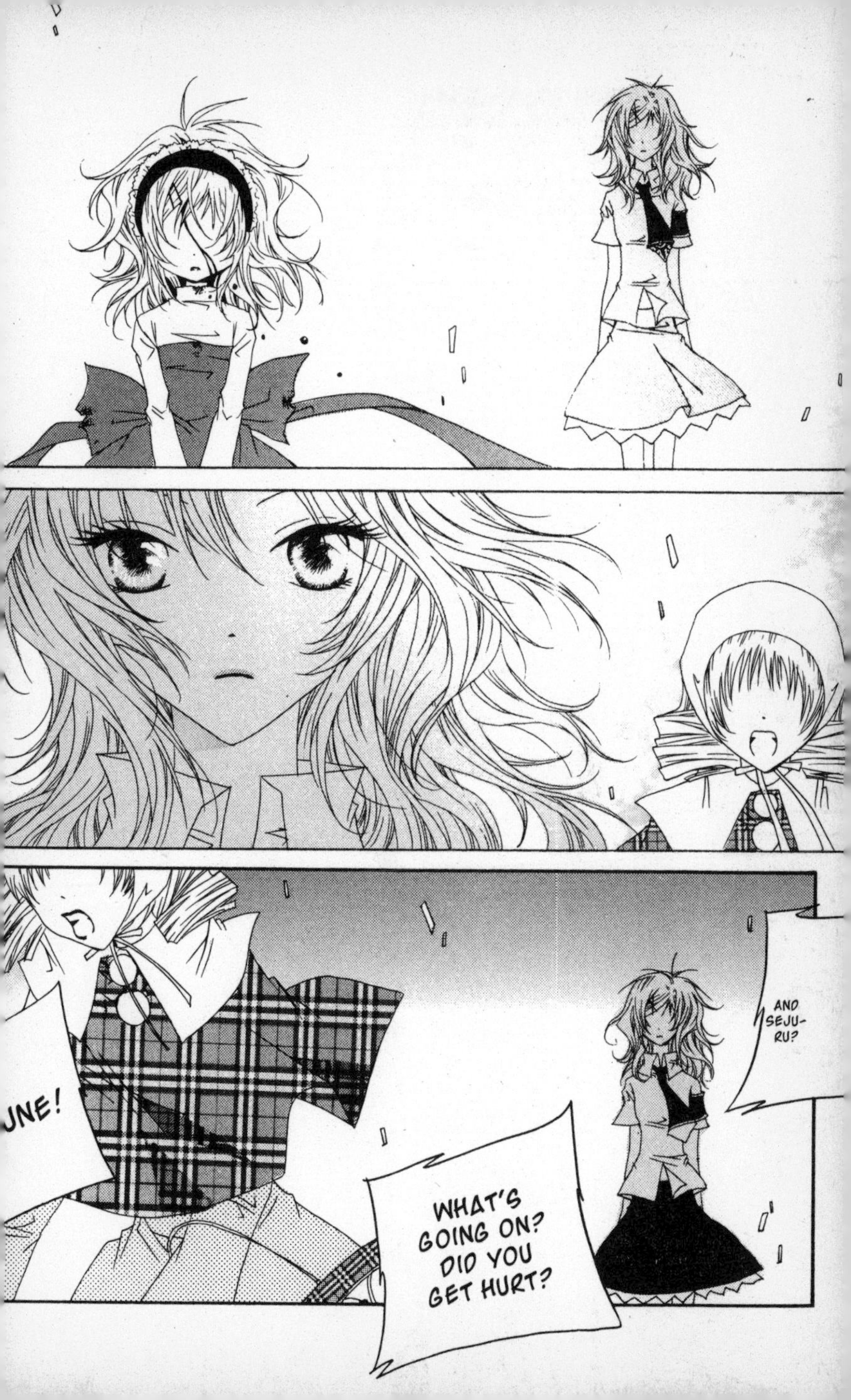
UNE!
AND SEJU-RU?
WHAT'S GOING ON? DID YOU GET HURT?

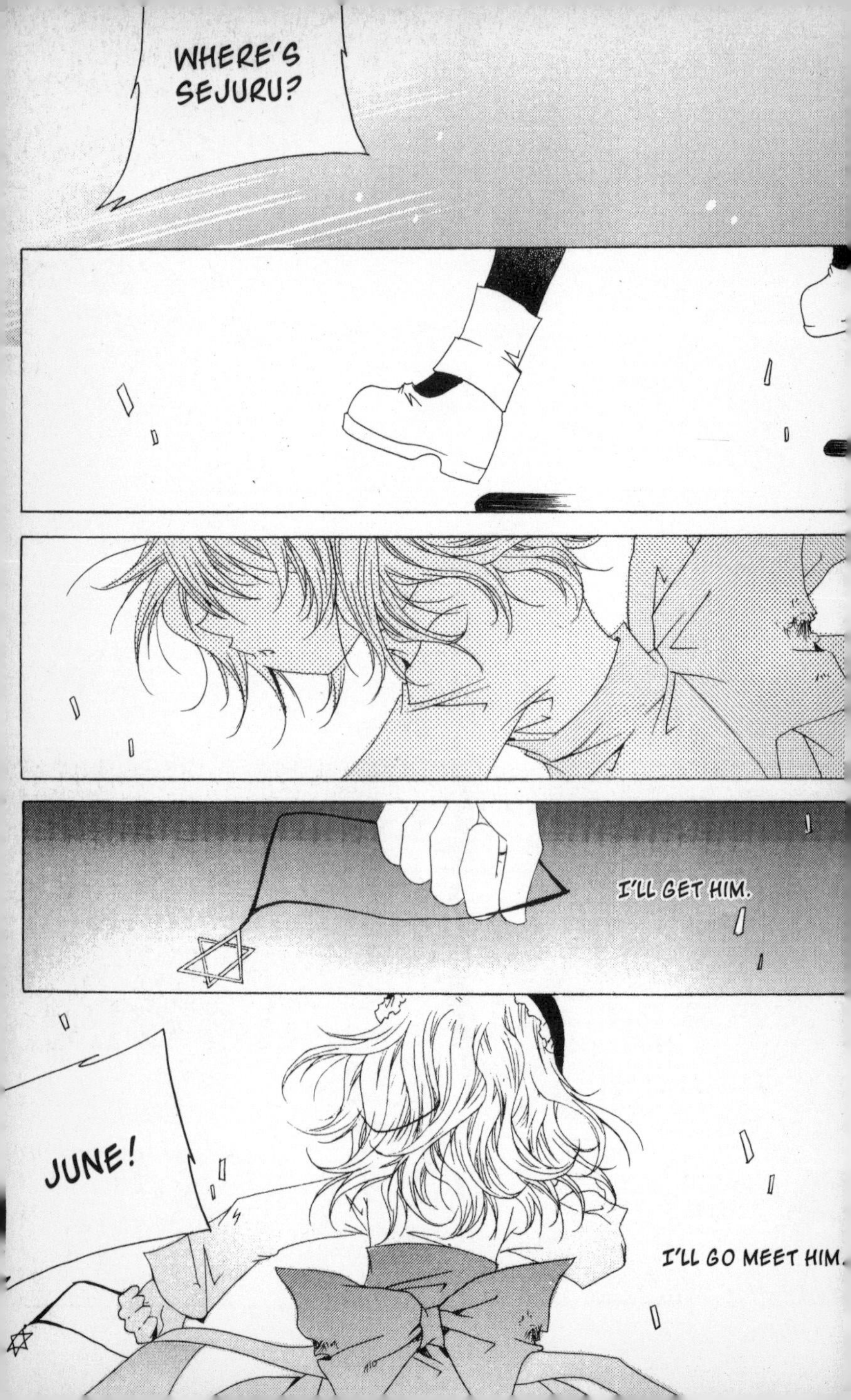
WHERE'S SEJURU?
I'LL GET HIM.
JUNE!
I'LL GO MEET HIM.

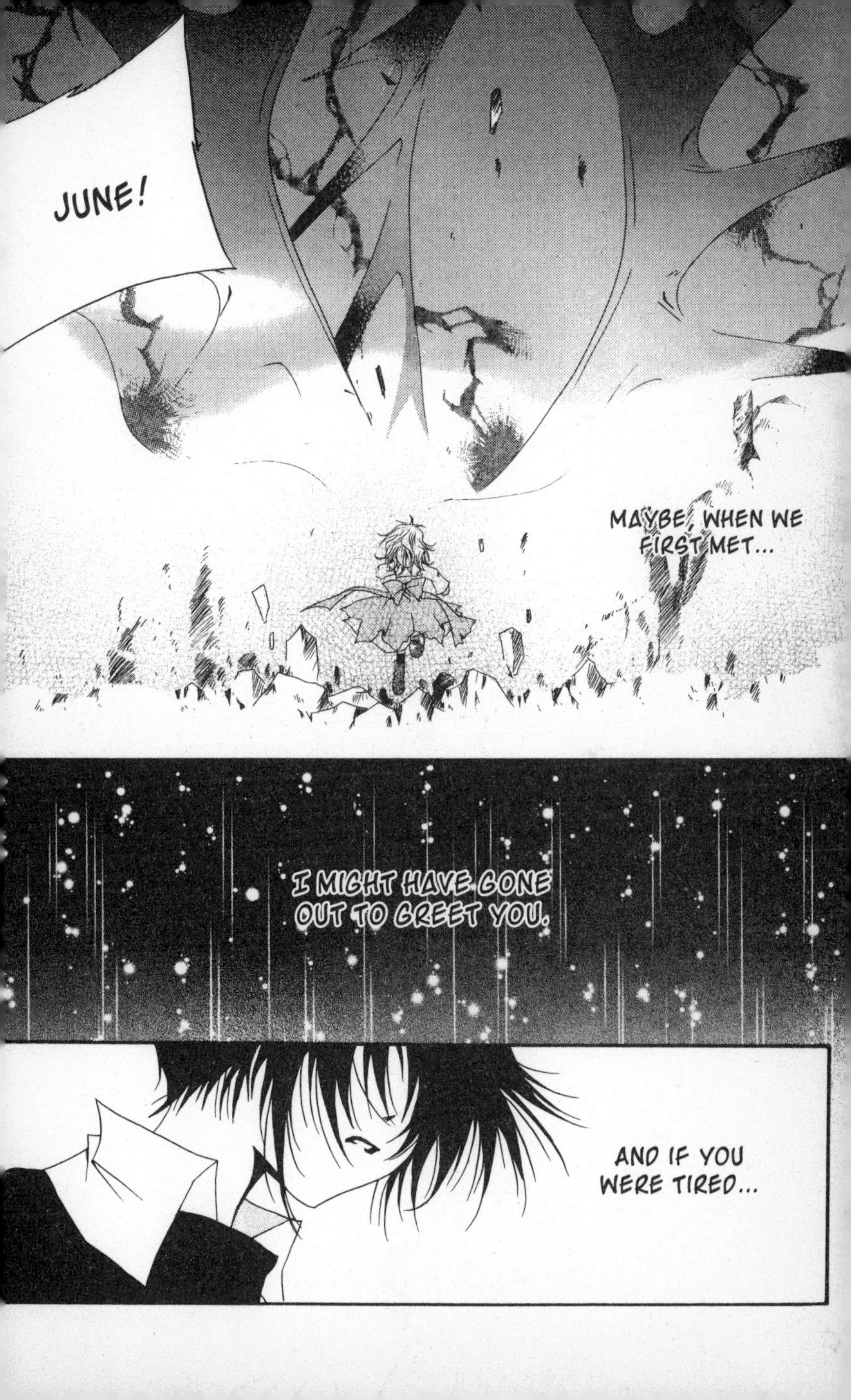
JUNE!
MAYBE, WHEN WE FIRST MET...
I MIGHT HAVE GONE OUT TO GREET YOU.
AND IF YOU WERE TIRED...

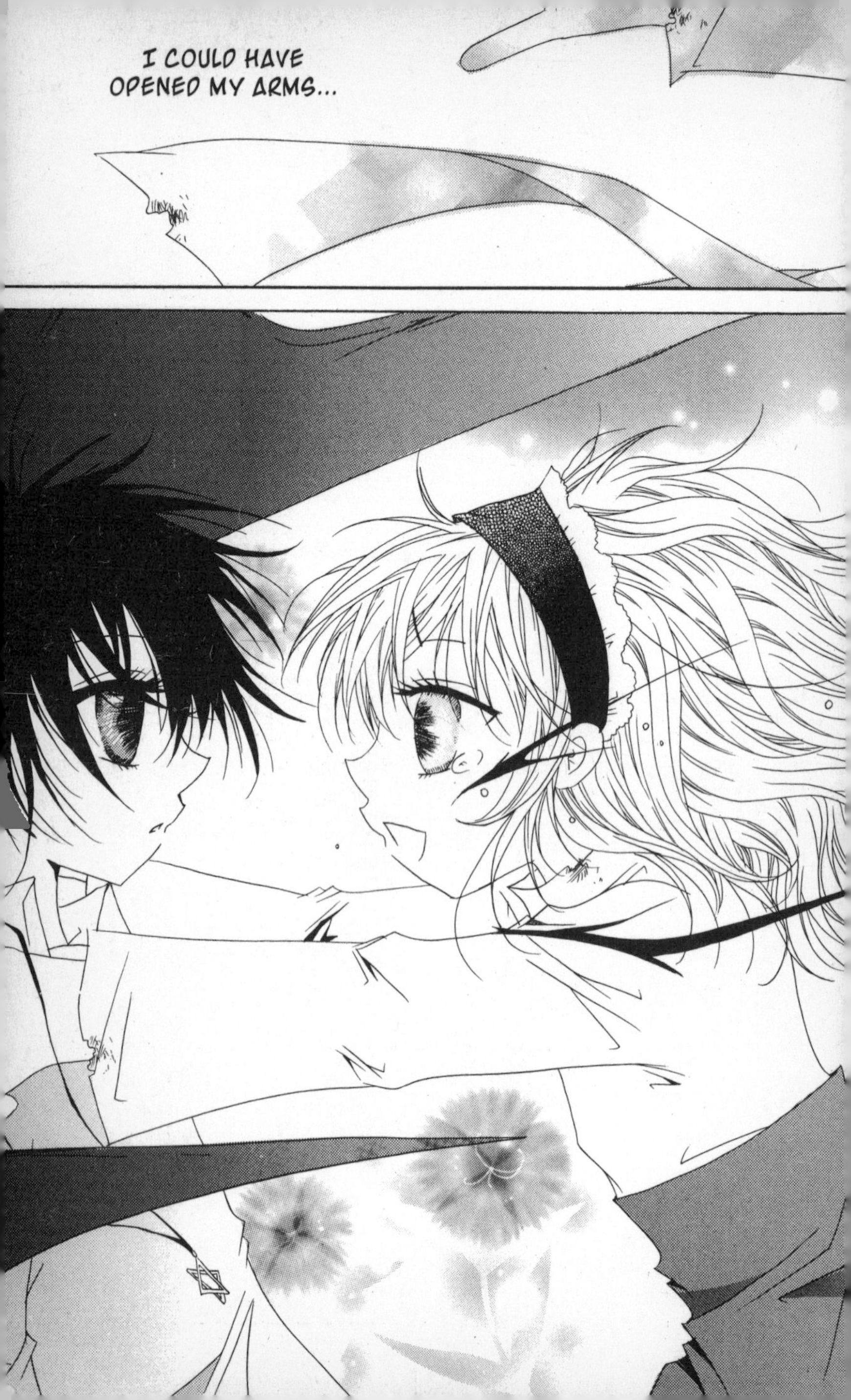
I COULD HAVE
OPENED MY ARMS...

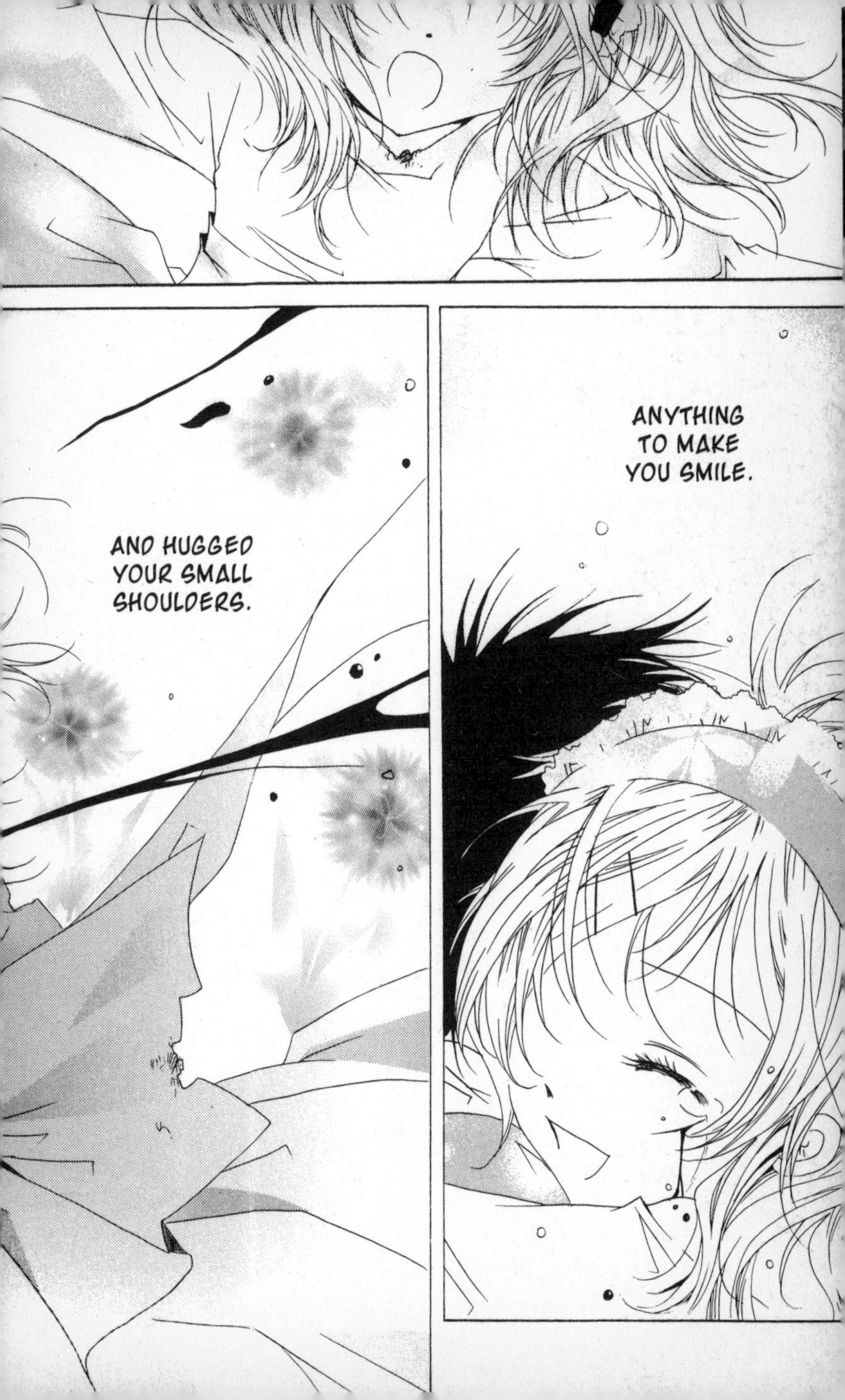
AND HUGGED YOUR SMALL SHOULDERS.
ANYTHING TO MAKE YOU SMILE.

SMILE

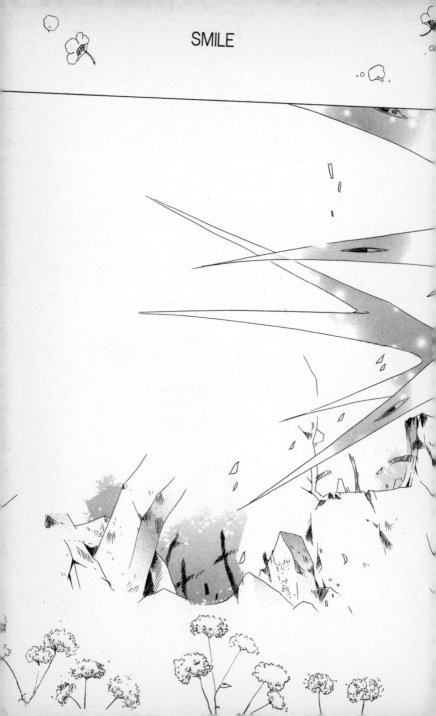

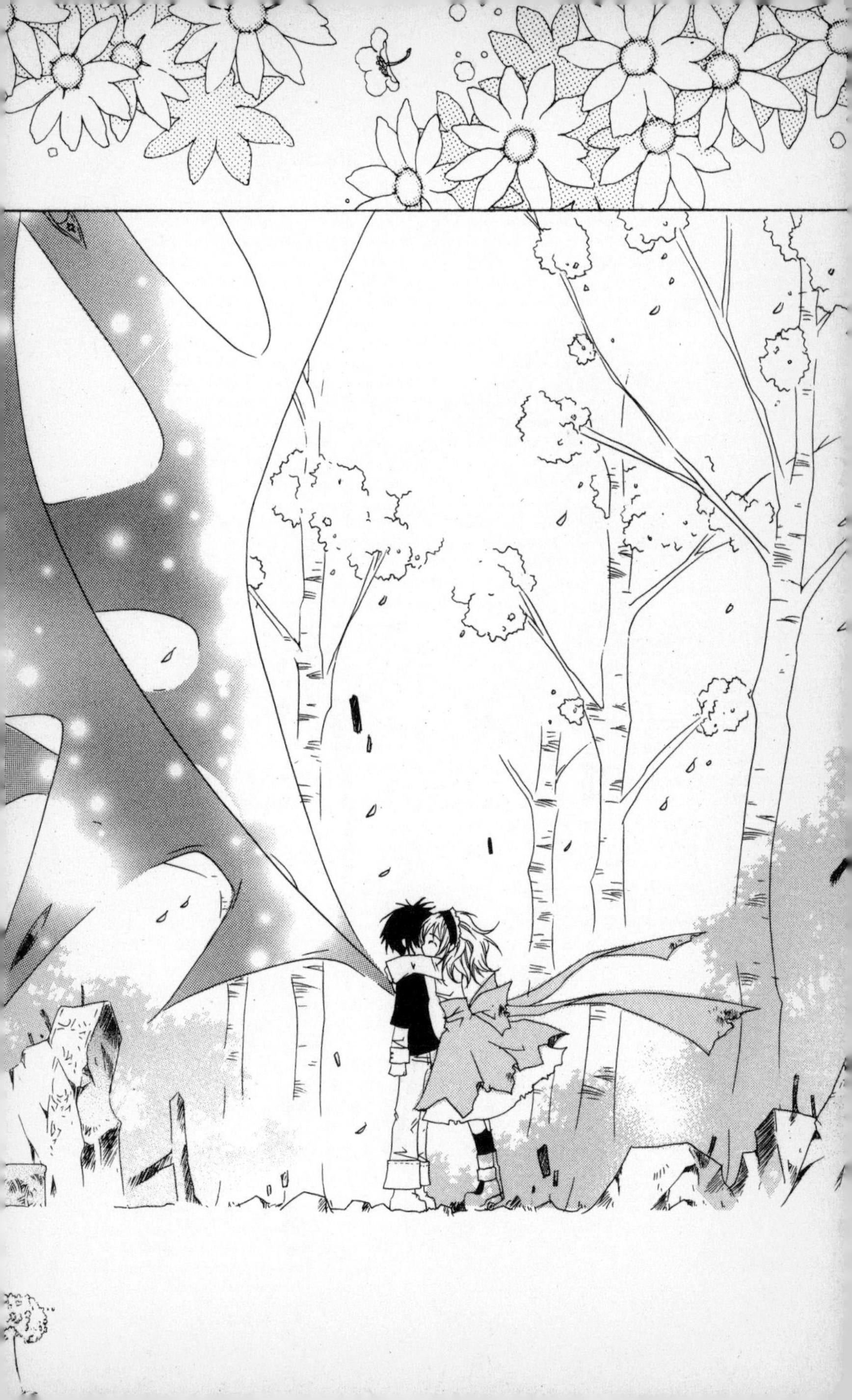

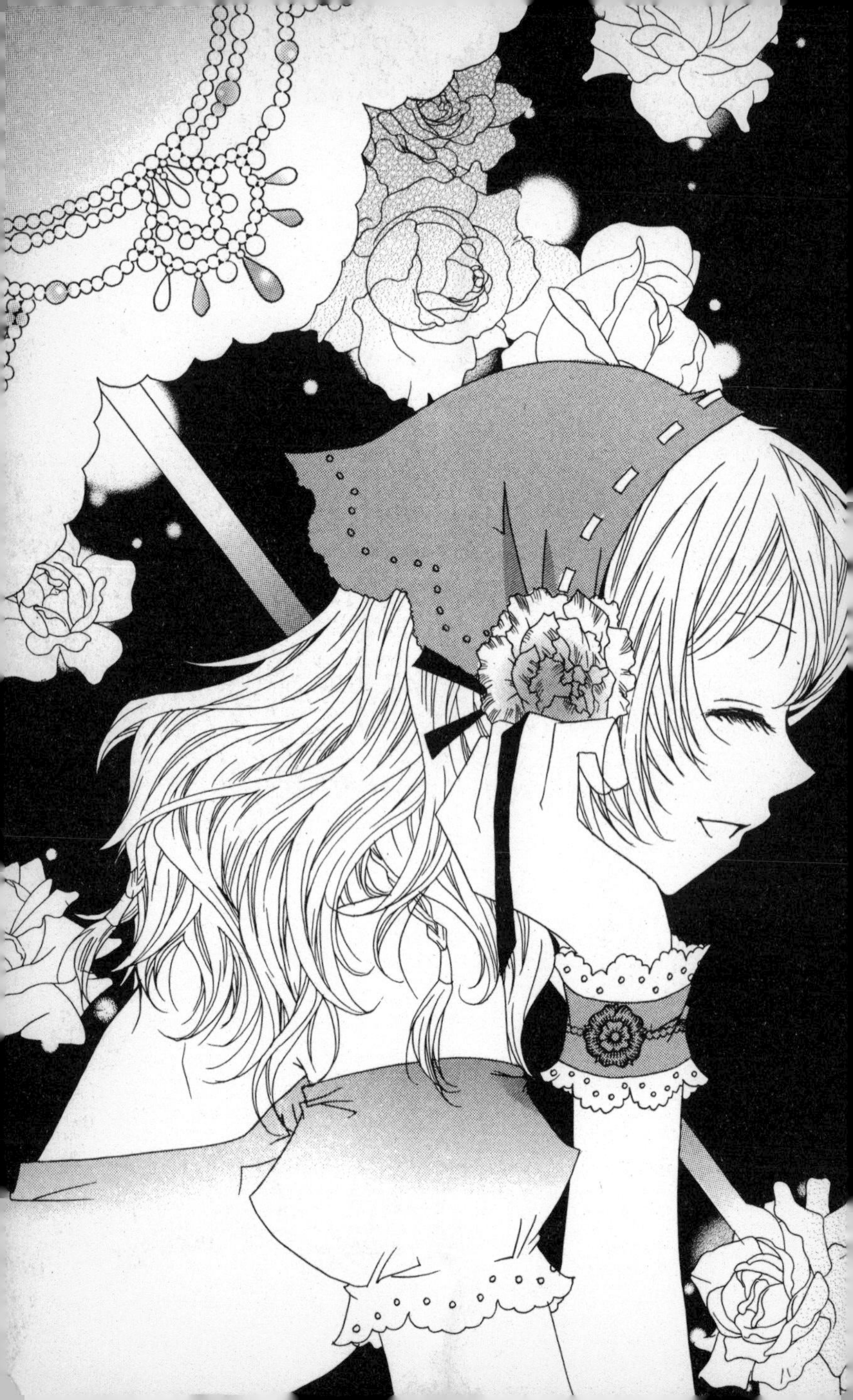

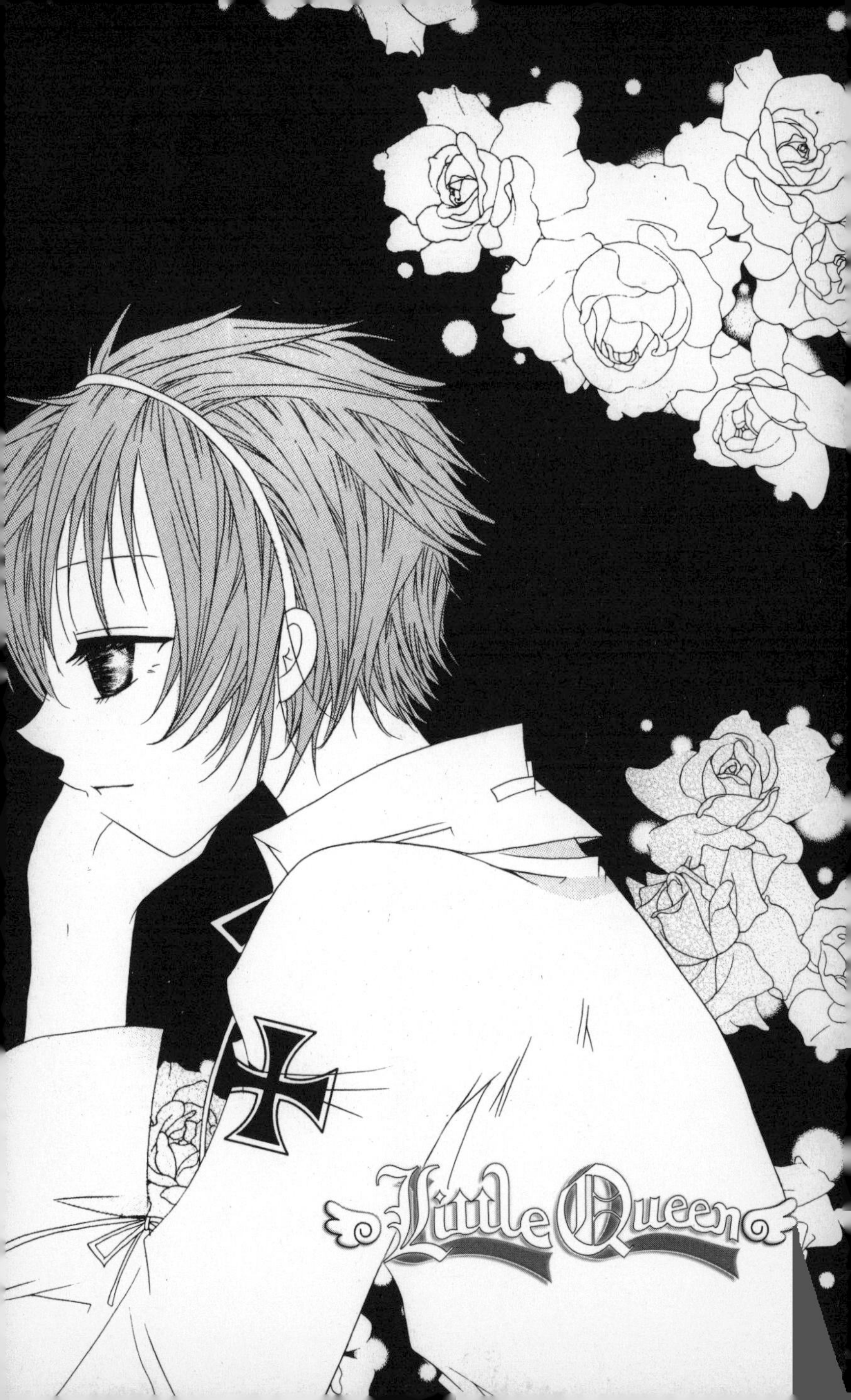
Little Queen

So Different, So Lovable

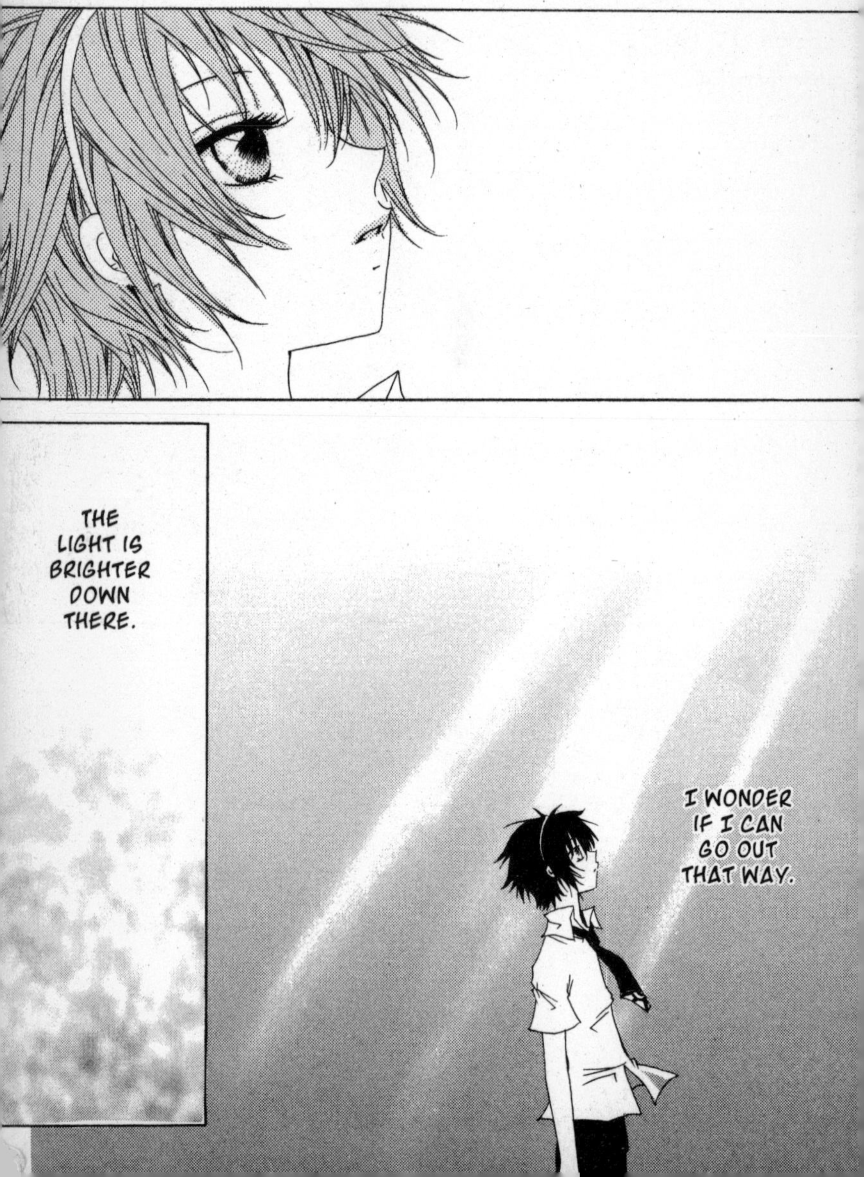
THE LIGHT IS BRIGHTER DOWN THERE.
I WONDER IF I CAN GO OUT THAT WAY.

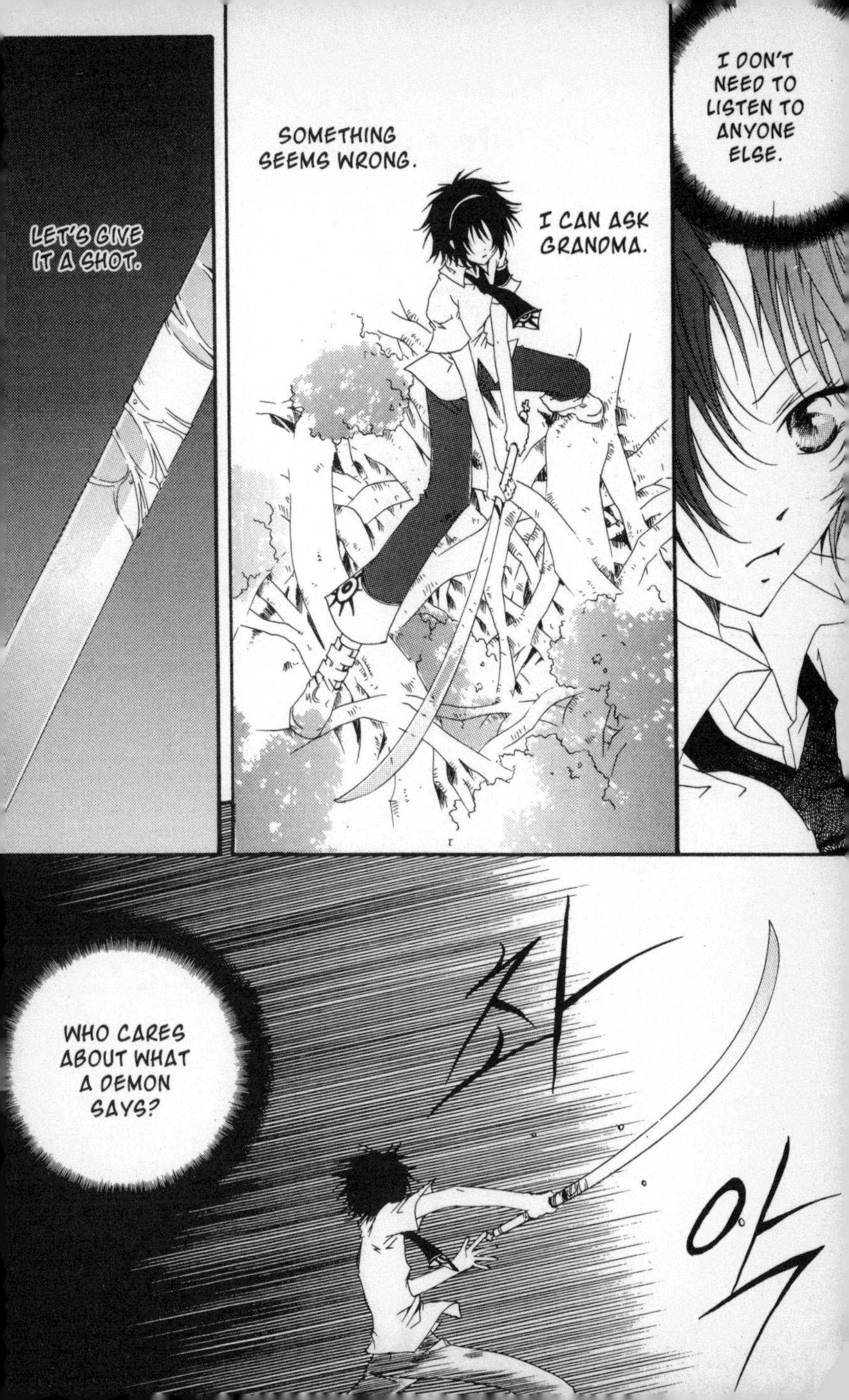
LET'S GIVE IT A SHOT.
SOMETHING SEEMS WRONG.
I CAN ASK GRANDMA.
I DON'T NEED TO LISTEN TO ANYONE ELSE.
WHO CARES ABOUT WHAT A DEMON SAYS?

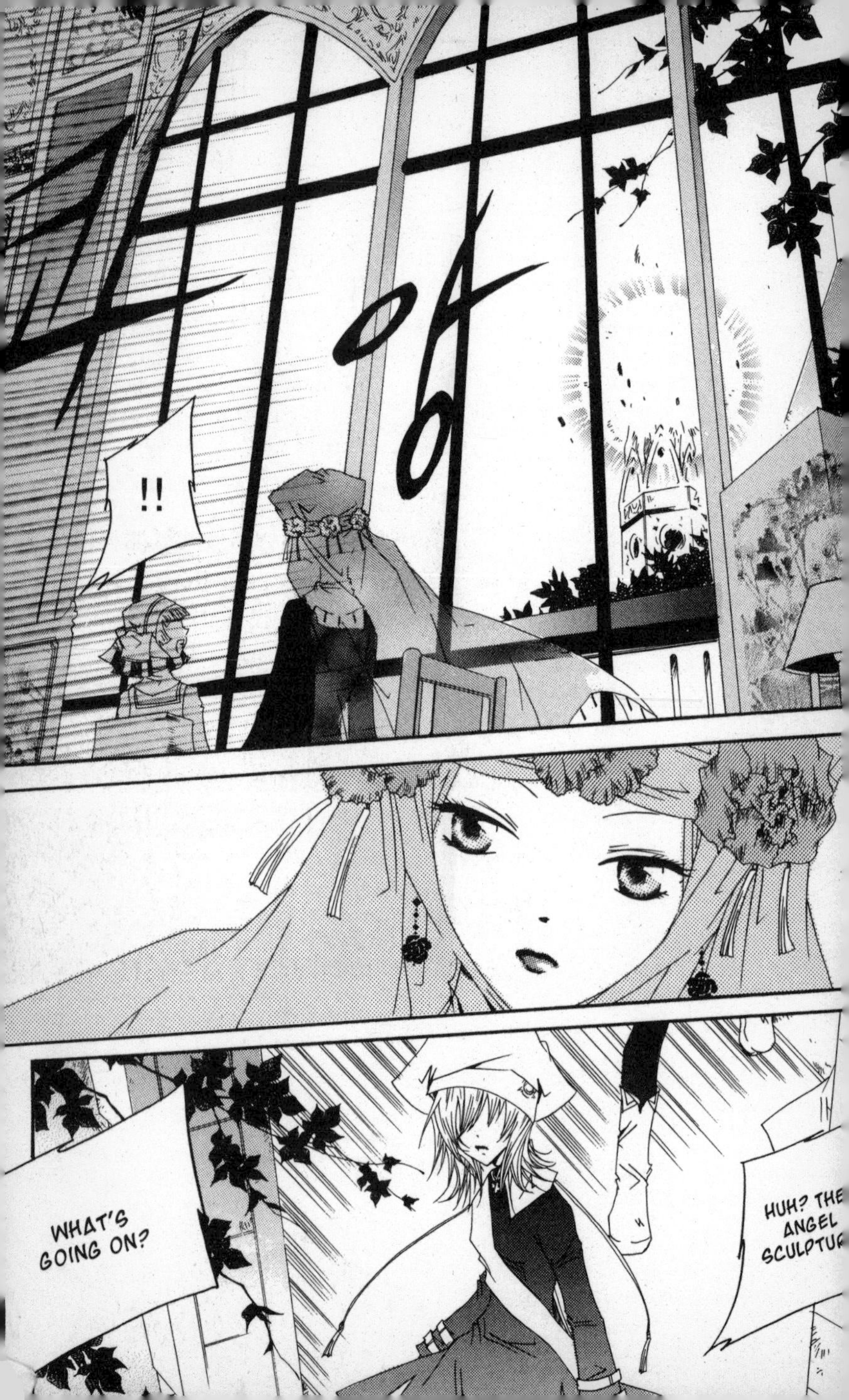
!!
WHAT'S GOING ON?
HUH? THE ANGEL SCULPTUR

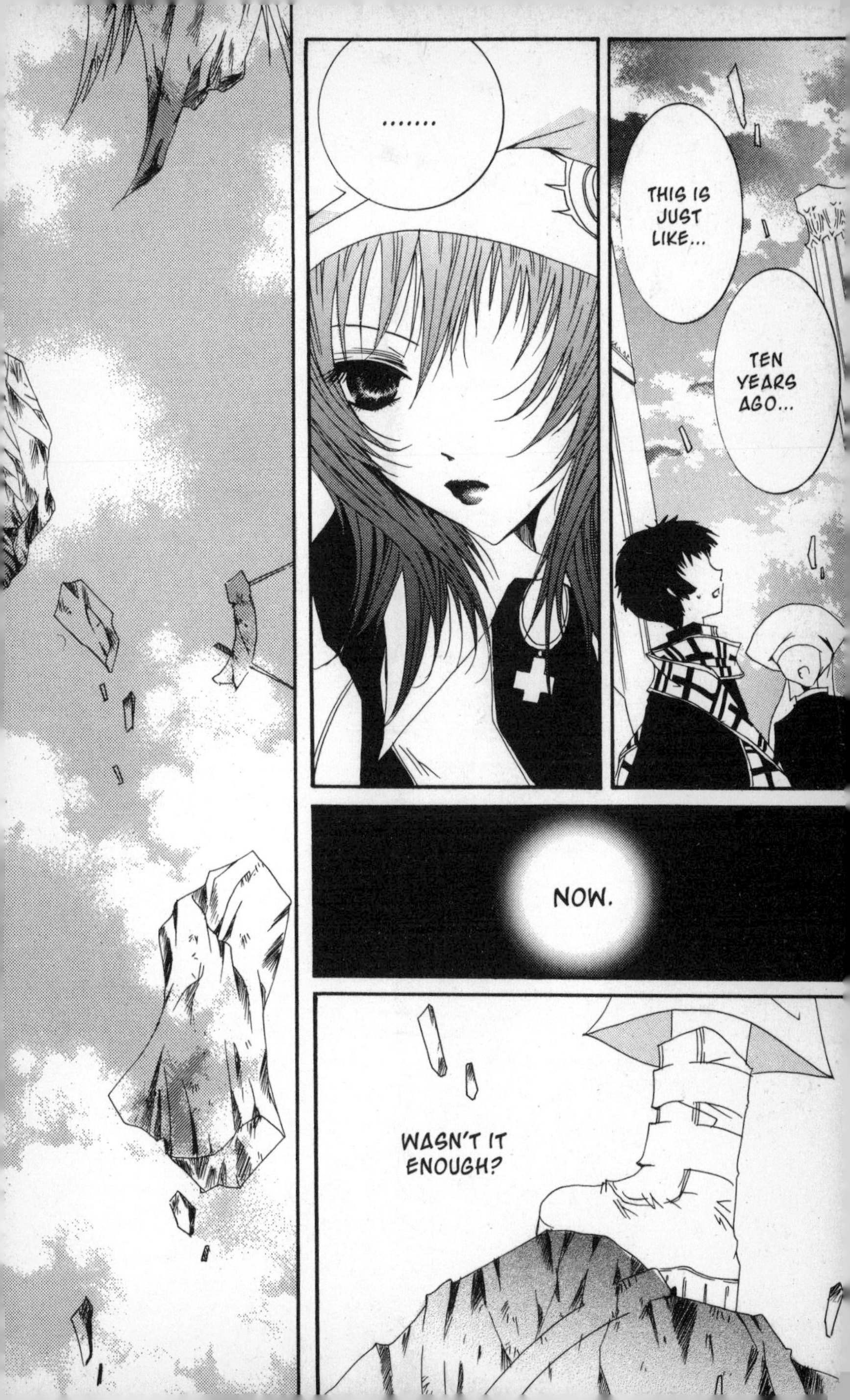
....
THIS IS JUST LIKE...
TEN YEARS AGO...
NOW.
WASN'T IT ENOUGH?

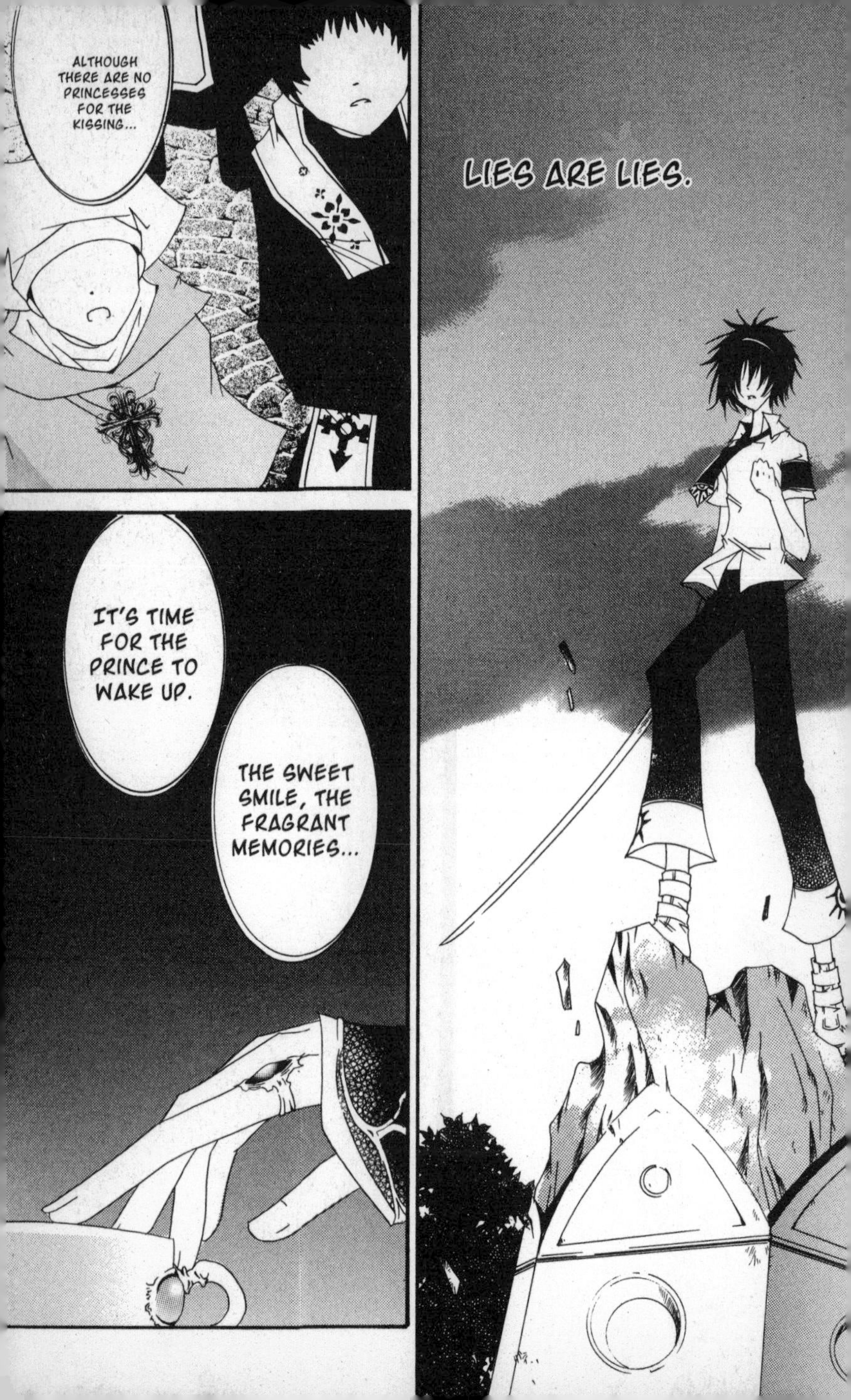
ALTHOUGH THERE ARE NO PRINCESSES FOR THE KISSING...
IT'S TIME FOR THE PRINCE TO WAKE UP.
THE SWEET SMILE, THE FRAGRANT MEMORIES...
LIES ARE LIES.

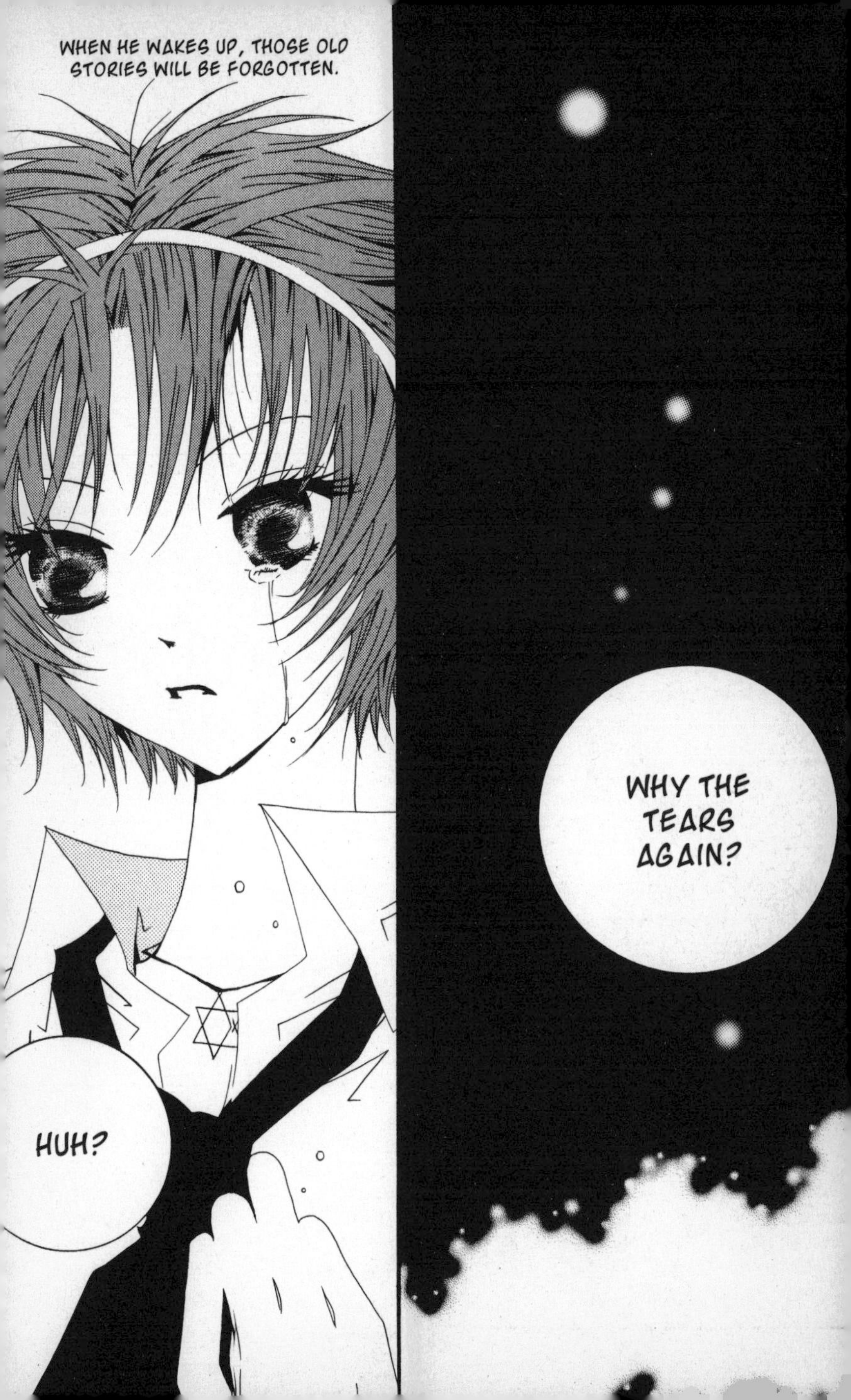
WHEN HE WAKES UP, THOSE OLD STORIES WILL BE FORGOTTEN.
HUH?
WHY THE TEARS AGAIN?

TO BE CONTINUED

In the next volume, things go from
bad to worse for Sejuru, after
Mayanne finally recognizes him!
What will his fate be? And despite
her conflicted feelings about Sejuru,
how will June respond to the
persecution of her longtime friend?
Don't miss the next exciting
installment of *Little Queen*!

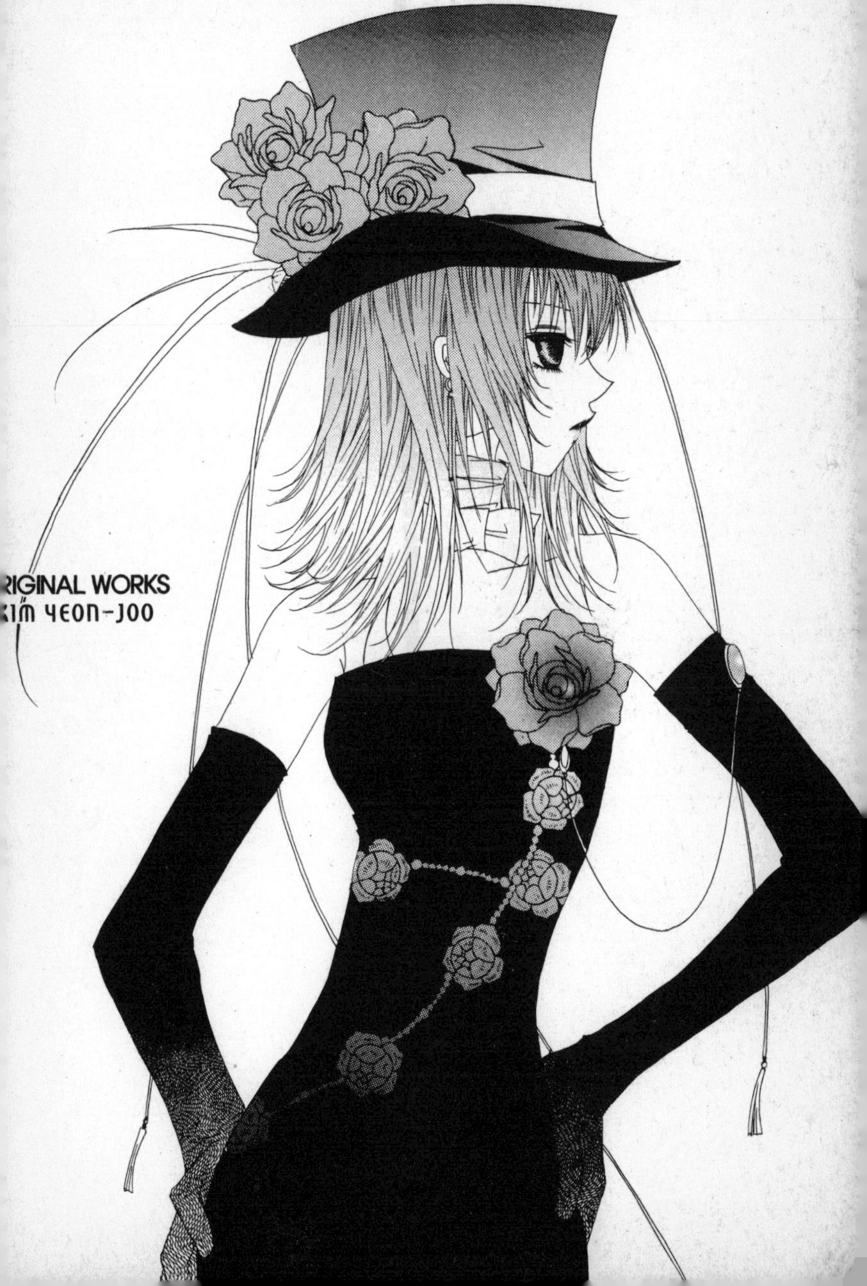
RIGINAL WORKS
KIM YEON-JOO

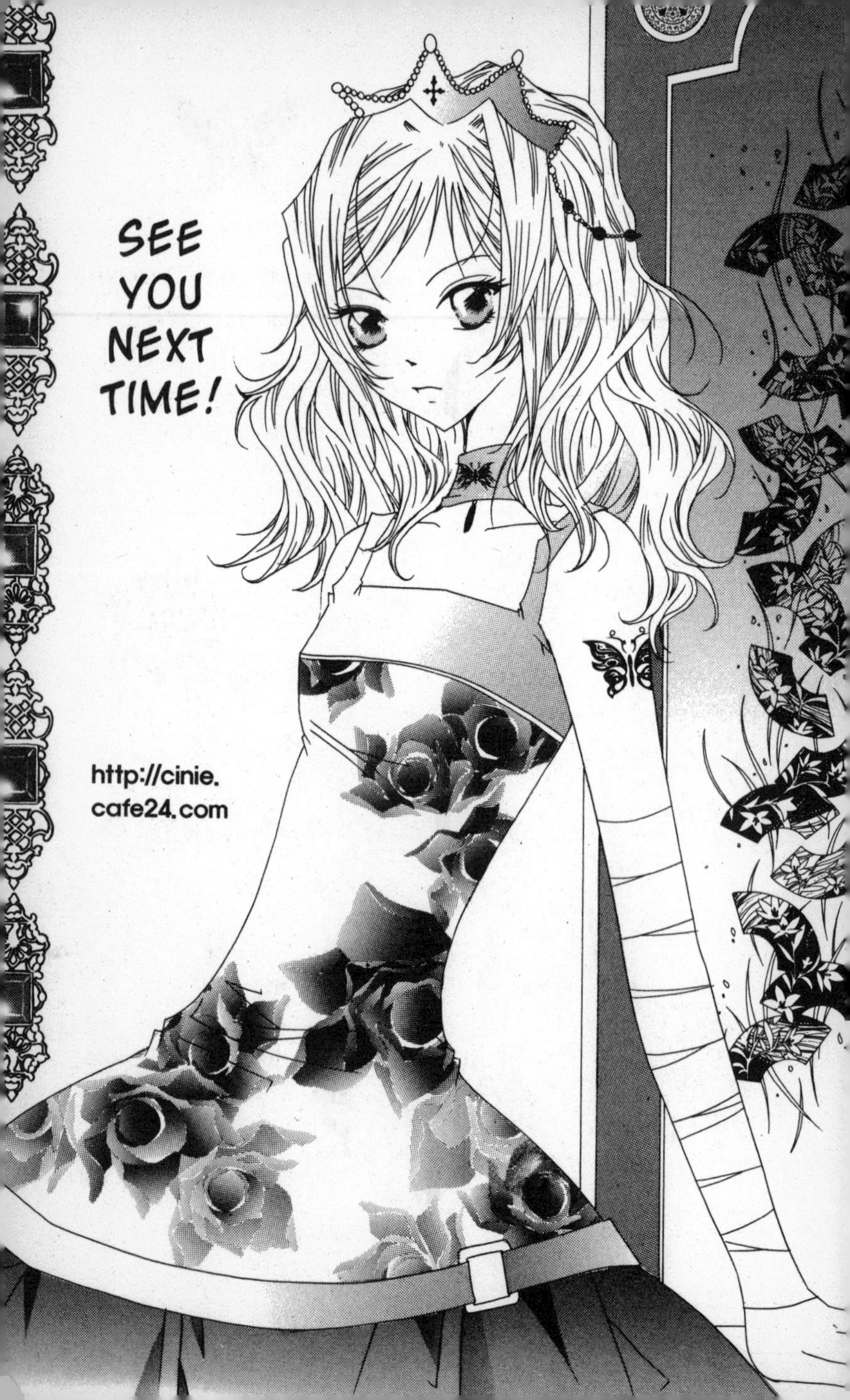
SEE YOU NEXT TIME!
http://cinie.cafe24.com

THANK YOU FOR READING VOLUME 4!

A LOT OF PEOPLE ASKED IF VOLUME 4 WOULD BE THE FINAL INSTALLMENT, BUT AS YOU CAN SEE, IT IS NOT. I'M ESTIMATING THAT WE'LL REACH A SIXTH OR SEVENTH VOLUME. THANKS TO YOU, MY BRAIN AND HANDS ARE BUSY! TIME TO RELAX AND THEN JUMP RIGHT ON TO VOLUME FIVE!

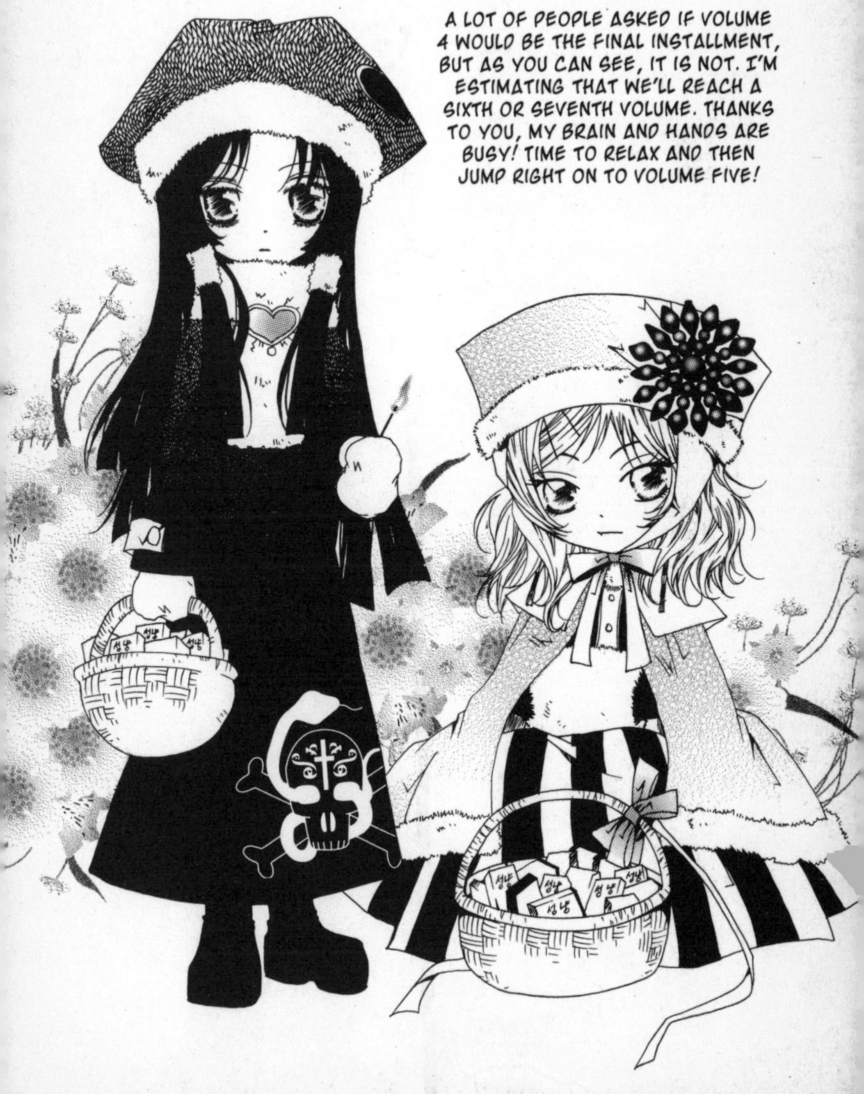
성냥
성냥
성냥
성냥
성냥
성냥
성냥
성냥